A PORTRAIT OF KATHERINE MANSFIELD

This substantial volume aims to provide a 'behind the scenes' view of the very tragic, depressing and, above all, moving story of the life of England's number one short story writer.

Having such an understanding and great respect for Katherine Mansfield, the author feels that in dying at so young an age, a light went out in the literary world.

A PORTRAIT OF KATHERINE MANSFIELD

Nora Crone

ARTHUR H. STOCKWELL LTD.
Elms Court   Ilfracombe
Devon

To Peter Crone

ISBN 0 7223 1862-6
Printed in Great Britain by
Arthur H. Stockwell Ltd.
Elms Court   Ilfracombe
Devon

Contents

LIST OF ILLUSTRATIONS

Preface

As a medical student, made restless by blackbird song outside
the University Library, I would stray for relief to the dim
recesses of the Literary Section. There I read the works of
Katherine Mansfield, her abstracted lover in his bow-tie, John
Middleton Murry and their friend, that 'free-floating flame'
D.H. Lawrence. It would be true to say that these three have
dogged my footsteps ever since. As the years passed and the
stage lighting of interest ebbed and flowed, illuminating first
one and then another, gradually the spotlight settled on
Katherine Mansfield, that bird of paradise from a southern
ocean and she will no doubt wheel and dive in my vision
forever.

Chapter I

Childhood

In the Tate Gallery, there is a painting by Charles Robert Leslie, RA (1794-1859) entitled *Uncle Toby and the Widow* and dated 1833. It depicts a rubicund gentleman and a comely lady with a heart-shaped face, who is gazing at him from amber coloured eyes. The gentleman was a Mr Bannister, an actor friend of John Constable, who wrote to the artist on January 20th, 1834:

My dear Leslie,
    I dined with Mr Bannister, who is much delighted with your print of 'Uncle Toby and the Widow' . . . .

The lady was the sister-in-law of C.R. Leslie and one of a family of six sisters called Stone, all notable beauties. She was the wife of John Beauchamp, the mother of the first generation of the pioneering Beauchamp stock of New Zealand and the great grandmother of Kathleen Mansfield Beauchamp, later known as Katherine Mansfield. This portrait was one of the Empire loan collection, exhibited in the New Zealand National Gallery at its opening in August 1936.

John Beauchamp, born 1781, lived in Hornsey Lane, Highgate. He had a gold and silversmiths business, established before 1660. Samuel Pepys recorded the purchase of a 'gilt tankard' at 'Mr Beauchamp's the Goldsmith' on November 14th, 1660. It cost £200. There were three further purchases noted in the diary. C.R. Leslie in his *Memoirs of Constable*, wrote in 1833:

*I had introduced Constable to Mr Beauchamp, to whose
manufactory of British plate in Holborn he paid a visit with his
sons, of which he gave me the following amusing account:*
January 20th (1833)

> *My dear Leslie,*
>
> *I went with John and Charles to Mr Beecham's (sic) last
> evening; their delight was great, not only at the very great
> kindness of Mr and Mrs Beauchamp and their boys, but at
> the sight of all that was to their hearts content: forges —
> smelting pots — metals — turning lathes — straps and
> bellows — coals — ashes — dust — dirt — and cinders; and
> everything else that is agreeable to boys. They want me to
> build them just such place under my painting room; . . . .
> Poor Mrs Beauchamp was suffering with the toothache, but
> her politeness made her assure me that I succeeded in
> talking it off.*

John Beauchamp had varied interests. He mixed with writers
and artists, he wrote and recited poetry, and was known as the
Poet of Hornsey Lane. His poem 'The Rook' was printed in the
local Hornsey newspaper. He also rode to hounds. Alas,
though he invented the process for silver plating, he did not
patent it, and failed to succeed in business. The Beauchamps
had nine children; their only daughter, Annette, died when
young. The boys were educated at the City of London School
in Hampstead, then apprenticed in business. When their
father's business inevitably failed they were encouraged to seek
their fortune — lucky young men!

Henry Herron Beauchamp, the fourth son, born 1825, was
the first to leave, encouraged by his Uncle William Mead de
Charms, who was married to another Stone girl. After working
in the office of Samuel Baker, Philpots & Co., Merchants and
Shippers, he was sent to the company's overseas agents in
Mauritius in 1848, at the age of twenty-three. Being a bright
young man, he went into trading and shipping on his own
account after only two years, sailing to Australia where he
lived for the next twenty years.

On January 20th, 1855, he married Elizabeth Weiss Lasseter
(Louey), daughter of a Baptist minister, and settled in Sydney.
They had six children: Ralph, born 1857, who was to run the

London School of Music; Charlotte (Chaddie), born 1855, who married George Waterlow, son of Sir Sydney Waterlow; Sydney, born 1861, who became a doctor and was eventually knighted; Walter, born 1862, who worked for a colonial wool-broker; Harry, born 1864, who became a farmer; and Mary Annette, born 1866, who married Count Henning August von Arnim in 1891. Thereafter she wrote the first of many books, *Elizabeth and Her German Garden*, which was published on September 20th, 1899 and was an immediate success. Henry returned to London in 1868 and on discovering he could carry on business deals in Australia from an office in London, decided to stay, taking a house at Bexley. He kept a journal all his life.

Arthur Beauchamp, born 1827, emigrated to Australia in 1848, becoming a clerk in Henry's office, later unsuccessfully prospecting for gold in Victoria, New South Wales. He married in 1854, at Port Fairy, a Miss Mary Elizabeth Stanley, a Lancashire girl aged eighteen, daughter of a silversmith. The first two children died in infancy. Their third son, Harold, born November 15th, 1858 on a goldfield at Ararat, became the father of Katherine Mansfield. A fourth son Arthur de Charms, was born two years later.

In the meantime, a sister of John Beauchamp, Miss Jane Beauchamp, who had been a cherished companion to Lady Laura Tollemache, was left £20,000 by her mistress, part of which she invested in Gibbon Wakefield's Colonial Land Scheme in New Zealand. In 1861, she bequeathed the lands, comprising of a thousand acres, to her favourite nephew Arthur. No doubt jubilant, he sailed with his family to Picton, New Zealand, where he became a general merchant and auctioneer. Alas, he was able to claim but a fragment of this legacy, as the New Zealand Company had surrendered its charter to the Crown.

Arthur Beauchamp was an extrovert, fiery, voluble, imaginative and witty. He also loved poetry and would recite *Childe Harold* for his young granddaughter, Jeanne Beauchamp, as she sat on his knee. He wrote numerous poems which he would include in his speeches in Parliament where he represented Picton, and also even in the course of his work as an auctioneer. A rolling stone by nature, he moved house thirteen times, ending his days in a small bungalow in Picton at the age of eighty-three. He paid a last visit to England at seventy, bringing back a watering can. He declared one could go anywhere in the world with just a clean pair of socks and a rook rifle, a true colonial!

Young Harold, a bright boy, sandy-haired and blue-eyed, attended Picton's Dames School, a houseboat on stilts. His parents adored him. He would help his mother to do the washing and manfully wore the trousers she made him, in which, in later years, he admitted ruefully that one did not know whether he was 'coming or going'. He was reported good at figures, and at fourteen, became a clerk to his father at auction sales which often lasted six hours daily. In his *Reminiscences and Recollections*, Sir Harold wrote:

. . . *during those years I travelled on horseback between Wanganui, Hawera, and Palmerston North . . . . I was sent to take delivery of sheep cattle and horses and to drive them to Wanganui*

This operation once took seven days, the horses having to swim across flooded rivers. They had to stay at a Maori whare. *'Our Maori host . . . . supplied us with a blanket, with no charge for fleas.'*

At seventeen, when the family moved to Wellington, he joined the firm of William Bannatyne & Co., importers of French and Spanish wine, English beer, Italian candied peel, Californian raisins, tinned salmon, kerosene, and Egyptian cigarettes. A fellow clerk, Joseph Frederick Dyer, introduced him to his sister Annie Burnell Dyer, aged fourteen, who eventually was to become Mrs Harold Beauchamp.

The maternal great-grandfather, John Dyer, was the son of a Baptist minister in Devizes. He married a Miss Burnell from Plymouth and had fourteen children. An introspective man, given to bouts of depression, he committed suicide by drowning himself in his rainwater tank in Battersea in 1841. His tenth son, Joseph, emigrated to Australia, where he became an insurance clerk in Sydney. There, in 1855 when he was thirty-six, he met and married Miss Margaret Isabella Mansfield aged sixteen, daughter of a publican. He was sent to open the first New Zealand branch of the Australian Mutual Provident Society in Wellington.

With their family of four sons and five daughters, the Dyers settled in Thorndon, a suburb of Wellington. The girls were lovely, dark-eyed, and chestnut-haired, with their mother's fine complexion. Belle, (Isobel Marion) the 'Aunt Beryl' of Kathleen's stories, was considered the 'family beauty' but I think Annie had the more exquisite face. The brothers were darkly handsome too; one, Sydney Dyer, appears on the *SS Niwaru* family portrait taken in Las Palmas, 1903, while *en route* for England.

Harold courted Annie Dyer for eight years. During this time she had rheumatic fever, and thenceforth was treated as a delicate flower. In 1884 they were married. Harold had infused life into the Bannatyne firm, and was promised a partnership. Mrs Dyer, now aged forty-five, had been a widow since 1876. She and her two unmarried daughters, Belle and Kitty, came to live with the Beauchamps presumably to help rear the family but also for financial reasons. Joseph Dyer had been deeply in debt when he died, and rather given to saying lightly, "It will be alright after the Maori Wars."

The Beauchamps' first child, Vera Margaret, was born on October 22nd, 1885, at Hill Street, Wellington; their second, Charlotte Mary on July 9th, 1887, in Wadestown, in the first house built by Harold. When the winds there became too boisterous, he decided to build a second home in Wellington.

The site was a delightful one at number eleven (now twenty-five) Tinakori Road, high up above the glittering water of the harbour. It had extensive views of the hills of the Orongo Orongo range. The house, of earthquake-proof design, was square, made of white painted wood and topped by a gay red, corrugated iron roof. The front faced the gorse-clad Mount Wakefield; the back overlooked a verdant gully containing a suspension bridge and zig-zag path leading down to the Esplanade and Lambton Quay, now alas containing a great concrete motorway. Downstairs there were two reception rooms, the drawing room being on the left, and the dining room on the right. There were four bedrooms, a box-room, and a bathroom. A small porch at the side, its door inset with coloured glass, led into a hall which contained the doll's house. In front there was a lawn edged with arum lilies.

There, in a bedroom facing the wooded Tinakori Hills, on Sunday October 14th, 1888, at 8.00a.m., Kathleen Mansfield Beauchamp was born. It was a fine spring day, and azaleas were blooming in the Botanical Gardens nearby. The colony was only forty-eight years old. Grandmother Dyer would be ministering in the wings, Vera and Charlotte (Chaddie) vaguely aware of something going on, and Mrs Beauchamp? no doubt very exhausted.

In a few weeks Mr and Mrs Beauchamp sailed to England for a holiday, and the brown-eyed baby Kathleen was left in the care of her grandmother. At three months she developed jaundice, at two years she had to suffer the advent of a rival, a little sister Gwen who, alas, died of enteritis three months later. She began to have night terrors, slept fitfully, and was afraid of the wind.

On May 20th, 1892, another sister, Jeanne Worthington Beauchamp was born. By now Kathleen was a plump dreamy child, 'fatty' to the boys next door, considered 'difficult' at home and given to temper tantrums. She looked different and was pale, with brown wavy hair and big, dark 'mossy' eyes. Her sisters were blue-eyed, rosy-cheeked with Beauchamp features, and pleasantly wide-mouthed. Kathleen's mouth was small, like a buttonhole, but potentially beautiful.

At Easter 1893, the family moved to Karori, a small village eight hundred feet above sea level and four miles from Wellington, which only fifty years before had been a dark totara forest — Maori country — now mostly cleared, leaving pleasant, gorse-filled gullies and wooded, hilly vistas for the scattered white bungalows.

There was a general store at the village serving as a post office, a bakery, an estate agent and café, a wooden church, a library, a smithy and a small school. Mr Beauchamp, a partner of Bannatyne's since 1889, had taken a five year lease on a larger house called 'Chesney Wold'. It was a lovely rambling old place, of white painted wood with big square bay windows, a slim-pillared veranda and a conservatory, set in fourteen acres of orchard, garden and paddock through which ran a stream.

There were two horses, some cows, pigs and poultry with an Irish gardener-handyman, Patrick Sheehan, to look after them. In front of the house was a large old aloe, set in a curved drive, all described so lovingly in Kathleen's story called *Prelude*; the winding mountain road to Karori was that taken by the 'Storeman' when 'Kezia' and 'Lottie' were transported to the new home. The doll's house arrived with the furniture. Chesney Wold was lit by oil lamps; indeed there were no street lights in Karori. Mr Beauchamp, when taking the family to church on dark evenings, would have to carry a lantern.

Further up the road was Monkey Tree Cottage, to which Mrs Beauchamp's sister Agnes and husband Valentine Waters had moved the same week with their two boys Barry and Eric, the 'Pip' and 'Rags' of *Prelude*. The Dyers were obviously a close-knit family and Mr Beauchamp, beset by them all, seemed to give vent to his irritation in Kathleen's stories, especially in *At The Bay*, when as 'Stanley Burnell' he fumes over his brother-in-law 'Jonathon Trout' (Valentine) who seems to trespass on the morning bathe.

Valentine Waters, a kindly, courteous, dreamy type, was a clerk in Wellington. He was organist at Karori church, had a fine baritone voice and was the instigator of the family charades and concerts. Alas, he was to die in the influenza epidemic of November 1918, the infection having been brought first to Wellington by the passengers on the ship *Niagara*, one of which was his niece Vera Margaret. She was visited later by her father and Uncle Val, both of whom became ill, Valentine dying one week later.

On February 21st, 1894 Mrs Beauchamp had a son in a private hospital in Wellington. Everyone was delighted. He was christened Leslie Heron Beauchamp after C.R. Leslie the artist, and great uncle Henry Herron Beauchamp.

There was now a living-in maid to help, also a village washerwoman, Mrs MacKelvie, mother of five children, two of whom figure as 'Lil' and 'Our Else', the two haunting waifs in the story *The Doll's House*. The children attended the village school one mile away, as did all the Karori children, regardless of class. They had to stay to lunch, taking with them nourishing mutton sandwiches. Having kissed all the children at the breakfast table, Mr Beauchamp would prepare to walk the four miles to Wellington each morning, when Jeanne would say, as a matter of routine, "Father dear, may I have a pony?" and his answer was always the same, "Yes dear, you may have a pony, some day."

"I had to wait until I was forty," Jeanne told me ruefully; but then she did things in style and was able to go hunting with her husband, Captain Renshaw.

Patrick Sheehan, wearing a brown bowler hat, collected and drove Mr Beauchamp home at night in the phaeton drawn by Violet the white mare. By now, as well as being the sole partner in Bannatyne's, he was a director of the Gear Meat Company, chairman of the New Zealand Candle Company, a member of the Wellington Harbour Board, elected representative of the rate-payers of Wellington City and a JP. No wonder he got a trifle testy at times. He then recruited his Jewish neighbour from Tinakori Road, Mr Walter Nathan, as his partner in Bannatyne's, whose children duly appeared in *Prelude* as 'The Samuel Josephs'.

Kathleen, now six, joined Karori school. As middle child of two age groups she was rather out on a limb. She felt less loved, which was probably true if she caused the family friction which became so evident in later years. A Miss Rose Ridler, an informally adopted orphan who lived with the Waters family, thought Mrs Beauchamp less well disposed to Kathleen. One can visualize the resentful, smouldering gaze of the gifted child, at odds with her environment. To make things worse, she had to wear unlovely steel-rimmed spectacles *and* she was fat. Undoubtedly she would have a sharp tongue, and sibling rivalry would make it the sharper. She was irritable and quarrelsome, causing much disharmony. Vera was the general favourite, and Kathleen seemed at times ill-disposed to her even on to the end, perhaps because of this. With her rosy cheeks, blue eyes and golden-brown plaits, Vera was considered a comfort to her parents and helpful in the home. Chaddie, gentle, amiable, with ringlets and hazel eyes, had a chronic cough and often complained of feeling 'tired in her knees and feet', especially when she had to concentrate on schoolwork. Jeanne thought Chaddie was less clever but that her warm personality made up for this. She seemed to like everybody. Kathleen was a good hater.

However, in Mrs Dyer, Kathleen found deep emotional security. She slept in her grandmother's room and basked in the love she extended to all the family; and they in their turn adored their grandmother.

Emotional insecurity in a child can lead to two reactions, overdependence or rebellion. Inevitably, perhaps because of her superior intelligence, this imaginative, unusual child Kathleen chose the latter, and was, in turn, to reject her family and even her country for a time. She was vagrant by nature, taking after her rolling stone Grandpa Beauchamp. While at Karori, Kathleen's teacher noticed her interest in writing, and thought she wrote as if under compulsion. She had to be taught restraint.

At eight, Kathleen won the school composition prize for an essay on 'A Sea Voyage'. A childhood letter to a friend survives; it is delightful and endearing.

Her white furs have come out of the hatbox — 'a little smelly but such a comfy smell'. She wears a small red jacket over her white frock and 'Look at my new woollen legs'.

Beyond the garden gate the road walks over a hill away from people and houses.

"It's running away from the shops," and we know, could we but walk far enough, it would run right into the sea.

"Does it go on then?"

"Why, of course, right through a coral forest, pink and white, where the Sea King's daughters play 'Here we go gathering seaweed grapes', and blow the loveliest tunes through little silver shells."

"Oh, look, a sparrow — a little boy sparrow. Whistling on top of that willow tree. Look at his fur blowing about . . . . he looks as though he was waving a hanky at me. I wish I could hold him inside my jacket here, and take him home — he'd be so warm."

The late Willa Catha, in her book *Not Under Forty*, gives us a delightful account of the young Kathleen as described to her by a fellow passenger on an American bound ship from Naples in Autumn 1920:

Mr J., a New Englander, on a business trip to Australia via New Zealand, saw a family join the ship at Wellington, a man and an old lady in charge of young children. One of the little girls impressed him by exploring the ship on her own, after which she sat by him and talked about the sights. He saw her again the following morning. She was wearing a dress embroidered with yellow ducks around the hem with a duck on each cuff. It was new apparently and she kept stroking it. She told him her name was Kathleen Beauchamp and they became fast friends for the rest of the voyage.

Because of this unusual and delightful little girl he remembered that boat trip, only one of many. Some years later, in London, he heard of a young New Zealand writer there who 'could knock the standard British authors into a cocked hat', and who was unconventional and consequently rather talked about. Her name was Katherine Mansfield. Later, when dining in a restaurant with a business client, she was pointed out to him. It was his sunny little friend of the duck embroidered dress; the face was unmistakable but she looked frail.

Mr J. longed to contact her but felt he had better read some of her work first. He was given a copy of her privately printed story *Je ne parle pas français*. Alas, he did not like that fine story and decided consequently to do nothing further about meeting her. He was to see her once more, at the theatre, and as the lights went down, looking along at her, he thought she looked ill and unhappy. He was disappointed in the story, he told Willa Catha, thought it affected, artificial and hysterical and very unlike his little shipboard heroine.

In spite of her problems, Kathleen spent many happy days at Karori, wading in the stream at the bottom of the garden and catching little fish there in a glass jar. She loved riding, which she did fearlessly and there were her cousins Eric and Barry Waters to play with.

In March 1898, Mr and Mrs Beauchamp sailed for England on a business trip, returning in November via Canada. The lease on 'Chesney Wold' was terminating and Mr Beauchamp made arrangements to move back to Wellington. The three girls were now attending the Wellington Girls' High School in Thorndon, travelling from Karori each day. There, a wonderful new avenue opened up for Kathleen in the School Magazine, the *High School Reporter*. Her first work to appear in print was an essay, 'Enna Blake', an account of 'the happiest holiday she had ever had'.

Many years later in a letter to Miss Ruth Mantz, Kathleen's first biographer, Vera still remembered with what triumph Kathleen brought home the magazine containing her first 'story': '. . . She could not have been more than nine at the time'.

In November 1898 the family moved into 75 Tinakori Road, Wellington, a large, square white wooden house, looking towards the Tinakori Hills and sunlit from morning till night. There was a large garden with a tennis court down which Jeanne remembered bowling green apples until they were soft enough to eat. "I can see myself and Leslie running about there with Kathleen and calling to the boy over the neighbouring fence, 'Guy will you come over?'" which led eventually to the famous wedding service held on the lily lawn, read from a seed catalogue by Kathleen, when Jeanne was 'married' to Guy with a daisy chain for a ring. As well as the lily lawn, there was a violet bed and a pink garden seat just large enough for three children.

There, in a photograph, we see Kathleen flanked by Leslie and Jeanne, all smiling at the photographer. On another, perhaps taken on the same day, Mr and Mrs Beauchamp stand on a gracious pillared veranda with their new Canadian friends the Ruddicks and their little daughter Marion. They had been fellow passengers on the trip from Canada. Mr Beauchamp looks as though he had just got in from work. The children in their hard straw boaters are arranged on the steps at their feet. The fact that the garden seat was pink casts, for me at least, a glow over that garden and that sunny afternoon so long ago.

Kathleen's bedroom looked over the harbour. She would watch the dawn turning the dark distant hills to violet. *Four o'clock*, she wrote years later, remembering that old house with love, *is it light now at four o'clock? I jump out of the bed and run over to the window. It is half light, neither black nor blue. The wing of the coast is violet, and in the lilac sky are black banners and little black boats manned by black shadows put out on the purple water. Oh! how often have I watched this hour when I was a girl! But then — I stayed at the window until I grew cold . . . thrilled by something — I did not know what.* (quoted in Mantz.)

A stone wall, from which nasturtiums tumbled, flanked the

terraced garden. There was a visitors' gate, a tradesman's entrance and two old carriage gates on which the children often swung. There were other fine old houses in Tinakori Road, the Prime Minister's residence 'Awarua' for instance, but there were some modest ones too and below, running at right angles, was Saunders Lane, a collection of rather poor little houses, the setting for the story *The Garden Party*.

In the white and gold drawing-room, with green wooden sun-blinds, Kathleen, writing to Chaddie much later, remembered the potted blue cinerarias there: *the faint light, big cushions, tables with photographs of the children in silver frames, some little yellow and black cups and saucers that belonged to Napoleon in a high cupboard and someone playing Chopin — beyond words playing Chopin.*

The Wellington Girls' College stood below Tinakori Road, and was within walking distance. Kathleen joined the second form on May 25th, 1898. The class consisted of seven girls, among them Chaddie and Marion Ruddick, who in her smart sailor suit was Kathleen's special friend. Their classroom had a view of the sea.

On a summer evening in December 1899, in the presence of her family, a prize-giving ceremony was held at school. Kathleen received three prizes for English, French, and Arithmetic. Christmas was spent at their holiday cottage at Island Bay on the shore of Cook Strait. Marion was a guest, bringing her doll with her.

She gave Kathleen a silver thimble in a green velvet case, Jeanne a pink and white dolls' teapot and Leslie a toy dancing bear. Another guest was New Zealand's Premier, the Rt.Hon. R.J. Seddon, who crowned the festivities with an offer of a Government Directorship, Chairman of the Bank of New Zealand, a great honour for Mr Beauchamp at the age of forty. His future was now secure.

Kathleen and Marion learned to swim at Thorndon Sea Baths below the quay. She remembered the seaweedy odour years after, planning to put it all into a story: *the feeling of the Thorndon Baths, the wet, moist, oozy . . . no, I know how it must be done*, she wrote in her notebook. They played tennis at Tinakori Road, and ate Canadian Maple sugar cakes up an acacia tree in Marion's garden, with its lovely view over the harbour.

Mr Beauchamp, flushed with success, acquired another holiday home at Muritai, south of Day's Bay, the only access to which was by steamer, a thirty-minute journey in the *Duke* or *Duchess* from Lambton Quay. Friendly ship's hooters would summon passengers to pick-up points, a wonderful sound, especially on sparkling days with the hinterland of untrammelled green bush.

As well as a fine beach, there was a wonderland for the children at Day's Bay, with a laughing gallery, swings, and even that childhood delight, a water-chute.

In December 1899, another essay by Kathleen M. Beauchamp appeared in the *High School Reporter*, called 'A Happy Christmas Eve', in which a party of four children are shown a Christmas tree at a party given by the rich 'Courtenay' children — a precursor of *The Doll's House.*

In June 1900 the Beauchamp girls were transferred to the more exclusive school, Miss Swainson's, built 1878, at 20, Fitzherbert Terrace. The headmistress was Mrs Henry Smith, a cousin of Charles Kingsley. According to Miss Mantz, Mrs Smith thought Kathleen 'a thundercloud', 'unruly', 'careless', 'plain', 'surly', 'imaginative to the point of untruth', and quite different from her neat polite sisters. She *was* different, right to the end.

Another teacher, Miss Eva Butts, thought her 'shabby, inky, dumpy and unattractive — not even cleverly naughty'. She also seemed unambitious. However, Miss Butts discovered Kathleen could act, and she was given the part of Mrs Jarley in a charity performance of *Mrs Jarley's Waxworks*. No doubt her wonderful sense of humour was beginning to shine through the 'thundercloud'.

About this time, Marion Ruddick departed and Kathleen was without a friend for a time. She was thirteen and adolescent, when a new interest developed. She met Tom Trowell, fifteen years old, a promising cellist, son of a Wellington music teacher. The boy's twin brother Garnet played the violin. A fund had been raised, contributed to by Mr Beauchamp to the tune of £25, to send the boys to Europe for further study. The first meeting was at 75 Tinakori Road at a 'musical'. Inevitably, she fell rapturously in love with him, with his thick red-brown hair, pale skin and rather prominent front teeth. She named him 'Caesar' and corresponded with

him until 1907. As one would expect, Kathleen being the
lonely, highly emotional girl she was, the relationship was
rather one-sided but it was an outlet. Now she had to have a
cello and a brown dress to match, taking lessons from Mr
Trowell. She was going to become a 'musician'.

There was someone else who interested her, a rich Maori girl
at school in the class above. She was Maata Mahupuku,
daughter of a brother of a tribal chief, Tamahau Mahupuku.
She had a lovely face and was absolutely bewitching.

It was now time for Leslie to start school. Jeanne told me
that she did not get to her first school until she was eight. "I
had to wait until Chummie was six. We were shown into Miss
Swainson's drawing room and asked to kneel on two hassocks.
Prayers were said over us. Tears were coming from Chummie's
eyes. 'Chummie, haven't you got a handkerchief?' 'No, I
haven't!' 'Then use your neck-tie!' Jeanne whispered. I was
'adopted' by the Samuel Bolton family, nine girls and two
boys, one extra made little difference. We used to round up
twenty ponies. Our bridles would hang above our beds. We
brought ourselves up. At night, carrying lamps, we went
fishing for eels, coming back for refreshments, ginger beer and
biscuits. There was never any alcohol. It was all on a lovely
platonic level, all happy and carefree. On my last visit to New
Zealand at eighty-seven, I found only one Bolton daughter
remained."

It had been decided to send the three elder girls to Queen's
College, Harley Street, London for their further education, on
the recommendation of Mrs Beauchamp's cousin Frank Payne,
a physician in Wimpole Street, whose daughters Evelyn and
Sylvia were already established there. On January 7th, 1903
the *New Zealand Mail*, Wellington's 'Illustrated Weekly', with
its nice, thick rose-red cover, announced the Beauchamps'
imminent departure, also noting the sad news of the
grandmother, Mrs Dyer, having suffered a seizure at the home
of her daughter, Mrs W.V. Waters of Karori, adding that she
was, however, progressing favourably.

The February 4th edition described an afternoon tea given
by Mrs Beauchamp. It was held on a wet and windy
afternoon in late January. Mrs Beauchamp's prune cloth

costume with cream collar and revers, topped by a black hat, was duly described. No doubt it was new for the trip to the Old Country and being tried out, for it appears on the *Niwaru* family photograph at Las Palmas.

Chapter II

Queen's College

Imagine the excitement with which the whole family sailed for England on January 29th, 1903. Mr Beauchamp had booked all of the passenger accommodation in the Tyser liner, *Niwaru*, the group including Aunt Belle, her brother Sydney and the canary. The route via Cape Horn took forty-seven days.

Jeanne, aged eleven, earnestly wrote an account of the voyage in her diary which she still has. They passed Cape Horn at 2.00 p.m. on Saturday February 21st, 1903 — Leslie's birthday. In the evening there was a fancy dress party until 11.00 p.m., with music and solos from the crew, Uncle Syd, and Chaddie. On Monday March 16th, the *Niwaru* docked at Las Palmas. Accompanied by Captain Crowe, they drove in two carriages around the town, taking lunch in 'a lovely hotel', and here they were photographed. The picture shows a happy group, with a mature young Katherine in a straw boater and Aunt Belle wearing a fragrant rose on a hopeful breast. On Tuesday March 24th they sailed up the Channel, anchoring at Gravesend for six hours, and eventually boarded an omnibus at Liverpool Street Station. *We drove all over town and had a lovely time. I think London is just wonderful, it is wonderfully big.* After dinner, at their apartment, *Aunt Belle and mother went to the dressmakers and left us children at home. I was awfully* Niwaru *sick and wanted to go back badly.*

On April foul (sic) day . . . mother went all day to see Queen's College, the girls are going there.

Sunday April 6th . . . went to Uncle Henry's place down at Bexley . . . when we were having dinner the maid came in and placed the dirty old cheese before father. It was black and Uncle Henry said it was lovely and he kept it live by brandy and water, we said we would give it a funeral but Uncle Henry said it was nice. . . .

Queen's College, 43-45 Harley Street, was founded in 1848 and still flourishes today. It was started as a training school for governesses, a project of the Governesses' Benevolent Institution and aimed to give a university education to the hitherto downtrodden, ill-paid governess. One of the founding professors was Charles Kingsley. Dr Sophia Jex-Blake, who established a medical school for women, was a former pupil, also Gertrude Bell who was to cross the Syrian desert alone.

The teaching staff in 1903 included Professor John Adam Cramb (1861-1913), a Scot who taught modern history, painting, music and philosophy. He sported a magnificent walrus moustache, spoke seven languages, and at that time, though married, was in love with a Lady Ottoline Morrell. He wrote her ninety-four letters and bought her gifts of 'Ladies No. I' gold-tipped cigarettes from Noteras, in Piccadilly.

Katherine in 1916, eulogizing in her journal about her college days, wrote: . . . *Cramb, wonderful Cramb . . . . he was 'history' to me. Ageless and fiery eating himself up again and again.* In 1903 she would have been intrigued by his background, as she herself was to become friendly with the same Lady Ottoline, who also thought Cramb 'brilliant and wonderful'.

Hall Griffin taught English Literature and Walter Rippmann languages. Rippmann was young, able, dark and charming.

In April 1903, the three girls in their velour hats and sailor coats, piped with red and decorated with brass buttons, were received by the lady resident Miss Camilla Croudace and taken to the hostel at 41 Harley Street, which was supervised by a Miss Clara Wood. Aunt Belle, who still had charge of the young Beauchamps, was to stay on there to help Miss Wood.

That day, Katherine met another student, Miss Ida Constance Baker, who showed them to their bedroom. So began the lifelong relationship which was to succour but torment Kathleen to the end of her days.

Ida was the elder daughter of Colonel Oswald Baker, a

former Indian Army doctor who had been in practice in Welbeck Street since 1895. His wife Katherine had just died of typhoid fever and the younger daughter May was disabled by polio. Colonel Baker was an arrid, moody, unhappy man who eventually committed suicide by shooting himself, at the end of World War One.

Ida six feet tall, with size nine feet, pale, fair, emotionally immature and self-effacing, showed the little party into a bay-windowed bedroom which looked across Harley Street to the Mansfield Mews.

At that time, there were forty boarders and some day-girls, including the Payne cousins, Evelyn and Sylvia.

In her novel *Juliet*, commenced in May 1906, Kathleen described those first impressions of her bedroom — the wall texts, intertwined with foxgloves and robins, the mews below the large windows and the sound of carriages being swilled with water.

The girls unpacked their large boxes, Kathleen briskly choosing her bed, the one by the window. She loved dreaming at windows, communicating with the world beyond. She would later lean out, elbows resting on a towel-draped sill and say, "Don't bother me girls: I'm going to have a mood."

Arnold's photograph was placed on her chest of drawers, and no doubt was often addressed as she would address her own face in the mirror and the pages of her notebook. There was no question of homesickness either, Mr and Mrs Beauchamp, Jeanne and Leslie, were to stay on in England until November.

Kathleen was reserved and considered unpopular with the other girls. She did make a few friends however: Ruth Herrick, a New Zealander, who thought her 'a strange girl, she had an intensity beyond the understanding of most of her school-fellows', Gwen Rouse from the Isle of Man who kept in touch with her for years, and Vere Bartrick-Baker (Mimi or Eve), who said in retrospect that Katherine's appearance did not attract her but her personality interested her very much. Vere eventually worked for John Middleton Murry, almost became his wife after Katherine's death, and ultimately married his friend, J.W.N. Sullivan.

Then there were the two Payne cousins, Evelyn and Sylvia. Evelyn was commissioned to check and correct Katherine's lecture notes. Under the strain of reading the almost illegible handwriting, no doubt skin and hair flew. Evelyn, who became Mrs M.J. Murphy, told Professor Alpers that Kathleen was 'impossibly conceited and perfectly detestable' — there now!

Sylvia on the other hand, artistic and clever with her long red hair and mischievous ways, became a favourite of Kathleen's and they corresponded long after leaving Queen's College. Sylvia kept the letters until her own death. Her nickname was Jug and she is immortalized as Constantia in the poignant story *The Daughters of the Late Colonel.*

Kathleen now had a new cello, purchased at Hills in Bond Street. She took lessons at the London Academy of Music. These had been arranged by her second cousin and official guardian in England, Henry De Monk Beauchamp, who taught there. He was the son of Henry Herron Beauchamp and brother of Elizabeth Countess von Arnim.

Kathleen attended concerts at Queen's Hall, she and Ruth Herrick pretending to be young Bohemian musicians. Ida Baker studied the violin and would spend long periods in Kathleen's room listening to her playing the cello.

Since Tom Trowell had adopted the professional name of Arnold, Kathleen decided that she and Ida would do similar. She chose Katherine Mansfield; Ida, who wanted to be called Katherine Moore after her mother, became Lesley Moore, to avoid confusion. Thereafter, the initials K.M. and L.M. came into being.

By now, following Katherine's sudden proposal to Ida 'let's be friends', Lesley had become her adoring slave, emotionally and physically. As Professor Alpers points out 'a form of imprinting had occurred'. L.M. fell into love with Katherine as though under the effect of religious conversion, a feeling that was to last even into old age.

Of course Ida, motherless and insecure, needed some love object. Her immature personality had a marked masochistic component, which made her ideally suited to the serving role which the dominant, self-assured Katherine required. She would order Ida to get her a handkerchief from a drawer. Ida would respond promptly and meekly, "Yes, Katie, darling," her adoring compliance sickening Ruth Herrick (according to Alpers).

Katherine loved life at Queen's College and wrote about it in her notebook in 1916: *I lived in the girls, the professor, the big, lovely building, the leaping fires in the winter and the abundant flowers in summer. The views out of the windows, all the pattern that was — weaving. Nobody saw it, I felt, as I did. My mind was just like a squirrel. I gathered and gathered and hid away, for that long 'winter'* . . . .

Her work was reported to be above average. French and German were her best subjects. She joined the Debating Society and the Swanwick Society which met each month to discuss poetry, where each member recited a poem of their own choice. I think Katherine would have loved this. She was composing poetry of her own, one little verse being particularly remembered by a schoolfellow, Isobel Creelman (Mrs Howard Ambrose of Hamilton, Ontario):

> I hope I may die in darkness
> When the world is so quiet and still,
> And my soul pass away with the shadows,
> Ere the sun rises over the hill.

She was still sending ardent letters to 'Caesar', of course. By August 1903 the Trowell twins were established in Frankfurt and perhaps on the crest of a wave from having Arnold nearby, Katherine wrote a story entitled *His Ideal*, as yet unpublished. It was about a young man who cherished the memory of a childhood dream when he lay ill and had a vision of a beautiful woman for whom he longed when he grew up. In a state of spiritual desolation and preparing to drown himself, he sees again his beautiful vision 'and her name was Death'.

On October 17th, 1903, perhaps as part of her fifteenth birthday celebrations, Katherine paid the Trowell boys a visit. One can imagine her rapture. A photograph of a torn-up picture of a demure Katherine playing her cello, dated 17. X. 03 and headed 'Eschersheimer Landstrasse' appears in Professor Alpers' *The Life of Katherine Mansfield*. I wonder who tore it up and why?

On November 10th, 1903, Mr and Mrs Beauchamp, Jeanne and Leslie sailed home to New Zealand. All would be feeling sad I think, but the fact that Aunt Belle was left behind as chaperon to the girls, no doubt eased any anxiety.

In December 1903, there appeared in the *Queen's College Magazine* a story by Katherine with the endearing title 'The Pine Tree, The Sparrows, and You and I', a story about children. On December 23rd the girls went to stay with Great Uncle Henry Herron Beauchamp and Aunt Louey at Bexley, Kent.

A word now about their famous daughter Mary Annette, Countess von Arnim. She was fair, small, with prominent Beauchamp blue eyes and a high colour. She did well at school, and on July 19th, 1883 her father noted in his diary: *May glorified by coming out first in History examination against all Ealing Schools.* She studied music at the College of Music, South Kensington, winning a prize for organ playing.

On January 23rd, 1889 she accompanied her father to Rome where she met Graf Henning August von Arnim Schlagenthin. He had heard Elizabeth playing the organ in the American Church there and was fascinated. He was related to the Imperial Family through his mother, née Elise von Prillwite, daughter of Prince August of Prussia, 1779-1843, a nephew of Frederick the Great. As a boy, Henning had been taught to play the piano by Liszt.

Henning August von Arnim, desolate after the death of his first wife Countess Anna von Törring-Jettenbach in 1888, and their baby daughter very soon afterwards, was captivated by May Beauchamp. He proposed to her in Florence and they married on February 21st, 1891, taking up residence in Berlin. The Count also had an early seventeenth century schloss (château) called Nassenheide, formerly a convent, situated in the depths of Pomerania and consisting of eight thousand acres of pine forest stretching to the Baltic. At his wife's instigation the family settled there in 1896 with their three daughters. Elizabeth's first book *Elizabeth and her German Garden* is a charming account of that time. No doubt her royalties of £40,000 financed much of the renovation.

A fourth daughter Felicitas Joyce (Martin) was born July 29th, 1899; and finally, on October 27th, 1902, a son at last, Henning Bernd von Arnim Schlagenthin. This was no doubt why Felicitas was sent to live with her grandparents in Bexley from 1902-1907, and so the little German girl was there to greet her New Zealand cousins that Christmas in 1903. Aunt

Louey, 'sweet and sunny natured', would make the girls very welcome. Katherine wrote a letter about Felicitas on a subsequent Easter visit.

To Edie Bendall (later Mrs G.G.S. Robison) 1906-1907:

Do they in New Zealand have a children's Thanksgiving Service? They do in the country in England. One Easter I was staying with my Grannie at the time down in Kent, her German grandchild of five was there, so we took her — I shall never forget how beautiful it was. She wore the shortest little white embroidery frock, and white stockings and red shoes, and under her little white satin straw hat with just a wreath of field daisies round it — her curls tinkled round her. There was a hymn — 'All things bright and beautiful' — when the children had to hold their offerings as they sang. We lifted the German baby right up on the cushions in the pew, and she sang very gravely, holding her white basket full of coloured Easter eggs, and flowers — and the sun streamed into the little old quaint church, and the children's voices, very thin and high — seemed to float in the air — above them all I heard the German baby — exultant joyful — her cheeks all rosy. Granny and I enjoyed ourselves so much that we both cried, to the baby's horror and astonishment. She pulled my sleeve — "Kassie, why are you lookin' so wistful?" — I can hear her now with a violent German accent — she was so precious . . . . —
More of Felicitas later.

That Christmas, among Katherine's presents was a concerto written by Arnold Trowell and in a letter to her cousin Sylvia dated December 23rd, 1903 she described a stormy morning in Bexley:

I have been fearfully cross this morning. It was about my music. Yesterday I got a concerto from Caesar for a Xmas present and I tried it over with Vera this morning. She counted loud and said wrong wrong, *called me a pig, and then said she would go and tell Aunt Louie I was swearing at her. I laugh as I read this now. At the time I felt ill with anger. So much for my excellent temper . . . .*

In the same letter, writing alone in the quietness of her bedroom,

O don't you just thank God for quiet? she made a sudden endearing declaration of loving friendship for Sylvia: . . . *I like you much more than any other girl I have met in England . . . . We just stand upon the threshold of each other's heart and never get right in. What I mean by 'heart' is just this. My heart is a place where everything I love (whether it be in imagination or in truth) has a free entrance. It is where I store my memories, all my happiness and my sorrow and there is a large compartment in it labelled 'Dreams'. There are many many people that I like very much but they generally view my public rooms, and they call me false, and mad, and changeable. I would not show them what I was really like for worlds. They would think me madder I suppose . . . .* — a charming letter.

New Year was spent with other relatives near Sheffield and after attending the midnight service, she sat down in her dressing gown and 'by the light of a tiny peep of gas', wrote an account of the service in her notebook to send to Tom Trowell. *What a wonderful and what a lovely world this is! I thank God tonight that I am.*

Thus began what was finally to become her Journal, addressing herself on the page, recording impressions, moods, fears, and ideas for stories, this habit becoming life long. *Nothing affords me the same relief,* she wrote later. As a young woman, Katherine was to refer to some of these early notebooks as her 'huge complaining diaries'. Alas, she destroyed them, presumably for the sake of privacy — what a pity!

Back at Queen's College Katherine began to be enamoured of young Professor Rippmann. *I long for German I simply can't help it . . . . when I go into class I feel I must just stare at him the whole time. I never liked anyone so much,* she wrote to Sylvia on January 24th. Young and as yet unmarried, dark, plump, with a lisp, Rippmann lived in 72 Ladbrooke Grove with two other men, an artist and a journalist. He held occasional literary evenings there for the brighter attractive students in his class. Katherine was included and later she described the salon in her unfinished novel *Juliet*.

> . . . *vivid yellow curtains hung straight and fine before the three windows. Tall wrought-iron candlesticks stood in the corners* . . . *there were prints of beautiful women on the walls and a graceful figure of a girl holding a shell in her exquisite arms stood on a table. There was a long low couch upholstered in dull purple* . . . . *The room was full of the odour of chrysanthemums.*

There she was introduced to the works of Oscar Wilde, Paul Verlaine, Shaw, Ibsen and Symons. Katherine had written some poetry for Rippmann's book *English for Foreigners* to illustrate the exercises. No doubt she told him about her cousin Countess von Arnim and her latest book *The Adventures of Elizabeth in Rügen*, which had been published in 1902. In it Elizabeth had written about her tour of Rügen, a fascinating island off Pomerania, mentioning the small watering place there with the beautiful haunting name of 'Die Einsame' (The Lonely One), so called, perhaps, because of its isolated position by a pine forest.

Katherine, no doubt fascinated, used the name as a title for her story 'Die Einsame', which was published in the *Queen's College Magazine* in March 1904. With a death-wish theme, it was about a romantic young girl, who lived a lonely life in a small, bare house on a hill, overlooking the sea. Walking on the shore one night she sees a wonderful boat fashioned of 'moonshine', containing a smiling, beckoning figure. In rapture, she cries 'take me', but she is submerged by a great wave and then 'there is Silence'.

The college continued to charm Katherine. Overlooking the entrance hall on the first floor was a square opening known as the Giraffe Hole. Girls would lean over the railing to watch the professors coming and going. At the college dances, girls, like white peonies in their evening dresses, danced with one another. One can see Katherine, lost in one of her reveries, manfully steering her partner. Sweets were thrown from the Giraffe Hole to one's special friend. No doubt L.M. would be an expert at this.

There was a bun shop below stairs, cosily heated by a stove. What more glorious a meeting place for young growing things, exchanging confidences as they sat round the square wooden tables, eating commodious cakes and being looked after by old Mrs Brown. Oh! that bun-room squash of all our college days, when one felt so well and the future was so rosy!

In the summer of 1904 Katherine visited Bollendorf in Germany and presumably saw the Trowells again. Fired by Arnold's musical compositions Katherine decided to compete. She wrote the words and Vera the music for two songs called 'Night' and 'Love's Entreaty'. They were published in Berlin, sponsored by the New Zealand Piano Company and sung by Uncle Val Waters at a Harbour Board dinner. 'Night' was headed by the endearing dedication 'To Our Darling Parents'. Katherine was not yet courageous enough to use her *nom de plume*.

A further two stories concerning children appeared in the *Queen's College Magazine*, 'Your Birthday' in December 1904 and 'One Day' in July 1905. By now Katherine was sub-editor, and L.M. treasurer.

The girls had met their cousin Elizabeth briefly on her frequent visits to London. At that stage Vera felt that Elizabeth considered them 'little colonial frumps'. However, the man engaged as tutor to the daughters of the Countess, E.M. Forster, was to be a literary colleague of Katherine's in the next four years and to have his novel *The Story of the Siren* reviewed by her in the *Athenaeum*. He duly arrived at Nassenheide on the evening of April 4th, 1905, entered the dark vaulted hall and was shown to an appallingly cold spare room, decorated with pink and green wallpaper. He found Elizabeth 'small, graceful, vivid, and vivacious . . . a merciless tease'. She informed him later that she had nearly sent him back to England since he was wearing a particularly ugly tie. However, he found the radiant flat country surrounding Nassenheide absolutely ravishing.

Katherine was now seventeen and there appeared in the December edition of the college magazine her last story, entitled 'About Pat'. It bore the stamp of her future work and was about Patrick Sheehan, the Irish cowman-gardener at

c

'Chesney Wold', Karori.

She now had a new friend Mimi — Vere Bartrick-Baker — aged nineteen, dark, enigmatic, 'eyebrows raised, her eyes half veiled'. She had lent Katherine *The Portrait of Dorian Gray*, in the original unexpurgated form published in *Lippincott's Magazine*. It was a revelation. Katherine's notebooks were now full of Oscar; *To realise one's nature perfectly — that is what each of us is here for.*

The two girls would meet in the lower corridor an hour before classes commenced, no doubt to mull over Dorian Gray, but on being questioned about these sessions by a vigilant and suspicious Miss Croudace they declared they discussed Tolstoy, Maeterlinck and Ibsen!

Another college friend was Eileen Palliser, daughter of Charles Palliser, manager of the Bank of New Zealand, and a friend of Mr Beauchamp. Katherine was invited to join their parties for concerts at Queen's Hall.

The highlight of this period was a jubilant meeting with Maata, who was on her way home from finishing school in Paris, chic, 'polished with a vengeance' and dressed like a Parisienne. After this meeting the girls decided to keep diaries, and Maata sent Katherine part of hers to be woven into a story. In the unpublished manuscripts in the Alexander Turnbull Library, there is a charming piece entitled 'Summer Idylle 1906' which I think reflects their relationship.

Hinemoa (Katherine) and Marina (Maata) are living by the sea. It is early morning and refreshed by sleep Hinemoa goes to Marina's room to wake her up. *In Marina's room the scent of manuka was heavy and soothing. The floor was strewn with blossoms. Great sprays stood in every corner. Marina lay straight and still in her bed . . . her lips slightly parted. A faint thin colour like the petal of a dull rose leaf shone in the dusk of her skin. Hinemoa bent over her with a curious feeling of pleasure intermingled with a sensation which she did not analyse. It came upon her if she had used too much perfume, if she had drunk wine that was too heavy and sweet, laid her hand on velvet that was too soft and smooth. Marina was wrapped in the darkness of her hair. Hinemoa took it up in her hands and drew it away from her brow and face and shoulders.*

"Oh come quick, come quick," cried Hinemoa. ". . . I want to bathe."

"I come now," Marina answered, and suddenly she seized a great spray of manuka and threw it full in Hinemoa's face and the blossoms fell into her hair.

"Snow maiden, snow maiden," she said laughing . . . and they ran . . . down to the shore. They . . . swam swiftly . . . towards an island. Hinemoa fell back a little to see Marina. She loved to watch her complete harmony . . .

"You are just where you ought to be," she said raising her voice . . . . . I like not congruity. It is because you are so utterly the foreign element . . . you see?" At breakfast Marina invites Hinemoa to a baked kumara, the New Zealand sweet potato which when cooked has a bluish colour.

"No, I don't like them. They're blue, they're too unnatural. Give me some bread." Marina handed her a piece, and then helped herself to koumara (sic) which she ate delicately, looking at Hinemoa with a strange half-smile expanding over her face. "I eat it for that reason," she said. "I eat it because it is blue." "Yes," said Hinemoa, breaking the bread in her white fingers.

In her notebook for 1908 Katherine nostalgically recalled their London meeting. *In the pocket of an old coat I found one of Ariadne's gloves — a cream suede glove fastening with two silver buttons. And it has been there two years. But it still holds some exquisite suggestion of Carlotta; still when I lay it against my cheek I can detect the secret of the perfume she affected. O Carlotta, have you remembered? We were floating down Regent Street in a hansom, on either side of us the blossoms of golden light, and ahead a little half-hoop of a moon.*

At Easter Aunt Belle took her three nieces to Paris and Brussels to see Arnold and Garnet, now at the Brussels *Conservatoire.* Bohemian to their coat tails, wearing very wide-brimmed black hats and smoking extra long cigarettes, they introduced Katherine to their friend Rudolph. She would be in her element. This was the life, *la vie de Bohème!*

She sent L.M. a photograph of herself she had taken there and inscribed it in a firm, mature hand 'Mes Mains Dans Les Votres', showing her hair with a centre parting, backcombed and fluffed out sideways from a plump, young, grave face, not yet fascinating.

On April 20th, 1906, the *Athenic*, bearing Mr and Mrs Beauchamp, arrived at Plymouth and the whole family went to stay at a hotel in 3 Manchester Street near Marble Arch. On April 24th, 1906 Katherine wrote to Sylvia Payne:

We have been staying here since last Friday with Father and Mother and have had a very good time. I don't think I have ever laughed more. They are both just the same and we leave for New Zealand in October . . . . A great change has come into my life since I saw you last. Father is greatly opposed to my wish to be a professional cellist or to take up the cello to any great extent — so my hope for a musical career is absolutely gone . . . . But I suppose it is no earthly use warring with the inevitable — so in future I shall give all my time to writing.

. . . I am enjoying this hotel life. There is a kind of feeling of irresponsibility about it that is fascinating. Would you not like to try all sorts of lives — one is so very small — but that is the satisfaction of writing — one can impersonate so many people . . . .

One can imagine the joyous reunion at the London hotel, the talk, the laughing, and the beds strewn with 'wedding cake hats, and perhaps a white feather boa or white fox fur stole which Mrs Beauchamp sometimes affected.

On returning to college Katherine seemed unsettled and changed rooms after a quarrel with her sisters, sharing instead with Eileen Palliser. Then came the news that Rudolph had committed suicide by shooting himself. This tragedy with its Wildean undertones upset Katherine very much. The Trowell twins had arrived in London to give a recital but there seemed to be some rift in the lute. She would come back to college after seeing Arnold and sob on her bed, no doubt due to her over-loving and Arnold's under-loving. He was more concerned with his cello playing, his image, his red hair, which was to be worn shoulder length in his 1907 portrait. It is a wonder that Katherine was so enamoured of him — his teeth were prominent; his students at the Guildhall School of Music used to call him 'Toothies', but affectionately, when he became their professor in 1924 — he was well liked. It was probably about this time that with the advent of *Dorian Gray* via Mimi, her meeting with Maata and the tragedy of Rudolph, Katherine began to suffer over stirrings of adolescent bisexuality. This was further complicated by her imminent departure for New Zealand.

On May 18th, 1906 Katherine began her novel *Juliet* into which she poured all this pent-up emotion. It was largely autobiographical and set in Wellington. It was written in one thick black notebook (Notebook I) in a series of episodes not yet gelled. The content was unrequited love, death, life in London contrasted with that in New Zealand, choice of careers *etc*.

Juliet Wilberforce is dressing for a musical evening to which a young cellist, David Méjin aged fifteen has been invited. She studies her reflection in the mirror as she brushes her hair:

. . . her face was square in outline, and her skin very white. The impression which it gave was not by any means strictly beautiful, when in repose it conveyed an idea of extreme thoughtfulness, her mouth drooped slightly at the corners; her eyes were shadowed — but her expression was magnetic — her personality charged with vitality. She looked a dreamer — but her dreams were big with life. Juliet's hands were as distinctive as any part of her. They were large and exquisitely modelled. Her fingers were not very long — and blunted at the tops, but no amount of work could change their beauty. She gesticulated a great deal, and had a habit of sitting always nursing one knee — her fingers interlocked.

Juliet was the odd moment of the family — the ugly duckling. She had lived in a world of her own — created her own people — read anything and everything which came to hand — was possessed with a violent temper, and completely lacked placidity. She was dominated by her moods which swept through her and in number were legion. She had been as yet utterly idle at school — drifted through her classes . . . . She absorbed everybody and everything with which she came in contact, and wrapped herself in a fierce white reserve. Of late she had quarrelled frequently with the entire family . . . . She had no defined path, no goal to reach. She felt compelled to vent her energy on somebody and that somebody was her family. [This was obviously a detailed picture of herself.]

The mother was a slight pale little woman. She had been delicate and ailing before her marriage and she never could forget it . . . . Mr. Wilberforce tall grey bearded with prominent blue eyes — large ungainly hands . . . was a general merchant . . . thoroughly commonplace and commercial.

Then a typical Katherine through Juliet leans out of the window with its 'great pine tree outlined against the night sky — and the sea stretching far in the distance . . .' *"O night,"* she *cried . . . turning her face up to the stars. "O adorable night."*

David's appearance is touched up a little: *Profusion of red-brown hair, very pale he was with a dreamy exquisite face.*

Juliet goes to London for three years to complete her education, David also, to study music. Juliet shares a room with a girl named Pearl or sometimes Vere in the manuscript, describing what must have been her room at Queen's College and her feelings on starting her new life there. At the end of the three years she refuses to return home, electing to share a flat with Pearl. She meets Rudolph who lives with David. Then comes evidence of Katherine's conflict:

"She hates me," Rudolph said. "I only wish she hated me," said David. "It is an impossible position — I feel as though I ought to love her . . . but I do not. She is too much like me. I understand her too well. We are both too moody, we both feel too much the same about everything . . . and so she does not attract me . . ."

The story hurtles to its tragic end, Juliet is seduced by Rudolph, becomes pregnant and dies after an abortion, with David and Pearl who are in love with each other standing by her bed.

She opened her eyes and saw the two beside her. "Ought I to join your hands and say bless you?" she whispered. Suddenly she raised herself. "O-o- I want to live," she screamed. But Death put his hand over her mouth.

Though naïve and melodramatic and the death scene energetically stormy, the work is full of precious subjective information.

The real conflict was of course that Katherine did not want to leave London. In *Juliet* she wrote:

If I do once go back all will be over. It is stagnation, desolation

*that stares me in the face. I shall be lonely, I shall be thousands
of miles from all that I care for and once I get there I can't
come back.*

Mr Wilberforce replies: *"What have I got for my money? . . .
You are behaving badly. You must learn to realize that the
silken cords of parental authority are very tight ropes indeed. I
want no erratic spasmodic daughter. I demand a sane
healthy-minded girl." (Juliet; p25)*

In truth, Mr Beauchamp was not at all pleased with the
situation. There were family scenes as he refused Katherine
permission to remain in London, and in consequence declared
darkly that he had no intention of sending the two younger
children 'home' to be educated.

On October 14th, 1906, Katherine was eighteen. A few days
later the family sailed for New Zealand in the *Corinthic*, sister
ship to the *Athenic*. A case of smallpox was discovered on
board and landed at Capetown. Aunt Belle Dyer remained
happily in London. She had become engaged to a wealthy
stockbroker and was to become Mrs Harry Trinder.

What of L.M. at eighteen, lonely, with no future career
prospects? She would feel bereft. In her book *Katherine
Mansfield, The Memories of L.M.* she wrote: *I waited, and
lived on Katherine's letters. They came irregularly at first,
posted at stopping places on the way, with photographs of the
group: boys and girls happy on board the slowly moving ship.
The favourite amongst the boys was called Adonis. Katherine's
grand despair at having to leave London inevitably dissipated
and she began* seeing *things again, but with a more mature
eye.*

On board, Katherine flirted with this 'Adonis', a member of
the English Cricket Team bound for New Zealand and
Australia and, describing in her notebook his beauty, his
Grecian mouth, wrote:

*When I am with him a preposterous desire seizes me, I want to
be badly hurt by him, I should like to be strangled by his firm
hands . . . . Last night we sat on deck . . . 'The more hearts you
have the better,' he said, leaning over my hand . . . . We*

exchanged a long look and his glance inflamed me like the scent of a gardenia.

Alas, all was not well within the family. Katherine resented her parents' vigilance. *They are prying and curious . . . my Father spoke of my returning as damned rot, said look here, he wouldn't have me fooling around in dark corners with fellows . . .* She *is constantly suspicious, constantly overbearingly tyrannous . . . .*

I cannot be alone or in the company of women for a half minute — he is there, eyes fearful, attempting to appear unconcerned, and then with the cruelty of youth, Katherine proceeded to vilify both parents. However, one must remember that these critical comments were private and that they were published posthumously for all the world to see, can only be a matter for some regret. She continued: *I shall never be able to live at home . . . . There would be constant friction. For more than a quarter of an hour they are quite unbearable, and so absolutely my mental inferiors.*

. . . . I have none of that glorious expectancy that I used to have so much. They are draining it out of me.

Chapter III

Return to Wellington

The *Corinthic* arrived at Wellington on December 6, 1906 on a fine sunny morning. Mr Beauchamp was interviewed. He had, after all, met King Edward VII. The big square house, 75 Tinakori Road, was occupied once more. Leslie was sent to boarding school, the Waitaki Boys' High School in South Island.

Grandmother Dyer, aged sixty-seven and in poor health, was now living with her widowed daughter Eliza Trapp, Aunt 'Li', in Tinakori Road. On December 31st at 11.00p.m. she died. Katherine had not yet visited her since returning from England. This omission had been noted gently by the old lady, and now it was too late! In a letter to Sylvia Payne on January 8th, 1907 Katherine wrote:

The New Year has come — I cannot really allow myself to think of it yet . . . life here's impossible — I can't see how it can drag on — I have not one friend — and no prospect of one — my dear — I know nobody — and nobody cares to know me — There is nothing on earth to do — nothing to see — and my heart keeps flying off to Oxford Circus — Westminster Bridge at the Whistler hour . . . . It haunts me all so much — and I feel it must come back soon — How people ever wish to live here I cannot think — I have been living, too, in the atmosphere of death. My grandmother died on New Year's Eve — my first experience of a personal loss — it horrified me — the whole thing — death never seemed revolting before.

Even dear uncomplicated 'sunshiny' Chaddie (Jeanne's

description) criticised New Zealand in her letter to Sylvia:

Well dear it is absolutely devoid of art and so naturally the people are most uninteresting. Take my advice dear and never come to the Colonies to live in, remain in England, how I wish I was there too. I would give the worlds to be back. I can't tell you how miserable it is as we have absolutely no friends. All the girls we used to know have grown up and got married and don't seem the least bit interested in us. So it is rather a sad state of affairs n'est pas?

Katherine's father also had problems. The *Auckland Weekly News* for January 3rd, 1907 reported that Mr Harold Beauchamp of Wellington had resigned his position as Consul for Chile owing to pressure of business. At the risk of sounding like the Scottish poet MacGonegal, another small piece of news reported and glossily illustrated could be mentioned: Wellington Corporation Tramways had launched their first fleet of tramcars, open double-deckers! New Year Merry-makers were travelling around Wellington for the fun of it, calling out greetings to the friendly onlookers. Alas, by May 18th, one had overturned, and a poor married woman in her forties had been killed.

In the *New Zealand Graphic* for March 16th, 1907, Mr Beauchamp figured yet again, this time in a splendid photograph taken in the boardroom of the Bank of New Zealand, Wellington. Sitting by the manager, Mr A. Michie, he was relaxed and smiling, with pointed beard, walrus moustache, butterfly-wing collar, elbows on the waist-high padded chair, hands clasped, legs extended comfortably in black boots.

Mrs Beauchamp was in the news too, reported attending the farewell tea for Mrs Michie, and wearing her petunia cloth with cream gold-braided vest.

Arrangements had been made to move to a bigger and better house at 47 Fitzherbert Terrace. The garden party at number 75, depicted in Katherine's famous story of 1922, had been given. There *was* an accident in Saunders Lane that day, and Vera it was who took the left-over food to the stricken family. Her garden party hat was too big for entry through the cottage door and it had to be tilted, much to Vera's embarrassment.

And how was Katherine faring? *Definitely I have decided not to be a musician. It's not my forte . . . I must be an authoress,* she wrote in her diary in January. It was summertime, and in spite of her frustration she was able to enjoy it and said so: *I am at the sea — at Island Bay in fact — lying flat on my face on the warm white sand . . . . I have no boots or stockings on — a pink dress — a panama hat — a big parasol. Adelaida, I wish that you were with me . . . Oh, what a glorious day this is! I shall stay here until after dark — walking along the beach — the waves foaming over my feet — drinking a great deal of tea — and eating a preposterous amount of bread and apricot jam at a little place called the Cliff House.* In the light of the future tragic years what a happy entry this is. 'Adelaida' was L.M. who waited eagerly for Katherine's weekly letters — 'she wrote reams!' L.M. told me.

Katherine spent a lot of time in her room, reading, writing and playing her cello, objecting strongly to the infringement of domestic matters on her domain, stockings to be darned, left on her bed by her mother, discussion of food and laundry lists on the landing outside her door. Katherine never was one for housework, she seemed always to have some domestic help throughout her future life in spite of being short of money, but of course her standards were obsessively high. She could not settle or work in an untidy environment.

She took cello lessons with Thomas Trowell, Arnold's father, who was the resident conductor at the opera house. This was a precious link with Arnold, with whom she continued to correspond and whom she thought she loved.

She met Maata again and a passionate friendship developed, a vehicle for all Katherine's tumult. In April Maata wrote in her diary: *Dearest K. writes 'ducky letters', I like this bit: 'What do you mean by being so superlatively beautiful as you went away? You witch: you are beauty incarnate'.* (Typed copy of *New Zealand Journal* by Maata, Mantz papers, Texas. Quoted by Professor Alpers.) Maata attended the house warming party at 47 Fitzherbert Terrace on May 4th.

The new house, in one of the few garden streets in the city, had a ballroom, a croquet lawn and a beautiful garden. Chaddie described it all in a letter to Sylvia Payne:

We have a lovely ballroom, which we of course use for music, and it is splendid for sound. Kass has been playing her cello so well tonight. I do wish you could have heard her the dear old thing. I hate to feel she is so unhappy here, isn't it a horrid state to be in so early in life?

There were forty guests, which included young men they had grown up with like the Nathans, the next door neighbours in Tinakori Road, Cheviot Bell, Siegfried Eichelbaum and Chummie, of course. An impromptu orchestra played cotillions, waltzes and lancers. George Nathan, talking to Miss Mantz, remembered asking Katherine for a dance. She answered abruptly. asking him why he asked her to dance when she knew he hated her.

He thought she was plump, had a quick way of speaking, rather putting people off.

The rooms were decorated with chrysanthemums, palms and cosmeas. Mrs Beauchamp received in a black silk poplin gown with ivory lace trimmings, complemented by a black feather hat. Katherine was wearing an ecru lace dress piped with flame-coloured silk, no doubt feeling her old self with Maata there.

Another guest was Miss Edith K. Bendall (Edie), still alive in 1976, who remembered meeting Maata that night. Edie, nine years older than Katherine, had recently returned from an art school in Sydney, her particular interest being portrayals of young children. She had made water colour sketches of Maori babies for Katherine's album and it was Edie who received the letter about the baby girl Felicitas at the Easter Thanksgiving Service in Kent, during Queen's College days. In the same letter Katherine wrote:

This afternoon on the quay I saw a charming little group. A little girl with very red hair and a green frock sat on the doorstep — with oranges in her lap. And looking at her — with more than envy was a small boy in a red pair of knickers and a tight holland bodice that buttoned down the back with three huge buttons — his sister — a young lady vainly trying to appear out of an enormous pinafore, held his hand. She was distractingly pretty, and her hair was braided in one stiff aggressive little braid that stood straight out behind, and was tied with a huge bow.

They were all so delightful I could have stood still and just rudely stared at them. Somehow they were so entirely picturesque, and the shop behind them was full of coloured beads. Do you see how nice that effect was? You would really have liked them, I know . . . . I am so glad you are not going to read 'In the Morning Glow'. Somehow I longed to read that to you . . . .

The child with the fringe is fascinating me — in fact, all of them are wonderfully beautiful.

Katherine was writing a book of child-verses and had asked Edie to illustrate them. Written in violet ink, they were sent to an editor in America but they were returned, minus the illustrations. They were published eventually, alas post-humously. Walter de la Mare thought them 'as true to childhood as any child poems that we know'.

The friendship deepened, the girls met daily by the spring in Grant Road, and Katherine wrote to Edie almost every day.

They stayed at the bungalow together at Day's Bay. Edie made a sketch of Katherine wearing her winged Mercury hat. The drawing was published in *The Mystery of Maata* by Pat Lawler, Beltane Book Bureau, 1946.

Talking to Mr Lawler in 1959, Edie described an evening with Katherine at Day's Bay. In the light of two candles Katherine leant over the side of her bunk and read 'In the Morning Glow'.

"I can see her now," she said, "even hear her soft caressing voice. Her delicate mobile hands were cupped together and when I remarked on their beauty, she told me that an English artist had wished to paint them on black velvet."

A humorous memoir given to Mr Lawler by Edie was of a trip made with the Beauchamps on the Picton boat, returning from Nelson.

"Katherine came bustling along the deck after the boat had left the Picton wharf. 'You know Mother,' said Katherine, 'this seasickness is all in the brain — all in the brain. *We* are not going to be seasick.'

"Half an hour later," added E.K.B. with a smile,

"Katherine came tottering back to us with the words, 'I am afraid, Mother, that seasickness is not in the brain, but entirely in the stomach,' and she fled to her cabin and was not seen for the rest of the voyage."

For May 20th, 1907 Jeanne wrote in the back of her *Niwaru* diary: *My birthday. I was 15, we came home from the Bay cottage Chad Les Dora and Eric Ray and Guy. Mother very ill with pleurisy, got numerous presents Fr. 2/6 whip book Kass. Chad 2/6 Syd 10/- Li 5/- Les purse Vera sweets not special happened in holidays.*

At the bungalow at Day's Bay on June 1st, 1907 Katherine described the interior in her black notebook:

I sit in the small poverty-stricken sitting-room, the one *and only room which the cottage contains, with the exception of a cabin-like bedroom fitted with bunks, and an outhouse with a bath and wood-cellar, coal-cellar complete. On one hand is the sea, stretching right up to the yard; on the other the bush growing close down almost to my front door.*

She was now in the midst of a passionate love affair with Edie and late on the Sunday night Katherine was facing some rift in their association while Edie slept in the other room.

I am here almost dead with cold, she wrote . . . . *I cannot sleep because the end has come with such suddenness that even I who have anticipated it so long . . . am shocked and overwhelmed . . . Last night I spent in her arms — and tonight I hate her — which, being interpreted, means I adore her: that I cannot lie in my bed and not feel the magic of her body: . . . I feel more powerfully all those so-termed sexual impulses with her than I have with any man. She enthrals, enslaves me — and her personal self — her body absolute — is my worship . . . .*

Gone are all the recollections of Caesar and Adonis . . . a week ago, I could have borne all this, because I had never known what it truly was to love and be loved — to adore passionately. But now I feel that if she is denied me, I must — the soul of me goes into the streets and craves love of the casual stranger, begs and prays for a little of the precious poison. I am half mad with love. *She is positively at present — above my music even — everything, and now she is going . . . .*

In my life — so much love in imagination; in reality 18 barren years — never a pure spontaneous affectionate impulse. Adonis was — dare I seek into the heart of me — nothing but a pose. And now she comes — and pillowed against her, clinging to her hands, her face against mine, I am a child, a woman, and more than half man.

In a deleted journal passage she writes: *This is madness I know — but it is too real for sanity it is too simply incredible to be doubted . . . . I am so shocked with grief, that I feel I cannot continue my hard course of loving — and being unloved — of giving loves, only to find them flung back at me.*

Edie, hearing Katherine return to bed, takes the grieving girl in her arms and all is forgotten. *What an experience!* wrote Katherine. *And when we returned to town, small wonder that I could not sleep, but tossed to and fro, and yearned, and realized a thousand things which had been obscure . . . .*

Oh Oscar! am I peculiarly susceptible to sexual impulse? . . . we shall go away again.

Yet four weeks later Katherine was admitting in her writings that E.K.B. bored her and she bored E.K.B: 'she never took the initiative' and in a deleted passage she admitted that: *E.K.B. is a thing of the past — absolutely irrevocably — thank heaven! It was, I consider, retrospectively, a frantically maudlin relationship and one better ended — also she will not achieve a great deal of greatness (?) she has not the necessary impetus of character. Do other people of my own age feel as I do I wonder — so absolutely powerful* licentious, *so almost physically ill?*

As an outlet to these feelings she wrote on: *I alone in this silent clockfilled room have become powerfully — I want Maata — I want her as I have had her — terribly. This is unclean I know but true. What an extraordinary thing — I feel savagely crude — and almost powerfully enamoured of the child. I had thought that a thing of the Past — Heigh Ho!!!!!!!!!!*

However, social events filled the void. The *New Zealand Mail* reported the Beauchamp girls at the Star Boating Club Dance on July 2nd, *stairs and lobbies were warm and bright*

with crimson baize . . . . plentiful supply of partners. What
more could a girl ask for?

Millie Parker, niece of Robert Parker, Katherine's piano
teacher, who was so well drawn in the story *The Wind Blows*,
wrote an endearing memoir for the *New Zealand Herald*,
February 3rd, 1923. A neighbour of Mr Trowell, she was
pianist to his violin and Katherine's cello. The three spent
hours playing Arnold's compositions. After the Trowells
departed for England, Katherine continued to visit Millie for
cello practice, arriving every Thursday morning 'windblown
hair clinging to a little round hat, her cello slung by a strap
over her shoulder, and almost invariably an offering of rare
flowers . . . . Quaintly Bohemian, seeming almost a little
foreign by way of strange temperament, she always found joy
in the unusual'.

Millie considered her very matured and experienced for her
age. She also admired the forcibleness of her handwriting,
thought it like a man's writing, valuing a piece of music
inscribed by Katherine 'with best wishes from the cello'. After
a particularly strenuous practice, when the two girls cooled off
on the balcony, the roses blooming there prompted Katherine
to recite:

> Red as the wine of forgotten ages,
> Yellow as gold by the sunbeams spun,
> Pink as the gown of Aurora's pages,
> White as a robe of a sinless one,
> Sweeter than Araby's winds that blow,
> Roses! Roses! I love you so!

At Millie's request Katherine made a copy of the poem, adding
a quotation, 'It cannot be possible to go through all the
abandonment of music and care humanly for anything human
afterwards, K. Mansfield 1908'.

Katherine had pointed out her new signature to Millie at the
time. Millie thought Katherine a remarkable cellist,
considering her short training, and vividly remembered a
quick dry comment from her after performing the 'Boellmann
Variation Symphonique'. On someone saying, "I do wish I
could play the cello!" "So do I," said Katherine grimly.

The following Tuesday at a nurses' dinner the hundred

guests were entertained 'with a brilliant duet for piano and cello by the Misses Beauchamp'.

On July 17th, 1907 the paper announced that Miss Martha Grace of Wanganui was paying a visit to friends in town. This of course was Maata. Her mother had re-married, a Mr Nathanial Grace. She was to be one of the guests at Miss Chaddie Beauchamp's birthday ball. The rooms were decorated with spring flowers and violets; coffee and ices were served all the evening, followed by a delicious supper. Mrs Beauchamp received in grey voile over pink silk. Chaddie wore pompadour silk with bands of pale blue velvet and Vera was in an empire gown of vieux rose Liberty satin. Katherine wore white silk with a lace overdress. Maata's dress was of ivory silk ninon, with frills of narrow Valenciennes lace. The dance of the evening was the cotillion and no doubt Katherine was wildly happy with Maata there.

August was wet and cold with much influenza about. There were fewer social events apart from the tea parties and Government House was virtually shut up. Katherine was moody and dispirited, abreacting in a letter to Arnold on August 11th:

Beloved, though I do not see you, know that I am yours . . . while my outer life is going on steadily, monotonously, even drearily, my inner life I live with you . . . . To me you are man, lover, artist, husband, friend . . . And so this loneliness is not so terrible to me.

And again on August 20th, with violent wind beating rain on the window-pane: *I cannot look ahead into the long unutterable grey vastness of future years . . . . Do you know that you are my life? I am tired and miserable tonight.*

By August 27th she was recording her progress with her cello playing and expressing her regard for Mr Trowell; but on the next day there came a letter from Aida (L.M.) with some gossip about Arnold, which made Katherine 'sorrowful...hurt...old...and angry.' Arnold was deposed! And now Mr Trowell had left Wellington for England. Katherine was bereft and isolated.

On September 2nd she wrote:

D

O let me lift it, ever, ever so slightly. It hangs before me . . .
this curtain which veils the future. Let me just hold a corner
up and peep beyond. Then maybe I shall be content to let it
fall. They have left N.Z. my people — My Father. It has come
of course. I used to think: So long as they are here, I can bear
it. And now — I shall somehow or other go, too. You just see.

For relief and to pass the winter days Katherine had been
writing steadily and she enlisted the help of her father's
secretary Mattie Putnam for the typing. Talking to Miss
Mantz, Mattie remembered her first sight of Katherine on her
return to Wellington. It had been on a Saturday morning in
the D.I.C. tearoom. She saw her pause in front of a gilt mirror,
raise an eye veil on her little round hat with Mercury wings,
then light a cigarette as she passed Mattie's table, extending
cool, formal greetings. Mattie thought Katherine had 'a fine
proud bearing, magnificent brown eyes, beautifully waved
hair, and distinction'. She noticed that though Katherine
always appeared serious, spoke in a monotone, showing little
change of expression, she frequently made dry, humorous
comments, for example calling a tenor soloist 'an elongated
clothes horse!' She confided in Mattie that her relations
thought her 'posey and affected'.

About that time Mattie received some of Katherine's work
with the following covering letter:

> *My dear —*
>   *Here is the work — it is written really in a 'faire*
> *hande' and will I hope — not be too much of a bother — I'm*
> *afraid you won't like 'Amore', I can't think how I wrote it —*
> *it's partly a sort of dream. Castles have been tumbling about*
> *my ears since Father came home. Do not mention — I pray*
> *you — my London prospects to him — he feels very sensitive —*
> *but — willy nilly — I GO — I'm determined —*
> *I wish you were not always so busy. I always feel when I am*
> *with you that there's so much I want to say — oh delightful*
> *sensation and so rare . . . . K.*

Mr Beauchamp, working behind the scenes, discussed
Katherine's writing ambition with an *Evening Post* reporter

friend, Tom L. Mills, who grudgingly offered to read some of her work. With prose pieces typed by Mattie and called 'Vignettes' and some child-verse, Katherine met Mills in a Lambton Quay tea room. He found Katherine a 'bright, well-read', confident girl. When he suggested that 'the sex-problem type' content, created placing difficulties in a local paper, she answered sharply, "That's my business." His, she said, was to judge the quality of the writing. He suggested *Harpers Magazine* in America for the poems (they were rejected) and *Native Companion*, a new monthly published in Melbourne by Mr E.J. Brady, for the 'Vignettes'.

In his autobiography *Life's Highway*, serialized in *Southerly* Vol. 16 No. 2 (1955), Brady remembered receiving the work.

He thought the material too sophisticated for an eighteen year old girl and that one of his contributors, Frank Morton, a most able writer, may have written it. Brady wrote back querying her identity.

On September 23rd Katherine replied, alas with a spelling mistake:

Dear Sir,
        Thank you for your letter. I liked the peremptatory (sic) tone with regard to the Vignettes. I am sorry that (they) resemble their illustrious relatives to so marked an extent — and assure you — they feel very much my own — this style of work absorbs me at present but — well — it cannot be said that anything you have of mine is 'cribbed' . . . . Frankly — I hate plagiarism. I send you some more work — practically there is nothing local — except the 'Botanical Gardens' Vignette — The reason is that for the last few years London has held me very tightly indeed — and I've not yet escaped. You ask me for some details as to myself. I am poor — obscure — just eighteen years of age — with a rapacious appetite for everything and principles as light as my purse. If this pleases you — this MSS — please know that there is a great deal more where this comes from. I am very grateful to you and very interested in your magazine.

E.J. Brady replied saying that it was a compliment to be

mistaken for Frank Morton, and enclosed a cheque for £2! to which Katherine replied on October 11th, 1907:

Dear Mr. Brady,
            Thank you for your note — and cheque — too. Encouragement has studiously passed me by for so long, that I am very appreciative. I like the name "Silhouette" — If you do print more than the "Vignette" in the November issue, please do not use the name K.M. Beauchamp. I am anxious to be read only as K. Mansfield or K.M.

Mr. Brady — I am afraid that so much kindness on your part may result in an inundation of MSS from me — but the kindness is very pleasant.
            Sincerely, Kathleen Beauchamp.

When the *Native Companion* went out of publication Brady consoled himself with the thought that his paper had opened the door to *the* literary find of his editorial career.

Brady preserved the letters, which included one from Mr Beauchamp dated October 10th which was a typical protective gesture from a good, loving father and unrevealed to Katherine, assuring him of the originality of the material and calling her a 'very original character'. These letters are in the Mitchell Library, Sydney.

The social scene was in full swing as Dominion Day September 26th, 1907 approached. On September 14th the Beauchamp girls attended a ball at Government House. There was dancing until 2.00 a.m.; a wonderful supper which included 'hot dishes'. On September 20th the Prime Minister's wife Lady Ward received 1300 guests at Awarua House, amid daffodils, freesias and ferns. The Governor and Lady Plunket were among the guests, Lady Plunket wearing heliotrope chiffon which would complement her dark good looks and magnificent blue eyes. Mrs Beauchamp, in black taffeta and flower-trimmed lace, had two daughters with her, dressed in reseda crêpe de Chine and lace-trimmed blue cloth respectively; if only the reporter had mentioned initials! If Katherine was there she would have enjoyed observing the crowds.

Finally on Dominion Day September 26th there was the Governor's garden party for 2,500 guests. The weather was mild and string bands played on the lawn. Mr and Mrs Beauchamp and their daughters attended, so did Edie Bendall, wearing a blue Eton costume and rose-trimmed hat. At night the Parliament Buildings were illuminated, banqueting members toasting the new Dominion at midnight.

Chapter IV

Early Success

On October 1st, 1907 'Vignettes' by K. Mansfield appeared in the *Native Companion*. Katherine and Leslie tore down to Lambton Quay to buy a copy. In a letter to her father on March 18th, 1922 she remembered that night 'standing under a lamp post with darling Leslie to see if my story had been printed' and there it was, heading the list of contributors.

Vignette I
>   (*London*)
> *Away behind the line of the dark houses there is a sound like the call of the sea after a storm — passionate, solemn, strong. I am leaning far far out of the window in the warm still night air. Down below in the mews the little lamp is singing a quiet song . . . it is the one glow of light in all this darkness. Men swilling the carriages with pails of water, their sudden sharp exclamations, their hoarse shouting, the faint thin cry of a very young child, and every quarter of an hour, the chiming of the bell from the church close by are the only sounds . . . impersonal, vague, intensely agitating.*

Vignette II expressed further nostalgic memories of London.

In *Vignette III* Kathleen, in melancholic mood on her return to New Zealand remembers her school days in London as she watches a downpour.

> *Oh, this monotonous terrible rain. The dull steady hopeless sound of it. I have drawn the curtains across the windows to shut out the weeping face of the world — the trees swaying softly in their grief and dropping silver tears upon the brown*

earth — the narrow, sodden, mean, draggled wooden houses, colourless save for the dull coarse red of the roof and the long line of grey hills, impassable, spectral-like. So I have drawn the curtains across my windows, and the light is intensely fascinating. A perpetual twilight broods here. The atmosphere is heavy with morbid charm. Strange, as I sit here, quiet, alone, how each possession of mine — the calender gleaming whitely on the wall, each picture, each book, my cello case, the very furniture — seems to stir into life. The Velasquez Venus moves on her couch ever so slightly; across the face of Manon a strange smile flickers for an instant and is gone, my rocking chair is full of patient resignation, my cello case is wrapt in profound thought. Beside me a little bowl of mignonette is piercingly sweet, and a cluster of scarlet geraniums is hot with colour. Sometimes, through the measured sound of the rain comes the long hopeless note of a foghorn far out at sea. And then all life seems but a crying out drearily, and a groping to and fro in a foolish, aimless darkness. Sometimes — it seems like miles away — I hear the sound of a door opening and shutting. And I listen and think and dream until my life seems not one life, but a thousand million lives, and my soul is weighed down with the burden of past existence, with the vague, uneasy consciousness of future strivings. And the grey thoughts fall on my soul like the grey rain upon the world, but I cannot draw the curtain and shut them out.

Professor Sylvia Berkman called the 'Vignettes' 'impressionistic explorations of mood, fusing subjective emotion with natural scenes'. It *is* floridly emotional writing, full of youthful yearning, but the 'Vignette III' — 'Oh! this monotonous rain' never fails to move me.

On Saturday October 12th Mrs Beauchamp gave a 'small and early' to celebrate Katherine's nineteenth birthday. It must have been a wet night because galoshes were mentioned in the newspaper report. Sensibly the party ended at midnight. Mrs Beauchamp received in her dove grey, over pink silk, Vera wore black with bodice of lace and black bretelles, Katherine also wore black and around her neck hung a carved bone Maori tiki. Chaddie was in lace-trimmed net. Large rhododendron blossoms graced the supper table and the drawing-room was filled with the scent of boronia blossom which would intoxicate Katherine. She loved its fruity smell. Home-made sweets were placed about the flower-filled room and no doubt the smell of Mr Beauchamp's cigar was irresistable.

I don't think I have ever enjoyed a dance so much before, wrote Chaddie to Sylvia Payne on October 14th. *Talking of my dear sister Kathleen she has been so lucky in getting such beautiful presents today. Mother gave her greenstone earings, Father two sweet liberty brooches, Vera a jewel case, I a back comb, Leslie a writing case, Jeanne a charming bag made and designed by herself . . . . I am sending you The Native Companion which has accepted a lot of her work . . . . Isn't it splendid, I can't tell you how proud and happy I am . . . . Fancy Kathleen going back to London after Christmas. I can't bear to think of it, but I know she must go, it is the only thing for her, and I feel her going will bring us all over the sooner. Oh! dear what absolute joy and bliss that would be.*

Since her return to Wellington, Katherine had read avidly. She was able to borrow books from the General Assembly Library and thanks to the librarian, Dr G.H. Scholefield, there is a record of her reading choice. She read the poetry of Browning, Whitman and Yeats, biographies of artists and poets, Ibsen, Maeterlinck, Ruskin, Shaw, Nietzsche, Heine, and the Brontës.

In later years she was to mention the Brontës in her letters, and I wonder whether she caught this little snippet of Brontë news in the *Dominion* for April 30th, 1908:

An old man Joseph Marsden Dixon — has a clear remembrance of Charlotte Brontë who used to visit Ellen Nussey nearby. "She was a 'lowish' woman and her eyes they looked a long way into her head . . . . She was thought nought about at that day. She and Miss Nussey used to walk out together in the wood behind where Wensleydale Mill stands now.

There is no record of her reading Chekhov then, but there was in the library R.E.C. Long's translation of Chekhov's *The Black Monk* and other stories. After her marriage in 1918 she had a large cupboard which she called 'The Black Monk'. It was painted black and decorated further with orange nasturtiums by her husband.

Now in October she was reading about and identifying with the tragic young Russian artist Marie Bashkirtseff, whose journal in two volumes culled from a hundred and three notebooks had been published three years after her death from tuberculosis, on 31st October, 1884. In July 1876 at seventeen Marie wrote: *What am I . . . . nothing! What do I want to be? Everything!*

Marie Bashkirtseff was born in Poltava in the Ukraine on January 24th, 1859, daughter of a Russian noblewoman of the Babanine family and Constantin Bashkirtseff, a landowner's son. Her mother, after separating from her husband, settled in Nice in 1870 after sampling other famous European resorts. With her daughter Marie and son Paul and accompanied by her aged father's sister, Princess Eristoff, niece Dina, faithful family doctor, governesses, nurses and dogs, she lived in a large furnished house — Villa Acqua Viva, on the Promenade des Anglais.

The journal opens in January 1873 with Marie aged fourteen, passionate, undisciplined, self-absorbed, declaring her love for the Duke of Hamilton whom she had seen but never even met. She wanted to marry him! *Oh God, give me the Duke of Hamilton. I love the Duke of Hamilton.*

Marie, with red-gold hair, grey eyes, and dressed in white, would sit in their garden by a marble fountain writing: *so fresh, so soft, so green, so lovely, I shall bring him here to show him the place where I've thought so much about him.* That verdant garden with its white marble fountain is somehow thrilling in the light of the heartless row of hotels on the Promenade today.

After the Duke inevitably married someone else, Marie, heartbroken, arranged hours of daily study in languages, drawing and music, trying to improve her writing style and railing against the dullness of her life.

The summers at Nice kill me, there is not a soul there . . . one only lives once . . . Oh if Mamma and the others knew what it costs me to stay here, they would not keep me in this terrible desert. The world — that is my life; it calls me, waits for me, I

want to run to it . . . St. Petersburg, London, Paris.
Katherine was writing in similar vein in 1907. Marie visited
Paris in 1874 and loved it: *it is my life . . . I begin to live and to
try and realize my dreams of becoming celebrated . . . I want
to be famous.*

She had a fine mezzo soprano voice 'three octaves less two
notes' and hoped to make music her career, but alas at sixteen
a haemoptysis and inevitable hoarseness prevented this.
Instead she concentrated on art, discovering at a Paris art
school, Julien's Studio, she had exceptional talent for one so
untrained.

The family moved to 71 Champs Elysée on October 2nd,
1877, Marie arriving at Julien's Studio dressed in furs, leading
a white dog and accompanied by Chocolat, her black pageboy,
wearing livery and jubilantly carrying the paint-box. 'I could
kill myself for not having begun 4 years sooner . . . . I am very
very happy' — her métier found at last. She worked eight
hours per day, and in her black Doucet dress with white
frills and crocodile belt, she was the envy of the other girls with
whom she shared her baskets of delicious food.

She did sculpture at home in the evenings; her art absorbed
her. She would walk about Paris in the early evening light,
observing the crowds, their form and movement, composing
pictures in her mind's eye. She longed for freedom to move
about more, 'to walk about quite alone to come and to sit on
the benches in the Tuileries garden'.

In January 1879 she was given a medal and in spring 1880
her portrait of a woman reading with violets by her side was
accepted at the Salon, and yet another in May 1881. She was ill
and burning herself away like a candle. 'I must produce
something that will make them jump with astonishment,
nothing else will bring me peace of mind.' She was ordered to
the south. 'Oh God, hear me, give me strength, take pity on
me.' She had no time to be ill.

She continued to paint in Nice and back in Paris worked
from eight till five. By now, both lungs were affected, her
lovely voice had gone, and a progressive deafness and tinnitus,
associated with the laryngeal pthisis was hard to bear. She
found stimulation in her new friendship with the young and

celebrated painter Bastien Lepage, who was also dying of tuberculosis. He kept her company in her last days and on seeing her in white lace and plush 'all different shades of white' said, "Oh, if I could only paint!" He was too ill to do so. She died at dawn on October 31st, 1884. Looking at the guttering candle by her bed, she murmured, "We shall go out together." Though she never received the coveted Salon Medal, she was an acclaimed success. Eighty-four paintings, fifty-five drawings and three sculptures are in Leningrad, the rest are in galleries in Chicago, Paris and Nice, all work executed after she became ill.

This then was the girl whose journal Katherine found so absorbing. Marie for that time and background was a new kind of woman, who questioned her role in society and strove for some kind of identity. She said and did things Katherine wanted to do herself, writing startling things like: *to marry and have children any washerwoman can do that — what do I want? Oh, you know well enough. I want glory . . . . I want to be the centre of a circle that shall be political, brilliant, literary . . . .*

And so on that cold morning of October 21st, 1907, Katherine had sat in her bedroom reading avidly. *Damn my family!* she wrote, objecting to being disturbed. *this morning I do not wish to write, but to read Marie Bashkirtseff. But if they enter the room and find me merely with a book, their tragic complaining looks upset me altogether . . . I have sat here for two hours and read. My right hand is quite cold . . . . If she comes into the room I put down Marie Bashkirtseff and seize my pen. She leans against the door, rattling the handle and says: 'Are you writing a colossal thing — or an ordinary thing — or anything exciting?' How completely inane! I tell her to leave the room* at once.

On October 31st Mrs Beauchamp and her daughters attended a dance at Government House, with its ballroom decorated with crimson azaleas, rhododendrons and red tulips.

I like to appear slightly condescending, very much du grande monde, and to be the centre of interest, wrote Katherine in her journal, *. . . at present, though I am damnable, I am in love with nobody, except myself.*

Perhaps the family were sick of this 'damnable' condition because Mr Beauchamp arranged a holiday for his rebellious daughter, a caravan expedition to Maori Tawharetoa Territory, from November 15th to December 17th. Exultant, Katherine took childish delight in the buffeting wind as she leaned out of the carriage window on her way to Napier to join the caravan. Millie Parker was one of the party. They travelled in a covered wagon, the luggage was on a dray behind, there were five horses and one partitioned tent.

From Napier they were bound for the Maori-speaking Urewera country, mountainous, with rivers cascading through gorges, dark forests and native bush. They camped in the valley of the Rangitaiki river, the beauty of which inspired her later poem 'In the Rangitaiki Valley':

> O valley of waving broom,
> O lovely, lovely light,
> O heart of the world, red — gold!
> Breast high in the blossom I stand;
> It beats about me like waves
> Of a magical, golden sea.
>
> The barren heart of the world
> Alive at the kiss of the sun,
> The yellow mantle of summer
> Flung over a laughing land,
> Warm with the warmth of her body,
> Sweet with the kiss of her breath.
>
> O valley of waving broom,
> O lovely, lovely light,
> O mystical marriage of Earth
> With the passionate Summer sun!
> To her lover she holds a cup
> And the yellow wine o'erflows.
> He has lighted a little torch
> And the whole of the world is ablaze.
> Prodigal wealth of love!
> Breast high in the blossom I stand.

On they journeyed through 'gorgeous blue mountains . . . in a great stretch of burnt Manuka', towards Rotorua, the air already 'heavy with sulphur and steam' exuded by the boiling mud volcanoes.

Recording all her experiences, she was happy to leave Rotorua, calling it 'loathsome and ugly — that little Hell' and found deep refreshment by the rushing Waikato River, with its blossoming banks of manuka. Thence to the magnificent Lake Taupo, 238 square miles by its group of volcanic craters, Mount Ruapehu, Ngauruhoe and Tongariro, standing in rough heather like any Scottish mountain range.

The rest of the trip was by train. Katherine arrived in Wellington on December 17th, sunburned but otherwise unchanged, with five poems and the germ of one of her strongest stories about the back-blocks and a woman she met there to be called *The Woman at the Store*.

In the November issue of the *Native Companion* there had appeared a piece called 'Silhouette' by K. Mansfield, Katherine's new writing name.

It is evening and very cold. From my window the laurestinus bush in this half light looks weighted with snow. It moves languidly, gently, backwards and forwards, and each time I look at it a delicate flower melody fills my brain. Against the pearl sky the great hills tower gorse-covered, leonine, magnificently savage. The air is quiet with thin rain, yet, from the karaka tree comes a tremulous sound of birds song ... And I, leaning out of my window, alone, peering into the gloom, am seized by a passionate desire for everything that is hidden and forbidden. I want the night to come and kiss me with her hot mouth, and lead me through an amethyst twilight to the place of the white gardenia. The laurestinus bush moves languidly, gently backwards and forwards. There is a dull heavy sound of clocks striking far away, and, in my room, darkness, emptiness, save for the ghostlike bed I feel to lie there quiet, silent, passively cold would be too fearful—yet — quite a little fascinating.

On December 2nd while Katherine was still away, further work of hers appeared in the *Native Companion*, a cynical sophisticated story, forerunner of her future style, called 'In A Café' and a further vignette 'In the Botanical Gardens', under a new masculine-sounding name, Julian Mark.

'In A Café' described the meeting of two young people in a Bond Street café, she a student, he a composer, and while they talk of 'Art, Art, Art . . . . Scarlet youth, and mortality, and life', she fervently waits and hopes for a proposal of marriage, while, on impulse, he asks for the violets she is wearing. Perhaps regretting the gesture, he suddenly takes his leave, accidentally dropping the violets on the pavement as he puts his hands in his pockets against the cold. She follows some way behind and white-lipped, she discovers the abandoned violets. *Then, very delicately and deliberately, she kicked the flowers into the gutter: and she, too, laughed, and continued laughing all the way down the street.*

'In the Botanical Gardens' is a study of the lush, flower-filled park near her home, with its encroaching 'silent and splendid' bush.

In the meantime Wellington's Parliamentary Buildings had been destroyed by fire on Wednesday December 11th, between 2.00 a.m. and 6.00 a.m. The portraits of Queen Victoria and the Prince and Princess of Wales were all lost.

On January 1st Katherine made a thrilling entry in her notebook: *The year has dawned — My Year 1908.*

Wellington was now taken up with the visit of the famous singer, Clara Butt. On January 20th, Katherine wearing white piqué, attended a reception for her. Miss Butt, six feet tall, in a dress of brown chiffon over gold tissue, with chenille tassels and a plumed tulle cloche hat, was deemed 'magnificent'. She later received a standing ovation at her two concerts in Wellington Town Hall, to which Katherine went and commented upon. Tickets were half to one guinea.

In February, there was a new experience recorded in Katherine's notebook. She described an assignation with some man at the cottage at Day's Bay whom she thought she loved. It seems obvious that this was a full-blooded affair and that it was her first experience of the kind.

However, the next entry refers to Maata, Katherine expressing nostalgic memories of their meeting in London. Then there follows the dramatic entry: *I shall end — of course*

— *by killing myself . . . I am unlike others because I have experienced all there is to experience . . . Of course Oscar — Dorian Grey has brought this S.S. to pass.* Katherine was seeing Maata again and feeling very guilty about her harmless, adolescent bisexuality.

On March 18th, 1908 the *Dominion* announced that Miss Kathleen Beauchamp was leaving the next month for London, where she intended to engage in literary work, and went on to describe 'a very enjoyable little impromptu dance given by Mrs Harold Beauchamp'.

The *New Zealand Graphic* also reported the event, describing the red cactus dahlia decorations, Katherine's white dress with bretelles of ribbon and lace, and Chaddie's lace-trimmed apricot chiffon taffetas. There were eight other girls and twelve men, including a Major Hughes, Captain Nelson and Doctors Harty and Holmes. Maata was not there. Mr and Mrs Beauchamp now disapproved of the friendship.

On March 25th Mrs Beauchamp held a sale of work at 47 Fitzherbert Terrace in aid of St Mary's Home for Girls at Karori. The *Weekly Graphic* and *New Zealand Mail* for April 4th reported that 'she and her daughters had gone to no end of trouble in making preparations' (Katherine would have liked that). There was an amateur orchestra of girls which included the Prime Minister's daughter, Miss Eileen Ward, and the Misses Beauchamp, who played 'nice tuney things', reported the *Dominion*. The price of admission was one shilling which included tea. Lady Ward was present, and though it rained most of the day, over £100 were raised.

On April 12th Katherine, in white crêpe de Chine and lace, attended the Polo Ball, along with Chaddie in her apricot taffetas. It may have been after this event that the blow fell. Katherine was not to go to England. Mrs Beauchamp had found some windblown notes on the floor of Katherine's room which described a sexual adventure 'with a sailor' at a dance, as Katherine later informed L.M. by letter. This may have been her cover-up for revelations of the Maata affair.

In his book *The Mystery of Maata* by Pat Lawler, 1946, Maata had told him that she had climbed up to Katherine's locked bedroom, presumably by the fire escape (years later in a letter to her husband, Katherine described sleeping in a room with a fire escape at 47 Fitzherbert Terrace). If Katherine was locked in her bedroom, she was indeed in disgrace. On the other hand, Katherine was clever enough to have arranged a secret assignation with Maata this way, locking the door from the inside!

May 1st: *I am now much worse than ever. Madness must lie this way. Pull yourself up!* wrote Katherine sternly in her notebook.

And on May 17th: *Be good . . . and brave and do tell the truth more, and live a better life — I am tired of all this deceit . . . Go anywhere. Don't stay here — accept work — fight against people. As it is, with rapidity unimaginable, you are going to the devil.*

One year later Katherine penned a regretful confession of her 'secret' which lay behind those desperate notebook entries of that autumn of 1908.

In New Zealand Wilde acted so strongly and terribly upon me that I was constantly subject to exactly the same fits of madness as those which caused his ruin and mental decay. When I am miserable now — these recur. Sometimes I forget all about it — then with awful recurrence it bursts upon me again and I am quite powerless to prevent it — This is my secret from the world and from you — Another shares it with me — and that other is — — for she, too is afflicted, with the same terror — We used to talk of it knowing that it would eventually kill us, render us insane or paralytic — all to no purpose — It's funny that you and I have never shared this — and I know you will understand why. Nobody can help — it has been going on now since I was 18 and it was the reason for Rudolf's death. I read it in his face today.
I think my mind is morally unhinged and that is the reason — I know it is a degradation so unspeakable that — one perceives the dignity in pistols.

> *Your*
> *Katie Mansfield '09*

Professor Alpers states: *When found it was folded within another piece of paper, a torn off sheet serving as an improvised envelope, on both sides of which Kathleen had written: "Never to be read, on your honour as my friend, while*

I am still alive. K. Mansfield" The name omitted is that of a Wellington girl . . . This letter to my mind was meant for L.M.

On May 8th, 1908, Katherine entered Wellington Technical College to take a shorthand and typing course. This would stand her in good stead in the future. Whether Mr Beauchamp was tired of the atmosphere at home or feared further social embarrassment, or had simply relented, he decided to let Katherine go to London that July. There is no journal entry to record Katherine's reaction, which is a pity but Professor Alpers believes she finally left with 'bitterness in her heart'. Certainly she seemed under a cloud, for her going away celebration at home was merely an afternoon tea for her girlfriends instead of the usual 'jolly dance'. In any case, Katherine had had her dance in March. Perhaps Mrs Beauchamp did not feel up to another. However, friends rallied round.

On June 19th there was the famous violet tea given by Mrs Rankine-Brown, wife of the Professor of Classics. The event was reported in the *Dominion* for June 20th. 'Festoons' of fresh violets trailed from a violet-shaded lamp to the table, on which stood 'wide bowls' of violets. The cakes were decorated with violet icing, there were crystallized violets in little dishes, and sandwiches were filled with real fresh violets. Each guest was given a nosegay of violets which were later sent to the hospital. Mrs Rankine-Brown received in a white lace blouse and white silk skirt, with violet chene sash. She wore her pearl and amethyst necklace.

Miss Eileen Ward, Miss McTavish and Chaddie 'sang songs about violets, and there were two violet competitions' for which violet coloured pencils were provided. The cakes each bore one word piped in violet icing from a quotation from Browning, 'Blue ran the flash across, violets were born'. Strangely, Katherine did not recognize this, but she won first prize for the next competition. The girls had to compose a poem on a violet. It was entitled:

> Why Love is Blind
> The cupid child tired of the winter day
> Wept and lamented for the skies of blue
> Till foolish child! he cried his eyes away —
> And violets grew.

The original MS was shown to Professor Alpers in 1947 by Mr Siegfried Eichelbaum of Wellington, who was present at the house-warming party at Fitzherbert Terrace in 1907. Miss Eva Butts won second prize, beaten by her 'shabby, inky' former pupil, to 'our wicked joy'.

On June 30th Lady Ward gave a farewell tea for Katherine at 'Awarua'. It was reported in the *Dominion* for July 1st, 1908. A crimson shaded light illuminated the table, with its centre-piece of glowing Venetian glass containing pale green and black grapes. It was winter in Wellington and the days were short. After tea there was music and fortune telling by teacup, then in an album later presented to Katherine, each girl, while blindfolded, drew an autographed picture of a pig. Katherine wore a brown, tailor-made costume, furs and matching brown hat, trimmed with purple asters. Chaddie wore green, with matching hat bearing feather rosettes.

Then there was the farewell afternoon tea at 47 Fitzherbert Terrace. Katherine, in wine coloured braided cloth and guipure lace, entertained seventeen girlfriends, who included Edie Bendall, Mattie Putnam, and Miss Butts. Chaddie, in purple shot silk and velvet, sang a solo.

Before the final curtain Katherine managed to send some work to *Triad*, an avant-garde periodical in Wellington. It was a study called 'Death of a Rose' which was published in the July issue, and described the colour of a dying rose changing as though bleeding from a wound.

Katherine was due to leave Lyttelton for London on Sunday July 4th, on the New Zealand Shipping Company's steamer *Papanui*. To everyone's consternation departure was postponed to 4.30 p.m. on Monday July 6th. This meant a long, difficult wait in Christchurch.

Wellington on that Saturday was, according to the *Dominion*, 'a crystalline city', the temperature being 38° F in the shade. How did Katherine feel, one wonders, looking around her bedroom for the last time, packing the little brass pig with bristly back, a gift from her father's desk to wipe her pen on, saying goodbye to Vera, Chaddie, and Jeanne, who would be very upset? I think she would be afraid, sad, but still determined. Mr and Mrs Beauchamp boarded the SS *Maori* with Katherine on Saturday evening and the lights of Lambton

Quay under which she had read her first published work with Chummie, receded into the distance. She was never to see those lights again.

On Monday July 6th the 3.00 p.m. weather report was of a south-easterly gale and a very heavy sea. It was raining hard. At 4.30 p.m. the *Papanui* drew away from Lyttelton in the darkening day, leaving Mr and Mrs Beauchamp forlorn on the quayside.

However, on July 22nd, no doubt recovered somewhat, Mrs Beauchamp gave an 'At Home'. The *Dominion* reported floral details of narcissi, purple cinerarias and 'a great central vase of holly'. Mrs Beauchamp received in a soft, grey silk dress trimmed with cream lace; Chaddie wore pale heliotrope silk with a lace yoke. There were thirty-one guests, including Edie Bendall. No doubt there was much talk of Katherine.

Meanwhile, the *Papanui* ploughed its way through the Southern Ocean. There were twenty-four passengers; twenty-two men and one other woman. The first port of call was Montevideo. After three long weeks at sea, Katherine, with the inevitable male admirer, went ashore and some adventure ensued. After a further call at Tenerife the *Papanui* arrived safely at Plymouth on Sunday August 23rd.

L.M., longing for the day, awaited Katherine's train which drew in on Monday August 24th. There was no one else to meet Katherine and L.M., overjoyed, took her straight home to Montague Mansions to stay, before taking up residence at Beauchamp Lodge.

Chapter V

Beauchamp Lodge and After

Beauchamp Lodge was a hostel for music students run by two professional musicians, Miss Ann Muckle and Miss Rosabel Watson. It had been recommended by Mr Beauchamp's cousin Henry. It was a large, square white mansion of five storeys standing on the Grand Union Canal, at 2 Warwick Crescent, Paddington. There was a pleasant atmosphere and few rules; each girl had her own latch-key and could practice any instrument in her room. There was one inviolable rule however: once married a girl had to leave.

Katherine's room was on the first floor, with a french window and small, curved wrought-iron balcony overlooking the canal. Weeping willows trailed into the glassy water which was broken only by the breeze or passing barges. The walls were painted green, there was an open fire, a carpet and a desk. It cost 25/- per week, which, out of her allowance of £100 per year, left 12/- to cover all other expenses. From then on Katherine was chronically short of money to the end of her days, except when at Fontainebleau — secure at last but tragically, too late — she was able to send L.M. a hundred franc note from the proceeds of her last book. Today a second-hand copy of her poems costs over £100! And her journal cost £15 in 1977.

At Katherine's table was a violin student, Miss Margaret Wishart, daughter of a Rear-Admiral. They had much in common, Margaret's father also disapproved of a musical career and allowed her only £60 per annum. They soon became fast friends; Margaret called Katherine 'Kassie', her family name in New Zealand. Both loved poetry and would walk in the evening to Browning territory nearby, then drink cocoa on the floor by the fire. Katherine, being the vital and attractive person she was, soon had others joining the fireside group, listening to her talk, watching her expressive face in the firelight and thinking, 'She must have some Maori blood'. This, of course, was not true.

This then was the longed-for room in London, with a desk and a view — her world! and all the fun of a musical population there, with rolling drums, always a merry sound, and a trombone or two in the background. She should have been happy, and probably was, until the novelty wore off and the greyness of London seeped into her, never to be eradicated. She came to detest London — and even England, alas.

However, she began to work, filling notebooks, writing 'masses of short stories . . . which had to be read aloud to me for criticism', Margaret Wishart told Professor Alpers in 1948. She also remembered the feeling of intimacy in her friendship with Katherine, never experienced before or since, and remarked on L.M. who visited frequently, and who 'worshipped Kassie in an abnormal fashion' being 'frantically jealous of her having any other associates'. As is the way of the besieged human heart, this degree of love was never really returned. Poor L.M. was tolerated for her great loyalty and spent the rest of her days on the sacrificial altar, while Katherine engaged in a lifelong rear-guard action against the onslaught.

Katherine happily sought out the Trowells who lived in a charming house in St John's Wood, 52 Carlton Hill, just off the Edgeware Road, a three storeyed, semi-detached Victorian house in brick, with front and back garden, and steps up to a portico. 'All the rooms were good — the top room's lovely,' Katherine wrote to the Hon. Dorothy Brett in 1921. When I saw it on a recent spring morning it looked very gracious still, a beautiful pale, flowering cherry growing nearby looking like a bride in a rain shower. The red granite horse trough still stands at the foot of Carlton Hill. Katherine must have passed it often.

The Trowells, with their daughter Dolly, were preparing for the return of the boys from Brussels and Katherine went to meet them at the station. Perhaps a little disillusioned with Arnold, with his long red hair and lack of romantic love for her, she turned her attention to Garnet, nineteen years old, tall, slender, pale and gentle, rather dreamy — more Katherine's type in fact. Having much to give where her heart was engaged, she soon fell deeply in love with him.

On September 13th Garnet left for Birmingham to join the orchestra of the Moody-Manners 'A' Company for a winter season in the provinces, battling for six nights a week with an extensive repertoire, which included *Aïda, Butterfly, Meistersinger, Tannhäuser* and *Maritana*. Drear Sundays were spent travelling. Just a day or two before he left, Katherine wrote her first letter to him:

My Dearest —
   I feel I must write you a little note — Fate has been so unkind to you both today. Dearest — I've wanted you ever since I saw you yesterday. I have been wretched — I don't know why exactly — but I feel we have so much to say and so little time to say it in before you go away. Dearest, I love you so intensely that I feel I could tell you so now until we are both old . . . I feel as though your kisses had absorbed my very soul into yours.

And only a few days had elapsed since their first meeting! impulsive, impetuous, passionate little being!
   I seem to see all with double force, she wrote a few days later. *You have transformed me utterly, I am a different person — or rather — pour la première fois — I feel so much myself.* By September 23rd she was calling him 'husband'. It seems they were hoping to marry. As they were penniless, one pales at the thought. *When I think for one moment of what the future holds for us together, what days, and oh my husband,* what nights — *I feel really that I do not belong to this earth — it's too small to hold so much.* With her wonderful sense of humour she added that a girl overhead was practicing 'The Policeman's Chorus' on her drums, while trombone scales stole from another room.
   On October 3rd Katherine took Garnet's young sister Dolly to a Saturday afternoon concert in the Bechstein Hall. The

artist appearing was the Venezuelan pianist Teresa Carreno, an acquaintance of Katherine. In a letter to Garnet she described the concert and her meeting backstage with Carrenno, who kissed her hands and said that she had played *Erlkönig* especially for her.

In the same letter, however, Katherine admitted that letters from home depressed her, 'the shadow of the old life creeps over me . . . . They hurt me bitterly.' Perhaps she felt rejected. Life was not really ideal, underneath she was emotionally insecure. Money was short, according to L.M. desperately short at times, the beloved cello had been sold for only £3, an ignominious end to her musical career.

Through the students at Beauchamp Lodge, she had embarked on another career, that of an entertainer at evening parties for a fee of one guinea, when she would sing, recite and act. She *must* have been desperate. For this, in spite of the lovely Wellington dresses she had brought to England, she felt she needed a new long dress. This was made by Amy Birch, one of the fireside cocoa drinkers, and was of expensive grey silk, the gleaming folds of which were to appear at a vital December evening meeting three years later, when she met her future husband for the first time.

On October 4th a further love letter to Garnet spoke of her loneliness and 'savagely passionate' feelings. *Let us go up the stairs together and look in at little Doll's room — she is sleeping. And, lying in your arms, I fancy the world is beating to the beating of our hearts. I love you — I love you passionately with my whole soul and body,* and yet underneath, like the melancholy tolling of a bell, came the premonitory fear of *that frightful sensation of grief that used to come over me in Wellington . . . . It is like suddenly finding myself face to face with this ghost which terrifies me.* These fears were crystallized in a fragmentary 'novel' she began some years later, drawing on this period of her life: *You know sometimes I feel I'm possessed by a sort of Fate — you know — by an impending disaster that spreads its wings over my heart, or maybe only the shadow of its wings — but it is so black and terrible . . . . I can't describe it —* alas, too true.

In February 1920 she wrote in her journal: *I feel today that I shall die soon and suddenly.*

Little allowance was made for Katherine throughout her life for these obvious depressive mood-swings, part of her cyclothymic personality — up in the clouds at one stage, plunging in the next. In the face of her high courage and effort at keeping her flag flying, however battle-stained, she was considered tough, self-sufficient, even cruel, but underneath was a highly sensitive, lonely, over-loving girl, who rarely received the kind of deep love she gave, especially from her lovers.

There was another worry gnawing in Katherine's mind, some real anxiety mirrored in a notebook entry for October 12th: *This is my unfortunate month. I dislike exceedingly to have to pass through it; each day fills me with terror* — the aftermath, of course, of the Montevideo adventure. To her joy, however, on October 14th — her birthday — Garnet sent her a ring. She happily displayed it at 52, Carlton Hill and left Victoria at four-fifty for Warlingham, for a five day visit to Aunt Belle.

Katherine no doubt gave a good performance of a happy, successful writer, but in her notebook she wrote: *Feel frightful and can't think why . . . . feel awful, shocking terrible — what is to be done I wonder . . . . I wonder if I will ever be happy again — that's the question . . . . It seems my brain is dead, my soul numbed with horrid grief.*

She had approached Ruth Herrick one day, asking about a woman doctor whom Ruth knew, admitting she was suffering from amenorrhoea and fearing she was pregnant.

On October 21st Katherine went to Paris with Margaret Wishart to attend a Naval wedding. The invitation was extended by Admiral Wishart, no doubt Margaret had talked him into it. They had a hectic time, visiting Versailles. Garnet was sent a glowing description of the palace with its chestnut trees 'burning a red bronze with the fires of autumn'. Later, at the reception, she sat on a sofa talking to a Naval Lieutenant until after eleven, but admitted to Garnet that she 'was so tired and ennuyée that I almost saw "double". You know that degree of fatigue? I came home my darling, and went to bed, thinking of you — dreaming of you all the night through'.

Happily, a notebook entry for October 29th which read: *Went to Mrs Charley Boyd and at last put my mind at rest,* seemed to dispose of her Montevideo problem. On that date she also wrote to Garnet: *Please take care of yourself for this poor little girl who cannot take care of you. I think — yes, I am rather afraid, Beloved — you'll have a very tyrannical wife!* . . . *I feel as though I've been married to you for years — As though I ought to be looking after you.*

On November 4th she and Margaret dined off boiled onions, cooked on the fire in her room, all very cosy, especially no doubt the conversation that went with it. Later that evening she wrote to Garnet about her writing and how she would like to perform her own work in public: *I want to write — and recite what I write — in a very fine way — you know what I mean. Revolutionize and revive the art of elocution — take it to its proper plane . . . and express in the voice and face and atmosphere all that you say. Tone should be my secret — each word a variety of tone . . . I should like to do this — and this is in my power because I know I possess the power of holding people . . . I could then write just what I feel would suit me — and would popularize my work — and also I feel there's a big opening for something sensational and new in this direction.*

She expressed justifiable confidence in herself. Her friends agreed that she had a 'faultless sense of drama' and great acting ability. L.M. said of Katherine in her memoirs that 'There was a bell-like quality in her rich low voice'. If it was anything like the voice of Katherine's younger sister Mrs Jeanne Renshaw, it would be most beautiful. Even at eighty-eight, Jeanne's voice is unforgettable, clear, low and wonderfully melodic. Katherine's idea was avant-garde.

At New Zealand House on April 30th, 1979 there was presented 'The Case of Katherine Mansfield' compiled and edited by Miss Kathy Downes, a charming New Zealand actress, born in Wellington. In the programme she wrote: *using only Mansfield's own words I have attempted to present a dynamic, dramatic portrait of this magical woman.* This she did thrillingly, by candlelight at a desk, pen picked up with such a flourish and poised, then restlessly pacing to the most realistic sound of a train, with arms folded and gripping her waist she cried passionately the familiar words, "Risk! Risk anything! Care no more for the opinion of others, for those voices. Do the thing hardest on earth for you. Act for yourself. Face the truth."

What a gal! It was a marvellous idea — what a pity

Katherine did not carry it out.

Her final letter to Garnet was on November 8th from Devonport. No doubt through Margaret, she had been present at the launching of the dreadnought battleship *Collingwood*, by Mrs Asquith.

Oh, Garnet, why is it we so love the strong emotions? I think because they give us such a keen sense of Life — a violent belief in our Existence. One thing I cannot bear and that is the mediocre — I like always to have a great grip of life — so that I intensify the so called small things — so that truly everything is significant.

And again that tolling of the bell to remind us of the impermanence of happiness and ecstasy:

I dreamed last night that we were at a Tchaikovsky concert together — and in a violin passage, swift and terrible — I saw to my horror, a great flock of black wide winged birds — fly screaming over the orchestra.

This idea of a black bird overhead was to recur. On February 3rd, 1918 she wrote from Bandol: *there is a great black bird flying over me and I am so frightened he'll settle — so terrified. I don't know exactly what kind he is. If I were not working here, with war and anxiety I should go mad, I think. My night terrors here are rather complicated by packs and packs of growling, roaring, ravening, prowl-and-prowl-around dogs.* She was very ill when she wrote this letter.

So what about her work? She had composed a poem for Vera's twenty-third birthday on 22.X.08:

October
(To V.M.B.)

Dim mist of a fog-bound day . . .
From the lilac trees, that droop in St Mary's Square
The dead leaves fall, a silent, shivering cloud.
Through the grey haze the carts loom heavy, gigantic
Down the dull street . . . Children play in the gutter,
Quarrel and cry: their voices are flat and toneless.
With a sound like the shuffling tread of some giant monster

I hear the trains escape from the station near and tear
      their way into the country.
Everything looks fantastic, repellant . . . I see from my window
An old man pass, dull, formless, like the stump of a dead tree
      moving.
The virginia creeper, like blood, streams down the face
      of the houses . . .
Even the railings, blackened and sharply defined, look evil
      and strangely malignant.
Dim mist of a fog-bound day.
From the lilac trees that droop in St. Mary's Square
The dead leaves fall, a silent, fluttering crowd.
Dead thoughts, that, shivering, fall on the barren earth . . . .
Over and under it all the muttering murmur of London.

As Professor Alpers said in his biography of Katherine 'so
recently so longed for, London now was filled with symbols of
barrenness and death'. However, re-titled 'November' the
poem was published in the *Daily News* on November 3rd,
1908.

    She also wrote a delightful story 'The Tiredness of Rosabel'
which was first published, posthumously, in *Colliers' Magazine*
in February 1924, the style of which was competent and a
harbinger of her later work. Briefly, it was about a tired little
London shop girl, going home to her cold, miserable room in
Paddington, hungry, after only a scone, a boiled egg and a cup
of tea at Lyons, and though yearning 'for a good dinner —
roast duck and green peas, chestnut stuffing, pudding with
brandy sauce — something hot strong and filling', had just her
wish-fulfilment fantasies to nourish her as she kneels in the
dark by the window. She thinks of the attractive young couple
she served that day, and wondered what marriage to such a
rich and handsome man would be like, with rose-filled rooms,
fires, and a silver ball gown laid out on the bed. Stiff and cold
she retires supperless to bed, until finally, in the grey light of
dawn, she wakes and smiles a little, 'because her heritage was
that tragic optimism, which is all too often the only
inheritance of youth.'

    Meanwhile in Wellington the officers of the ship *Encounter*,
a fast cruiser guarding the Pacific, were being entertained by
Mrs Beauchamp, the report of which appeared in the *Weekly
Graphic*. She wore her grey chiffon taffetas, Vera, her

beautiful flowing white satin Empire gown and Chaddie a pale yellow silk dress, frilled with lace. There was dancing, and white roses decorated the supper tables, a far cry from the grey English austerity.

As the letters to Garnet end on November 8th it seems likely he came home for his one week's holiday about then. The Trowells by now were in financial difficulties, with little coming in. To alleviate the situation, Katherine suggested becoming a paying guest. There was, after all, plenty of room. Mrs Trowell must have been worn out with all the housework involved. Towards the end of November, no doubt at Katherine's instigation, and unknown to the Trowells, she joined the chorus of the Moody-Manners Opera Company, pretending to be Garnet's wife. Two of her poems belong to this period.

Sleeping together

Sleeping together . . . how tired you were . . .
How warm your room . . . how the firelight spread
On walls and ceiling and great white bed!
We spoke in whispers as children do,
And now it was I — and then it was you
Slept a moment, to wake — 'My dear,
I'm not at all sleepy,' one of us said . . . .

Was it a thousand years ago?
I woke in your arms — you were sound asleep —
And heard the pattering sound of sheep
Softly I slipped to the floor and crept
To the curtained window, then, while you slept,
I watched the sheep pass by in the snow.

O flock of thoughts with their shepherd Fear
Shivering, desolate, out in the cold,
That entered into my heart to fold!
A thousand years . . . was it yesterday
When we, two children of far away,
Clinging close to the darkness, lay
Sleeping together? . . . How tired you were . . . .

The Arabian Shawl

'It is cold outside, you will need a coat —
What! This old Arabian shawl!
Bind it about your head and throat,
These steps . . . It is dark . . . my hand . . . you might fall'.

What has happened? What strange, sweet charm
Lingers about this Arabian shawl . . . .
Do not tremble so! There can be no harm
In just remembering — that is all.

'I love you so — I will be your wife,'
Here, in the dark of the Terrace wall,
Say it again. Let that other life
Fold us like the Arabian shawl.

'Do you remember?' . . . 'I quite forget,
Some childish foolishness, that is all,
Tonight is the first time we have met . . .
Let me take off my Arabian shawl!'

L.M. believes that Katherine was away only about two weeks
and then became redundant. Years later, talking to Leonard
and Virginia Woolf, Katherine described the cooking of
kippers over a fishtail gas-light flame in dingy theatrical
lodgings — not her scene! Also she later admitted to L.M. that
she 'could not really bear to see the way that Garnet ate his
egg'. She returned to Carlton Hill and in the light of future
events, no doubt saw Garnet over Christmas.

Suddenly, in the New Year, Katherine returned to
Beauchamp Lodge to a cheaper room. There had been some
catastrophic rift with the Trowells. Plagued by money worries
and strained by the uprooting from the safe, comfortable soil
of New Zealand, Mr Trowell had discovered the extent of the
love affair between Garnet and Katherine and was extremely
angry. It was one thing to sit in the sunlit music room of a rich
businessman's house, encouraging and teaching the ardent
young daughter of the house how to play the cello, quite
another to have his nineteen year old son, as yet precariously

balanced on the bottom rung of the ladder of success, taken from him in marriage. In any case, foolishly, he considered it a disastrous alliance. New Year's Day, 1909, found Katherine sitting in the Leicester Square Gardens, weeping into her muff. An old woman in a jet bonnet sitting by her said, "Well, that's 'ow it is, my dear!" So wrote Katherine years later when she described that unhappy time.

In February, Katherine met a Mr George Bowden at a dinner party in Hamilton Terrace given by a Dr Caleb Saleeby and his wife, who was the daughter of the poetess Alice Meynell. Dr Caleb Saleeby, thirty, a temperance campaigner, was interested in eugenics and the medical value of sunshine, and wrote a book about this later. George Bowden, aged thirty-óne, son of a Baptist minister, was a professional singer with a fine tenor voice and had been to Cambridge on a choral scholarship from 1899 to 1902. He was, therefore, a contemporary of E.M. Forster. He taught singing and speech training at a London College of Divinity, and also gave singing lessons in a studio in Bond Street. He shared a studio-flat in St Mary's Terrace with an engineer friend, Lamont Shand, and there was a manservant, Charles, in the background, an all-male household.

George Bowden, who according to L.M. 'wasn't much but he wrote beautiful letters', neat, dapper, with pink cheeks and small moustache, a mild and amiable man, approached the 'inconspicuous and somewhat demure figure' sitting by the piano and introduced himself. There were 'some rapid exchanges', so he wrote to Professor Alpers in 1949, illustrating Katherine's facility for immediate contact with people. There followed another meeting at the flat of a young continental soprano, then Bowden held a musical party, at which Katherine made an impressive entrance as Charles announced, "Miss Kathleen Beauchamp." His training in the household of the Marchioness of Ailesbury no doubt gilded the perform-ance. Bowden thought she carried herself with 'regal simplicity' and 'it was she who "received" rather than we who hastened forward to greet her'. Such is the way with fine actresses.

From then on she was a frequent visitor. Bowden said that Katherine seemed detached and preoccupied. She would be detached, alas. Her mind was in a turmoil, for she knew now that she was pregnant by Garnett Trowell; 'penniless, friendless, hopeless, loveless alone', she wrote about these desperate weeks in a document called 'The Little Episode' in 1909.

By now, Bowden, unsuspecting, was in love with her and sent daily passionate love letters 'beautifully expressing his humble devotion and understanding', according to L.M. These Katherine read out to Margaret Wishart and Amy Birch, commenting caustically on them and sometimes laughing at them. She was doing this for a purpose of course, the scene was being set, and no one was to see the anxiety behind the mask except perhaps L.M. She was very frank with L.M., she needed her support but would not always admit it. Being the staunch friend she was, L.M. did her best to help.

During that time Bowden entered hospital for a tonsillectomy and Katherine dutifully offered to collect him in a taxi on his discharge. They then 'became engaged'; the announcement was made at a Saleeby dinner party. Mr Bowden met Katherine's guardian Henry Beauchamp, also the Countess von Arnim. Henry wrote to Mr and Mrs Beauchamp and awaited their reaction and ultimate permission to marry, as Katherine was not yet twenty-one.

As yet unaware of these momentous happenings, Mrs Beauchamp was entertaining a friend, a Mrs Milward bound for England, at a farewell tea on February 17th, 1909. On that happy summer day the hostess received in reseda green shantung trimmed with lace, Vera was resplendent in purple velvet-trimmed taffetas and 'sunshiny' Chaddie wore white muslin patterned with pale blue flowers. Doubtless a description of this party would be sent to Katherine, including news of the tragic wreck of the ship *Penguin*, which foundered in Cook Strait *en route* for Wellington from Picton about that time, with the loss of seventy-four lives. All were buried at Karori. The association of Karori, so near to Katherine's heart, must have deepened the misery of her wretched state.

It was obvious in the document 'A Little Episode' (typed copy, not dated, Texas), that she felt no joy in her engagement. Bowden was merely a port in a storm.

*"Oh," she said impulsively, childishly, "I have been so
miserable." She felt she must tell him everything — confide in
him — ask his advice — win his sympathy — she felt she must
hear again that curious, caressing tone of his voice.*

The account goes on:

*Wishing to appear pleasing to them she not only thru herself
into the situation, whole-heart, absorbing all of it — but she
seemed (to herself, as well as to them) to lean completely for a
moment, though she always really stood alone.*

With obvious reference to the last days at Carlton Hill she goes
on: *When I came from Paris here, O, I really felt I should have
died. I cried every night — they tortured me with everything.
It went on for weeks — until at last I made up my mind that
whatever happened — I should leave them.* If this account is
true to fact, the Paris visit being only in October, it seems to
me she can never have been truly welcome at the Trowells'.

   Then came the illuminating entry: — *came and engaged
himself to me — Yes, that's the way to put it,* finally ending,
*Never before had she needed so much love in her life.
Primitive woman she felt. All scruples were thrown to the 4
winds —*
   "I walked, and the wind has blown me about."
*She saw a bottle of eucalyptus, and the two clean
handkerchiefs at his pillow. She was filled with disgust.* This
about sums up her attitude to poor Bowden and is a clear
indication of the basic reason for the hasty marriage on March
2nd, 1909. She felt she had to procure a father for her child.
The picture of the singing teacher Mr Reginald Peacock in her
later story *Mr Reginald Peacock's Day* was based on Bowden.

   An intelligent girl like Katherine would never have entered
so solemn a contract but for this deepest, most desperate
reason and yet, in view of her courageous unconventionality,
one is also surprised that she bothered, but financially there
were too many problems, and it was still only 1909.

   Clearly, news of the engagement had reached Wellington
and coincided with an 'At Home' at 47 Fitzherbert Terrace, in
honour of a visiting world famous contralto, Madame Ada

Crossley, for in the newspaper account Mrs Beauchamp wore black. However, as usual the *Weekly Gazette* reported the house was filled with flowers, sweet peas, carnations, and coreopsis and a string band played. Madame Crossley was resplendent in pale green marquisette over hydrangea changeant taffetas, enhanced by tourmaline and pearl jewellery. White plumes drooped from a black picture hat. Vera wore puce chiffon taffetas, with a black hat trimmed with pink roses and white wings, and Chaddie, pale blue eolienne with black sash and hat trimmed with white roses.

Meanwhile at Beauchamp Lodge, Miss Rosabel Watson heard of the engagement and plans for an early marriage. She advised Katherine to write of these plans to her parents. Needless to say, Katherine had no intention of complying, even though it seems she earnestly assured Miss Watson she would do so. She married George Bowden on March 2nd, 1909 at Paddington Register Office, without consent, giving her age as twenty-two.

Much has been written about her all-black wedding outfit and the 'dreadful shiny black straw hat' worn to give her courage, according to L.M.'s account, who was a witness. The Register Office was the usual dusty, heartless place, without a flower in sight. Katherine and L.M. alike would be in despair. After the ceremony, Ida went home leaving Katherine with a new dressing-case borrowed from her, with its 'Bear up' note tucked into one of the pockets. The day passed with wining, dining and a show. The hotel bedroom with conventional pink satin bedspread and tasselled pink lampshade offended Katherine, according to her later account for L.M. On retiring Katherine's iron resolve gave way. She lay inert and frigid. Poor Katherine — poor Bowden; she could not go through with so terrible a deception. Deeply perplexed, he suggested she telephone L.M.

I doubt whether she really did, but that night she returned to Beauchamp Lodge, appearing at breakfast next morning 'cool as a cucumber', wearing a pink and white striped blouse and brown tweed skirt, with the news that she had just been married. Though under great strain it seems she was composed, on the surface at least. She must have spent a terrible night. Without contacting Margaret Wishart, she

F

packed some of her belongings and left Beauchamp Lodge for ever.

It appears she went straight to her Swiss hairdresser in George Street, begging asylum. They had a spare room above the shop and they kindly took her in. Behind the locked door, she cried for a week, refusing to leave with Bowden, who had found her whereabouts ultimately. Then she vanished, without leaving an address, to join Garnet in Glasgow, ending up in Liverpool.

One does not know how much she told Garnet, but news of the announcement of the marriage in the *Morning Post* for March 17th must have reached him somehow. Undoubtedly he would know of the pregnancy and perhaps this was just the loophole he looked for, because at the end of the month Katherine left for London. She knew there was no future with Garnet and one wonders if she ever saw him again. However, she wrote lovingly to him in June. From Liverpool she went to stay with L.M. Meanwhile, news of the marriage had been cabled to Wellington by Mr Kay and consternation would reign.

Mrs Beauchamp arranged to sail to England on the *Paparoa* which left on Good Friday, April 8th. At least four months away from home, with all the expense and inconvenience, Mr and Mrs Beauchamp would be furious but also deeply anxious. A shrill note sounded from the *Weekly Graphic* for April 14th, 1909: *The cabled news of the marriage of Miss Kathleen Beauchamp came as a surprise to most people here, as they had not heard of her engagement. Miss Beauchamp went to England last year in order to take up literary work, for which she had a decided bent. Mrs Beauchamp left for the Old Country by the* Paparoa *on Thursday and her sister, Mrs Derry (of Auckland) and Mrs Trapp (Wairapa) came to Wellington for a few days to see her off.* One cannot help feeling that their curiosity got the better of them but perhaps that is being uncharitable. Finally even the North Island itself seemed dyspeptic. Mount Ngauruhoe was in eruption. *Several Aucklanders recently ascended the mountain when the eruption was at its height, the ash covered cone belching forth steam and smoke*, reported the *Weekly Graphic* for April 28th.

In England on Good Friday Katherine was expressing her

misery in her writing. *It is the evening of Good Friday; the day of all the year, surely, the most significant* . . . . *I* thirst *too — I hang upon the Cross. Let me be crucified — so that I may cry 'It is finished.'* She was sleepless with anxiety and had to buy tablets of Veronal, a barbiturate, to alleviate this. She was never a drug addict as some of the ill-informed imply, just desperate.

She had found a flat in Maida Vale, poorly furnished with wobbly bamboo. L.M. would visit early and they shared breakfast of coffee and stewed fruit, not really nourishing for two young people. According to L.M. Katherine wrote often to Garnet, begging him to visit but he failed to come and, it appears, failed to answer her letters, 'pearls before swine'!

Perhaps to cheer herself up, perhaps because of some tempting low-price excursion, Katherine took a trip to Brussels towards the end of April. In her journal she wrote: *The carriage is full but Garnie I feel that I am going* home. *To escape England — it is my great desire. I loathe England. It is a dark night, full of rain* . . . *Everybody sleeps but I. The train shatters through the darkness. I wear a green silk scarf and a dark brown hat.*

Alas for the London she once loved. *April 29th* . . . *Packed again, I leave for London. Shall I ever be a happy woman again?* . . . . *I can't rest. That's the agonizing part* . . . . *my* body *is so selfconscious* . . . *Sick at heart, till I am physically sick — with no home, no place in which I can hang up my hat and say here I belong, for there is no such place in the wide world for me* . . . *I wonder when I shall sit and read aloud to my little son.* Two stories written in 1910 *Journey to Bruges* and *Being a Truthful Adventure*, were no doubt inspired by this trip.

On May 27th, wearing her shiny black straw wedding hat, Katherine stood quite apart and unacknowledged by the crowd of relations awaiting Mrs Beauchamp's arrival. One can imagine the cold dread under the shady brim. L.M. who was with Katherine, described the meeting in her memoirs: *I had never known, and I think Katherine had forgotten, the unquestioned assurance, security and authority of the rich, represented by her mother. There was no question of where she was staying: it must be at the dignified private hotel in*

Manchester Street where they always stayed . . . Presently, she looked at the black hat. 'My dear child! The chambermaid can have that!'

Then for the next two weeks Mrs Beauchamp had much to do. She saw Dr Baker, and innocent, mystified L.M. was packed off to the Canary Islands for a holiday. 'I did not know then what a "Lesbian friend" meant,' said L.M. in later years. Mr Bowden was interviewed, one wonders what transpired, and what they thought of one another. One speculates too on the exchange between Katherine and her mother. I cannot believe that the question of pregnancy never came up. Mrs Beauchamp knew of Katherine's regard for Arnold and Garnet Trowell. It is unusual for a pregnant woman to desert the father of an unborn child. In addition, it was now June, Katherine could have been showing signs of pregnancy in her face, subtle changes, a blurring of contours, rarely missed by any sharp-eyed woman; women's eyes in general are sharp, experience over the centuries has made them so, and none so sharp as a mother's eyes!

Then it was decided that Katherine should go abroad, for obvious reasons one supposes — out of sight, out of mind; London was too exposed. A watering place in Bavaria, Bad Wörishofen, was chosen; one wonders why. Perhaps Great Aunt Louey, via Countess von Arnim, had suggested it. It was noted for hydrotherapy and cold water hosing, guaranteed to rearrange one's thoughts, especially if they erred on the wicked side.

They arrived at the expensive Hotel Kreuzer on June 4th, and on June 10th Mrs Beauchamp sailed for New Zealand on the *Tongariro*. Katherine registered as Käthe Beauchamp-Bowden, Schriftstellerin, London, her new name sporting an umlaut like a jaunty feather in a cap! Occupation — authoress. The ordeal was over for the moment. By June 12th she had moved to a less expensive address, the Villa Pension Müller, Türkheimer Strasse 2, where she stayed until July 31st.

Some time in June she was ill, febrile and shivering, which last suggests a high temperature. In an unposted letter to Garnet, headed 'A.C.F. letter. Night' she blamed a barefoot woodland walk taken the previous day. Incubation periods being what they are, this cause can be ruled out; in any case, people, rather than wet June grass, infect one. She went on to describe her symptoms: *I think it is the pain that makes me shiver and feel dizzy. To be alone all day, in a house whose every sound seems foreign to you, and to feel a terrible confusion in your body which affects you mentally, suddenly pictures for you detestable incidents, revolting personalities, which you only shake off to find recurring again as the pain seems to diminish and grow worse again.*

This is a description of the colic of uterine pain, and mild delirium. It is likely that she was having the miscarriage then, and the pain which she described in the letter to Garnet appears to have continued through the night to the inevitable sad end. *It was a night of agony*, she wrote. *Now I know what it is to fight a drug. Veronal was on the table by my bed. Oblivion — deep sleep — think of it! But I didn't take any*, no doubt fearing interference with parturition.

It would have made little difference to the outcome. All she could do for comfort was to lie and think of her Grandmother Dyer and imagine her standing by the bed with the bowl of hot bread and milk, along with the loving wrapping-up of cold feet in 'a little pink singlet, softer than a cat's fur'. It was all over finally and Katherine was bereft. Her last tie with Garnet was gone. All she had was her pen.

A poignant note in German appears in her notebook for that time, vowing to work hard and so make every effort to respect herself again.

She began to write her bitter satirical stories which, when collected, formed her first book *In a German Pension*, published in 1911. The setting of the stories was the Pension Müller, which is mentioned by name in the story *Frau Fischer*. She must have been unable to cope with the depressive reaction of her bereavement because she acquiesced in a wild, loving scheme of L.M.'s to compensate for the loss, which was to send a little boy of eight, Charlie Walters, from a Welbeck Street Mews, suffering from the after-effects of pleurisy, distension of the abdomen and dear knows what else in the way of an underlying lesion, to convalesce with Katherine in Wörishofen. This boy, a poor shopkeeper's son, had been found by L.M.'s nursing friend Miss Good. They tied a label on him bearing his name and address and sent him alone across Europe by train.

From August 1st Katherine stayed with Fräulein Rosa Nitsch, the owner of a lending library, with whom she must have got acquainted early on, for the scent of lilac always carried her back to the Wörishofen library. (There were lilacs growing outside.) Katherine and Charlie stayed there until September 22nd. He called her Sally — yet another name change! One wonders how they got on and whether Charlie is still alive.

On September 23rd they moved to another address with the family of Johann Brechenmacher, on Kaufbeurerstrasse. Charlie eventually returned to London, one hopes invigorated. The only child she was ever to care for, he is probably the sick boy 'Peter' in the haunting story *Elena Bendall*, written in 1914, but thought by some to have been written in 1909. It appears in *The Unpublished Manuscripts of Katherine Mansfield*, in the Alexander Turnbull Library in Wellington.

It is set in Wörishofen, with descriptions of pansies and lilac bushes in Kasino grounds, and is about a beautiful, selfish, histrionic singer Elena Bendall and her delicate, sick son Peter. They are living in a pension and the boy lies gravely ill. Then there occurs a piece of writing which dates the story and can be seen on p63 of the *Journal* for December 28th, 1914: *She loved to think of the world outside white under the mingled snow and moonlight. White trees, white fields, the heaps of stones by the roadside white, snow in all the furrows. Mon Dieu how quiet it was.* Elena expresses an urgent desire to sing, in spite of the boy's eyes imploring her not to. *But she would only sing gently, only softly Peter. Listen. Snow is falling. Out of the sky falls the snow, like green and white roses and nobody sees but the moon. From her cloud pillows the moon arises and floats with the falling snow and gathers the green and white roses, the little white buds of snow, in her gleaming fingers . . . . As she sang she stood up and singing still she went to the window and put her arms along the frame. Peter shut his eyes. He floated into his mother's singing bosom and rose and fell to her breath. His wonderful mother had wings. Yes, she could fly. She flew with him out of the window to show him the snow and to give him some of the roses. He felt the snow on his chest and creeping up to his throat it formed a little necklace round his neck. It crept up — but not to my mouth Mother. Mother, not over my eyes.* Her singing was interrupted by the arrival of the doctor, who by the light of a lamp held over Peter discovers he is dead.

Meanwhile, Mrs Beauchamp on the *Tongariro*, no doubt feeling rested but still angry, arrived at Hobart and was met by Mr Beauchamp, who was dismayed to learn that a fellow passenger, a Mr D.M. Niven, had died at sea in Mrs Beauchamp's arms. "Yes it did happen," Vera told Professor Alpers. "Cut him to the quick, poor dear." This event was the basis of the fine story *The Stranger* written by Katherine in November 1920 at the Isola Bella. Once in Wellington, Mrs Beauchamp visited her lawyer to disinherit Katherine. She must have been feeling very bitter to do so. It was too soon for forgiveness.

Exciting preparations were in hand for the marriage in September of Vera, who had become engaged to Dr James Mackintosh Bell, a Canadian geologist and director of the New Zealand Geological Survey. There was a happy whirl of social engagements, a naval ball given by the officers of HMS *Encounter* on the polished decks of the Union Company's *Mararoa* on September 3rd, Vera wearing mauve crêpe de Chine and ivory lace, and Chaddie an Empire dress of emerald green crêpe-de-soie with gold fringe.

On September 22nd, 1909, Edie Bendall became engaged to Mr Gerald Robieson of Wellington College teaching staff, and on September 23rd Vera, in blue-braided shantung with matching hat, and Chaddie in a hat with wings, no doubt matching her happy mood, attended Miss Aileen Russell's tea (Vera's bridesmaid), amidst violin solos and narcissi and daffodils.

On September 23rd, 1909 in St Paul's pro-Cathedral, Vera and Dr Bell were married by the Bishop. Admission to the church was by ticket only. Choristers sang 'The King of Love My Shepherd Is', as Vera in white satin charmeuse and scarf of Limerick lace, a gift of her great aunt in London, came up the aisle on her proud father's arm. A wreath of orange blossom crowned her Brussels net bridal veil, and on her arm was a sheaf of white irises. The bridesmaids, Chaddie and Jeanne, Aileen Russell and Kitty McKenzie, wore 'ivory satin with overdresses of silk spotted net terminating in tasseled ends'. 'Clusters of pink flowers' held the white tulle veils, their bouquets were of pink and white flowers. Mrs Beauchamp had chosen grey radium silk with a silk embroidered lace yoke, her grey matching hat was decorated with cabochons and ospreys of black. The reception was at 47 Fitzherbert Terrace; spring flowers were everywhere. Presents were laid out in an upstairs room. Vera, wearing the bridegroom's present, a fur coat of Canadian caribou, edged with ermine and lined with pale blue silk, had chosen 'a grey striped tweed tailor made' and 'a large black satin hat draped with iris blue panne' as her going away outfit. The happy couple left in a taxi-cab decorated with white flowers, for a honeymoon in the South Island.

Needless to say, after two or three days of rain the afternoon weather was delightful. No doubt news of this event would reach Wörishofen and our little black sheep with her waif Charlie must have reflected bitterly on her own ghastly wedding of March 2nd. Edie Bendall was duly married in December, the dresses for the child bridesmaids having been happily designed by Edie, no doubt they also sported fringes. Another door was closed gently.

Katherine stayed on with the Brechenmachers until January 1910. It seems she was not truly well. In an apologetic letter to Margaret Wishart in autumn 1909 she described her efforts to sort out 'the tangled web' she had made of her life, and went on: *Heaven knows I look well enough — but I am not at all well — my heart is all wrong — and I have the most horrible attacks of too much heart — or far too little.* It seems she was having palpitation which could have been paroxysmal in character and of nervous origin, but more likely was due to her poor physical health.

She became friendly with a literary group in Wörishofen, an Austrian journalist 'S.V.', with whom she had some sort of love affair, a Polish couple called Yelski, and another Pole Floryan Sobieniowski, critic and translator, described in later years by Katherine's husband, who became acquainted with him to his cost, as 'charming, distinguished, and completely untrustworthy'. However, through his burning interest in the Polish dramatist Stanislaw Wyspiański, Floryan inspired Katherine to write her poem which he translated into Polish for publication in a Warsaw paper in 1910. Sobieniowski ultimately left Wörishofen, presumably in the course of his work, and wrote a love letter to Katherine from Warsaw on 12.12.09: . . . *you can't know how I long for you, how my thoughts are full of you all the time . . .*, to which Katherine responded by saying she loved him. They planned to meet up again in Munich or Paris; he was looking for a place in which to live together but it is clear that Katherine's heart was not really engaged, for he wrote again from Paris on January 9th, 1910 asking if she had received his last two letters addressed to 'the hotel'.

Katherine had returned to London just after Christmas 1909, her fare of £6 having been telegraphed by L.M. on December 21st, 1909, and was living in the Strand Place Hotel. *Are you well again, or still sick?* Floryan wrote. *Oh, write me immediately, dear, write to me, Kathleen, so I can be at ease* . . . . By the end of January, no doubt money was running out and Katherine turned to George Bowden for support. One deduces that this move was taken in desperation.

He was at a house party at Easton Hall in Lincolnshire and received three urgent telegrams from Katherine asking him for a meeting in London. She wanted to rejoin him. Bowden was apprehensive but agreed. They met and Katherine lived with him at the flat in 62 Gloucester Place until the end of March. According to Bowden, though they were the best of friends, the venture was only partially successful.

L.M., who was instructed to visit only when Bowden was out, thought that Katherine was not happy and was much distressed by his 'lack of delicacy'. However, Katherine visited his studio in Bond Street, and recited some of her sketches at a concert he had organized. He noticed she had periods of depression, the melancholy of which she expressed in her poem 'Loneliness'. If only one had had a glimpse of her 'huge complaining diaries'!

She did, however, have a glimmer of hope. She showed Bowden her Bavarian stories and he was impressed enough to suggest she take them to A.R. Orage, the editor of a bright weekly, the *New Age*. This was in February. They were accepted — some good fortune at last! — and her poem 'Loneliness', reflecting all her insecurity and sadness, was printed in the *New Age* on May 26th, 1910.

Loneliness

Now it is Loneliness who comes at night
Instead of Sleep, to sit by my bed.
Like a tired child I lie and wait her tread,
I watch her softly blowing out the light.
Motionless sitting, neither left nor right
She turns, and weary, weary droops her head.
She, too, is old; she, too, has fought the fight.
So, with the laurel she is garlanded.

Through the sad dark the slowly ebbing tide
Breaks on a barren shore, unsatisfied.
A strange wind flows . . . then silence. I am
    fain
To turn to Loneliness, to take her hand,
Cling to her, waiting, till the barren land
Fills with the dreadful monotone of rain.

Chapter VI

Orage and the New Age

James Alfred Horrage, a name he changed to Alfred Richard Orage and known as Dickie in childhood in the Cambridge-shire village of Fenstanton where he was born in 1873, had been an elementary school teacher in Leeds. Poor, bright and inspired, strenuously rejecting his working-class background, he read extensively, produced a book on Nietzsche, and formed the Leeds Arts Club along with two friends, Holbrook Jackson a lace merchant, and a ycount architect, A.J. Peaty. He joined the ILP, lecturing for his hero Keir Hardie. By 1915 he and his wife Jean, daughter of a Scottish Inspector of Schools, were in London, sharing a flat with A.J. Peaty.

Orage was now thirty-two, tall, slim and dark, with hazel eyes and a faint birthmark on his left cheek. With a soft felt hat on the back of his head, he moved like a cat, as though he was going to pounce on something, according to Holbrook Jackson. He was a fascinating talker, a warm, cyclothymic personality with whom one made immediate contact — he had charisma.

In April 1907, along with Holbrook Jackson, Orage took over the weekly called *New Age*. His offices were two rooms in a passage called Tooks Court, near Chancery Lane. S.G. Hobson, formerly on the staff of *New Age* described the new editors thus: 'two tall men, dark-haired and noticeable in any company', 'upstanding and lithe'.

Orage, had become involved with a green-eyed siren of a woman, twenty-seven years old, dangerously and viciously outspoken, but well informed and hard-working, called Beatrice Hastings. His marriage had broken down, his wife, a lesbian, had left him to live with Holbrook Jackson. Beatrice, having joined the staff of the *New Age,* was Orage's mistress for the next seven years.

Beatrice, born Emily Alice Haigh in Hackney, 1879, was the fifth child of a couple formerly from Huddersfield, on holiday in England from Port Elizabeth, Cape Colony. At twelve she was sent to a boarding school at Pevensey near Hastings, returned to South Africa in 1893, finally leaving at twenty after her marriage to a Mr Lackie Thompson broke down. He was reputed to be a pugilist. A tempestuous, highly-sexed and violent woman, her quiet respectable family were probably glad to see the back of her.

Other members of the *New Age* team were A.E. Randall, literary critic, who was to die of tuberculosis, J.M. Kennedy, foreign editor on the *Daily Telegraph,* 'a fat squeaky man', who lived with his mother, so described for Professor Alpers by Carl Bechhofer Roberts on November 16th, 1949.

Miss Alice Marks was the adoring and devoted secretary. Orage being the bright, enterprising light he was, encouraged famous contributors to say exactly what they pleased, the price being no remuneration. Likewise, unknown authors were welcomed with much kindly interest but unpaid, for the pleasure of seeing themselves in print. Any payments made at all were nominal. He met his numerous contributors on Monday afternoons in the basement of a nearby ABC Café where no doubt over tea and sticky buns, their material was finalized for the Thursday issue.

Among contributors were Shaw, Wells, Chesterton, Arnold Bennett, and Hilaire Belloc. Arnold Bennett reviewed books under the pseudonym of Jacob Tonsen. Welcome new writers were Ezra Pound, Edwin Muir, Ruth Pitter, Richard Aldington and Michael Arlen. Articles poured from Beatrice's pen under names like D. Triformis, Beatrice Tina, Roberta Field, T. Robert West, T.K.L. and Alice Morning. She was an ardent Feminist; one of her first articles was 'a lurid plea for State Protection for women from the horror of giving birth', declaring that child-bearing was a gross infirmity of the weaker sort of woman. She had socialist sympathies and wanted women to have the vote. 'Notes of the week' at the front of the paper were written by Orage, the new cover was designed by Eric Gill, and the price was one penny.

And so one day in February Katherine and Bowden mounted the two flights of stone steps leading to the office, which contained a roll-topped desk, two chairs and a coat-hook. She was received by Alice Marks, Bowden remained on the landing, and Orage met Katherine for the first time. Swiftly reading the MS, but retaining no clear memory of what the story was about, he agreed to publish it in the next issue . . . .

Under an overheading 'Bavarian Babies' her story *The Child-who-was-tired* appeared in the *New Age* on February 24th, 1910. Her literary career had begun. One can imagine her excitement.

Much has been written about the similarity of this story to Chekhov's tale *Sleepyhead* which appeared in R.E.C. Long's collection *The Black Monk and other stories* in 1903. Both deal with an overworked child who in desperation smothers the crying baby in her charge in order to get some much needed sleep. Whether Katherine had read the Chekhov story or not, she was in her favourite medium, writing of childhood. It is highly unlikely that she would present a plagiarised story, knowingly, as her first offering at such a vital interview. A second story *Germans at Meat* appeared on March 3rd. Between February and August 1910 nine further stories were published in the *New Age*.

Some time near the end of March 1910, L.M. received an urgent message from Bowden. Katherine was ill in a nursing home and had asked him to send for her. *I found her in a second-rate nursing home where they told me she had been operated on for peritonitis*, wrote L.M. in her memoirs. Katherine was in great pain. *After a dreadful operation I remember that when I thought of the pain of being stretched out, I used to cry. Every time I felt it again, and winced, and it was unbearable,* she wrote in December, 1920 to Sylvia Lynd, as she recalled that terrible time. She asked L.M. to take her away as she felt the surgeon had more than medical interest in her body. A horse-drawn, four-wheeled conveyance, a growler, was called and to spare the pain of jolting, the driver was instructed to drive slowly; but to little avail. Katherine was taken to L.M.'s sister's flat in Luxborough House off Marylebone Road, and the wound, as yet unhealed, was dressed daily by Miss Good. L.M. would be deeply anxious but glad to have her beloved Katherine under her wing again, for Katherine never returned to Bowden. The marriage was over.

Katherine had had a specific infection of the reproductive system requiring removal of the left salpinx. There was associated inflammation of the peritoneum, the inner lining of the abdominal cavity. She had been and was very ill. Recovery took months and was alas only partial. It was decided the convalescence should be spent by the sea and rooms above a grocer's shop in Rottingdean were taken in April.

Inevitably, new complications had developed, rheumatic pains in her hip and feet, and the local doctor was called in. In desperation, Katherine wrote to Mr Kay, manager of the Bank of New Zealand, who kindly came to Rottingdean, saw the doctor and arranged payment of the fees, no doubt also informing Mr and Mrs Beauchamp. When walking became a little easier, the two girls moved to a cottage by a daisy-filled meadow. L.M. collected books from the library at Brighton, bringing back one day a black and silver Egyptian scarf. A photograph taken by L.M. shows Katherine wearing the scarf as she sits on a divan. No amount of brave draping of the Egyptian scarf could mitigate the sickly looks of the patient. However, a little stray dog joined the household and was much loved. He lurks on a further photograph of Katherine taken outside in the sunshine. She stands, head up proudly, a walking stick in her left hand. On it she had written: *This is the first photograph which shows some character.*

While sitting by the sea, she composed some sad little poems:

The Sea Child

Into the world you sent her, mother,
Fashioned her body of coral and foam,
Combed a wave in her hair's warm smother,
And drove her away from home.

In the dark of the night she crept to town
And under a doorway she laid her down,
The little blue child in the foam fringed gown.

And never a sister and never a brother
To hear her call, to answer her cry,
Her face shone out from her hair's warm smother
Like a moonkin up in the sky.

She sold her corals — she sold her foam;
Her rainbow heart like a singing shell
Broke in her body: she crept back home.

Peace, go back to the world, my daughter,
Daughter, go back, to the darkling land;
There is nothing here but sad sea water,
And a handful of shifting sand.

Bowden visited once or twice, also Orage and Beatrice who
looked at some of her work. When she was stronger, Katherine
went to stay with them in their cottage in Seaford, Sussex,
happier at last in this most stimulating environment.

On July 29th L.M. was commissioned to write to Garnet
Trowell and send back the birthday ring, adding that, *she will
never join G. Bowden again . . . . Now she is Katherine
Mansfield, 39 Abingdon Mansions, Pater Street, Kensington.
That is her writing name and she is taking it almost entirely
now.* As much as Katherine loved writing letters, it is
interesting that she declined to write this one.

She stayed with Orage and Beatrice until August. Three
further Bavarian stories were published in the *New Age*. She
was invited to the ABC Monday meetings; she would be in her
element there, and joining Beatrice under the pen names of D.
Triformis and Beatrice Tina, wrote vitriolic pieces on other
writers such as Chesterton and Bennett. The ménage would be
an abrasive one because of Beatrice. With her youth, beauty,
and ability, Katherine was a constant threat to her. Not long

before her suicide in October 1943, when conversing with Mrs Charles Lahr, Beatrice still insisted on how much she had always hated Katherine. The poet Davis Gascoigne, who met Beatrice in the early thirties, also remembers her telling everybody how she detested Katherine.

Orage, from whom Beatrice had parted in 1914, was also assassinated by her pen. John Carswell in his book *Lives and Letters* considered *both Beatrice and Katherine had an ambi-sexual side which drew them to one another yet was a source of horror and embarrassment.* This would be the basis of the degree of hatred engendered in Beatrice. It seems she never ever wrote anything kind or complimentary about Katherine. Beatrice was rather given to lying and one must treat her vitriolic account of those early days after meeting Katherine with some reservation. *Beatrice said Orage nicknamed Katherine the Marmozet and largely ignored her. She considered Katherine furtive and obsequious as she sat among them, extracting material from their conversation for future sketches.* 'Marmozet' bears the unkind stamp of Beatrice's invention, but the rest is probably near the truth. Katherine had not come 11,500 miles for nothing. This was her milieu, Orage had the key which opened the door to future success and probably she felt bound to sing for her supper. As Edmund B. d'Auvergne, a contributor to the *New Age* recalled after inviting the three of them to dinner that summer, he felt that Katherine 'was like an actress trapped in comic roles — she had to sustain the part she had created in her sketches'. He noted too that she was 'a cool young lady with a cynical view of love' — and she was but twenty years old! and so far from home.

In August, Beatrice or Orage managed to procure a flat for Katherine. Though this was advantageous for her, one cannot help wondering whether Beatrice in fact got rid of her, because for the next nine months no work of Katherine's appeared in the *New Age*. The flat in 131 Cheyne Walk, Chelsea belonged to Henry Bishop who had gone to paint in Morocco for five months. It was pleasant and situated on the Embankment, looking south to Battersea Park, with plane trees and river barges under her window. Sun poured into the large front room which Katherine used as a bed-sitting room. Vera Brittain, who lived in 2 Cheyne Walk during the Second World War, described her house as *typical 18th Century with one or two rooms on each floor, each perfectly proportioned, bringing a sense of serenity combined with a consciousness of sunlight never far away.*

L.M. often visited Katherine, staying the night in the small back bedroom. She thought that Katherine loved her new home. There was music from a street musician stationed outside the nearby public house. Katherine, writing about it to a friend, commented: *A man is singing outside the Cremorne Arms. Do you know that tree of mine believes every word of it — and is wideawake — with excitement.*

One night, Katherine surprised L.M. by saying that she might go to Japan; there had been a Japanese exhibition in Shepherds Bush that summer. This was a sign often repeated in the following years that Katherine wanted to be on her own. From time to time she felt constrained by the depth of L.M.'s regard for her. Though L.M. tried hard to please and was mostly useful to have around (a 6ft young Amazon, she was good at humping and carrying), she depended too much on Katherine emotionally. Hers was a subservient personality; she was, in a way, a responsibility, or at least Katherine felt she was. 'What shall we do now Katie' was a favourite expression later when, stranded and ill in Paris, Katherine needed all the counsel she could get. But L.M. had her uses, acting once as a very refined 'bouncer' against an undesirable male caller. 'I was sent to guard the door and send him away'.

Among new acquaintances Katherine made at this time was Gwendoline Otter, a Chelsea hostess, at whose house she met Aleister Crowley. There she took some of his famous narcotic potion, as did the rest of the company. It only made her nauseated and unduly irritated by a picture hanging crookedly on the wall. She also spent much time arranging shed matches in a pattern on the floor.

Another friend was a handsome young man, Z— —, who worked in the city and with whom Katherine fell in love. He brought her a present of a painted miniature Russian village, the tiny houses and church of which they arranged on the floor by the fire. At Christmas he bought her an illuminated tree. This affair was ended by his family on their discovering that Katherine was married — sadly, too late, for she now was pregnant by him. He failed to answer her many letters, L.M. was sent to his office to prevail but without success. So once again Katherine was deserted by her lover, and even on to the end.

Some years later in a café, Katherine was to see Z— — again. Coldly noting his thickening figure and rather common face under a hard black bowler, she remarked wryly to L.M. that she considered she had had a lucky escape and straightaway wrote a story about him called *The Dill Pickle*.

Between August 1910 and May 1911 no work of Katherine's appeared in the *New Age*, but a periodical called *The Open Window*, run by Vivian Locke-Ellis, published *A Fairy Story* by Katherine Mansfield, on December 3rd, 1910, a cynical tale of a 'woodcutter's daughter' who is persuaded to avoid the Seven Deadly Virtues.

A more stable and secure relationship she made was with a young schoolmaster, William Orton. They met in the late summer of 1910 at a tennis party given by Paula Berling, the decorative young Austrian wife of a German scientist, who were friends of William Orton, but it is not clear how Katherine came to be there.

William Orton, born in 1888, was a sensitive, gifted young man, with interests similar to Katherine's: music, literature and art. As a child, he also had had an adoring grandmother living with him. At school he had been solitary and subjected to much sadistic bullying, but in spite of that, he managed to win a scholarship at fourteen to University College School in Gower Street, where he discovered he could draw, being awarded two prizes. He read Carlyle, Emerson and Ruskin avidly, filling exercise books with essays, three of which were published in the *Westminster Review* from August 29th, 1908. After drifting into an architectural apprenticeship he discovered he lacked interest and application, preferring to study history in office hours and at Holborn Public Library, which led eventually to the History Tripos at Cambridge. Like Katherine he was frustrated at home, filling diaries with : *why*

do I never write how sick I get of these people I live with! . . .
no fine passionate blood in them . . . *The pater has just come
down from his room (11.15 pm) to send me away from the
piano, where I was playing splendidly* . . . . *perhaps it is good
that we Bohemians are dropped into the world singly*
(especially if they play the piano at 11.15 p.m.!) Though he
had had many girlfriends, he was sexually innocent and was
likely to remain so for some years, due to some unresolved
sexual conflict. Spiritually he was lonely.

So at that tennis party, Orton, slight, dark-haired, with
dark eyes in a pale, broad face, met Katherine for the first
time and *a sort of instant recognition passed between them.* So
he described the meeting in his autobiography *The Last
Romantic*, devoting a chapter to his friendship with
Katherine.

Two days later William visited her at Cheyne Walk. He
found her in a pink kimono and white flowered dress. On the
floor were lamplit yellow chrysanthemums, candles stood
about. In a corner were stacked canvases and a bundle of dried
rushes. He thought the room looked beautiful.

It was a good friendship for both, neither hearts were
involved, a sort of child-love. They exchanged confidences
freely and gave each other emotional support. They shared a
diary and wooden bowl of money on a shelf, to which they each
contributed for gay little meals out. In the diary they were
'Michael and Catherine'; his present girlfriend, Edna Nixon,
was called 'Lais'. She was four years younger with a Hungarian
mother and English father. She was beautiful, with flashing
brown eyes, rosy cheeks and hair the colour of port wine. Their
relationship was a tempestuous, sterile one. She fascinated
Katherine when she visited the flat. Orton recognised
Katherine's burning desire to write. *She lived to write* . . . . *all
her writing was a kind of poetry in its extreme intensity.* He
thought that the collapse of her marriage had done far more
harm than she realized, for at heart he considered her
idealistic and deeply religious. He thought she was often
'very lonely' and her description of 'a bitter mood' would
appear in the communal diary: In lighter mood she added this

bright poem, drawing no doubt from her girlhood trip to the King Country.

> A gypsy's camp was in the copse,
> Three felted tents with beehive tops,
> And round black marks where fires had been
> And one old waggon painted green.
> And three ribbed horses wrenching grass
> And three wild boys to watch me pass
> And one old woman by the fire
> Hulking a rabbit warm from wire.

Katherine acquired a grand piano while at Cheyne Walk from a Madame Alexandra, a teacher of opera singing, who lived in the flat above. This piano, originally on hire purchase terms, was to cause some anxiety later when Katherine recklessly sold it before the transaction was completed.

After two years away from New Zealand, Katherine's wardrobe was replenished by a dressmaker in Redcliffe Road, an address of later significance. L.M. in her memoirs wrote: *It was she who made those small coats of lovely colours and soft velvet materials that Katherine wore for so many years; warm, full skirts for the winters; and dresses with long fitting bodices and pleated skirts. Life was an orgy of dressmaking at that time.*

Gwen Rouse, of Queen's College days, would join the dressmaking circle and L.M. obligingly took a photograph of the two girls, sitting on the floor by a merrily burning fire in a marble fireplace. Katherine, with smooth hair and a centre parting, no fringe as yet, looks healthier.

Early in 1911 Henry Bishop returned and Katherine moved to 69 Clovelly Mansions in Gray's Inn Road, a four-roomed top floor flat looking into a timber yard at the back. The cold cement stairs with iron balustrade to the top floor must have been a great trial. She covered the sitting room floor with cheap bamboo matting and cushions. L.M. provided a roll-top desk, an armchair and basket chair which had belonged to her mother. She also scoured London for gay travel posters for the kitchen walls. The other room, known as the Buddha room, because of a stone Buddha placed on the floor and brought originally from India by Dr Baker, contained the grand piano and a divan draped in a black cover, very Bohemian that. The tiny bedroom contained a camp bed and a chair; there was also a bathroom. The rent was £52 per year, and Katherine was to stay there until September 1912.

L.M. thought Katherine loved the flat, but though now more settled, she was still troubled with insomnia which had plagued her for so long. The girls would sit talking past midnight by the fire, not a good habit pattern for an insomniac to adopt. L.M. frequently stayed the night. In spite of Z's — — behaviour Katherine seemed happy in the pregnancy, perhaps on the premise that 'women need men like fish need bicycles'.

There have been doubts expressed about this pregnancy, but in the light of ensuing pleurisy, the disappearance of the £60 left in Katherine's account by L.M. in April, before she left to join her father in Rhodesia, the imminent arrival of the family from Wellington for the Coronation, and the return of Beatrice Hastings to the scene, as clerk of the works, no doubt, it is likely that Katherine had indeed been pregnant and had an abortion, deciding that the whole venture, at such a time, was a lost cause — sadly, for she was never to fall pregnant again.

Meanwhile in Wellington, the *Weekly Graphic* for November 9th, 1910 reported that the Beauchamp family were booked on the passenger list of the *Ruahine*, due to arrive in England in May 1911. There would be much excitement in the air, it was summer and the *Graphic* reported Chaddie in a berry-trimmed black hat attending a 'Rose' tea — 'roses everywhere in silver bowls' and 'roses rioting in a music filled old garden'. Mr and Mrs Beauchamp attended a dinner party on February 8th, 1911, given by their Excellencies, the Governor and Lady Islington. The dining room was newly panelled in New Zealand woods, a deeply satisfying décor. Then on March 15th, 1911, little Jeanne Beauchamp appeared in the society gossip columns for the first time. She was now nineteen and was reported attending Mrs Mile's tea, amidst pink and white lilies, crimson phlox and carnations, wearing pale blue muslin with a matching blue hat, an excellent foil for her fair hair and large blue eyes, Beauchamp eyes. On April 12th, 1911, the *Ruahine* departed, carrying Chaddie, Jeanne, Chummie and the parents.

As usual, Katherine was somewhere going through the mill, paying the price, while everyone else was having a good time. On May 18th, 1911 she had a story published in the *New Age* entitled *A Birthday*, the subject matter being highly significant, describing the birth of a son to the wife of a harassed businessman, the character obviously based on Mr Beauchamp in spite of the foreign-sounding name, Andreas Binzer.

In April L.M., grasping a bunch of carnations, a present from Katherine, sadly left for Rhodesia where she stayed five months. On her return she . . . *found no baby and a closed bank account. We never discussed the matter; obviously it had all been horrible.* In the meantime, William Orton had found a job in Tanford Hills Grammar School, Kent, teaching music and drawing, and it is likely that he and Katherine now saw less of one another.

The *Ruahine* duly arrived in May 1911. It was a great joy to be reunited with Chummie after three long years; he was now seventeen. The bitterness with which Mrs Beauchamp had returned to New Zealand in 1909 had died away. In letters to L.M. Katherine described her deep feelings for Chummie, and her discovery of a new and loving relationship with her mother. Mr Beauchamp joined the family some weeks later, from Canada, where he had been visiting Vera and her husband, who had left New Zealand on March 12th. Alas, he missed the coronation of George V on June 22nd and probably also the satirical piece in the *New Age* written by Katherine and called 'The Festival of the Coronation'.

In July, in spite of the hot, happy summer days of 1911 with the family, Katherine became acutely ill with pleurisy, severe enough to make her delirious. Katherine told L.M. later, that while lying alone in her flat with a high temperature, she felt that she was floating on the ceiling and described visual hallucinations when she thought she saw the elephants in the pattern of her Indian bedspread marching around the border and waving their trunks. This attack heralded her tuberculosis which was probably precipitated by the strain of the second pregnancy. In the light of this illness, the occurrence of the febrile illness in Wörishofen is also ominous and it seems likely that without the two pregnancies, a serious factor in the breakdown of old healed scars of much earlier tubercular infection, Katherine might never have succumbed to the infection at all. There was also the risk of cross-infection from the child Charlie Walter to consider.

After convalescing, the family sent Katherine to the Continent, to Bruges and Geneva, where she contacted the old Wörishofen friends the Yelskis. The collected stories *The Journey to Bruges* and *A Truthful Adventure* were written during this period.

L.M. on her way home from Rhodesia via Paris, had failed to meet up with Katherine as arranged. On her arrival in London she was visited by Chummie the same evening, who disclosed the Geneva address. In a typical flurry of love, L.M. scraped the £5 fare together and went back to seek out her ailing Katherine. She found her anxious, with less than £1 left. L.M. manfully got some money sent out and they shared a top floor room at a pension in a leafy street. She thought that Katherine seemed stronger. After a few days, L.M. returned to London alone; there wasn't enough money for two and anyway she felt *de trop*.

Katherine followed in September, meeting up again with William Orton for whom 'the world sprang to rights at her touch'. His relationship with Lais had been a deeply frustrating one, and remained so.

On September 6th Katherine noted in the communal diary that she had entertained 'the man' the day before, and there follows a torrid description of the evening, reproduced in the *Journal* p45. Surprisingly he turned out to be Professor Walter Rippmann of those far-off Queen's College days. One wonders what he thought of his former pupil! However, she went on to express disillusionment: *I want to begin another life; this one is worn to tearing point . . . . I am very lonely and ill today. Outside my window the buildings are wreathed in mist.* One feels that the previous evening had mattered little and was perhaps a mere panacea for the underlying mental and physical weariness. *I live merely from day to day — taking in everything apart from my work, the line of least resistance for the sake of my work. Do other artists feel as I do — the driving neccessity — the crying need — the hounding desire that (will) never be satisfied . . . Then Katherine what is your ultimate desire — to what do you so passionately aspire? To write books and stories and sketches and poems.* Nothing else really mattered. She had written three stories around Geneva: *Pension Seguin*, *Violet* and *Bains Turcs*.

By October 29th she must have been feeling better for she noted: *. . . I am at Peace. I am writing in Michael's book . . . I am become a little child again. I know not the world, the flesh and the devil. I live only in my imagination . . . It is not that I wish so much to renounce the world — it has gone.* Michael replied: *from far away, I know you mine for ever and ever . . . I am sealed with your mark and you are sealed with mine . . . . I too, my own, my Catherine, I am at Peace. All Saints Day, 1911.* Theirs was a special relationship, ephemeral like a raindrop irradiated by the sun. There was no further communication until April 1912 when Katherine wrote to William: *My life has been sad lately — unreal and turbulent . . . . But now I am utterly happy. I am at home again here . . . . I wander alone . . . . smiling, a silk shawl wrapped round my body, sandals on my feet. I lie on the floor smoking and listening . . . I think of you more often than you think of me. You are always in my heart — even when my heart — my beloved and my dear — has been most like the sand castle and nearest the waves — you have been safe and secret and treasured. I shall always love you . . .*

William finally broke with Lais and in October 1913 entered Cambridge to study history, philosophy and economics. In 1914 he joined the Public Schools Brigade of the Royal Fusiliers, leaving a message for Katherine in the communal diary. They had not communicated for many months. *Tomorrow 18.9.14 I leave here for camp in Epsom . . . To Katherine I need send no word save perhaps — what by this time she already knows — that the attitude of the Buddha room, premature as it was, was fundamentally the right one, and at least the gate to what is final: and that there is the one thing she must do, this time without mistake.* This she finally did but by then the bell was tolling.

Meanwhile in December 1911, Katherine's first book was published by Stephen Swift and Co., consisting of thirteen stories, ten of which had first appeared in the *New Age*. It was entitled *In a German Pension* and cost 6/-. One can imagine her joy, especially when handing a copy to the family. She had been paid £15 in advance by 'Stephen Swift', otherwise Charles Granville, a friend of Orage. It was not quite the initial success that her cousin's *Elizabeth and her German Garden* was, but it can be seen still on the shelves of any decent book shop, never having been out of print. There were glowing comments in the newspapers and periodicals.

Meanwhile she had written a fairy story. A friend and contributor to *New Age*, a Mr W.L. George of Hamilton Terrace, had sent it to a magazine called *Rhythm*, a quarterly launched during the summer term of 1911 by two Oxford undergraduates. Through ensuing correspondence Katherine at last met her Prince Charming who was to be the last and best man of her life. He was John Middleton Murry. The fairy story had 'puzzled' him but he was impressed enough to request another. Back came the story *The Woman at the Store*, strong, tense, with its New Zealand outback setting. It was promptly accepted. So much was his interest engaged that he bought a review copy of *In a German Pension* in Dan Rider's book shop in St. Martins Court, a meeting place and haven for young aspiring artists. Murry also knew W.L. George, who told him that Katherine Mansfield was 'terribly clever', and suggested they should meet. A dinner party was arranged at Hamilton Terrace, the setting, ultimately, for Katherine's story *Bliss*.

Chapter VII

John Middleton Murry

John Middleton Murry of Brasenose College, Oxford, born in
Peckham, August 6th, 1889, was the first son of a clerk in
Somerset House. A hard, tyrannical, ambitious man, then
aged twenty-nine, bent on improving his conditions and seeing
his son in the higher Civil Service, he worked fifteen hours a
day, the evening hours being spent as ledger-clerk to a Penny
Savings Bank. He left home at 8.00 a.m. and returned after
midnight. His wife of nineteen took in lodgers to help the
family budget. During the week the little boy was the centre of
an adoring female environment, the gentle pretty mother, a
loving maternal grandmother and an aunt, who, when they
were together, did a lot of laughing we are glad to hear. When
the father was home there was much restraint and education
on Sunday mornings for young Murry; sums, spelling, the
learning of history dates, useless facts, and Latin tags.
Disapproval was shown if the sums were wrong. Happily the
child was brilliant, could read at two, commenced school at
two and a half and by seven was in the top standard along with
boys of fourteen.

Murry, in his autobiography *Between Two Worlds*
considered that 'the grim education involved the complete
obliteration of a child's childhood'. His aunt in later life said
that he had been like 'a little old man'. He was timid, very
much a mother's boy, given to night terrors which often
required the comfort of the mother's big bed. At eleven he won
a scholarship to Christ's Hospital, Newgate Street, a
tremendous change in direction in a young life, especially in
view of his humble origins. In his wonderful new uniform, he

entered the school in January 1901 as a weekly boarder, with weekends spent at home. The difficulty of fusing the two worlds inevitably led to his becoming a snob. He became ashamed of his parents and his home. Some would not have survived. In fact he soon began to falter, depressed probably, becoming lethargic and losing interest. The father, intent on success, was badgering him about his position in class. Murry had to cover up with lies about his rival, a boy called Allen, who was by now a whole form above him . . . 'summer holidays were a torture'.

He became happier when the school moved to the country in 1902, becoming a Grecian and winning the Charles Lamb Medal for an English essay and finally overtaking Allen. At thirteen his brother Richard was born and Murry discovered he had great tenderness for little children. During the holidays, the little boy would sit patiently by while his brother studied, content to wait to be taken out for walks. Richard bridged the ever-widening gap between Murry and his parents. After the father visited the school in connection with the lack of progress, and during some intercurrent infection, the hysterical component of Murry's personality became overt. He was overheard talking in his sleep on one occasion, by a senior monitor in the dormitory who, being interested in hypnotism, decided to sit by Murry's bed on following nights. Aware of this interest, Murry proceeded to give further nightly instalments while pretending to talk in his sleep, elaborating on the theme that he was the illegitimate son of the Duke of Aosta. His histrionics must have been convincing, because the monitor took copious notes and delivered them to the housemaster, who thereafter seemed to take more interest in Murry.

In later life Murry confessed in his journal, 1st November, 1953, that he had suffered a homosexual assault at fourteen. He was thereafter to show violent repugnance to homosexuality.

In his last year, 1908, he won the gold medal for classics and a scholarship worth £100 per year to Brasenose College, Oxford which he brilliantly managed even after a sleepless night listening to the chiming clocks of Oxford, and suffering an overwhelming feeling of panic and inferiority on entering the examination hall. He felt his clothes were all wrong.

In October 1908, in fear and trepidation, he entered Brasenose to find to his delight a firelit study and later that evening another student, genial Frederick Goodyear, called to welcome him. He was to become a good friend. Other contemporaries were Michael Sadleir, Leonard Duke, Joyce Cary and Arnold Toynbee, one of whom recalled that Murry was noticeably reticent about his origins. Cary thought him brilliant on dialectics, Leonard Duke thought: *with his white face, black hair, and aquiline features he always reminded me of the portrait of Dante; there was a look almost of spirituality humanized by his quaint way of holding his head on one side, and his smile — rather shy than sly.* According to Donald Gladding, Murry gave the impression of a future poet or saint. Sadleir thought his good looks spoilt by 'his ungainly lunging walk'. He acted and spoke like a gentleman, merging into the enchanted life of Oxford, but underneath there was emotional and sexual immaturity, a bashfulness and a craving for affection.

In the heady atmosphere of university life, and particularly after a month-long reading holiday spent with his adored classical tutor H.F. Fox, in his first long vacation in 1909, when they and three other undergraduates splashed about in an old sailing dinghy at Snape, Murry found he could not face further vacations at home with its intellectual isolation — sad for his parents, particularly for the mother. The only justification was that he had arrived at this point in his life by his own efforts and not by the sweat of his father's brow.

He found himself lodgings on a farm at Waterloo in the Cotswolds, for the Christmas vacation. Murry had come to detest his 'lower middle-class existence'. He let the farmer, Mr Thornhill, believe that his mother was a widow, living abroad. He also persuaded his mother to give him her precious legacy of £30 to buy a horse, on which he eventually rode to hounds — reprehensible! He won a first in Honour Moderations and with Thornhill celebrated with whisky in the time-honoured way, both crawling up to bed on all fours.

The summer vacation was spent in style, tutoring Lord Charles Hope in Latin at Hopetoun House. Murry was valeted, dressed for dinner and walked around the golf course with Lord Charles and A.J. Balfour. He was amazed how well he adapted to this exciting new environment. On the Easter vacation at Waterloo, Murry met another guest, Maurice Larrouy, a French naval officer who persuaded him that he ought to spend some time in Paris. They corresponded for the rest of the year and Christmas 1910 found Murry shivering in Rue Gay-Lussac, Paris, with only £25 to see him through a seven week vacation. He had left Waterloo for ever, without a word of explanation to his kind host. Though he did not know it, he was at the parting of the ways now. He was gradually withdrawing from Oxford, unable to settle to any real work.

In his lonely room, for the first two weeks, he studied Bergson, taking fourpenny meals of coffee and croissants at left bank cafés during the day, and his main meal at night, after which he would retire to the Café d'Harcourt, or the Closerie des Lilas for coffee and wine, to observe the left bank literary men until midnight; he also watched the girls congregating there in their big hats and muffs. It was cold outside.

'A lamb among wolves' was Joyce Cary's verdict when he joined Murry later, considering drily that 'in introducing Murry to Bohemian life he had ruined a good civil servant'. One of the girls called Yvonne embarrassed Murry by sitting on his knee, amusing a couple nearby — a Scot in a bow tie and bowler hat, J.D. Fergusson, and his American companion, blue-eyed Anne Rice, both artists and destined to become lifelong friends of Murry. Another girl, Marguéritte, tall brown-eyed and wearing a small black velvet hat trimmed with cherries, attracted him, and in the saturnalia of New Year's Eve, he finally plucked up courage to speak to her. After that they dined together each evening, Murry politely escorting her to the door of her lodgings near the Sorbonne. In a bitter-sweet turmoil of sexual innocence he would have let this situation drag on, but Marguéritte, who had other ideas such as marriage in mind, finally seduced him by sending for him to visit her, pleading illness; a lamb to the slaughter, a most reluctant hero.

In an attempt to turn over a new leaf, Marguéritte procured a job as a seamstress, wheedling ten shillings per week out of Murry to augment her puny income. This left him with one franc a day to live on, apart from his meal-ticket. Fergusson, inviting him to tea at the studio, noticed he looked ill and made him eat as much brown bread and butter as he could, interspersed with kindly 'but look now, Murry lad!' sort of remarks. This mental and material sustenance was just what Murry needed, and they talked at length about art, especially rhythm in art, and so the idea of the future literary magazine of Murry's called *Rhythm* was born.

Murry met friends of Marguéritte, notably Francis Carco, a cynical young writer from Nouméa who was to be for a time part of the fabric of Murry's shaky future. It was now time to leave Paris. Bidding Murry goodbye, Marguéritte hurried away weeping.

In emotional turmoil, he returned to Brasenose to find he could not concentrate on work. He was ill for some days and complained of a feeling of revulsion from Oxford, in a letter to P. Landon on 30th March, 1911. As far as Marguéritte was concerned, he felt trapped. He was afraid to open her misspelt letters. He found himself unable to confide in anybody, a lifelong failing of his.

At Easter he returned to Paris. Marguéritte now lived with her married sister. Murry occupied her old room at 36, Rue des Escoles. Confident of her future, she was wildly happy, which made Murry even more apprehensive, especially when she asked him about her returning with him to England.

Joyce Cary came to stay with Murry, introducing him to some of his artist friends, one of whom was a Scottish painter, Dot Banks, who called herself George, a large beautiful woman with a heavy face like Oscar Wilde. She dressed in mens' clothes and cried a lot as she denounced her friends. Murry believed she was in a condition of permanent hysteria due to sexual repression. He would, to his grim amusement, be required to comfort her with a friendly arm around her broad shoulders. The perk was a good, much-valued tea.

Cary described events in his *Paris Diary 1910-1911*, how Dot Banks, who was his own girlfriend and a pupil of Augustus John, hit him in a jealous rage and Murry, with whom they were walking, turned somersaults in the street to divert them. According to Cary, Marguéritte was very jealous and after seeing Murry with Dot one night, was enraged. She once told Cary she would knife Murry if he left her, she depended on him to save her from prostitution. Mistily, Murry was beginning to realize this and discovered the beginning of a hardening process within him.

The end of the holiday was marred by the loss of his wallet. With his lifelong flair for such carelessness, he had left it on an outside table at the Closerie des Lilas. A *cri de coeur* came to Joyce Cary on April 1st, 1911, with a request for two or three pounds.

The parting with Marguéritte was less harrowing than he feared. He was growing up a little. Back at Oxford he was able to do some work, and began learning German which was to be most useful to him in later years. He collaborated with Michael Sadleir on the new magazine *Rhythm*, the first quarterly edition of which appeared in June 1911, with its thick grey cover bearing a drawing by J.D. Fergusson showing a naked girl, sitting with an apple in her right hand. Inside was a reproduction of a Picasso drawing. There was also a glowing account of an exhibition of paintings by Anne Estelle Rice. J.D. Fergusson was now art editor of *Rhythm*.

Murry still foolishly sent money to Marguéritte and wrote about their reunion in Paris, but in reality he was a haunted and miserable man, wishing to end the affair. When he did return to Paris in the summer vacation without informing Marguéritte, he fled after a twenty-four hour wait in a hotel, never seeing or writing to her again. He was growing up! He made for home then, there was nowhere else to go. Marguéritte's letters went unopened. According to F.A. Lea, Murry's biographer, that betrayal was to haunt him to the end of his life.

In the autumn of 1911, Murry as editor of *Rhythm* was welcomed to Dan Rider's bookshop. A dealer in second-hand books and a champion of young struggling authors, Dan Rider would receive in the 'lion's den', a room at the back of the shop, laughing uproariously with the likes of Frank Harris, J.D. Fergusson, Lovat Frazer, sitting on a pile of *Decline and Fall*, Enid Bagnold and Hugh Kingsmill, who thought that Murry looked defeated.

On returning to Oxford there was a terrible aftermath to the Marguéritte affair. Apropos of the lively talk at Dan Rider's, with Harris *et al.*, holding forth on life and love affairs, Murry was advised that the best way to exorcize the ghost of Marguéritte was to have an adventure. Alas, this was duly arranged by Joyce Cary in some seedy Oxford brothel. Murry found he could scarcely face the experience and one week later discovered he had contracted gonorrhoea. He had reached the depths of degradation from which he eventually rose, Lazarus-like, a few weeks later, a sadder but wiser man — a sort of resurrection had begun.

So in December 1911, at the dinner party at Hamilton Terrace, Murry, nervous but intrigued, awaited Katherine Mansfield. She arrived late looking aloof and reserved, wearing the grey silk evening dress, grey gauze scarf and a single red flower. They dined by candlelight off German red plum soup, made in honour of her first book. W.L. George called her 'Yekkaterina' as they discussed Russian translation. Murry, watching her poise and cupped, expressive hands, felt clumsy and subtly out of it. Later though, in the drawing-room, he relaxed as they discussed the problems of writing.

Katherine, looking into that handsome face, seeing those 'eyes of unexampled beauty' and listening to the deep, slow voice, no doubt felt, as the heroine did in her story *The Dill Pickle: the strange beast that had slumbered so long within her bosom stir, stretch itself, yawn, prick up its ears, and suddenly bound to its feet.* At long last, she had met a man of her own mental stature. On leaving, Murry declined her offer of a lift, saying untruthfully that he was going in the opposite direction. Knight-errants need money, he had none. She invited him to tea, but strangely did not give him her address.

In January 1912 he asked her to review a book of poetry for *Rhythm*. In February, Katherine wrote to him from Geneva, saying that she had been ill but would give him brown bread and Russian cherry jam for tea on her return. She was still on friendly terms with Orage and Beatrice, for she stayed with them on February 28th at Crawley.

On March 8th the Beauchamp family sailed for home, arriving in Wellington about May 18th, 1912, after being delayed by quarantine regulations in Melbourne. No longer the rebellious teenager, Katherine would be sad to see them go. She was never to see her mother again.

Murry duly visited Katherine at 69, Clovelly Mansions, noting with inner surprise the sparse furnishings, as she handed him a bowl of tea from the floor. She soon put him at his ease however and he began to air his problems, mainly the catastrophic idea he had of actually leaving Oxford before taking his final examination. He confessed that he could not concentrate on work and found life at Oxford unbearable. Incredibly, Katherine thought he should leave; like many gifted people, they both had their blind spots. Being the suggestible, indecisive shipwreck of a young man he was, Murry acted on her advice and sought an interview with his tutor, who was furious but promised to help him find a job. Murry left Oxford at Easter and went back home, busily decorating his bedroom, no doubt in an effort to dissipate the general air of disapproval which must have pervaded the place.

In April, Fox arranged an interview with J.A. Spender, editor of the *Westminster Gazette*, who offered Murry book reviewing and daily comment on condition he took his examinations in June. He was given a cheque for £5 in advance, which he showed Katherine over lunch in a Soho restaurant, the Isola Bella. Dressed in a navy serge suit of boyish cut and a cream straw hat trimmed with flowers, she was jubilant. Some nights later she dined with Murry and Frederick Goodyear at the Dieppe; dinner there was 1s/3d. Goodyear, who admired her work, had expressed a wish to meet her. Afterwards as they walked around the fountain in Piccadilly Circus, enjoying the April evening and discussing accommodation in London, Katherine suddenly offered Murry a room in her flat.

No doubt mesmerized, he moved into the Buddha room a few days later on April 12th. He was to pay 7s/6d per week. L.M. who had been around and about all this time, was so forlorn at this influx that Katherine wrote a poem especially for her in the front of a treasured book of hers:

The Secret

In the profoundest Ocean,
There is a rainbow shell,

H

> It is always there, shining most stilly
> Under the greatest storm waves
> And under the happy little waves
> That the old Greeks called 'ripples of laughter'.
> And you listen, the rainbow shell
> Sings — in the profoundest ocean.
> It is always there, singing most silently!

As an old lady of eighty-seven, L.M. told me that she had sold this book a few years previously.

Two months later, L.M. and her friend Miss Good opened The Palma Rooms at 59, South Molton Street as 'Specialists, Scientific Hairbrushing and Face treatment, hours 10-7'. They advertised in *Rhythm*.

Katherine's story *The Woman at the Store* duly appeared in *Rhythm* Vol. 1, No. 4, Spring 1912, also two poems of a Boris Petrovsky translated by Katherine; very mysterious, that. Katherine, ousting Michael Sadleir, became assistant editor. J.M. Kennedy of the *New Age*, with whom Katherine had been friendly, was duly dropped, in spite of her having accepted his gift of a fur coat quite recently. It takes a stout heart to refuse such a gift.

Murry worked diligently on his paragraphs, seeing Katherine only at the end of the day when they would have tea and bread by the fire, talking until 2.00 a.m. Shaking hands to 'Goodnight Murry' — 'Goodnight Mansfield', they would go each to their bed. In her journal she wrote of Murry, 'how charming he looked — walking like a god'. Eventually they began to eat out, eels and penny pies mainly, taking beer at the nearby Duke of York public house to eradicate the taste, where they were deemed to be out-of-work actors. This platonic relationship with the vivid Katherine suited Murry very well. Throughout their life together it was Katherine who loved more deeply. He was afraid to enter into a further sexual relationship, in the light of Paris and Oxford. Discussing all this one evening by the fire, Katherine said, "Why don't you make me your mistress?" Murry, lying on his back on the floor, suddenly raised both legs and waved them saying, "I feel it would spoil — everything." Katherine answered coldly, "So do I," admitting later that this reply had been wounding. So life went on as before. Katherine was good for Murry; he felt at ease with her.

From time to time during his life Murry had felt unreal and de-personalized; Katherine had a unifying effect on him. She gave him emotional security and being the stronger outgoing personality, much support. Basically, he feared life and in arriving at this sort of oasis, he had been through a kind of spiritual upheaval. Now he had to face a new set of circumstances. He was having to work very hard on the *Westminster Gazette,* 'gutting' German books for review and writing political comments etc. Undoubtedly he would have repressed regrets and guilt feelings over leaving Oxford, he also had grave financial worries with *Rhythm* which was not selling. He had discovered, after arranging to make the magazine monthly, that less than five hundred copies out of three thousand printed, had been sold. Inevitably, some of his mental adjustments failed.

One afternoon, alone in the flat while reviewing one of Dr Wallis Budge's translations of the Egyptian sacred books, an oft-repeated phrase, 'the boat of a million years' seemed to trigger off a depressive panic attack with its content of futility, desolation, unreality and de-realization, when even the world seems unreal. Weeping and sobbing he was shaken to the core. Katherine, arriving home a little later, found him very upset. "Murry I love you. Doesn't that make any difference?"

They began to kiss each other goodnight instead of shaking hands. A further panic attack was precipitated in the Duke of York's by the sight of one of the *habituées,* a woman called Lil, presumably a street-walker, staring at her haggard reflection in a large mirror, with what seemed to be a tragic expression. Murry made to leave abruptly. Katherine admitted later that she also had caught Lil's expression. Both were quiet as they sat by the fire, clasping each other close, and no doubt for mutual mental comfort became lovers that night.

Murry felt had Katherine been free, they would have married the next day. They went blissfully to Paris for a few days' honeymoon, meeting an approving Fergusson, Anne Estelle Rice and Francis Carco, who noted Katherine's "Je ne parle pas francais."

Anne, in her memoir of Katherine Mansfield, described that

first meeting in the spring of 1912, on a sunny terrace of Boudet's restaurant in the Latin Quarter. *I well remember the impact of a compelling and vivid personality. Unforgettable was the round oval face like ivory, the nose, full face — how shall I describe it? Two dots indicating the nostrils gave its position, and her mouth was a blob of cosmetic scarlet. The evenly cut fringe of dark brown hair was topped by a straw boater trimmed with a profusion of cherries. She was short of stature and dainty in appearance. The arresting feature was the beautiful eyes, dark, sombre and questioning . . . there was no escape from the searching scrutiny, often disconcerting and I am sure not always flattering.* They met again at the Closerie des Lilas. Katherine in a black cloak and black and white fez, looked and was mysterious. *Only the yashmak was missing . . . she assumed the character of the costume she wore . . . . dressing up was a very important part of Katherine Mansfield's imaginative nature.* Anne thought her: *great fun, witty, satirically assessing friend or foe and quite capable of turning her wit against people she liked and loved . . . she was a chameleon, being all things to all people and, like a divining rod, sensitive to every aspect of friend or stranger . . . Secrecy played a part and friends were kept in separate compartments . . . One found her not always communicative; there were aloofness and moods.*

Returning to the ailing *Rhythm* as editor and sub-editor, they shortly adopted the nickname 'The Two Tigers' originally suggested by the novelist Gilbert Cannan, a contributor. Through W.L. George, Katherine had met Gordon Campbell, a young Irish barrister, father of the much-loved TV personality of 'Call My Bluff', the late Sir Patrick Campbell. Visiting the flat one day he was surprised to hear Katherine say, "You can come out now, Tiger." Murry, in his navy blue fisherman's jersey, suddenly appeared and was duly introduced. Murry was to become very attached to Campbell and he in turn a very good friend to both. In fact Murry became emotionally dependent upon him.

Katherine, happy and established on *Rhythm*, gladly left the *New Age*. She had been particularly hurt by a venomous six week serial in May by Orage, under the pseudonym 'R.H. Congreve', about a flighty widow, Mrs Marcia Foisacre, obviously based on Katherine and her jilting of a political scientist called Tremagne (J.M. Kennedy) for 'that spark Stornell' (Murry). One is surprised that it was Orage and not Beatrice who made such an attack. Perhaps he was sorry for poor Kennedy. One's sympathies are with Katherine.

To ease the financial difficulties of *Rhythm*, Stephen Swift was approached about taking it over. He agreed with pathological lightness of heart, to pay them an editorial salary of £10 a month, handing over a cheque for four months' payment in advance. *Rhythm* Vol. I No. V, now a monthly, duly appeared in June in a new bright blue cover, bearing the name of Stephen Swift & Company Ltd., 16 King Street, Covent Garden, London. There were reviews by John Middleton Murry and Katherine Mansfield with a tart note from K.M. on *Moods, Songs and Doggerals* by John Galsworthy: *We have neither time nor space to speak of this volume further. Mr. Galsworthy is wise in that he avoids all mention of the word "poetry" in connection with his verses.* Katherine was in her element!

In mid June, Murry with Katherine and Gordon Campbell, went up to Oxford for the final examination. By now he and Campbell were good friends: One is surprised at the threesome in this honeymoon period, and one wonders how Katherine viewed the situation. Murry achieved a second class honours degree, with which he was satisfied in view of his lack of preparation.

It must have been about this time that he took Katherine to meet his parents. The visit was a disaster. Cold disapproval hung over the tea table like a fog. The sight of his nine year old brother Richard, rounded-eyed with bewilderment and misery, was unforgettable. A sequel to his visit occurred two weeks later. Murry's mother and Aunt Doll arrived at the flat, hysterical, poor things, and trying to pass Katherine who had opened the door to their ringing. Murry, absolutely horrified at the scene, pushed them out and shut the door on them, terrible for all concerned. Murry put a very shaken Katherine on to the couch and covered her with a rug while the distraught women continued to bang on the door. They were trying to save their chocolate soldier from the toils of a married woman! Murry did not see his family again for three years.

Murry introduced Katherine to Dan Rider and his group, which one day included Enid Bagnold who remembered Katherine in her autobiography. *The first time I met her, she rushed in in a rage, with a key in her hand. 'Tell him I've left!' she cried out to Dan Rider, slamming down the key. 'Left who?' 'Left Murry!' (she called him that). She looked like a white-faced cat with a tiger in its eyes. Whirling out as she had whirled in, she was gone. I knew enough to know who they both were, she and Middleton Murry, and listened breathlessly. But it was only a row and it mended . . . 'I knew her' is just what I didn't. Never till I read "Bliss" fifty years later and found the girl! — I missed when I met her — imprisoned for ever in the crystal of her own words.*

As one would expect, Frank Harris had become a hero to Murry. Katherine had not yet met him. One day in June, Harris strode into Dan Rider's waving the current issue of *Rhythm* in which Murry had compared the poet James Stephens with Milton, finding his poem 'The lonely God' better than 'Paradise Lost'. Harris roundly ridiculed him in front of Katherine, Hugh Kingsmill, Kenneth Hare and Harold Weston. Then he picked up the contents bill of the July issue, which unknown to Harris contained the extravagant eulogy about him, 'Who is this man?' written by Murry in which he considered Frank Harris the greatest creative critic in the world. Cursorily reading the bill of fare Harris threw it down saying, "By God, Murry, this paper of yours is going to make a stir." Murry, upset and tearful, ran out of the shop. "He'll kill himself." cried Katherine as she followed him. Astounded, Harris was told that this was Katherine Mansfield. He persuaded Kingsmill to bring them back. He found them sitting by the fire in their flat. Both had been crying. Harris took all three for a meal at the Café Royal. The atmosphere was subdued but friendly. Quoting this article on Harris in *Between Two Worlds,* twenty-three years later, is evidence of Murry's basic, almost pathological honesty. Most, wisely, would have suppressed it.

That summer Katherine met Gordon Campbell's fiancée Beatrice, who described the meeting in her book *Today We Will Only Gossip: When we arrived Katherine was sitting on a laundry basket at the top of the stairs, carrying on a gay conversation with the laundry man in a high pitched voice. She and Murry wore fisherman's navy blue jerseys and her hair was bobbed with a fringe across the forehead . . . Katherine probably looked on me as a sort of interloper . . . we all sat on the floor of her flat . . . The conversation was about people going to bed with each other and other things that I had never heard mentioned in public before. I felt Katherine was trying to shock me and frighten me away. She was hard and bright and hostile. I never spoke a word.* No doubt Katherine was jealous, guarding her territory and feeling more of 'a little Colonial' than usual.

Among the drawings sent to *Rhythm* were some impressive animal studies by a young Frenchman, Henri Gaudier-Brzeska, which led to another vital meeting. Born Henri Gaudier, October 4th, 1891, at Jean de Braye near Orleans, he was the son of a carpenter, whose ancestor had worked on Chartres Cathedral. He began drawing at six years, insects mainly. Via two scholarships in 1906 and 1908, ostensibly to study business methods in London and University College Bristol, he became engrossed in architectural drawing, animal and flower studies. In 1909 he was in Paris studying anatomy, and there in the St Geneviève Library, he met Sophie Suzanne Brzeska, a Polish woman of thirty-eight from Cracow. She was trying to learn German. He observed her closely as they shared the same table. Sophie, a rejected child of a family of eight sons, was the daughter of a feckless, unfaithful solicitor father and a self-absorbed, uncaring mother. She had been refused an education by her parents, who called her stupid and a 'useless encumberance'. Failing to marry, she left home, but could not hold down even menial jobs for more than two weeks. She was highly unstable, emotionally labile and paranoid, showing signs of the eventual florid psychotic illness which led to her dying in a mental hospital in 1919, when she believed she was God. At the time of meeting Henri, she was poor, desperately lonely and fighting a depression which contained suicidal ideas. She had had a love affair lasting one year with a man of fifty-three, which had been terminated two months previously after discovering that he was married.

Now, to their mutual delight, a close loving friendship developed with Henri, which lasted until his death in battle at

Neuville St. Vaast on June 5th, 1915. It was a mother and son relationship. Writing to a friend, Dr Uhlemayr in Nuremburg, he described his new friend: *I am in love . . . she is 30 years old . . . I love her with a purely ideal love . . . she is an anarchist . . . lithe and simple, with a feline carriage and enigmatic face . . . last Sunday we talked from 8 to 4.* He painted her portrait which now hangs in the Tate Gallery. They came to London in 1910, where they lived as brother and sister, Henri calling himself Gaudier-Brzeska. They were extremely poor, renting two rooms for 7/- per week. One contained a dreadful old bed costing 5/-, the top mattress of which was packed with rags and was bug-ridden, where Sophie slept under padded travelling rugs. Henri lay on the bare lower mattress at the foot. The other room contained a deck-chair, a kitchen chair, a bench, two tin plates and two broken mugs. Here Henri worked on borrowed clay from daylight to late evening, curling up in the deck-chair to sleep, weary from overwork and ill-nourishment. The place was pervaded with the smell of fermenting stew, which was made once a week. They lived on Henri's meagre wage of £1 as a clerk in a Norwegian shipping office. He sold some of his drawings in public houses at 1d each. Once Sophie, with a rag doll wrapped in a shawl, begged 6d in the street.

In appearance Henri, in his square-necked red shirt, was short, black-eyed and unshaven; he had never shaved and his cheeks bore soft pale down, with two wisps of hair sprouting from his chin. Though poorly-nourished and given to nose-bleeding, he was lithe and moved like an animal. He reminded Murry of a panther. Enid Bagnold, whose head Henri sculpted, thought he was *like a dagger in the midst of us. He had a hungry face . . . and a mind made of metal. He talked like a chisel and argued like a hammer. Sophie . . . easily affronted . . . seemed mad even then.* He also was unstable, admitting to mood swings: 'after violent joys I find myself in the most pessimistic state of mind'. He had bouts of crying, and explosive outbursts of anger. There were violent quarrels with Sophie, soon dissipated 'mid floods of mutually penitent tears. He also told lies, admitting that lies were indispensable to an artist. Though he modelled in clay, his great creative interest lay in stone. He told Murry if he could only have a Pyramid, a hammer and a chisel and a life time, then he would build a temple. Some of his work is in the Tate Gallery, strong, harsh and eternal. He did a bust of Ezra Pound, who asked him to make him look like a sexual organ. It stood in the garden of Violet Hunt's house, South Lodge, Campden Hill Road for years and surprisingly, reached San Remo at one stage.

So one night in the summer of 1912, Henri and Sophie visited Murry to discuss the drawings for *Rhythm*. He was immensely taken with the Tigers, finding Katherine 'a curiously beautiful person, Slav in appearance and very strong minded'. Murry charmed him so much that Henri embraced him violently on leaving, kissing him passionately as he arranged to model his head. Katherine, astute and watchful, noted Sophie's problems, her garrulity, abreacting and over-excitement, carefully withdrawing her hand which Sophie clutched so wildly as she described her unhappy past. Being paranoid, Sophie noticed this action of course. Murry admired the Gaudier-Brzeskas.

In the meantime Murry had found a house in the country at Runcton, near Chichester, and during August he and Katherine had the pleasurable task of getting it ready. Unfortunately, Henri, on being told about it, suggested airily that Sophie would like to live with them, which suggestion, at an open window there some days later, Katherine pronounced upon vehemently. Poor Henri, paying a surprise visit, after having walked thirty miles, overheard Katherine say, "I don't want to see her here — she's too violent . . . I don't like her . . . . She'll make me ill again." In anger and anguish, he returned to London without presenting himself.

On September 1st, 1912, *Rhythm* appeared with Henri's drawings, but the friendship was over. He became an implacable, aggressive enemy; he and Sophie stoned the clay head of Murry until it was completely destroyed. Murry returned the rest of the drawings and was to see Henri only two more times.

The house at Runcton, standing 'mid pasture and salt-marsh, was charming, with a walled garden, medlar trees and a magnolia tree by the door. They moved in on September 4th, 1912 with furniture on hire purchase from Maples. They

engaged a rascal of a soldier servant. Strangely, their days
there were shot with melancholy. Both were restless, unsettled,
and insecure; Katherine's hoped-for child did not materialize.
However, they were visited by kindly Eddie Marsh, upon whose
shoulders Murry climbed to gather the medlars. Other callers
were Rupert Brooke, Frederick Goodyear, Ford Maddox Ford
and Violet Hunt. L.M. also spent some uneasy weekends
there. She thought it 'a lovely little house'.

Alas, Floryan Sobieniowski also descended on them, with
two big black trunks, no money and a propensity for breaking
into mournful Slav songs. They manfully put him up.

In October disaster struck. Charles Granville, alias Stephen
Swift, had absconded with a lady called Louise Hadgers,
leaving Murry with a printing debt of £150. He was arrested in
Tangier on October 28th for two bigamous marriages and
fraud of £2000, and sent to prison for fifteen months on July
2nd, 1913. Inevitably Maples removed the furniture. Life at
Runcton was over. The forlorn Tigers moved into one room in
Chancery Lane at 10/- per week. The furniture consisted of
one camp bed, two chairs, and a packing-case. Katherine
arranged to pay the whole of her allowance, £8-6-8 per
month, to the printers and also saw Gilbert Cannan's
publisher Martin Secker, who agreed to take over the
publishing of *Rhythm*. Edward Marsh gallantly guaranteed
£150 and Wilfred Gibson, a young man from Hexham,
became permanent assistant editor at £1 per week. There were
five more issues of *Rhythm* and two further under a new name,
Blue Review.

The Murrys then moved into a flat at 57, Chancery Lane,
which was 'really horrible' according to L.M. A large
cupboard without a window became Murry's office, there was
a gloomy sitting-room, bedroom and kitchen. Orage lived in
number 59! Beatrice was sharpening her claws. Each day in
November gloom, Katherine canvassed for advertisements.
Her little pet canary died to add to the general misery. L.M.
thought Katherine 'was fading away too'.

Far away in New Zealand, on November 22nd, Mrs
Beauchamp in white and rose ninon and hat with rose plumes,
was present at a sunny garden party at Government House.
Jeanne, in white lawn and lace and a hat with roses,

accompanied her. Chaddie was in Canada on a long visit to
Vera because Mr Beauchamp thought anxiously that Vera
might be lonely. I doubt whether Mrs Beauchamp knew of
Katherine's misfortune. Reprehensibly she often left her
parents in the dark about her whereabouts and what had been
happening. Katherine was a law unto herself, and no doubt
her independence of spirit was laid down *in utero*.

However, there was one bright spot on her horizon. They
were going to Paris at Christmas with Gordon and Beatrice
Campbell, Gilbert and Mary Cannan. Anne Estelle Rice was
giving a party in her large studio in Montparnasse. Beatrice,
who thought Katherine had accepted her by now, heard Murry
say 'in his funny slow way', "Tig, I told you she was alright," as
they drove from the station. Beatrice remembered their visit to
a café and Katherine removing her big black hat with a gay
flourish, as she hung it with the men's hats on a rack,
delighting in the male approval from a nearby table.

Fergusson with George Banks joined them in their gay
café-crawl. Anne showed off her paintings, exhibiting each
one from an easel. After seeing about twelve, Katherine, to
everyone's astonishment, suddenly burst into sobbing. As she
was led away she said, "The colour, the form, the light — it is
all just as I feel it myself." Perhaps she was overwhelmed by her
predicament; perhaps this was indeed a genuine, non-
histrionic emotional overreaction. She was a highly emotional
girl. In later years she was to admit to almost fainting at the
sight of a beautiful flower illustration in a magazine.

The *New Age* appeared on January 2nd, 1913 and
contained two vitriolic attacks on the Tigers by Beatrice
Hastings, following kindly articles on them by Hugh Kingsmill
and Enid Bagnold in the *Hearth and Home*.

The first article called *Rhythm* a nest of crickets or rats. The
other article entitled *The Changeling* was directed against
Katherine, calling her 'Dinky's Baby' and made veiled,
unpleasant references to her former lovers. Orage, perhaps
beginning to realize that some pathology was creeping into the
paper, took over Beatrice's column.

The following year Beatrice left Orage for good, going to
live and work in Paris.

Sobieniowski was still around, ostensibly the Murrys' lodger at a rent of 15/- per week, but borrowing 25/- a week to pay it. It is incredible that they put up with him.

Rhythm was still afloat, some of the writers agreeing to give their services free. They included Gilbert Cannan, Hugh Walpole, Frank Swinnerton, James Stephens, Walter de la Mare, Wilfred Gibson, J.D. Beresford, Max Plowman and later the incomparable D.H. Lawrence. Katherine had written first to Frank Swinnerton about his novel, which she had reviewed for the *Westminster Gazette*, and said she wished to meet him. He was invited to tea at 57, Chancery Lane along with Richard Curle and Gilbert Cannan. He wrote of his impressions of Katherine: *I found myself enchanted by a small, very slim, very dark girl who spoke in a carefully modulated murmur, hardly parting her lips, as she hummed or intoned her words. She sat very still and explained in this low voice, with much sweetness, that she did not know quite what she should do in the future . . . The beautiful idol-like quietness of Katherine Mansfield made a great impression upon me . . . she was one of the most enchanting young women I had ever met.*

I had never previously met any young woman who talked so frankly or who looked so distinguished in her prettiness. That is to say, no young intellectual woman who did not look more markedly intellectual than in fact she was. She was so assured that I felt shy and clumsy, but in no way resentful of her assurance. For one thing I think she had great tact. She had that uncommon gift of encouraging one's self respect by subtle deference — the outcome of politeness and an air, to which at that time I was unused in my contact with superior young intellectuals, of respect and comradship. Certainly she had a cool judgement as her critical work showed. At that period I saw her perhaps a dozen times, always with the same feeling of admiration and affection because I think it was impossible to know Katherine Mansfield without being strongly attracted by her personality.

Frank Swinnerton also recorded his memory of Murry on that first meeting: *Murry then a handsome, rueful, and always ingratiating fellow in his early 20's . . . moved himself about the room, and talked with the ease of one long used to aesthetic discussion . . .*

Another occasion was an H.G. Wells party at St James

Court, Buckingham Gate and Swinnerton remembered feeling indignant over criticism of Katherine: . . . . *a brilliant but forgotten woman novelist Alice Herbert indicated Katherine at the other side of the room and exclaimed: "Hasn't that girl got a decadent face!" Indignation turned to embarrassment when I found Murry at my side, well aware of the speech. The observation was repeated "That girl; d'you see? Opposite!" I rolled appealing eyes to the lady, she grew silent. Katherine soon approached bade me farewell in a manner combining affection with dignified composure, and reduced A.H. to unwonted incoherence.*

Katherine had written also to D.H. Lawrence on January 29th, 1913. She received a reply from the Villa Igéa, Gargnano in Italy:

Dear Miss Mansfield,
  I cant send you a story from here, not at once, because I haven't one. But the Forum is publishing one either in March or February . . . . called 'The Soiled Rose' — a sickly title, but not a bad story I think. If it were for March, might you not publish it simultaneously? . . if 'The Soiled Rose' is no go . . . ask Mr. Garnett to give you another of my stories . . . . I left most of my M.S. at his place . . . I am as poor as a church mouse, so feel quite grand giving something away — Oh but I make two conditions — First, that you send me a copy of Rhythm for I've never seen your publication, only somebody said you wrote nasty things about The Trespasser; and second, that you let me have something interesting to review for March — German if you like. I shall probably be in London at the end of March — immediately after Easter — and then, if your tea kettle is still hot, I shall be glad to ask you for the cup you offered me.

Katherine, sending this letter on to Edward Garnett, wrote: *Here it is, — I am sorry, I explained to Mr. Lawrence that we don't pay: I made it quite clear.* Writing to a friend later, Lawrence spoke of *Rhythm* as 'a daft paper, but the folk seem rather nice'. D.H. Lawrence reviewed the first collection of *Georgian Poetry* by Edward Marsh, in the last edition of *Rhythm*, March 1913.

That spring, Gilbert Cannan and his wife Mary, who had been previously married to J.M. Barrie, were decorating their new home, The Mill House at Cholesbury. Seeing how wretched 57, Chancery Lane was, they suggested that the Tigers should rent the semi-detached red-brick villa next to the Mill House. It was called The Gables. Gordon Campbell was to share this tenancy which meant their weekly rent would be reduced to 3/-. So in March 1913 they moved in thankfully, getting rid of Sobieniowski in the process. Katherine was to stay there permanently while Murry continued to work at 57, Chancery Lane from Monday to Friday. The first collection of Katherine's published letters to Murry was sent from Cholesbury. I always find a poignancy in their undated heading 'Summer 1913'. It seems so long ago.

Back in Wellington, Chaddie's engagement to Lieut. Colonel Perkins DSO, of Poona, India, was announced on April 2nd. A charming man nearing sixty, he was a widower with a son. They were married at St Paul's Pro-Cathedral on May 26th, 1913. The organ was played by Millie Parker's father. Chaddie in 'white brocaded crêpe-de-Chine, the draperies of Limerick lace caught up with lotus blossoms', wore the bridegroom's gift of pearl, tourmaline and diamond pendants. Jeanne and Aileen Russell were chief bridesmaids 'wearing saxe-blue velours' trimmed with ermine, their berets 'each with an osprey'. Chummie was best man. Mrs Beauchamp in white fox furs presided at the reception at 47, Fitzherbert Terrace. The rooms were decorated 'with autumn foliage and hot house flowers'. Chaddie sailed to India, where her husband was controller of Military Accounts for the Western Circle.

Katherine would receive a full account of the happy day and, cut off from Murry and in such a quiet backwater, no doubt felt discontented. One cold wet weekend they were visited by Gordon and Beatrice Campbell, who found that Katherine had been ill. The leg of mutton which Beatrice had bought had made a nightmare of the washing up, and the sink was blocked with fat, there was little hot water and no washing powder. *I tried to make a joke of our predicament but Katherine was beyond jokes; she started to weep ceaselessly and hopelessly. I felt there must be some deeper reason for her tears than the grease, and this idea was reinforced when she suddenly cried out in her distress, 'I want lights, music, people!'*

She was probably very dissatisfied with Murry who was very dependent on Gordon emotionally. L.M., visiting Katherine, also noted certain tensions. Katherine was wanting to write, her poverty irked her. She was lonely through the week and afraid at night, locking her door 'three times three'.

Meanwhile, at Chancery Lane, Murry had received menacing letters from Henri Gaudier, who, on the afternoon of May 12th, 1913, accompanied by George Banks, burst into the office threatening to choke Murry and demanding payment for the drawings published in *Rhythm*. Then he slapped Murry's face after snatching two framed drawings from the wall. "We've only begun," said Gaudier ominously as they left.

Deeply shaken, Murry wrote to Katherine a highly emotional, rather girlish account telling her he had been crying and was scarcely able to work. However he also threatened to kill George Banks.

In May the first issue of the *Blue Review* appeared, with the same blue cover but bearing print only. It contained *The Soiled Rose* by D.H. Lawrence also *Pension Seguin* by Katherine, written in Geneva, July 1911. In the same number there was a further story by Katherine about the New Zealand backblocks entitled *Millie,* then alas, Murry had to admit defeat. The magazine was losing £15 a month. Contributors were informed and the *Blue Review* was terminated. In the last few days Murry had an important caller at 57, Chancery Lane. It was D.H. Lawrence. He had returned to England after eloping with Frieda, the wife of Professor Weekley of Nottingham University, in May 1912.

Chapter VIII

Meeting with D.H. Lawrence

Like Murry, Lawrence came from a modest working class home. Born on September 11th, 1885, in Eastwood, Nottingham, he was the fourth son of a miner who had worked at Brinsley Colliery since he was seven. After winning a scholarship at thirteen to Nottingham High School, Lawrence left after three years to take a job as office boy to Haywards of Nottingham, makers of surgical and orthopaedic instruments, which position he had to abandon after three months because of an attack of pneumonia. His convalescence lasted six months. In the autumn of 1902, he and his younger sister Ada became pupil teachers at the British School in Eastwood, eventually transferring to the Ilkeston Pupil-Teacher centre in 1903, where he stayed until 1906, being joined by his friend Jessie Chambers of Haggs Farm, who for deep love and admiration of him, was responsible for his first appearing in print in November 1909, having sent unbeknown to him, two of his poems to Ford Maddox Hueffer of the *English Review*.

After passing the London University matriculation examination in June 1905, he spent the next year as an uncertificated teacher in the British School at Eastwood, entering Nottingham University in 1906 for a two-year teacher training course, passing the final examination with the highest marks in England. For the next five years he was a junior assistant master at Davidson Road School, Croydon. He began writing at twenty.

What manner of man was this, later called 'the starry genius of our times' by Middleton Murry, who felt immediate rapport with Lawrence? Jessie Chambers, looking across the Ilkeston classroom at Lawrence, saw 'his uniqueness, how totally different he was from any of the other youths' . . . . 'his look of concentration of being more intensely alive' than others . . . .'his sensitiveness and delicacy of spirit' which made him 'so vulnerable, so susceptible to injury' . . . . 'But there was another quality of lightness about him something that seemed to shine from within' . . . . 'I felt I was in the presence of greatness' . . . but she also noted his 'dark' moods.

Her brother, Dr J.D. Chambers, remembered from boyhood days how irresistible Lawrence was, but 'there was the streak of the incalculable almost the uncanny about him that drew him apart even when he was most intimate'.

William Edward Hopkin, a good friend from Eastwood, thought his conversation brilliant, 'like someone reciting free verse'.

Jan Juta, a young South African painter who was to illustrate Lawrence's book *Sea and Sardinia* felt he was in the presence of an indefinable force, powerful yet disciplined.

However, Ford Maddox Hueffer, later Ford Maddox Ford, did not like Lawrence. His first sight of him, leaning against the doorpost, 'fox coloured hair and moustache . . . deep wary sardonic glance . . . as if he might be going to devour me — or something I possessed', reminded him of a fox. On reading Lawrence's story *The Fox* some years later: *I really jumped when I came to his description of the fox looking over its shoulder at the farm girl . . . I experienced then exactly the feeling of embarrassment I was to feel when I looked up and saw Lawrence . . . that fellow was really disturbing . . . . the perturbation and dying down of emotion attended my every meeting.* The Indians in Taos called Lawrence 'Red Fox'.

Frieda on the other hand was a Silesian aristocrat, daughter of Baron von Richthofen, a professional soldier. Born 1879 into a patriarchal society, she was the middle child of a family of three daughters. Baron Frederick von Richthofen, from an old Prussian *Junker* family, was a Prussian officer with the Iron Cross who, subsequent to losing the use of his right hand, became an administrator in the German garrison town of Metz. Frieda was a spoiled, zestful, self-assertive child, defining herself as 'primitive', and dedicated herself to Eros, renouncing *Kultur*. Though intelligent, she was inexpert with words at times, expressing herself badly and abrasively, being frequently undiplomatic and foolish. She craved the admiration of men and would leave home duties and study to entertain the young soldiers of the garrison, singing folk songs while standing on a table and loving their applause. At twenty, she married an Englishman of thirty-four, Ernest Weekley, who via hard work and lectureship became Professor and Dean of the Arts Faculty at Nottingham University. She met him on a walking tour in the Black Forest and agreed to marry him mainly for his dignity and stability. She came from an emotionally insecure home where there was much marital disharmony. For the first time she felt a sense of security.

In Nottingham she had her three children, Else, Montague and Barbara, and accommodated happily and stoically to her humdrum existence. She was, however, what is now known as a liberated woman, and livened her days with exciting extra-marital affairs, the most important of which was in 1906, with Dr Otto Gross aged twenty-nine, assistant at the Neurolog-Psychiatrische Institut at Graz. The brilliant only son of the criminologist Dr Hanns Gross, he was one of the most important disciples of Sigmund Freud, and colleague of Carl Gustav Jung, who eventually adopted Otto's theory of personality types, introvert-extrovert classification. Tall, fair-haired and blue-eyed, Otto was, according to Ernest Jones, who met him in Munich in 1908, 'the nearest approach to a romantic idea of a genius I have ever met'. He stood for total sexual freedom and sexual immoralism; but he also took cocaine and morphine, which was to lead to sexual orgies and his early death in March 1920. In 1906 he met Frieda and her elder sister Dr Else Jaffe. Both sisters fell in love with him, Else giving birth to his son Peter in 1909. At one stage Frieda thought she was pregnant by him.

In September 1907, telling Ernest that she was visiting Else and her husband, Frieda joined Otto in Amsterdam where he was attending the Neuro-Psychiatric Conference, the principal speaker being Freud who was to deliver his paper on Hysteria. Writing to Frieda and calling her his 'bright fire', 'the woman of the future' and 'golden child', Otto said she had chosen him in her 'great magnificent way' and begged her to leave Ernest and join him with the children. This she fortunately did not do, but she was ready for Lawrence when he came along in 1912. Because of Otto she now had a roseate view of her own worth; all her life she had fought insignificance. With the glamorous Lawrence she could leave England, journey to strange countries and be her 'atavistic' self. She was very bored with her marriage.

In November 1911 Lawrence was so ill with pneumonia that after a prolonged convalescence, he decided to give up teaching. Writing to Edward Garnett, he said he felt his life burning 'like an oil flame'. He had also been devastated by the recent death of his mother. Wishing to become an English lecturer in a German University (he already had an aunt living in Germany), Lawrence contacted Professor Weekly in April 1912, who invited him to lunch. There Lawrence saw Frieda, a handsome sturdy creature of noble carriage, with blonde wavy hair, eyes like a lioness and finely-cut Prussian features, her personality outgoing and sunny; and Frieda, observing Lawrence, asked herself, "What kind of bird is this?"

So on this sunny Saturday morning, as the door of Murry's office opened, Murry saw Lawrence for the first time. Slim and boyish, wearing a large straw hat, he was accompanied by Frieda, her flaxen hair glinting in the sunshine. They all went upstairs to meet Katherine who was sitting on the floor of the bare room beside a bowl of goldfish. Describing this meeting later to Catherine Carswell, Lawrence was interrupted by Frieda exclaiming Katherine's legs were pretty. However Lawrence grudgingly thought them like the legs of the principal boy in the pantomime. Alas, there is no record of Katherine's impression of the Lawrences but no doubt she would be observing them closely as they went out to Soho for lunch, sitting in opposite pairs in the bus, the Tigers making faces at one another to Frieda's delight. It was summer, all were young and happy.

They invited Murry and Katherine for a weekend to Kingsgate near Broadstairs, where they had rooms. Unfortunately, when the day came to go, there was no money for the train tickets. Lawrence furiously disappointed, cooled down somewhat when Edward Marsh, to whom he was complaining of this non-arrival, suggested that the reason would be financial. This was a complete surprise to Lawrence who had believed Murry was wealthy. Dated July 22nd, 1913 Lawrence sent a further invitation: *Oh, but why didn't you come and let us lend you a pound . . . Come for the week-end and bathe. We've got a tent in a little bay on the foreshore, and great waves come and pitch one high up, so I feel like Horace about to strike my cranium on the sky . . . . So you come and bathe . . Then you'll feel much jollier. I am not poor, you know. But I didn't know you were really stoney . . . .*

The week-end was a hugh success. All bathed naked, ate beefsteak and gleaming tomatoes, and coming home in the train, Murry and Katherine read Lawrence's *Sons and Lovers*. They were deeply impressed.

In July, with the termination of the *Blue Review*, the Chancery Lane flat was given up and Katherine and Murry took another small flat at 8, Chaucer Mansions, Barons Court. Murry, now free of the wretched magazine, was able to earn £12 a week book reviewing for the *Daily News* and the *Westminster*.

The flat was furnished with Dr Baker's furniture which had been in storage since May, following the departure of L.M.'s sister for Rhodesia. According to L.M. Katherine did not seem happy there, she had further joint pains and she was not working well. There was a tension in the atmosphere.

Murry had the sitting-room to work in, leaving Katherine the living-room table. With his desk piled high with books, he was totally immersed in his reading. He was withdrawing from Katherine, desiring the society of men with whom to indulge his intellectual mysticism. Katherine had never been much in sympathy with this. Brooding on the effect on him of Milton and Plato he wrote the poem 'The Critic in Judgement', with its final line.

> I will be
> The master of my soul's lost harmony.

He found no harmony in himself now.

So he wrote of that time in his autobiography. No wonder Katherine was not happy and felt a trifle rejected. It seems to me that Murry was not suited to domesticity and remained the seclusive intellectual mystic for many years. Katherine the extrovert was quite a different personality and this side of

Murry must have had a chilling effect.

Via Miss Good's Nurses' Home in Welbeck Mews, L.M. now lived in a poorly furnished room above a butcher's shop in Dorset Street, the rent of which was 6/- per week. Still working in the Parma rooms, she sometimes resorted to eating the oatmeal face-packs, out of the hunger born of long hours waiting for non-existent customers, and sheer poverty. Katherine had a key to L.M.'s room and would go there during the day, when she needed to be alone.

In August, the Campbells invited the Murrys to stay with them in a cottage on the Hill of Howth outside Dublin. The famous Sir Patrick Campbell, born in the spring of 1913, was to be a member of the group. Katherine did not want to go but agreed for Murry's sake. She was ambivalent towards Beatrice whom she thought a little spiteful at times because Beatrice informed on adverse criticism of her. Also a holiday *à deux* would have been preferred, and Katherine was beginning to resent Murry's engrossment with Campbell.

Katherine must have felt strongly about this, because she asked L.M. to join them, but in different lodgings, planning to meet up with her daily, probably as an excuse to get away from the party. In her autobiography *Today We Will Only Gossip* Beatrice wrote: *I watched Katherine go to her (L.M.) and the two figures sat on a rock and talked earnestly for some time. I had the feeling that Katherine was telling her how much she disliked being in Howth.* Beatrice thought Katherine was a very difficult person to know. *Behind her little expressionless mask of a face an endless turmoil of emotion and thought seemed to be going on . . . . complex . . . self-critical . . . . self-centred . . . sometimes hard to approach; she could be so false and unreal that you shrank from her . . . at other times . . . warm and gay and sympathetic . . . Her courage was enormous, and so was her capacity to make fun of her sufferings . . . beside her, I used to feel . . . almost a simpleton.* Mary Cannan also found Katherine 'remote and reserved, unapproachable, impossible'. It is odd, but typical that Katherine made such elaborate plans to have L.M. available. Inevitably L.M. was invited to the Campbells'. No wonder Murry became disapproving. Beatrice knew of L.M.'s devotion to Katherine, who admitted to treating her badly at times, but 'could not live without her'. Of course Katherine was indebted to L.M. and perhaps she thought, rightly, that L.M. was much in need of a holiday. It is also possible that L.M. invited herself!

That autumn, Murry was harried with debt, dulled and dissatisfied with the monotonous grind of journalism.

Meanwhile Lawrence, from a vine-filled garden on the edge of the sea at Lerici, was roundly lecturing him by post, perhaps in answer to a whining letter. He was trying to persuade them to join him, and live on Katherine's money.

It looks to me as if you two . . . . are snapping the bonds that hold you together, Lawrence wrote . . . . *you and Katherine must heal, and come together . . . . It strikes me you've got off your lines somewhere, somewhere you have not been man enough . . . . And you don't know what you are . . . . You've always been dodging around getting Rhythms and flats and doing criticism for money . . . . If you are disintegrated, then get integrated again . . . use Katherine — her money and everything — to get right again. You're not well, man . . . I think Oxford did you harm . . . Don't be a child — don't keep that rather childish charm.*

The warm affection in this letter produced feelings in Murry which he had never felt for a man before.

Feeling unable to live on Katherine's allowance, Murry decided impulsively that flight was the next best thing. Both eventually chose Paris. Murry felt that once in France, he would become inspired and write well and easily. He hoped to work for the *Times Literary Supplement*, perhaps reviewing French books. Foolishly they shipped their furniture there at a cost of £25, eventually renting a flat. Murry had cabled Francis Carco, who duly met the Dieppe boat-train at Gare Saint-Lazare.

Carco in his book *Bohéme d'artiste* remembered meeting them and escorting them to a hotel in *Rue Gay-Lussac*. He noted that Katherine drew from her bag squares of old embroidery, framed photographs, a kimono and a pair of satin mules. She was pale and tired with a fringe of glowing brown hair and wore a long dark coat trimmed with nickel buttons. She said to him 'je ne parle pas français'. He thought Murry had changed, he seemed more confident. Carco noted his deferential attentiveness to Katherine.

All three went out into the wet windy night walking by the
dripping trees of the Luxembourg Gardens. Carco wondered
what would happen if Murry met an old flame. Sure enough
the next day at the *Café d'Harcourt,* a blonde called *Gueule
d'Amour* (mouth of love) approached their table. Carco hastily
intercepted her. Over the next few weeks they visited museums
and cafés, taking a cab sometimes to the woods. Katherine
helped Carco to read his manuscripts.

Murry took a year's lease on Flat 31, Rue de Tournon which
looked on to a cobbled courtyard, near the Luxembourg
Gardens. Very soon, things began to go wrong. Seven of
Murry's articles were returned. His income dwindled from £12
to 30/- per week. Added to this was the penetrating cold of
Paris; it seemed impossible to heat the flat adequately. One
day they found they could not pay the printer's debt and
bankruptcy proceedings began like the snap of a steel trap.
Murry went to England alone, staying with the Campbells at 8,
Selwood Terrace, that Salvation Army Citadel for intrepid
literary folk. On Gordon's advice, he went to see the
bankruptcy court official who considered that the debt was not
in fact Murry's. All was settled satisfactorily one month later
on March 27th.

Meanwhile, alone in Paris Katherine was afraid and
sleepless. She wrote about it in her notebook: *It is as though
God opened his hand and let you dance on it a little, and then
shut it up tight — so tight that you could not even cry . . . The
wind is terrible to-night. I am very tired — but I can't go to
bed. I can't sleep or eat. Too tired.*

Towards the end of February the tide turned; Murry was
offered the post of art critic on *The Westminster.* To pay for
the release from the flat agreement, they had to sell all the
furniture, eventually to a brothel-keeper, a friend of Carco's,
for £10. An unfinished letter of Katherine's described this last
day.

Dear —
   *Everything is packed of ours . . . and we are waiting for the
man to come and take away the furniture. Grimy and
draughty . . . tea leaves in the sink . . . you never saw an uglier
place — now — or a more desolate . . . Yes, I am tired . . . but*

it's mostly mental. I'm tired of this disgusting atmosphere of eating boiled eggs out of my hand and drinking milk out of a bottle . . . . Oh, how I love Jack! There is something wonderfully sustaining and comforting to have another person with you . . .

For good measure the *femme de ménage* stole Katherine's long dark overcoat with the nickel buttons. However they did have a glimpse of Marcel Proust in the Café Weber late one night, tall, slim with a yellow complexion. Under her belt Katherine had a new story, *Something childish but very Natural* and Murry, the beginnings of his novel *Still Life*, an apt title. Sadly, Dr Baker's furniture ended its days in a brothel.

Arriving in London at the beginning of March, penniless, with books and clothes only, they had to borrow money from Gordon. They were offered a furnished flat belonging to a colleague, Richard Curle, for two guineas a week in 119, Beaufort Mansions, Chelsea. Murry commenced work as art critic. Katherine searched for yet another home. She was depressed and having difficulty in writing, tearing up much of what she wrote. L.M. was leaving for Rhodesia on March 27th to help her sister, who was getting married. Though a relief for Katherine, *When I get by myself, I am always more or less actively miserable. Nobody knows, or could, what a weight L. is upon me. She simply drags me down and then sits on me, calm and page. The strongest reason for my happiness in Paris was that I was safe from her.* L.M.'s imminent departure stirred up old guilt feelings over this curious, octopus-like relationship, expressed in *The Toothache Sunday* in the *Journal*.

Have I ruined her happy life? . . . She gave me the gift of herself. 'Take me Katie, I am yours. I will serve you' . . . . I ought to have made a happy being of her . . . Yes, I am altogether to blame. They spent the last few days together, walking in old haunts and talking. Writing about their last evening Katherine admitted she was: *frightened* in private *. . . . At the last moment Ida never said Good-bye at all but took the fiddle and ran.* She would be heartbroken. Katherine did not see L.M. to the boat-train, she probably could not face seeing her cousin Evelyn Payne who kindly did so, but she wrote a poem which revealingly marked the occasion:

The Meeting

We started speaking
Looked at each other, then turned away.
The tears kept rising to my eyes
But I could not weep.
I wanted to take your hand
But my hand trembled.
You kept counting the days
Before we should meet again.
But both of us felt in our hearts
That we parted for ever and ever.
The ticking of the little clock filled the quiet room.
"Listen", I said "It is so loud,
Like a horse galloping on a lonely road,
As loud as that — a horse galloping past in the night"
You shut me up in your arms.
But the sound of the clock stifled our hearts beating,
You said "I cannot go: All that is living of me
Is here for ever and ever"
Then you went.
The world changed. The sound of the clock grew fainter,
Dwindled away, became a minute thing.
I whispered in the darkness, "If it stops, I shall die."

Katherine remained wretched addressing her notebook thus: *a hideous day . . . Life is a hateful business . . . when G. (Gordon) and J. (Murry) were talking in the park of physical well-being and of how they could still look forward to 'parties' I nearly groaned . . . I hate society . . . Nothing helps . . . J. is far too absorbed in his own affairs . . . to even do so . . . terribly lonely.* However, she was able to write of Murry: *I love him to the inmost.*

At last they found two top floor rooms in 102, Edith Grove, Chelsea for 10/- a week, with two tables, two chairs and a large mattress on the floor. The day they moved in, Murry became ill with pleurisy. His articles as art critic had to be written from his sick bed and delivered by Katherine. One week later, Katherine also became ill. Beatrice Campbell visiting was met by Murry who looked 'wild and distracted' saying that Katherine had had a heart-attack. Beatrice found her seated in a chair, white, gasping, with loss of voice and palpitation. Dr Croft-Hill arrived, diagnosed pleurisy, lectured them both gently and never sent a bill. Both were miserable, debilitated, and having to endure their squalid bare rooms with the common WC, and pervading smells on the gloomy staircase.

Don't be so miserable, wrote Lawrence to Murry from Lerici on May 8th, 1914 . . . *Frieda is set on England in June — we shall come in about a month's time . . . . I wish you had come out here instead of going to Paris*; and Katherine, addressing her notebook: *I long and long to write, and the words just won't come.* On May 28th, 1914 in the case of 'Weekley v. Weekley and Lawrence' the decree nisi was final. On June 11th Lawrence and Frieda were walking over the St. Bernard Pass on their way to England. By June 27th they were dining at the Moulin d'Or, London, with Sir Edward Marsh and Rupert Brooke, and staying with Gordon Campbell at Selwood Terrace, Beatrice having gone to Ireland to have her second child.

The Lawrences eventually visited the Murrys who were feeling ruffled at the delay, which was real enough because of Lawrence's involvement with new friendships. They had been to tea in Hampstead with Catherine Carswell, then Mrs Jackson, and within days he was reading the MS of her first novel.

There also he re-met Ivy Low, whom he knew well from her visiting him in Lerici, and Viola Meynell. Katherine and Murry were jealous of these new friends. Indeed there was to be a sort of enmity between Murry and Mrs Carswell for many years.

Over supper in Edith Grove, Katherine complained bitterly to the Lawrences about their squalid conditions, to Murry's inner fury. After Lawrence had gone, he quarrelled with Katherine until 1.00 a.m. He felt betrayed. In any case, Lawrence's success, his third novel *The Rainbow* awaiting publication, for which he had been offered £300, and Frieda's bounce at the idea of spending some of it, just accentuated the Murrys' poverty. In the healing light of the day the Tigers decided they must find somewhere better to live. Soon, to their joy, they found a delightful upper floor flat in Arthur Street (now Dovehouse Street), Chelsea, with a tree looking in at the old-fashioned windows at the back. Alas, the decorator they had hired found bugs, this after an agreement had been signed; but they moved in and were duly attacked, a horrible, defiling experience. Over tea, during the small hours, they decided, with some ultimate rueful laughing, to fight back with paraffin, petrol and sulphur with some little success.

It was now time for the Lawrences' wedding which was to be at Kensington Registry Office on July 13th at 10.30 a.m., with Katherine, Murry and Gordon as witnesses. Alas, Lawrence had neuralgia in his left eye and felt rather nervous.

Frieda gaily lent her discarded wedding ring to Katherine who was wishing she could marry Murry. The four were photographed later beside that killer of backyard amateur photography, the large unruly towel drying on a clothes-line, buxom Frieda unwisely sporting a waist-belt, Lawrence in a celluloid butterfly-wing collar and gay straw boater, Murry in an Al Capone trilby hat, and Katherine, enigmatic in her navy suit, tartan taffeta waistcoat and large dark hat, at a rakish tilt. Eddie Marsh sent Lawrence the complete works of Thomas Hardy as a wedding present. Thanking him Lawrence wrote that he had rushed round the room with joy. It was a happy day for everybody concerned.

Later, in July, all five were invited to a picnic in Hampstead, presumably by Ivy Low, who, dressed in a kimono, greeted them off the Tube, arms outstretched, and calling, "Lawrence!"

"I won't have that," said Katherine and fled around the corner followed by Murry and Campbell. Meeting up later, when Lawrence returned furious, Katherine tried to pacify him by explaining her objection to effusiveness. In any case, the Murrys were very exclusive; in Campbell and Lawrence they had all the friends they wanted, not so Lawrence.

On July 30th he and Frieda were invited to dinner at the Berkeley by Amy Lowell, the American poet, illustrious relative of the future Robert Lowell. Other guests were Hilda and Richard Aldington who found Lawrence's 'fiery blue eyes and the pleasing malice of his talk' memorable.

On July 31st Lawrence went on a walking tour in the Lake District. He was hoping to meet up with an engineer called Lewis who lived in Barrow-in-Furness and with whom he had walked into Switzerland in June. With Lewis was a lawyer called Horne from the Russian Law Bureau in Holborn, and a colleague, Samuel Solomonovitch Koteliansky, a research worker on a scholarship from Kiev University who had preferred to stay on safely in England. Lawrence, with water lilies around his hat, had enjoyed himself in the fresh windy countryside and Koteliansky was captivated by him. There developed in him a protective allegiance to Lawrence which lasted to the end of his life. On reaching Barrow on August 5th, they heard from Lewis that war had been declared.

Meanwhile Murry and Katherine, who had been visited regularly by Elliot Crooke, a former student of Brasenose from the year below Murry, were horrified to see him in officers' uniform of the Special Reserve. Carrying kit and sword he warned them of the imminence of war. They were never to see him again. The next day, standing by the railings of Green Park, they saw the Highland Regiment Black Watch marching to the station. Life would never be the same again.

Chapter IX

War

On August 15th H.G. Wells invited the Lawrences and the Murrys to dinner. Lawrence insisted on wearing his new dinner jacket, much to Murry's gloomy misgiving, who felt that Lawrence did not look his best in such formal clothes. Also it was specially irritating for Murry to have to wear a dinner jacket, as his boiled shirt lacked suitable links and studs. These had had to be ingeniously produced by Katherine with the aid of pearl buttons and ginger beer wire. Going around to Selwood Terrace to tie Lawrence's bow, which as feared, seemed determined to settle into pious folds, Murry saw that Lawrence looked like a noncomformist parson. The problem was probably that low-slung, commodious, butterfly-wing collar. Even more exasperating was the fact that Frieda, totally absorbed with her own appearance, was insensitive to the pathos of the situation. It was a very scratchy group which arrived at Hampstead. Lawrence disapproved of Katherine's attempt at gaiety. All spent a miserable evening in spite of H.G. Wells warmly welcoming Lawrence. Talking of his wife, Wells said later that she deeply admired Katherine, he less so.

Murry and Katherine were to have two weeks' holiday in Cornwall at St. Merryns, near their good friend J.D. Beresford of *The Westminster*. On August 30th Katherine wrote in her diary: *We go to Cornwall to-morrow. I do not trust Jack. I'm old tonight. Ah I wish I had a lover to nurse me, love me, hold me, comfort me, to stop me thinking.* Murry's job had dried up with the war and they were living on Katherine's allowance of 35/- a week, eating eggs, blackberry jam and cream mainly. They searched for a cheap cottage to save on the rent of

Arthur Street, finding a wooden shack on a hill at Udimore, Rye, for 10/- per week. Always happier on their own they would have liked to stay on indefinitely, but the place was uninhabitable in winter.

The Lawrences had moved to the Triangle at Bellingdon on August 22nd, the rent being only 6/- a month. He wrote to Edward Garnett: *We are quite isolated, amid wide grassy roads, with quantities of wild autumn fruit. This is curiously pale-tinted country, beautiful for the blueness and mists of autumn.* Back in London after giving up the cottage, the Murrys were invited to stay with Lawrence for the weekend. "We're a bit bothered about them," he told Gordon.

There, on Sunday October 11th, the Tigers met Koteliansky, who became Katherine's firm friend for life; not so Murry's. Koteliansky, a Russian Jew, was born in the Ukraine in 1882, the son of a mill-owner. After suffering persecution and pogroms in which he lost most of his family, he came to London in 1911 via the Kiev University scholarship. He worked as a secretary and translator at the Russian Law Bureau, 212, High Holborn, with compatriot R.S. Slatkowsky. With curly black hair, very dark eyes set rather close together, extremely broad shoulders, Murry thought he looked like an Assyrian king.

Leonard Woolf in his autobiography leaves the most memorable description: *His eyes . . . looked at, through, and over you, sad and desperate, and yet with resigned intensity. When he shook hands with you, you felt that all the smaller bones in your hand must certainly have been permanently crushed. The hand shake . . . was merely an unconscious sympton of Kot's passionate and painful intensity and integrity . . . not at all a comfortable man . . . Kot's passionate approval of what he thought good, particularly in people; his intense hatred of what he thought bad; the directness and vehemence of his speech, his inability to tell a lie, all this strongly appealed to Lawrence . . . when Kot approved of anyone, he accepted him absolutely; he could do no wrong and Kot summed it up always by saying of him: 'he is a real person'. This ethical accolade was given by him to very few people — Lawrence, Katherine Mansfield, and Virginia Woolf . . . Lawrence liked this sort of thing in Kot, just as he liked Kot's ruthless condemnation of people like Murry* . . .

Kot had some endearing sayings, "It is hor-r-r-ible," like the roll of thunder on Mount Sinai, according to Woolf. Dealing with people he disapproved of, he would say, "He must be beaten, plainly, but to death," an old Russian custom no doubt, when dealing with unruly serfs.

Kot fell in love with Katherine, telling Ruth Mantz many years later, "If Kat'run ever wanted a greater relationship with me, she had only to indicate it." His dislike of Murry was probably tinged with jealousy. He did not like Frieda either, perhaps for the same reason.

The house in Bellingdon Lane was a wood and brick cottage, *the ugliest cottage I had ever seen,* wrote Sir Compton Mackenzie, after visiting Lawrence with the Cannans. Overgrown nettles at the window cast a 'green gloom' over the sparsely furnished sitting-room, out of which a curved staircase went up to a couple of rooms above. He found Lawrence scrubbing the floor *with his small red moustache and reddish hair and . . . attractive pink-and-white complexion he looked much younger than his twenty-nine years . . . . he went to the bottom of the staircase and shouted, "Frieda!" . . . a pair of legs in ringed black and white stockings came into view . . . . "Shut that door!" he called. The legs kept on their way down "Frieda, shut that bloody door!" he shouted . . . Frieda . . . shedding a warmth and geniality . . . went out . . . to prepare tea.*

On that weekend, Lawrence persuaded the Murrys to live nearby. Though they were loath to return to a part of the country where they had lived before, they decided to look for a cheap cottage, which Murry, on his bicycle, ultimately found in a village three miles away, called The Lee, near Great Missenden, Bucks. Rose Tree Cottage at 5/- per week was mean and damp, with an outside privy and a leaking roof. *It was so small that conversation with its inmates Middleton Murry and Katherine Mansfield was almost impossible,* according to David Garnett who visited them along with the Lawrences and the Cannans, with their sheepdog Nana of *Peter Pan* fame. He found Katherine 'mysterious and attractive'. Lawrence had helped them decorate. Murry carefully applying white paint to a door had the brush seized by Lawrence who exhorted him to get it done.

Thanking Amy Lowell for her most kind offer of a typewriter, Lawrence wrote on October 16th to say he had been seedy and grown a red beard.

The Murrys moved in on October 26th. The Lee was a charming village with old red-brick houses grouped around a triangular-shaped village green. *Out of the front door a field of big turnips, and beyond, a spiky wood. Out of the back door an old tree . . . and a moon perched in the branches. I feel very deeply happy and free . . . awake and stretching . . . so that I am on tip-toe . . . Can it be that one* can *renew oneself?* wrote Katherine in her diary on November 3rd describing it all.

On November 16th, and out of the blue, Murry received a letter from Francis Carco, the life of which intrigued Katherine. *I wish he were my friend*, she told her diary.

The Murrys visited the Lawrences frequently, walking the three miles across fields of rotting cabbages. Soon it became evident that the Lawrences were quarrelling seriously. Now that the glamour was wearing thin, Frieda was missing her children, particularly as she had been given no access since the divorce. It took two years for Professor Weekley to be persuaded to allow Frieda to see them for half an hour in a solicitor's office. Then the war, 'the spear through the side of all sorrows and hopes' as Lawrence put it, laid him low. Unable to bear the horror of it, he had once walked over in the dark to Murry, sitting, head bowed, rocking to and fro in a chair and moaning. There had been no quarrel. This was the first time Murry had lived close to Lawrence for any length of time, and his feelings, he discovered, were ambivalent. He was deeply fascinated by Lawrence's 'sensuous spontaneity' but repelled by his darker side, which contained so much sexual conflict. The ambivalence was mutual. Lawrence had been very taken with Murry too, but was eventually to turn against him to the extent of being unable to resist mentioning and denigrating him in letters right to the end of his life. That Lawrence was in love with Murry was covertly implied in *Son of Woman*, Murry's biography of Lawrence, written in 1931. It seemed to be a case of unrequited love, and the degree of vehemence in Lawrence's lifelong denunciation of Murry was commensurate with this. As in the case of Henri Gaudier,

Katherine, like Murry before her, bore the brunt too.

Lawrence came from a divided home based on incompatibility, in the marriage of the dominant educated woman to an uneducated ordinary but decent man, whose moderate drinking as a panacea for the incompatibility only widened the breach and turned the children towards the mother. The devouring, possessive, unusual mother, with the fearless, intensely blue eyes, turned to her three sons for satisfaction. Writing to Edward Garnett on November 14th, 1912 about his autobiographical novel *Sons and Lovers*, Lawrence described the situation which no doubt had existed at home.

> *A woman of character and refinement goes into the lower class, and has no satisfaction . . . as her sons grow up she selects them as lovers — first the eldest, then the second. These sons are urged into life by their reciprocal love of their mother . . . But when they come to manhood, they can't love, because their mother is the strongest power in their lives, and holds them . . . As soon as the young men come into contact with women, there's a split . . . the battle goes on between the mother and the girl, with the son as object. The mother gradually proves stronger, because of the tie of blood . . . It's the tragedy of thousands of young men in England.*

In an essay on the subject he urged women to beware the mother's boy. In this atmosphere, modelling himself on and identifying with the mother, he followed the feminine pursuits of sewing, cooking and cleaning, preferring to play with girls. He was very close to his two sisters. Being delicate and obviously special in his mother's eyes, she even went so far as to nurse an ill Lawrence, then a boy of sixteen, in her arms, on her knee, his long thin legs dangling to the floor. A visitor described the sight of those thin legs.

Jessie Chambers, his friend in adolescence, considered he was 'mother sapped — as a boy he could not have mated . . . the whole question of sex had for him the fascination of horror'. None of his encounters with women before Frieda seemed satisfactory. He told Jessie, "I shall go from woman to woman until I am satisfied," and again, "it doesn't matter who one marries." After becoming engaged on impulse to Louie

K

Burrows at the time of his mother's illness, he admitted to
Jessie, "As soon as I am alone with her, I want to run away."
After his mother's death he broke with Louie and finally with
Jessie, to whom he once confessed, he had loved his mother
like a lover.

As sometimes occurs in such mother-tied men, there is an
unconscious turning to a male relationship, which seems oddly
permissible, because it poses less of a threat to their allegiance
to the all-powerful mother, than a female relationship would.
In some, overt homosexual activity eventually results, in
others, mere homosexual tendencies, which are repressed to
varying degrees commensurate with the strength of the
super-ego structure of the personality, the conscious
manifestations of which are often paranoid personality trends.
I think Lawrence fits into the latter category.

Richard Aldington considered Lawrence had a streak of
homosexuality and a streak of sadism in him. Lawrence
himself thought he was 'two men in one skin' and that his
intrinsic sexual makeup was dual. Consciously he longed for an
ideal male relationship, which idea, like a leitmotiv, was
expressed in his writing so often. In later years he wrote in his
novel *Kangaroo: he had all his life had this craving for an
absolute friend, a David to his Jonathon . . . a blood brother . .
but not affection, not love, not comradship, not mates and
equality and mingling . . . what else? he didn't know.*

In a letter to Henry Savage he admitted that one was kept by
all tradition and instinct from loving men or man. He told
Catherine Carswell that, sexual perversion was for him "the sin
against the Holy Ghost". She thought that apart from his
mother and Frieda it was men who really counted.

His repressed homosexual desires were revealed in his novels,
in the swimming episode in *The White Peacock*, the wrestling
match between Birkin and Crich in *Women in Love*, the
nursing episode in *Aaron's Rod* and the initiation scene in *The
Plumed Serpent*. Once, in a frank moment, Lawrence
admitted to Sir Compton Mackenzie, he believed that the
nearest he had come to perfect love was with a young
coal-miner when he was about 16.

Meeting Frieda as he did was a liberation for him. On
August 19th, 1912 he wrote to Mrs S. Hopkin: *Frieda and I*

have struggled through some bad times into a wonderful naked intimacy . . . that I know at last is love. I think I ought not to blame women, as I have done, but myself, for taking my love to the wrong woman, before now.

It was now near the end of 1914 and Frieda, isolated in the backwoods of England through poverty and the war, was also feeling strained, her starry dream of freedom to roam in foreign lands being very much in cold storage. Lawrence was far from well and an abrasvie companion for her, who in turn easily irritated him with her bombastic arrogance. Katherine liked Lawrence, who however, with his puritanical streak inherited from his mother, did not always seem to approve of her as instanced in his frequent, "Kath-erine!" Frieda and Katherine rather walked carefully around each other. Katherine did not suffer fools gladly, but Frieda though decidedly no fool, did sometimes act and speak unwisely. Her size, ebullience, emotional lability in quarrelling 'tired' Katherine 'to death'; she hated things which rushed at her. On May 11th, 1915 Katherine, in a letter to Murry, was to say of poor Frieda: *What a great fat sod she is . . . Lawrence has got queer blind places, hasn't he?* which was a bit unkind. Murry seemed critical too, and wrote in his journal on 18th November 1914, about Frieda. Murry thought Frieda did not love Lawrence but was in love with the idea of him as a brilliant novelist. Murry considered her stupid and thought that Kot and Gordon hated her. He also believed that Frieda was jealous of Katherine and loathed her — a nest of hornets and Frieda out of her depth, also she resented Lawrence's interest in Murry.

Toiling away at his moribund novel *Still Life*, Murry admitted in his journal to grudging jealousy of Lawrence's superiority, his easeful creativity, deftly writing on Hardy as well as revising *The Rainbow*. As compensation Murry turned to intellectualism to preserve his self-esteem, drumming up an emotional haze of intellectual mysticism when he had long involved talks with Gordon about Dostoevsky, which led to an excitement which he enjoyed. Since reading and reviewing Constance Garnett's translation of *The Brothers Karamazov* in 1912, Murry had been deeply influenced by its author Dostoevsky. Katherine, though also enthusiastic about

Russian writing, felt shut out and was deeply hostile to the
'intellectual ghoul' figure Murry was becoming. She thought
him 'just like a little dog whining outside a door'. I doubt
whether Gordon was particularly excited. He later referred to
these discussions as 'those great Dostoevsky nights when
Mansfield was at her worst'. Basically Gordon disapproved,
but reluctantly went along with it all. The fact was that
Murry's hero at that time was Gordon, with whom he
identified, depending on him emotionally. He thought he was
more his kind, and considered that Lawrence, like Henri
Gaudier, was of a 'different kind' from himself. Gordon was
the solid £1800 a case man, which appealed to the
impoverished, largely out of work Murry.

So Katherine turned away to thoughts of Francis Carco, who
was beginning to write love letters to her, much to her
delighted surprise. A cryptic entry appeared in her diary on
December 18th: *That decides me . . . . I'll play this game no
longer . . . For him I am hardly anything but a gratification
and a comfort.* Unfortunately, prying into the red book
containing Murry's journal she had read this: *Jack, Jack, we
are not going to stay together . . . . Yes, I have already said
Adieu to you now,* she wrote in her diary.

On the same day, Lawrence wrote to Amy Lowell:

> *. . . It is Christmas in a week . . . we shall have a little party
> at Christmas Eve. I at once begin to prick my ears . . . . we
> shall have a great time, boiling ham and roasting chicken, and
> drinking Chianti. There will be eight of us, all nice people . . .
> I shall spend 25/- on the spree . . . . It is very rainy and very
> dark . . .*

On December 19th Lawrence advised Gordon Campbell on
the Murry sessions: *. . . mistrust and beware of these states of
exaltation and ecstasy . . . . there is no real truth in ecstasy . . .
Ecstacy achieves itself by virtue of exclusion . . . .*

Describing the Christmas party in her autobiography Frieda
noted: *We made the cottage splendid with holly and mistletoe,
we cooked, boiled, roasted and baked . . . Campbell and
Koteliansky and the Murrys came and Gertler and the
Cannans . . . . we danced on the shaky floor. Kot sang his*

Hebrew song "Ranain Sadekim Badenoi" Katherine sang "Ton sirop est doux, Madeleine". This occasion was the last time for years to come that we were really gay.

Mark Gertler, 1891-1939, one of the guests at the party, was a protégé of the Cannans. The youngest child of a family of five of poor Jewish emigrées from Austrian Poland, he lived in Whitechapel and had studied at the Slade. He was a friend of Edward Marsh who described him thus to Rupert Brooke: *a beautiful little Jew, like a Lippi Lippi Cherub . . . and has a funny little shiny black fringe, his mind is deep and simple and I think he's got the feu sacré.* He had been befriended by Gilbert Cannan with whom he was a long-term house guest, partly for his health's sake (Gertler was poor, struggling and delicate), but also for his great talent, delightful personality and boundless humour, expressed in a 'running commentary of laughter'.

The Cannans' party held on Christmas Day started on a low key at the sight of the little roasted suckling pig, which no one could carve. Much alcohol was taken to disperse an inner chill and later they began play-acting. At Koteliansky's instigation, Murry was to enact the actual situation between him and Katherine, with Gertler as the rival. However, in the final scene of reconciliation, Katherine discarded the scenario and amid violent love-making with Gertler, abandoned Murry. Lawrence angrily rang down an imaginary curtain, asking Murry if he was blind.

To Lytton Strachey on 1st January 1915 Gertler sent an account of the party: *The only exciting thing that happened were parties — one given by Lawrence and the other by Cannan . . . On both occasions we all got drunk! The second party I got so drunk that I made violent love to Katherine Mansfield! She returned it, also being drunk. I ended the evening by weeping bitterly at having kissed another man's woman and everybody trying to console me . . . This party was altogether an extraordinary one. So interesting was it that all the writers of Cholesbury feel inspired to use it in their work.*

To his Slade friend, Dora Carrington, a further account was sent on 15th January, 1915: *the next day everybody decided to take it as a joke — the Lawrences were the last to come to this decision . . . .*

By December 28th it had begun to snow. Back in Rose Tree Cottage, trying to make amends perhaps, Katherine had moved her desk away from the window to help her to write, and she settled to her new story *Elena Bendall*. Seeing the New Year in, she walked in the moonlit garden, 'opened the gate and nearly — just walked away', with the words of Francis Carco's letter, *'je suis jaloux de vous comme un avare'* in her ears. *I live within sound of a rushing river that only I can hear . . . a curious sort of life . . . more real than this three years idyll*, she wrote. She was suffering from joint pains, mainly in the hip and small bones of the feet and had a cough, Murry remarking on it in his journal. She felt she was getting old. *I don't feel like a girl anymore, or even like a young woman. I feel really quite past my prime. At times the fear of death is dreadful (she was only 27). I feel ever so much older than J. and that he recognises it . . . he often talks like a young man to an older woman.* She was depressed, not working well, and the cold dark winter days, made endless by depression, were not relieved by Lawrence discussing Rananim, his island dream, with its select group; *for me I know it has come too late*, she wrote. Katherine longed to be on her own for a while and dreamed in sleep of happier days, 'of Lilian Shelley's legs' for instance, a beautiful generous young singer at The Cave of The Golden Calf, a night club off Regent Street, where in former days Katherine, dressed in a Chinese kimono, occasionally compèred an evening's entertainment. She managed the odd visit to London, looking for rooms, to no avail, seeing the Pantomime and Marie Lloyd and having her photograph taken for Carco. She did finish a story *Brave Love*, which Gordon praised. Alas, it was published only in New Zealand and not until 1972.

On January 14th she received a letter from Carco asking her to join him in France, which idea thrilled but also tired her. She told Murry four days later, and he was 'rather amused than otherwise. He said he would have to tell Gordon!' It seems to me that Murry went through the motions of love only, even on to the end of Katherine's life. With all her comings and goings, it was Katherine who knew how to love. In her longing for Carco a hatred of England enveloped her. He was to be her deliverer from the dreary English winter and 'sad little rose tree cottage' where at times her pains sent her to bed, to listen to the doleful drip of rain from the deteriorating roof. *I am dreadfully tired in head and body, this sad place is killing me,* she wrote on January 21st.

On January 23rd the Lawrences left for Greatham near Pulborough, Sussex, driving through snow to a fine cottage lent them by Viola Meynell. It had white walls and oak furniture. One could have a fire in the bedroom and there was a bathroom. In a letter to Kot on February 5th he wrote: *I have got a new birth of life since I came down here . . . I shall never forget those months in Bucks . . . every moment dead, dead as a corpse in its grave clothes.*

By January 31st Katherine was feeling really ill with a febrile cold.

On February 6th she received another urgent request from Carco to come immediately. How to go? She had no money.

In New Zealand, on the outbreak of war, the *Weekly Graphic* had this to say: *All social gaieties have been abandoned.* Never again did Mrs Beauchamp's name appear in the social column until March 1918, when they reported her return from a holiday in Sydney, Australia. The former pleasant, leisurely photographs of women in fluttering draperies were replaced by massed soldiers about their duties. Chummie gaily volunteered, arriving in England early in February 1915. He went to stay with Aunt Belle in Tadworth, and one wonderful day, somewhere about February 11th, he ran into Katherine in the Bank of New Zealand. Over lunch he gave her £10, misguidedly, as is evidenced in his letter of February 11th to his parents: *She is more than ever in love with J.M. Murry . . . and with a new contract with one of the monthlies for a series of war sketches . . . They are going over to Paris at the end of this week to collect materials for the new job. I do not expect to see K. again for some time* (A.T.L.) Poor Chummie! with those white lies fluttering around his head like moths.

On Tuesday February 16th Murry waved goodbye to Katherine at Victoria. She was happy and excited and curiously Murry wasn't jealous. He had been and was going through a Gethsemane of his own, which Katherine knew nothing about.

On January 23rd Gordon Campbell, without warning or explanation, had failed to come for an arranged weekend. Murry felt shattered, pathologically so. On February 1st he wrote a long letter about it to Gordon. It was not posted for thirty-seven years. In it he admitted he must have needed Gordon badly and loved him. Sending it to Gordon in 1952 he reassessed it, protesting his innocence and naivety at the time and blamed it all on Katherine's imminent departure.

In the evening of February 16th Murry made his way to Lawrence, walking four miles and feeling low and seedy as he trudged through pools of water in the darkness. Lawrence ordered him to bed and nursed him like a woman, like Lilly nursed Aaron in his future novel *Aaron's Rod*. He also proceeded to lecture Murry on his friendship with Gordon, informing him that Campbell had said to him, "What there was between Murry and me was the most regrettable part of each of us." For good measure he added that Gordon was a callous materialist. Murry had the feeling he was being pressurised into some admission, the heat of which seemed to cool with his admission that all was over between him and Campbell. Recovering, a wiser man, Murry helped Lawrence to lay some green linoleum, finding what Lawrence called 'flow' in the simple harmony of a shared task.

To tie up loose ends, Lawrence wrote to Campbell after mid-February 1915 suggesting that Murry was in the position of a jilted lover; Lawrence admitted he also needed Gordon as well as Murry.

Chapter X

Francis Carco

Francis Carco (François — Marie — Alexandre — Carcopino — Tusoli) was born in Nouméa, New Caledonia, in 1886, son of a Corsican Inspector of State Prisons and a French Nicoise. As a child he was much opposed to his stern father and much beaten for it. From eleven years old he came to live in Nice. He was of pyknic build, short, broad, with soft contours, which matched up with his cyclothymic personality given to mood swings, in later life, mainly depressive in type. Charlotte Haldane thought him 'sympathetic and nearly first rate'. He had a passionate interest in writing, especially poetry. Normally a cheerful extrovert, humorous and given to entertaining, he would sing his own songs in cafés, and recite Greek stanzas from the *Iliad* in parks, rounding off the entertainment with a little dance as the hat went round. His family wanted him to become a government functionary, but this he strongly resisted.

After military service he drifted to Paris in 1910, residing in Butte Montmartre amongst the poets, artists, criminals and prostitutes. He first met Murry there. His father removed him to the family home in Villefranche-sur-Saône after seeing him return drunk from a brawl. Eventually he lived on his own in Nice where he met Frank Harris. There he wrote his novel *Jesus-la-Caille* which was published in 1914, and a volume of verse *La Bohème et Mon Coeur*. Returning to Paris he rented an apartment at 13, Quai Aux Fleurs, a pleasant-sounding address, becoming a literary drudge for Henry Gauthier-Villars, husband of Colette. On the outbreak of war, Carco enlisted, and became postman to a bakery unit in Gray near

Besancon. Bored and drinking heavily, he started to write to
Murry and then to Katherine.

He was always fascinated by the underworld, particularly by
its vice and depravity, gathering material for his writing in
opium dens, homosexual dance halls, bars and brothels.

So on February 16th Katherine set off to meet her deliverer.
In Paris she visited Beatrice Hastings in whom she confided,
borrowing her Burberry — perhaps it was raining, or perhaps
it was to wear as a comely disguise over her 'gay purple peg-top
coat with the real seal collar and cuffs' — to influence the stern
French authorities when trying to gain permission to enter the
army zone. Nearing Gray on February 19th she felt very happy
as she leaned out of the window, but on alighting, there was
the dreaded interview with two French colonels. One, with
hard grey eyes, seemed dissatisfied, but he was overruled by
the other.

Outside the station Carco, pale and carrying a postman's
bag, smiled and saluted. "Follow me," he sang, "but not as
though you were doing so." Then they were off, the doors of an
old cab which awaited them barely shut as they galloped away.
"Bonjour ma cherie," said Carco with a quick kiss, throwing
down his post-bag. By five o'clock, they were together in their
ground floor room, embracing amid much laughter. Carco lit
the stove while Katherine washed; then they went out to
dinner. Katherine sat quietly as Carco talked the evening
away. Returning by moonlight, they lit the little lamp on the
table and slowly undressed. Carco, first into bed said, "Viens,
ma bébé. Don't be frightened. The waves are quite small" —
charming. *With his laughing face, his pretty hair, one hand
with a bangle over the sheets, he looked like a girl,* Katherine
wrote later.

The next morning he felt ill, was cold and complained of a
sore throat as he dressed, finally leaving at 8.00 a.m., flicking
over his hair with Katherine's ivory hairbrush! At *déjeuner*,
Katherine, in a state of reaction, felt rather heavy-hearted,
and unable to still a deep feeling of doubt as to whether he
really loved her at all, admitting to another sad truth that she
did not really love him either *now I know him — but he is so
rich and so careless — that I love.* He was an exotic change
after Murry's intellectualizing. The notebook entry ended with

revival over lunch together, and in an unposted letter to Frieda written at five o'clock on February 20th: *Voila le petit soldat joyeux et jeune. He has been delivering letters. It is as hot as summer. One only sits and laughs.*

The idyll lasted only five days and she was back in England by February 25th. It is difficult to say what went wrong, but she returned disillusioned. Perhaps Carco's illness dampened everything; perhaps because of it he failed to keep an appointment; perhaps in the new intimate relationship she divined something not quite to her taste, a faint breath of the underworld. She seemed to avoid him after that even though she gladly used his flat in Paris for two separate stays there. She immortalized him as Raoul Duquette in her story *Je ne parle pas francais* written in February 1918 and he, in his next novel *Les Innocents*, modelled his heroine Winnie on Katherine, which was eventually made into a film, *Panam* starring Charles Boyer.

Murry met Katherine at Victoria at 8.00 a.m. on February 25th, finding her hostile and very much on the defensive. Her hair was cut short, a sure sign in a woman of a desire for renewal. She fell ill the next day, probably with arthritis and their estrangement deepened, she did not want to see anybody. By March 13th things had improved, she went to stay with the Lawrences, and wrote a loving letter from there to Murry saying she felt much better but she couldn't walk quite to the Downs, mentioning the fire in her bedroom, the flames dancing in the darkness.

Katherine's second visit to Paris was quite different. She had begun to write again, completing the story *The Little Governess*, and she hoped a period in Paris would produce further 'flow'. *It is agony to go; but I must go,* she wrote to Kot. She arrived in Paris after much delay and found all dull and depressing.She piled her coats and shawls on her bed for warmth and tried to sleep. Writing to Murry she told him she loved him deeply.

The next day was cold with a biting wind which suddenly brought snow. Katherine, taking shelter in a café, watched the snowflakes falling as she sat in a reverie over her coffee. Suddenly, with a feeling she likened to that felt in a theatre when a hush falls on the audience as the lights fade and the

curtain slowly rises, she knew that in Paris she would be able to
write again.

Carco's flat on the third floor looked over the Seine, near the
Île Saint-Louis with its big trees, fragrant in summer, now
bursting into leaf. Tugs and barges went to and fro, calling
incessantly. The room with its two corner windows illuminated
the golden curves of the Modigliani nudes on the walls. Carco
was a friend of Modigliani and had wisely bought some of his
paintings. By night it was lit by lamplight, but there was a gas
fire. There was also an occasional bug foraging, even a large
black louse. The snow gave way to warmer days, but Katherine
complained to Murry that her lung hated the weather, no
doubt due to the infinitesimal ache of bronchitis to
atmospheric change. She dined with Beatrice Hastings at the
'Lilas' and during the night there was an air raid warning. A
Zeppelin passed overhead through a clear starry sky.

Meanwhile Murry had found a top floor flat in 95, Elgin
Crescent, South Kensington, a pleasant place, looking on to
trees at the back. He was happily renovating old furniture,
decorating, and living on porridge bread and butter. At night
he and Kot translated Chekhov and Kuprin in the thick
atmosphere of Russian cigarette smoke.

A further meeting with Beatrice Hastings in her flat, ended
in a terminal quarrel when, in a drunken fury after imbibing
half a bottle of brandy, Beatrice bawled at Katherine and
called her a *'femme de rue'*. Katherine, coldly sober after
drinking only soda water, had noticed that her beautiful friend
was deteriorating; she was now an alcoholic. This was the final
break. Katherine took her leave and they never met again.
Beatrice remained her enemy to the end and beyond.
Katherine had always been her rival and Beatrice found this
intolerable. Murry replied to Katherine's account of her last
evening with Beatrice, the essence of which went thus. Murry
felt that Beatrice was a smaller specimen of Katherine, the
eternal woman type who reacted to the envy and hostility of
women in general in an extravagant and outrageous way.
Katherine had survived this, Beatrice had not. He believed
Katherine was a more real and good person with him and
because of that she would stick to him even though he
considered himself a funny little chap who would never grow

up. He thought he stuck to her because she was the only woman for him.

After this drama Katherine seemed to settle to work on her novel *Brave Love* but returned to England earlier than planned. She missed Murry too much. She spent five weeks at Elgin Crescent, then somehow restless, she returned to Paris on May 5th describing the masses of lilac everywhere.

Almost immediately after a long walk, Katherine developed a painful leg. In spite of this, she settled to work and began *The Aloe*, an important forerunner of the New Zealand stories and what was to become *Prelude;* but somehow on this trip, she lacked well-being and felt dead to the crowds in Luxembourg Gardens, normally so stimulating. Though managing to work hard, she felt emotionally isolated, which made even a meal out difficult, because of having to mix with other people. Overhearing another tenant call her 'La Maitresse de Francis Carco' infuriated her. *F.C. simply doesn't exist for me,* she wrote to Murry.

Her rheumatism went on unabated, she felt ill and lonely. By May 14th she decided to leave and anyway she had heard that Carco was coming to Paris on May 21st. She wrote Murry a loving letter about her return and in answer to his reply, asked him why he seemed disgruntled. She feared that he no longer seemed to need her so much. *Somehow I do always have to be 'needed' to be happy.* Alas this *was* the case. She arrived at Victoria on Wednesday May 19th.

This was to be her last visit to Quai aux Fleurs. A second floor tenant there, Madame de Kergintoul, remembered Katherine, the simplicity of her manners and extreme modesty of her dress, her grey tailor-made costume. She thought her a secretive, shy creature, a little cold and rather intimidating, a strong personality in fact; she also thought her ravishing with her brown hair, ardent black eyes, and virginal smile. She did not seem keen to converse, but when she did, she expressed herself in correct French. When meeting on the stairs Katherine would caress the Kergintoul children and smile at the mother, then disappear, in contrast to her landlord Carco, who sometimes slid down the banister, to the horror of the concierge! Katherine seemed to live a solitary existence. She looked undernourished, did not often eat out, and nibbled sandwiches at home, livened with local wine kept in cold water in her washing-up bowl. She seemed to consider eating out a real extravagance. She was absorbed in the life of the street below.

Preparations were being made to move to yet another home, but a really nice one this time, No. 5, Acacia Road, St. John's Wood with steps up to an imposing front door by the side of a large gracious sitting-room window. At the back was a long walled garden with a lawn and a fine pear tree. She never saw it flower, but it appeared with wonderful effect in her later story *Bliss*.

Near the end of December 1914, Gilbert Cannan arranged a meeting between the Lawrences and Lady Ottoline Morrell, half-sister of the sixth Duke of Portland, of Welbeck Abbey. Married for twelve years to a Liberal MP, Philip Morrell, she resided in 44, Bedford Square, London. Born 1873, and descended from Bess of Hardwick, Ottoline Violet Anne Cavendish-Bentinck, was a fascinating colourful personality, romantic and imaginative. As a child, her playthings included a dagger belonging to King Henry VIII and a pearl ear-ring worn by King Charles I at his execution. Her letter casket had been the property of William of Orange, and her pearls, those of Marie Antoinette. She was striking to look at, almost six feet tall, with a large long nose, glacier blue-green eyes, masses of auburn hair, and a prominent lower jaw. She spoke slowly, with a sing-song musical voice, ranging in pitch from soprano to baritone, emphasising separate syllables such as 'Roo-pert' (Rupert), or 'ye-e-es' (yes) with different notes. David Garnett thought she had 'a lovely, haggard face'. Lord David Cecil considered her 'the only person I have ever seen who could look at one and the same moment, beautiful and what I can only call grotesque'. She expressed her imaginative personality in the clothes she wore: full, trailing gowns, cut on Grecian, Cossack, and oriental lines, and made of silk, taffeta or brocade. For example, she appeared in Oxford High Street, among the short skirts and cloche hats of 1921, wearing an ankle-length, canary yellow silk dress topped by a royal blue hat trimmed with royal blue feathers. Henry James called them 'window curtaining clothes' in 1912; Virginia Woolf thought that Ottoline was 'like a Spanish Armada in full sail'.

Leonard Woolf was less complimentary, 'she was highly sexed, her taste disorderly flamboyance'.

Ottoline was passionately interested in people and their ideas, and though a lion hunter, she encouraged and took a warm interest in unknown young struggling poets, artists and even scruffy undergraduates. At 44, Bedford Square, she held her famous Thursday evenings, when up to thirty people would be invited for 9.00 p.m. for cider, cordial, occasionally champagne and light refreshments. In her rôle as patroness of the Arts, Ottoline was in her element. In a rarified, intellectual atmosphere, she craved and received spiritual rapture. Lawrence was fascinated by Ottoline, who, equally captivated, arranged a dinner party for him on January 25th.

The Lawrences and the Cannans duly arrived and were received by Ottoline wearing a Spanish lace mantilla. Among the guests were Mark Gertler and E.M. Forster, who sat next to Lawrence at dinner. Later on, there was dancing, and Duncan Grant who was partnering Ottoline, became ensnared in her train and fell heavily to the floor. Lawrence, dazzled by her title, wrote some days later saying he honoured her birth and that he would have given a great deal to have been born an aristocrat.

On January 27th Ottoline visited Greatham and Lawrence set about converting her to his idea of 'Rananim'. *I want you to form the nucleus of a new community*, he enjoined her in a letter on February 1st, 1915. Ottoline decided to introduce Lawrence to Bertrand Russell, her current lover (she tended to take lovers). The meeting took place towards the end of February. Lawrence felt he had found in Russell that ideal male friend and Russell thought Lawrence 'amazing', arranging to take him up to Cambridge on March 6th to meet his don friends. *I feel frightfully important coming to Cambridge*, he wrote to Russell on March 2nd, 1915: *Don't make me see too many people at once, or I lose my wits*. On the same day he wrote to Viola Meynell saying he had finished, and sent off *The Rainbow*, a wonderful day for him.

The visit to Cambridge was not a success. Remembering the occasion, John Maynard Keynes, still in his pyjamas at 11.00 a.m., much to Lawrence's disgust, noted in his memoirs that Lawrence was morose and irritable, sitting on the right side of the fireplace in a crouching position with his head down. He considered Lawrence jealous of the Cambridge world, attracted yet repelled by the brittle conversation, especially that of Frankie Birrell.

It was true Cambridge made me very black and down. I cannot bear its smell of rottenness, marsh stagnancy. I get a melancholy malaria, wrote Lawrence to Russell on March 19th. When David Garnett brought Birrell to visit him at Greatham, it was the last straw. Describing the visit in a letter to Koteliansky on April 20th, Lawrence complained of *the perpetual wash of forced visitors under the door. I like David, but Birrell I have come to detest. These horrible little frowsty people, men lovers of men, they gave me such a sense of corruption, almost putrescence, that I dream of beetles* — a violent, significant, pathological reaction. Lawrence told Garnett not to bring Birrell to see him again telling him to leave his friend.

Lawrence had introduced the Murrys and the Campbells to Ottoline some time in February 1915 at Bedford Square. Katherine had been *very silent and Buddha-like on the big sofa — she might almost have held in her hand a lotus flower!* Ottoline wrote in her memoirs. There was a reason for this coldness. Katherine, embarrassed by Lawrence pronouncing violently on some political point, had reacted by behaving coldly towards Ottoline. She felt Lawrence had cheapened himself. As Katherine and Beatrice did a tour of the large drawing-room at one stage, looking at the pictures, Katherine, in the same mood, whispered to Beatrice, "Do you feel that we are two prostitutes and that this is the first time we have ever been in a decent house?" Beatrice, describing the evening, recalled that they had all arrived bedraggled by rain, and even Kot was quarrelling in Russian with a fellow Russian. Lawrence also accused Gordon of being 'the devil behind the cross' and with arms flailing, accused him of lying. No wonder both Katherine and Murry were silent. Lawrence, of course, would be thoroughly enjoying himself and feel not the least bit put out.

Frieda had her reservations about the dashing new friends. She felt that Lady Ottoline considered her a blowsy German *hausfrau*, which in view of Frieda's background was hard to bear and inflaming to her touchy Prussian pride. Ottoline, passionately possessive of Lawrence, considered Frieda a mere appendage.

The Morrells were expecting to move to Garsington Manor in Oxfordshire in May and had suggested converting an outbuilding there for Lawrence, which prospect filled him with delight. By mid April, in view of poor Frieda's attitude, Ottoline had second thoughts and made an excuse, by letter, of insurmountable expense for the conversion. To Koteliansky on April 20th, 1915 Lawrence wrote: *Probably we shall not have Lady Ottoline's cottage. In my soul, I shall be glad . . . we will look out for some tiny place on the sea . . . I must write to the Murrys about it. But why don't they write to us? It is their turn. Nevertheless I will write tomorrow.* Really, he was deeply disappointed.

This may have led to him sending the following severe sermon to Ottoline on April 23rd, 1915, following a suicidal attempt by Maria Nys, a young Belgian refugee on her staff, and the future Mrs Aldous Huxley. Over-devoted to Ottoline, who had sent her to London to get rid of her when she was hoping to settle at Garsington, Maria had taken, in her misery, a poisonous mercurial mixture. *We were shocked about Maria,* Lawrence wrote. *I am not sure whether you aren't really more wicked than I had at first thought you. I think you can't help torturing a bit. But I think it has shown something — as if you, with a strong, old-developed* will *had enveloped the girl, in this will, so that she lived under the dominance of your will: and then you want to put her away from you, eject her from your will. So that was why she says it was because she couldn't bear being left, that she took the poison . . . Why must you always use your* will *so much, why can't you let things be, without always grasping and trying to know and to dominate.* Lawrence had great flair for calling a spade a spade. This letter upset Ottoline very much and trying to make amends, he wrote back: *Don't be melancholy, there isn't time.*

On May 17th Ottoline moved to Garsington. It was a fine, gabled house of grey Cotswold stone, with mullioned windows. The estate, which included a farm, covered two hundred acres and the house looked over the Thames Valley to the Berkshire downs and the lovely wooded hills, the Wittenham Clumps,

L

nearby. The two oak-panelled drawing-rooms on the ground floor Ottoline had painted Venetian red and sea-green, oak or no oak, with edges gilded, making a dramatic backcloth for the Chinese cabinets, ornate screens, little boxes and rich old Eastern carpets. Oranges stuck with cloves, and bowls of faded rose petals scented the air. There were paintings by Augustus John, Gertler, Lamb, and Conders. The hall was painted dove-grey and finished off with a thin coat of pale pink, as though flushed by a sunset glow. The curtains were of Cardinal red silk; those of the bedrooms were honey-coloured. Guests ate in the green room, at a heavy long table, drifting to the red room for music and endless talk. In front of the house one of the group of old ponds below the rolling lawn was made rectangular, in the centre of which was a small rectangular island. A spaced, clipped yew hedge gave vistas of the old orchard beyond. There were white statues about the edge of the lake and a white temple stood at one end. Guests bathed there and sat on the lawn or under the fine ilex tree to the left. By moonlight the garden was exquisite, with the lamplit windows of the house glowing in the background. There was, however, only one bathroom, which made Ottoline anxiously delay the house-warming.

However, for her birthday on June 16th she invited the Lawrences, Gertler, the Cannans and Russell. All helped with the finishing of the painting, Lawrence gilding and Russell touching up the ceiling beams. Alas, Frieda, at her worst, sat idle on a table, criticizing. She was jealous and consequently having a bad time, her inner storm breaking into a fierce quarrel in the bedroom. She left for London the next morning, leaving Lawrence a defeated man. What went wrong with what must have seemed to Lawrence a wonderful vista opening up for both of them? Well, Frieda, who had been to Otto Gross his 'bright fire', could not accept second position. Ottoline no doubt made it very clear that she had some divine right over Lawrence. For the moment he was her discovery, a sort of soul-mate. What was between her and Lawrence was what Frieda termed 'soul mush' and she could not stand it. It is possible that Ottoline ignored her, for she would be aware of rivalry between them. Frieda was not just anybody, she was a Prussian aristocrat. Later, Frieda admitted that at Garsington she had felt 'a Hun and a nobody'.

Many years later, when the passionate fires of youth had died down in both women, Frieda admitted how jealous she had been of her, and Ottoline, some time after Lawrence's death, when offering Frieda tea when she called one day at 10, Gower Street, said kindly, "Frieda I must tell you that I never was fair to you." As a sour footnote, however, it seems that Ottoline suggested to Russell that Lawrence should get rid of Frieda. One hopes that it was to be a civilized casting-off, with no blood-letting.

Chapter XI

Acacia Road

During the summer the Murrys moved into 5, Acacia Road, St. John's Wood, furnishing it with their pieces from Rose Tree Cottage and Elgin Crescent. Katherine took over a beautiful attic room as her own, which Kot was eventually to occupy and cherish for the rest of his life. The rent was £52 per year. Murry was now reviewing French books for the *Times Literary Supplement*, and Katherine's allowance had been increased. A housekeeper, a Mrs Peach, went with the house which eased Katherine's burdens.

The Campbells also lived in St. John's Wood, and by early August, the Lawrences had moved to 1, Byron Villas, Vale of Health, Hampstead, next door to the poetess Anna Wickham. It was a ground floor flat, and today it proudly bears a blue plaque in memory of his stay there. Lady Cynthia Asquith, visiting them 'in a dear little clean room', thought the flat 'delightful'. Lawrence had brightened with the stimulus of home-making, begging contributions from friends. Catherine Carswell, who gave him a gilt mirror, was amused by his singing 'Sun of my soul, Thou Saviour dear' as he polished pots and pans both inside and out. They bought cheap second-hand furniture in the Caledonian Market, and as a special luxury Lawrence bought a blue Persian rug for £10, which he called his Endymion rug. He also made a loose cover for an old sofa.

In June Lawrence had discussed the idea of lectures in London with Bertrand Russell and wrote enthusiastically to Ottoline: *We think to have a lecture hall in London in the autumn and give lectures: he on Ethics, I on Immortality: also to have meetings, to establish a little society or body around a* religious belief which leads to action . . . *You must be president . . . . Murry must come in, and Gilbert — and perhaps Campbell. We can all lecture, at odd times, Murry has a genuine side to his nature: so has Mrs Murry. Don't mistrust them. They are valuable, I know.* Russell, having been introduced to the Murrys by Lawrence one day in July, at the Russian Law Bureau, had other opinions. *I thought that Murry was beastly and the whole atmosphere dead and putrefying,* he wrote to Ottoline. Perhaps his impression had been soured by the inevitable kippering process engendered by three chain-smokers with a liking for strong Russian cigarettes. Later Leonard Woolf, on a similar visit to the Holborn Law Bureau, was to remark on the incessant smoking. However, Russell and Lawrence met regularly to discuss the lecture project.

A small room above a grocer's shop at 12, Fisher Street, off Red Lion Square, was rented at 10/- per week. Lawrence had the floor scrubbed and gave the walls a coat of distemper. A table and windsor chairs were bought in the Caledonian Market for £3.10.0. Frieda helped to hang the curtains, Lawrence carried a lamp, oil and sticks over. Kot was enjoined to bring a little bit of coal. Poor Lawrence was not well enough to carry coal as well.

There was to be an associated magazine, named *The Signature*, with Murry as technical editor. Both he and Katherine were to contribute. Kot was business manager, arranging the printing of the 32-page pamphlet, with a cheap printer in the Mile End Road called Narodiczky. The target was £30 from subscription, 2/6 for six numbers. Among the many circularized and agreeing to take *The Signature* were W.L. George, F. Swinnerton, S.P.B. Mais, E.M. Forster, Dr Ernest Jones, Gertler, Lady Diana Manners, Lytton Strachey, Alice Dax and O. Raymond Drey. Lawrence wrote a fine essay called 'The Crown', spread over three copies; Murry contributed a three-part autobiographical study entitled 'There was a little man'; Katherine, under the name of Matilda Berry, proffered her beautiful story 'The wind blows'. One of the subscribers, O. Raymond Drey, remarked, 'Matilda Berry is simply terrific'. He was the husband of Anne Rice.

'The Crown' was intimately connected with *The Rainbow*. Lawrence believed his 'philosophical' idea evolved from his imaginative work. In 'The Crown' he tried to clarify the conflict of light and dark in the being symbolized by the lion and the unicorn fighting for the crown, symbol of the true self.

Alas, only £15 was received, and about twelve people attended the lectures. The project foundered after the third number. Ten years later, in the preface to *Reflections on the Death of a Porcupine*, which collection of essays included 'The Crown', Lawrence regretted offering 'The Crown' in a sixpenny pamphlet and had felt shame over failing the few faithful subscribers. It was a sad affair; but second-hand copies of *The Signature* sold for £10 in 1933.

In the meantime the stench of war permeated the atmosphere, and casualties continued to arrive at Charing Cross. Those ghastly telegrams were on the increase. In Gallipoli, one sunny morning, William Orton minus two front teeth from a fracas with an army biscuit, was in a shell-burst while on reconnaissence with another comrade, and noticed his left arm 'hanging as though from a nail, shoulder very wet' as he lay, giddy, in soft mud. He survived, waking later to a dark sky in which one or two stars twinkled.

In May, Rupert Brooke died in the Aegean. On June 5th, 1915, Henri Gaudier-Brzeska was killed in a charge at Neuville St. Vaast. He left a Last Testament from the trenches:

I have been fighting for two months. Human masses teem and move, are destroyed and crop up again. Horses are worn out in three weeks, die by the roadside. With all the destruction that works around us nothing is changed . . . . the bursting shells . . . . do not alter in the least the outlines of the hill we are besieging.
. . . . My views on sculpture remain absolutely the same.

He had broken the butt off a brutal looking enemy rifle and carved on it his own design, trying to express 'a gentler order of feeling'.

Chummie was on an officers' training course in March and was housed in Balliol College. In April he was moved to

Bournemouth, sadly noting the trampling of spring flowers on route marches. By June, in camp near Aldershot, he was training in the handling of hand-grenades. In August, on a six-day course on Clapham Common, he had to instruct 'the whole Battalion, officers and men' how to cope with 'these frightfully deadly bombs'. He visited 5, Acacia Road whenever he could, gallantly describing life there in his letters home:

25th August, 1915
I had a most comfortable roost at Kathleen's dear little house in Acacia Road, St. John's Wood — Jack Murry is a very kind quiet soul and he and Kass are perfectly sweet to each other — in fact I was awfully glad to see how smoothly things were running — they pay £52 per year for the house and it is the acme of comfort and cleanliness — marvellously cheap, don't you think?

The brother and sister would walk in the garden beneath the pear tree and reminisce endlessly about that other garden with its lily lawn, violet bed, and beloved wobbly pink garden seat. Arms around each other, Katherine would say sadly, "You know I shall always be a stranger here," and Chummie in answer, "Yes, darling I know." So ran her journal, and this is likely how things were then. Out of those summer days together her story *The Wind Blows* emerged.

Chummie left for France at 6.00 a.m. on September 22nd and was stationed near Armentières at Ploegsteert Wood, the same 'thick wood of tall thin trees' from where Roland Leighton sent four violets and later his poem 'Villanelle' to Vera Brittain in April 1915, before dying of wounds on December 23rd, 1915.

Villanelle

Violets from Plug Street Wood,
Sweet, I send you oversea.
(It is strange they should be blue,
Blue, when his soaked blood was red,
For they grew around his head;
It is strange they should be blue) . . . .

On October 4th, Chummie wrote to Katherine and Aunt Belle. On October 7th at Ploegsteert Wood, while demonstrating how to throw a hand-grenade, it exploded, and Chummie and his sergeant were killed. As he lay dying he said, "God forgive me for all that I have done," and, "Lift my head, Katie, I can't breathe."

On October 11th Murry wrote in a notebook, later found among Koteliansky's papers, probably left behind, an account of that tragic day when the telegram arrived for Katherine. White-faced and incredulous she did not cry, taking some wine for support before going off to see Mr. Kay.

That night, Katherine, wearing her Russian peasant dress, had to face guests at her dinner party. Only Kot knew of the tragedy. Beatrice learned a few days later, on enquiring about Chummie as she held his photograph, and noticed Katherine looked at her 'in a queer wild hard way' and then said, "Blown to bits." Shortly after, Katherine received Chummie's cap, and his piece of greenstone on a matching ribbon given to him before he sailed by their much loved general practitioner Dr Martin of Wellington, who had brought him into the world, and whose silk hat Chummie and Jeanne, when children, would stealthily sniff at to catch the lovely smell of eau-de-cologne from its satin interior, as it lay in the hall when the doctor visited the Beauchamps. Katherine's passport photograph for 1918 shows her wearing the greenstone and it was left to Jeanne in Katherine's will. Acacia Road was now unbearable and to assuage Katherine's misery, they decided to flee to France. It is a measure of Katherine's rootlessness that she gave up a house that she loved in her favourite district, in the face of her bereavement and that Murry stood by, allowing himself to be shorn of home and security. It demonstrated, too, the dominance Katherine had over him.

Meanwhile Lawrence was in dire trouble. On September 28th he had given the Murrys a signed copy of the newly issued *Rainbow*, a book over which he had lovingly toiled and rewritten. On reading it, they did not like it. Neither did the critics. Robert Lynd, in the *Daily News* for October 5th, thought it 'a monstrous wilderness of phallicism'. Clement Shorter of the *Sphere* considered it 'an orgie of sexiness' and wondered whether Methuen had read it before publication. On November 3rd Detective Inspector Albert Draper of Scotland Yard seized 1000 copies at the publishers, and a court case against the book was to be held at Bow Street Police Station on November 13th. The magistrate, Sir John Dickinson, banned the book and ordered its destruction by burning; the *Daily Express* reported the proceedings under a headline — *Obscene Novel to be Destroyed* — *Worse than Zola*. Methuen was fined 10 guineas. All this and Lawrence was not even informed, nor given a chance to defend his book on which he had worked for three years.

Philip Morrell raised the question of the banning of the *Rainbow* in Parliament on November 18th and December 1st, to no avail. Like Katherine, Lawrence wanted to flee the country and chose America. On November 9th he wrote to Lady Cynthia, thanking her for help with passports, saying that his life was ended in England and he must find new ground. In her diaries for Friday November 12th she mentioned that Lawrence had also said in his last letter that *he heard I had said, 'The Rainbow is like the second story in the Prussian Officer only worse'. I asked who it was. And it was that little sneak Murry, who had eavesdropped on Basil and me at that water-colour exhibition whilst pretending not to recognise me.* She had visited Byron Villas that day and thought Frieda looked 'wonderfully Prussian. With a helmet she would do well as a picture of Prussia'.

The American prospect fell through; Lawrence was too proud to seek exemption from war service through ill health, and permission to leave England was denied. Ottoline, who had kindly contributed £30 to Lawrence for his American expenses, invited them both to Garsington for November 29th. Writing to Lady Cynthia he mentioned the proposed visit, saying he'd got a new suit and Frieda a new coat and skirt. He had made her a hat out of pieces of fur and also intended to buy her a big warm coat for the cold weather. He felt that his heart was smashed.

Katherine, in her grief over Chummie, expressed her bitterness in a satiric sketch 'Stay-Laces' (which appeared in *New Age*, November 4th, 1915), around the war seen through suburban women's eyes — *I love the wounded, don't you? Oh,*

*I simply love them. And their sweet blue and red uniforms are
so cheerful and awfully effective, aren't they?* Making
preparations to leave, she arranged to let Acacia Road to a
Russian journalist friend of Kot, Michael Farbman, his wife
and daughter, from November 11th who offered a room to
Kot, presumably Katherine's attic. The rent was to be £1-10-0
per week. Kot kept the house on after the Farbmans left.

A little light relief was provided by a party on November 5th
at the studio of the Hon. Dorothy Brett, near Earl's Court
Road. Her parents were Viscount Esher, governor of Windsor
Castle and Sylvain van-de-Weyer, daughter of the First
Minister of King Leopold of Belgium, who was so devoted to
her cold, handsome husband that she largely ignored her two
daughters. The boys of course were spoilt by the father, who in
turn rejected his daughters. As children living in Windsor
Park, they played with the Prince of Wales, Prince Albert and
Princess Mary. They had dancing lessons with Princess
Beatrice's children at Windsor Castle in front of Queen
Victoria, who would thump the floor with her stick. Dorothy
with golden hair, blue eyes, soft rounded cheeks and receding
chin was duly presented at Court, then bobbed her hair and
left home to study art at the Slade. There she met Dora
Carrington and Mark Gertler. She was very deaf, poor girl,
and used an ear trumpet. However, she had hidden depths. At
one stage she played the side-drums in a girls amateur
orchestra, organized by Margaret, Ranee of Sarawak, wife of
the second white raja who lived at Ascot, and who was on the
lookout for eligible, well-bred young girls for her sons to
consider marrying. Her sister the Honourable Sylvia Brett,
who played the big drum, cymbals and triangle, was happily
caught in the ranee's butterfly net.

Through Gertler, Brett already knew Lawrence and the
party was really in his honour. The guests included Kot, the
Murrys, Anne Rice, Lytton Strachey, Gertler and Dora
Carrington, also, alas, some amiable gate-crashers with bottles
— full ones. She described her guests as they arrived: *Kot . . .
an air of distinction, of power, and also a tremendous capacity
for fun . . . a little later Katherine Mansfield and Murry
appear. Katherine, small, her sleek dark hair brushed close to
her head, her fringe sleeked down over her white forehead, she*

*dresses nearly always in black with a touch of white or scarlet
or a rich deep purple. This evening she is dressed in black. Her
movements are quaintly restricted; controlled, small, reserved
gestures. The dark eyes glance about much like a bird's, the
pale face is a quiet mask . . . But she is cautious, a bit
suspicious and on her guard. Middleton Murry rolls in with his
gait of a sailor, his curly hair is getting a bit thin on top. He is
nervous, shy, a small man. The eyes are large and hazel with a
strange unseeing look; the nose is curved on one side and
perfectly straight on the other, due to its having been broken
. . . when the shyness wears off him, he also is full of fun.
Carrington is one of my Slade friends . . . Her heavy bobbed
golden hair falls round her face like a curtain; she looks up
from under it with her two sly blue eyes.*

After the gate-crashers, Brett manfully played the pianola
and persuaded the company to play charades, the star turn
being Carrington. "How well she does it," Gertler noticed
Katherine telling Murry. All were drunk, especially H.M.S.
Murry who, winily foundering, was being propped up against
the wall, as he kept sliding to the floor.

Let us have a last word on the party from Lytton Strachey,
writing to David Garnett on November 10th: *There were a
great many people I didn't know at all, and others whom I only
knew by repute, among the latter, the Lawrences, whom I
examined carefully and closely for several hours, though I
didn't venture to have myself introduced. I was surprised to
find that I liked her looks very much — she actually seemed
(there's no other word for it) a lady; as for him I've rarely seen
anyone so pathetic, miserable, ill, and obviously devoured by
internal distresses. He behaved to everyone with the greatest
cordiality, but I noticed for a second a look of intense disgust
and hatred flash into his face . . . caused by ah! whom? (Lytton
I presume.) Katherine Mansfield was also there, and took my
fancy a great deal.* It was inevitable that Lawrence would
dislike Lytton Strachey, with his squeaky voice reminiscent of
his own 'blond' tones, the puny appearance and red beard, a
kind of mirror image of himself. Then there was the irritant
quality of Strachey's upper middle-class background, his
seeming never to engage Lawrence in inspired conversation;
instead, a sort of hostile walking round each other like two

animals of the same species. Worst of all, it is likely that
Lawrence knew or guessed at Lytton's homosexuality.

Katherine and Murry arrived in Marseilles about November
19th. She wrote to Kot giving him her address and asked him
to retrieve Chummie's cap from a drawer and keep it safely.
She also invited him to use her fur rug on his bed. After a few
days they moved along the coast to Cassis. In spite of the cold,
the fire would not burn, and a dreary mistral blew, she found a
sort of comfort in the sea she told Kot, *the sound of it after
such a long silence is almost unbearable — a sweet agony, you
know . . . like moonlight is sometimes.* There was an inner
weeping going on for her lost Chummie. She described her
room for Kot: *my room is nice darling. The walls are blue with
small flowers standing on their feet at the bottom of the wall,
and the same flowers standing on their heads at the top . . .
Jack has just read to me what he wrote to you. Don't believe the
conjugal 'we' . . . it's not really true of me — never. In my*
heart *I am happy because I feel that I have come into my own.
You understand me?* This may imply that she felt a certain
freedom away from the confines of home and England.

She had withdrawn from Murry; it was obvious that she was
depressed and suffering from a mourning reaction. Under
normal circumstances she would have been wildly happy there
on the Riviera. In her depression she was physically and
mentally estranged from Murry, and her lost, loved object
Chummie was enshrined in her thoughts to the exclusion of all
else. Murry felt isolated and actually jealous of the dead
brother, which probably led to his rage at Katherine's
seemingly endless weeping on the rocky headland one day. It is
typical of the very clever to have incredible blindspots. With
'his heart of sensitive stone', described thus later by his good
friend Max Plowman, Murry did not recognise a depression
when he saw one. He would be the type to suggest that the
patients pull themselves together. He came up with the bright
idea of deserting the poor bereft creature. Anyway,
rationalizing, he felt he wanted, so earnestly, to revive the
dying *Signature*, suppose it meant printing it himself on his
non-existent printing press, paid for by his well nigh
non-existent bank balance.

In his defence, he was out of his depth in his assessment of

Katherine's malady; he was a worker, there was a war on, and in drifting about the Mediterranean in bad weather he 'felt like a fish out of water', justifiably so. To make amends, he searched for a better place for Katherine. They moved to the Hôtel Beau Rivage at Bandol and he left three days later on December 7th.

Manfully writing to him on 8th Katherine said he was quite right to go back', but she addressed her journal thus: *Bandol France. Brother. I think I have known for a long time that life was over for me, but I never realized it or acknowledged it until my brother died. Yes, though he is lying in the middle of a little wood in France and I am still walking upright and feeling the sun and the wind . . . I am just as much dead as he is. The present and the future mean nothing to me . . . . 'Do you remember, Katie?' I hear his voice in the trees and flowers . . . why don't I commit suicide? Because I feel I have a duty to perform to the lovely time when we were both alive. I want to write about it, and he wanted me to. We talked it over in my little top room in London . . . very well: it shall be done.* The phoenix was to rise out of the ashes and her writing, newborn and bathed in delicate radiance.

Back in England Murry found himself a cold attic in Devonshire Street for 5/- per week. Goodyear, on leave, slept on the floor and accompanied him on a visit to Lawrence, who wrote to Katherine about it on December 12th: *Murry turned up on Friday . . . he doesn't look well . . . is very chirpy . . . he came yesterday with Goodyear whom I like, but who is on the same Oxford introspective line . . . which bores me . . . I am tired of this insistence on the* personal *element . . . I want some new non-personal activity . . . . a harmony of purpose . . . I am weary of personality. It remains now whether Murry is still based upon the personal hypothesis: because if he is, then our ways are different. I don't want a purely personal relation with him; he is a man therefore our relation should be based on purpose . . . Let us be easy and impersonal not forever fingering over our own souls and the souls of our acquaintances . . . Murry irritates me . . . He makes me false.*

On December 12th Katherine fell ill with a temperature, sore throat, enteritis, and the dreaded 'rheumatism'; she could not walk at all. A letter from Murry cheered her a little. But in her journal she wrote: *Ten minutes past four. I am sure that this Sunday is the worst Sunday of my life. I've touched bottom. Even my heart doesn't beat any longer . . . I faint — I die.* Her illness was complicated by anxiety over letters, a pattern which was to be repeated often in the years to come. Unwisely Murry had been silent, waiting for word from Bandol; Katherine's letters had been delayed, and she was without communication when she felt the most ill.

On December 15th she wrote desperately: *Oh Jack, I appeal even to your imagination as a novelist — do not leave me like this without news. It is so cruel — I weep bitterly.* But after a letter arrived by afternoon post she wrote: " — — once away I suppose you 'forgot'." This was an abnormal reaction to a normal situation, but understandable in view of her low threshold for distress, her laying such passionate store on Murry's letters amidst emotional disturbance, inevitable under the stress of physical illness. Murry's letter of the 12th was a loving one and full of contrition.

Trying to make amends she wrote on December 16th: *I am afraid you will think my last letters very silly . . . since I have been alone here the loss of my little brother has become quite real to me. I have entered into my loss . . .*

In her misery she had written to Lawrence who, as always, answered promptly even if he did sometimes include a lecture but with what healing breath, like a sea breeze.

1, Byron Villas Mon. December 20th
Your letter this morning __ Murry was here when the letter came. I am so sorry you are so ill. . . . I knew you would have to die with your brother: you also go down into death and be extinguished. But for us . . . there is a resurrection and a clean life to begin . . . You have gone further into your death than Murry has. He runs away. But one day he too will submit, he will dare to go down, and be killed, to die in this self which he is. Then he will become a man; not till. He is not a man yet. When you get better, you must come back and we will begin afresh, it will be the first struggling days of spring . . . There remain only you and Murry in our lives . . .

At the same time Lawrence took Murry to task, who, dazed by

the body-punches, sent Katherine a blow-by-blow account. Lawrence blamed Murry for Katherine's illness and misery. He accused him of being cowardly and indecisive and reproached him for leaving her at Bandol.

However, in spite of this lecture, Murry felt that Lawrence was still deeply attached to them both. Having arranged to give up Byron Villas, Lawrence had decided to give the Murrys his beautiful 'Endymion' Persian rug, as well as his clock, his fender, his kitchen table and chairs, and a camp bed. After spending Xmas with his family in Ripley, he and Frieda went to the Beresfords' house in Cornwall.

By December 20th Katherine was better and beginning to love Bandol. She was writing again and by December 24th, had the beautiful prose piece 'Et in Arcadia Ego' ready for *The Signature*. She told Murry about it in her daily letter and went on: *I feel I only really know you since you went back to England. I feel as though a miracle had happened to you and you are rich and bathed in light . . . I am one with our love for ever.* Her depression had lifted.

This was the beginning of a period of inspired happiness for Katherine, the like of which she was never to see again. It is significant that it developed in the wake of bereavement, incomprehensibly this can happen, even progress to a state of mania in a susceptible, unstable person. Bereavement, however crippling, is associated with a certain simplification of life, resulting at times in a sense of release which expresses itself in a dissociated state. Perhaps this also explains some of the celebration associated with funerals, when spirits of the departed seem to be cheered or perhaps eased on their way? However, in Katherine's case it is also possible that this near exaltation was associated with her precarious health, a sort of auto-intoxication.

Murry, shaken by Lawrence's dressing-down, and feeling cast off and desperate to restore the status quo, asked Katherine to find a villa in Bandol. Meanwhile her ecstatic letters were now arriving and he wondered if he had been too precipitate, or at least now that she was better, he could perhaps sink back into inertia and await her return. With typical indecision, putting the onus on Katherine, he wrote *that if she wanted him he would* come immediately. No doubt chilled, Katherine sent a wire: *Letters received, implore don't come, don't want, understand perfectly.* It arrived on his return from Garsington, where he had been for Xmas. On December 26th he had written to Katherine, delighting in their reunion when she would lie in his arms with their feet entwined.

Ottoline in her memoirs thought Murry: *an odd remarkable-looking man, with a rather cavernous looking face, large unseeing vague dark eyes, and a slender lithe figure. He is rather like a southern welshman. He had a romantic love for Katherine Mansfield and seemed quite absorbed by the thought of her . . . . I feel he was lost and unhappy without her and advised him to go back to her (I gave him £5 for his journey).* Disregarding Katherine's last telegram, which awaited him, he sent her a wire to say he was coming. The £5 no doubt made his feet the more fleet and his mind the more clear.

While Murry had been vacillating, Katherine, wildly happy, was searching Bandol for a villa to rent. She was too excited to sleep, sitting by an open window at 4.30 a.m., watching the dawn light bathe the black mountains. Celebrating, she bought new relief nibs, then penned the beautiful passages: *Love presses on my forehead like a crown — my head is heavy — heavy . . . . I feel we are coming together for the first time. I send you everything I have got — yes, yes, even this throbbing sweet anxiety that beats in my forehead and makes my hands so cold and my heart intent and ready.*

She found a small detached villa standing on a hill top, near jonquil fields, with a terraced garden and stone veranda overlooking the sea, called the Villa Pauline. Receiving the final telegram, on December 29th, she ran along the *quai* to settle the transaction and wrote to Murry that evening. *I have loved you before for 3 years with my heart and my mind, but it seems to me I have never loved you avec mon âme as I do now. I love you with all our future life — our life together which seems only now to have taken root and to be alive and growing up in the sun . . . love possesses me utterly — I have never felt anything like it before. In fact, I did not comprehend the possibility of such a thing . . . Bogie, come quickly, quickly. My heart will break.* She was in a state of euphoria which affects most of us some time, if we are lucky. He arrived in Bandol on January 1st, 1916 and stayed until mid-April.

M

Chapter XII

Villa Pauline

The Villa Pauline — it was to be a memory of beatitude between us for ever, Murry wrote in *Between Two Worlds*. They rose at six, shopped in the market, and were at work at a small kitchen table by 8.30 a.m. Murry was writing a book on Dostoevsky, to repay a debt to Secker, so he was absorbed, enviably so. It was a sort of abreaction following all those Dostoevsky evenings with Campbell. Commenting on those days in Bandol in his journal, July 11th, 1934 Murry believed an inner change had occurred then when he lost self conciousness and became a real person. Katherine eventually wrote *The Aloe*, the final version of which was published as the long story called *Prelude.*

They lived on less than £1 per week, and no doubt both were undernourished. Murry bought a dark brown corduroy suit in Toulon for 19/-, which seemed in its odoriferous splendour, indestructible, probably requiring eventual death by shooting. With it he wore a broad-brimmed felt hat, originally Gordon's, and sported sturdy side-whiskers. The local people called him 'L'Espagnol'. Katherine wore her 'goblin hat', a broad-brimmed felt. It is obvious from her journal that this euphoria did not last, she was still caught up in her brother's death, but a sense of peace developed, a 'settled' feeling. Katherine had a burning desire to write but could not get started. Coming through the refining fire of her tragic loss, she wanted to write differently, she wanted to discard her old style with its satirical plots, and write instead of New Zealand. In this she felt a curious prompting from Chummie — *Each time I take up my pen, you are with me . . . .* She wanted *to make*

*our undiscovered country leap into the eyes of the Old World
. . . . But all must be told with a sense of mystery, a radiance,
an afterglow, because you, my little sun of it, are set. You have
dropped over the dazzling brim of the world.*

By February 13th she noted she had written very little and
blamed this on lack of willpower. At times she imagined she
saw Chummie lying outside in the field and felt deeply sad.
However, by February 16th she: found "The Aloe" . . . *"The
Aloe" is right . . . it simply fascinates me, and I know that it is
what you would wish me to write.* Her story with its revised title
was to be considered one of her best.

Meanwhile the Lawrences were still living in Cornwall in the
big grey house by the sea, belonging to J.D. Beresford. Staying
with them were two young men whom he had met at
Garsington in November; Peter Heseltine, aged twenty-one,
who composed songs under the name of Peter Warlock, and a
young writer, Michael Kouyoumdjian, later to become known
as Michael Arlen. Heseltine, greatly taken with Lawrence,
wanted to help him and planned, via a printed circular (1000
copies) inviting subscription, to issue *The Rainbow* at 7/6.

Writing to the Murrys about the venture, Lawrence received
a heated reply, for they had hoped to start printing themselves.
On February 24th, from Porthcothan St. Merryn, Padstow, N.
Cornwall, Lawrence implored them to calm down. *Now don't
get in a state, you two, about nothing . . . . I begin to tremble
and feel sick at the slightest upset: your letter for instance. Do
be mild with me . . . . I've waited for you for two years now,
and I am far more constant to you than ever you are to me . . .
I have been in a sort of 'all gone but my cap' state this winter,
and am very shaky.* He had indeed been very ill, probably with
bronchopneumonia.

There had been a rift in the friendship with Ottoline, who
declined an invitation to Porthcothan in January after an
exchange of angry letters with Frieda. Heseltine had repeated
some unpleasant remarks made by Ottoline about Frieda over
Xmas. Relations took weeks to heal, and perhaps the germ of
Lady Hermione Roddice, a virulent caricature of Ottoline, in
the future *Women in Love* was laid, as indeed was another
unpleasant character in the book *Peter Halliday*, based on
Heseltine.

No doubt as a result of a mutual wearying, Heseltine eventually returned to London. However, it was decent of a young man of twenty-one to take up arms on behalf of Lawrence. He was a gifted composer, and his songs are popular still. He did not have a good singing voice, so he whistled the different parts when composing, which seems endearingly bird-like. With his charming manner and good looks, blue eyes and long fair hair, it is very sad that he died when only thirty-six, and by his own hand. He was a friend of Delius and corresponded with him regularly.

By March 31st Lawrence had to give up Porthcothan and moved on to the Tinner's Arms, Zennor, St. Ives. On March 5th he wrote to the Murrys, inviting them to join him. He had found a little cottage by the sea for £5 a year, with another available cottage *only twelve strides from our house . . .. we can talk from the windows: and besides us, only the gorse, and the fields, the lambs skipping and hopping like anything . . . . and sometimes a fox, and a ship on the sea.* Katherine in particular was dubious about communal life, especially in Cornwall, which she did not care for. Murry was bewildered by Lawrence's idea of being a *'Blutbruder'* with a *'Blutbrüder-schaft'* between them; also, some of Lawrence's ideas on Dostoevsky for future publication, he found incompatible with his own.

So they gently prevaricated, but both knew, with war news of the German onslaught at Verdun trickling through, that their days at Bandol were numbered. Some time in March, Katherine went away for two days to Marseilles to meet Chaddie, sadly now a widow, her husband having died suddenly on February 27th, 1916; and who, on board the P.&O. liner *Sardinia*, was returning to England from India where she had been since her marriage in 1913. The girls had not met since 1911 and it was with much nervous anticipation that Katherine prepared to go. She stayed in the Hotel Oasis, in the same room as in November, writing two letters to Murry whom she was already missing. She spent *"a funny night. All my fever came back. I shivered and my blood buzzed as though bees swarmed in my heart"*. It seems that she was not well.

Back in Bandol, Katherine resumed her writing of *The Aloe*, the greater part of which was rewritten and published in

1917 by Leonard and Virginia Woolf, under its new name. However, in 1930 Murry had the original story published by Constable; 750 copies were made in large print, like a child's story book, on thick paper with a hard brown cover bearing the title in gold letters. Included was an introduction by Murry.

It begins: *The Samuel Josephs were not a family. They were a swarm. The moment you entered the house they cropped up and jumped out at you* . . . . It contained much material about the Burnells (Beauchamps) which is not in *Prelude* and was probably very true to life. 'Beryl', based on Aunt Belle, perhaps has a little of Katherine in the character. *Days, weeks at a time passed without her ever for a moment ceasing to act the part, for that was really what it came to and then, quite suddenly when the unreal self had forced her to do something she did not want to do at all, she had come into her own again, and for the first time realized what had been happening.* Then the following note appeared in the manuscript: *What is it that I am getting at?*

. . . for a long time, she hasn't even been able to control her second self . . . There was a radiant kind of being who wasn't even spiteful or malicious . . . who was grave — who never would have dreamed of doing the things that she did. Has she banished this being . . .? I want to get at all this through her, just as I got at Linda through Linda.

There follows a hairbrushing episode with friend Nan Fry brushing Beryl's hair, and it savours very much of the relationship of L.M. to Katherine and L.M.'s 'scientific hair brushing':

In the glass Nannie's face . . . was like a round sleeping mask. Slowly she brushed, with long caressing strokes . . . she would say with a kind of moaning passion . . . looping the hair in her hands: 'It's more beautiful than ever, B . . . But nearly always these brushings came to an unpleasant ending. Nannie did something silly. Quite suddenly, she would snatch up Beryl's hair and bury her face in it and kiss it, or clasp her hands round Beryl's head sobbing: 'You are so beautiful! — beautiful, beautiful!' And at these moments Beryl had such a feeling of horror, such a violent thrill of physical dislike for

Nan Fry. 'That's quite enough . . . Goodnight, Nan'. She didn't even try to suppress her contempt and her disgust . . . And the curious thing was that Nan Fry seemed to understand this, even to expect it, never protesting, but stumbling away out of the cubicle . . . whispering 'Forgive me' . . . And the more *curious thing was that Beryl let her brush her hair again, and let this happen again . . .*

L.M. told Professor Alpers that she 'used to brush K.M.'s hair by the hour throughout their friendship, but that she couldn't bear it if I *touched* her'.

At another point in the manuscript, a domestic note is struck: *Prepare charcoal fire every night before turning in. Then one has only to go down, put a match to it and stick on the funnel, and it's ready by the time you're dressed! How clever.* Presumably it was by the warmth of this little fire that they wrote at night. By the beginning of April they prepared to leave.

On March 5th Lawrence sent them a sketch of his 'little monastery', Higher Tregerthen, near Zennor:

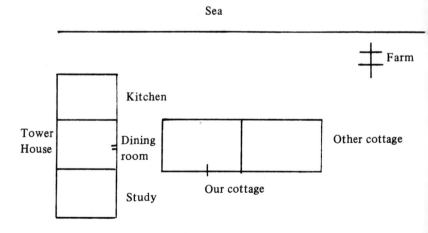

He suggested that Heseltine had one bedroom, with lunch and dinner to be taken communally in the Tower House — not what the Murrys really wanted! By the beginning of April, Villa Pauline was closed and Katherine tearfully handed over the key to Madame Allègre.

Lawrence met them at St. Ives railway station on April 7th, a cold grey day, journeying the rest of the way by cart, sitting on top of the trunks like immigrants. They stayed at the Tinner's Arms while getting the Tower House ready. "I shall never like this place," Katherine told Murry; a bad beginning. Cornwall had no chance when compared with Bandol. To Ottoline, on the same day, Lawrence wrote: . . . *the Murrys have come. We are very busy getting their cottage ready . . . But they neither of them seem very well in health.*

The tower room, accessible from the study only, they painted yellow. Unfortunately the roof leaked. There were three bedrooms. Lawrence's cottage had two bedrooms and a scullery. He had painted the walls pale pink and a dresser he had made 'like a rabbit hutch', royal blue. Yellow curtains with green spots hung at the large deep window, on the sill of which were to be massed foxgloves when in season. Two Staffordshire figures riding to market, 'Jasper and Bridget', stood on the mantelpiece, and embroidery by Ottoline after a painting by Duncan Grant, hung on the wall. There was an outside privy and a spring on the hillside, 10 feet up. The Lawrences cooked on the small oil-stove. Kindly Mrs Hocking, the farmer's wife nearby, sometimes cooked a joint or chicken for them on a Sunday.

In spite of the austere beauty of the Cornish coast and wonderful immense skies over the sea, there was trouble almost immediately. By April 16th Lawrence was writing to Catherine Carswell: . . . *It is queer how almost everything has gone out of me, all the world I have known, and the people, gone out like candles. When I think of Viola, or Ivy, even perhaps, the Murrys, who are here, it is with a kind of weariness, as of trying to remember a light which is blown out . . . even I myself am unknown, to myself as well.* He wasn't well, either physically or mentally.

None were happy except Frieda, who liked the place, and splashed happily at the hillside spring, trying to whiten clothes in bowls of bluing water. In spite of the quarrelling she always considered life with Lawrence to be glamorous, which it would be. Ottoline had written to Murry enclosing an angry letter from Frieda, who had discovered this treachery before handing over the mail to him, obviously having steamed open the Garsington missive because Lawrence said, "O. sent you Frieda's letter." He declared he was on Frieda's side and expected the Murrys to be likewise. Writing to Ottoline on April 12th, 1916 Murry admitted they were frightened of Frieda. However, he enjoyed walking to St. Ives with Lawrence to buy second-hand furniture, fascinated by the irresistible charm of the man. He came home with six chairs with rush seats costing 6/- and a bed painted green for 1/-. The chairs survived all the rigours and were handed down to Murry's son Colin, many years later. Frieda, trying to be nice to Katherine, brought her flowers and told her she was exquisite and really beautiful which infuriated instead of pleased Katherine, because she did not really believe it, considering Frieda a liar and riddled with ideas of 'sexual symbols'.

By the first week in May Katherine wrote to Kot that she and Frieda were not even speaking to each other, and Lawrence seemed 'one million miles away'. She said she could not stand the situation between Lawrence and Frieda, alternating between loving playfulness and terrible quarrelling. Katherine felt Lawrence had 'gone a little bit out of his mind', going into a frenzy when contradicted about anything, which exhausted him so much that he had to go to bed. She as well as Frieda precipitated these brainstorms, though with Frieda, Lawrence used verbal abuse and physical violence, threatening to cut her throat.

She went on to describe the evening of May 5th when, after a simple difference over Shelley's 'Skylark' at tea, Frieda ordered Lawrence out of the house, which fracas erupted into a full-scale attack over dinner at the Murrys, when Frieda came over to the Tower House saying, "I have finally done with him." *Suddenly Lawrence appeared and made a kind of horrible blind rush at her and they began to scream and scuffle. He beat her — he beat her to death — her head and face and breast and pulled out her hair . . . they dashed into the kitchen and round and round the table. I shall never forget how L. looked. He was so white — almost green and he just hit — thumped the big soft woman. Then he fell into one chair and she into another . . . L. sat staring at the floor, biting his nails. Frieda sobbed . . . suddenly, after a long time — almost a quarter of an hour — L. asked Murry a question about French literature . . . then F. poured herself out some coffee. Then she and L. glided into talk, began to discuss some 'very rich but very good macaroni cheese'. And next day . . . . he was running about taking her up breakfast . . . and trimming her a hat . . . I can't stand it. And what is hardest of all to bear is Lawrence's 'hang-doggedness'. He is so completely in her power and yet I am sure . . . . he loathes his slavery . . . I can't be sorry for him . . . The sight of his humiliating dependence makes me too furious . . . A policeman came to arrest Murry . . . . he will have to go I think. I am very much alone here . . . . I don't belong to anybody here . . . I am making preparations for changing everything . . . .*

Katherine was not working, and re-reading *The Aloe* she told Beatrice on May 11th that she could not believe she had written it.

In a letter to Barbara Low on May 1st Lawrence said that he had begun the second half of The Rainbow adding that he was unwell. This was of course the future *Women in Love,* which was to contain the germ of all the conflict at the time which was so damaging to their friendship, for in those weeks under that Cornish hillside, Lawrence and Murry came to the parting of the ways. Murry knew nothing of the new book yet, with its suppressed Prologue which he was never to read in his lifetime. Lawrence was still proposing *Blutbrüderschaft*, the blood-brothership ceremony which frightened Murry.

One night Murry heard Lawrence crying out from his bedroom next door, "Jack is killing me" — rather unnerving. Murry, completely mystified, pretended the next day that nothing had happened. Walking on the moors together Lawrence talked again of *Blutbrüderschaft*, the old German custom of German knights swearing eternal allegiance to one another over a blood-mingling, by rubbing each other's blood into a small cut on the arm. Murry, apprehensively denying the need for sacrament, picturing druid blood-letting among the boulders, said, "If I love you, and you know I love you, isn't that enough?" which infuriated Lawrence who turned on him with, "I hate your love, I hate it. You're an obscene bug sucking my life away." Murry felt nauseated.

The whole situation was frightening and incomprehensible and to Lawrence it was probably likewise. He was expressing ideas from a whirlpool of mental conflict generated by underlying homosexual longings which, through physical illness and consequent mental disturbance, were breaking from the moorings of repression, appearing in consciousness, disguised, after a fashion, as symptoms, because unfit to be faced. Lawrence's make-up was strongly puritanical; a direct conscious homosexual advance would be untenable and equated with 'death', 'annihilation'. It could only be tolerated in his consciousness, de-eroticised and dressed in the fancy dress of the impersonal, a kind of religious ritual like that of a Masonic Lodge, a symbolic close relationship between men. His heterosexual impulse, thanks to his Oedipus complex, was flawed and he believed he needed a relationship with a man to bring about a flowering in his relationship with the woman. If Lawrence had been an overt full-blown homosexual, he would have sought a partner in the ordinary way and he might not have married. I doubt whether he married Frieda to have children. He did not seem to like the Weekley children, nor was he sympathetic to Frieda's natural grief over their abandonment.

One could say that Lawrence had 'sex in the head', an emotionally toned complex of ideas, pathological, unusual, atypical, in line with the strangely constituted genius of a man, whom Murry called 'a man with a daemon'. If only Murry had been able to read *Women in Love* that early summer of 1916, or had it explained to him, he would have been less mystified, but perhaps even more repelled. With unheeding courage in the suppressed prologue, not published until 1968 in *D.H. Lawrence Phoenix II,* Lawrence gave vent to his longings through his hero, Rupert Birkin, modelled on himself, who feels unable to love women in the way he desires and is attracted to two kinds of men — the 'white-skinned keen-limbed men with eyes like blue flashing ice,' and the other kind 'with dark eyes that one can enter and plunge into',

the 'dark-skinned, supple, night-smelling men', at one with the
'viscous universal heavy darkness'. In the novel, the
Blutbrüderschaft is discussed (and ultimately carried out) by
Birkin and his friend Gerald Crich, 'fair good looking . . . eyes
blue as the blue-fibred steel of a weapon', and Birkin
meditates on *the problem of love and eternal conjunction
between two men . . . it had been a neccessity inside him all his
life — to love a man purely and fully. Of course he had been
loving Gerald all along, and all along denying it.*
"Shall we swear to each other one day?" said Birkin
"We'll leave it till I understand it better"
*Birkin watched him . . . . a touch of contempt came into his
heart. Birkin . . . looking at Gerald . . . seemed now to see . . .
the man himself . . . . doomed, limited to . . . . a sort of fatal
halfness;* Lawrence's predicament exactly. Reading what
rejection did to *The Prussian Officer*, releasing the terrible
upsurge of sadism towards the unknowing young orderly, one
gets a hint of a like propensity in Lawrence, and the depth of
his reaction to being rejected by Murry, for reject him he did,
making plans to move from Higher Tregerthen forthwith,
finally leaving in the middle of June.

Lawrence's manoeuvring in his neurosis for adjustment to
the pressures of reality, resulted in the absurd solution to his
problems which were solved only after a fashion. Instead of
straightforward homosexuality, he had to make an excuse for
the homosexuality by implying that it was only a step towards a
better relationship between man and woman. The neurotic
solution is acceptable really only to the blinkered neurotic
(none as blind as those who will not see), comical and bizarre
to the non-neurotic. Following the desertion by Murry, there
was some close friendship with the handsome young farmer
William Henry Hocking at the nearby farm. Frieda admitted
she was very unhappy about it. Nightly, Lawrence left her
alone to go down to see William Henry. *Lawrence seemed to
run against me, perhaps on account of the bit of German in
me,* wrote Frieda naïvely. Lawrence had told Catherine
Carswell of the friendship, assuring her that it was not 'the sin
against the Holy Ghost stuff'. He also made conscious efforts to
cover up his homosexual tendencies.

Meanwhile Katherine was not the only Beauchamp to have

shown early rebellion and individualism. The youngest daughter of Elizabeth, Felicitas (Martin), the delightful German baby of that faraway English Eastertide, who had so charmed Katherine at the children's Thanksgiving Service with her little basket of eggs and piping song, had had to leave her finishing school in Lausanne in 1914 due to some unacceptable behaviour. Elizabeth, coldly disapproving and unforgiving, had packed her off in tears to a stricter institution in Germany, where, with the advent of war, she was cut off from all her loved ones, never seeing her mother again. On June 6th, 1916, Felicitas died in a few hours from a virulent pneumonia, in a Bremen hospital where, just seventeen, she had begun nursing. Elizabeth, grief-stricken and suffering bitter regret for her parting in anger with her 'little Martin', wrote *Christine*, the story of Felicitas, under the pseudonym of Alice Cholmondeley. I wonder if Katherine ever read it?

The Murrys had found a very nice cottage set in trees near Mylor Bridge, at £18 a year. It had four bay windows and a porch and the garden was lapped by the tidal waters of the River Truro. Katherine went there by train; Lawrence helped Murry to load the furniture on to a cart. When Murry asked Lawrence to visit them, alas he did not answer. Murry cycled down to Mylor with relief but also sadness. On June 19th Lawrence wrote to Catherine Carswell: *The Murrys have gone over to the south side . . . Murry and I are not really associates. How I deceive myself . . . fox-gloves are everywhere.*

Katherine should have been happy in Mylor, but she wasn't. It was a beautiful spot. They had a maid and a kitten called Peter Wilkins. Murry hired a dinghy at 5/- a month and rowed to a sale at Falmouth, bringing home two easy chairs at 10/- each and numerous French books for 1/-, which absorbed him for weeks. He was still reviewing French books for the *Times Literary Supplement* and he was finding a new confidence in his work, and enjoying what he did. He also read prodigiously that summer and no doubt inevitably was drawn down into that enviable whirlpool of absorption, withdrawing from Katherine who was idle. To Koteliansky she wrote on June 24th: *I have been wanting to write to you for days. But I am too sad, my dear one. I hope to be in London within a fortnight . . . Life is so hateful just now that I am quite numb . . . you are so often in my thoughts — especially just lately . . .* One can only presume the trouble was her relationship with Murry, but what a contrast to those golden Bandol days!

On Saturday July 1st, 1916, the Battle of the Somme commenced, and during that terrible day, 20,000 men were killed. Goodyear, on leave, and preparing to go to France, came to stay with Jack and Katherine. He was to die on May 23rd, 1917. A letter from Katherine to Murry in August recalled the visit, which seemed below par: *. . . it's ages since I talked to you, for when Goodyear was here — no — you wouldn't respond. But it's all of little account. What misery I have known!*

She escaped on July 8th and was met by Koteliansky at Paddington, who was to receive a letter from Lawrence, in which he considered the Murrys relationship was wearing out and that Katherine needed to learn to live independently. Lawrence had a discerning eye.

In London Katherine, after a few days with the Campbells, went to Garsington for the first time. "Life feels wonderful and different for at least I am free again," she told Kot. One wonders what she thought of Garsington. Though it was very beautiful, and one would have given one's eye teeth to stay there, there was the fact of only one bathroom and one water-closet, the water for which had to be pumped up by long-suffering servants, who inevitably also had to empty the 'overflowing jordans', a written remark made by an unappreciative Carrington. When there were too few beds, guests overflowed to the estate cottages. Ottoline, in white-flaking face powder and stiff peacock silk, presided over a party of fifteen guests which included David Garnett, Carrington, Fredegond Shove, J.T. Sheppard from 'M.I. 7', Lady Constance Malleson, an actress married to actor Miles Malleson and Lytton Strachey, who sent a most lively account of the party to Virginia Woolf saying he had gone into a trance after losing count of the arrivals, only awakened by the stamping of thirty feet to the frenzied pianola playing desperate ragtime.

. . . Among the rout was 'Katherine Mansfield' — if that's her

real name — I could never quite make sure. Have you ever heard of her? or read anything of her productions? She wrote some rather — in fact distinctly — bright storyettes in a wretched little thing called the Signature, which you may have seen, under the name of Matilda Berry. She was decidedly an interesting creature I thought — very amusing and sufficiently mysterious . . . . She had expressed a wish to meet the author of *Voyage Out . . . . I may add that she has an ugly impassive mask of a face — cut in wood, with brown hair and brown eyes very far apart; and a sharp and slightly vulgarly-fanciful intellect sitting behind it.*

In her memoirs Ottoline suspected that Katherine came as a novelist looking for a copy and that she was suspicious and envious of her — she thought Katherine looked *like an early Renoir . . . also . . . . like a Japanese doll, a smooth mask as if she kept it still and impassive to hide behind, as anyone else might hold up a fan . . . she is brilliant, witty in describing people and is certainly not kind or charitable. She and Lytton got on very well together . . . but I love her vivid awareness of the trembling beauty of life.*

Katherine wrote to Lawrence from Garsington what he considered 'a mere note', saying she was returning to Mylor July 17th and inviting them to stay at Sunnyside Cottage. Launching forthwith into an attack, Lawrence asked her to ask Murry why he did not answer his letter and why he did not even put a word in with the money he sent on? Murry had done much the same to Katherine apparently, for she answered him from London: *I received a book and a note and a shilling on page 50 . . . I'll read the book on my journey to Garsington. You could not have given me much less news of you. Not a personal note nor half a phrase . . . You are a funny boy, and you do rather offend me.* However, as Murry had posted the book separately to a long letter, he was justifiably enraged and despairing on receiving the curt note, writing that he missed her very much. Lawrence went on to tell Katherine they had taken over the tower, furnishing it with a large rosewood table, four chairs, and a bed with *Endymion on the floor and plenty of flowers . . . . It is a great business to have a sitting room —* poor Lawrence!

He and Frieda went to Mylor for the weekend of July 29th,

where they picnicked and rowed the dinghy in choppy waters. Murry described the visit in his autobiography in which there had been a coolness between Lawrence and himself, even a degree of hostility, for on returning home Lawrence sent him a most violent letter, so Murry informed Ottoline. Alas, he destroyed it.

By now Murry had received call-up papers, being classified B2 at Bodmin Barracks, fit only for home service due to his short-sightedness. At a further examination, and after a rough passage with rather a stupid young medical officer, who naïvely declared he could not find a trace of the attack of pleurisy of two years previously, Murry was classified B1 and sent before the colonel, who kindly suggested he find a suitable job if he did not want to become a navvy. Visiting Garsington in August he had the good fortune to meet J.T. Sheppard who arranged for him to become a translator in his department at £5 per week — riches indeed — where he worked extremely hard for the next six months, commencing at Watergate House, Adelphi on September 4th, 1916.

While arranging all this in London, Katherine, alone at Mylor with Mary the maid and Peter Wilkins, wrote to Murry to say she loved him but was feeling miserable and rather abandoned since Murry had not insisted on her being with him. He really had begrudged the £2-10-0 rail fare. A further letter told him she was simply prostrate with misery . . . . *Are we never to be happy — never? We haven't had any 'life' together at all yet — in fact it's only on the rarest occasions that we have any confidential intercourse . . . . If it goes on like this, I'll make an end to it in October. I can bear no more.*

The trouble was, Murry had found his feet and if the truth were known, he was no longer so abjectly dependant on Katherine. His novel *Still Life* was published by Constable soon after, albeit very like the title, making only £8-10-0; there was also his book on Dostoevsky which appeared in August. Lawrence did not like *Still Life: merely words, words. It is the kind of wriggling self-abuse which I can't make head or tail of,* he told Kot and for good measure: *Murry is a small stinker . . . a little muckspout . . . . I don't like him any more . . . .*

To Campbell he also enlarged on the new novel. He thought that Murry was not a creative artist but a clever rearranger of ideas but wanted to be on a par with great writers like Tolstoy and Dostoevsky by identifying with them.

Katherine shut up Sunnyside Cottage, leaving the manuscripts of *The Aloe* and bits of furniture. Mylor was really at an end. Regretting her 'horrid letter' she joined Murry at Garsington on August 26th. There they met Aldous Huxley, Dorothy Brett, J.M. Keynes and Clive Bell. Brett remembered her first meeting with Katherine at Garsington. Having heard of her 'reputation of brilliancy, of a sort of ironic ruthlessness towards the small minds', Brett felt apprehensive as she awaited Katherine's arrival in the red room. Katherine, wearing black and white, was very guarded. In the afternoon, all walked to the old monastery on the estate to see the newly painted frescoes there and each, amid giggling, painted some more. In the evening Katherine sang to her guitar in a 'low whispering voice'. *Later Katherine came to my room. She asked me to be her friend. We made a secret pact of friendship . . . . The following day I watched Katherine holding her own with what we called the Bloomsburies.* She described Katherine thus — *her features were small and delicate, the eyes dark in a pale clear skin, beautiful even white teeth and her polished black hair rolled on top of her head in a sort of fan shape. The fringe brushed smoothly down over a forehead that bulged at the top then straightening down to the dark eyebrows . . . her changes of mood were rapid and disconcerting, a laughing joyous moment would suddenly turn through some . . . . remark into biting anger . . . Katherine had a tongue like a knife . . . She could be cruel. She had no tolerance of the stupid . . . .*

Returning to London Katherine stayed at Brett's studio, 4, Logan Place, Earl's Court. Murry had to go to a cheap hotel as Brett had only one bed. Brett, arriving at Garsington in July, was still there three years later! Ottoline thought her 'a shy squirrel' but liked her companionship, especially her witty, comic observations about guests, and both gossiped happily together during the quiet moments.

Sir Harold Beauchamp [*1925*].

52, Carlton Hill, St John's Wood.

The site of the former Casetta Deerholm, Ospedaletti.

Villa Pauline, Bandol.

Villa Pauline, Bandol.

Annie Burnell Beauchamp [*née Dyer*].

Charlotte Mary Pickthall, 'Chaddie'.

Katherine Mansfield [1913].

Jeanne Worthington Renshaw [née Beauchamp].

'The Elephant' with its plaque.

Katherine's sitting room was on the first floor, at the back.

Villa Isola Bella.

Villa Louise

John Middleton Murry [*1918*].

Katherine Mansfield [*1917*]
'*By permission of the British Library*'.

Diary

of

Jean Beauchamp.

we got out
at Liverpool
street and
jumped on a
Omnibus and
drove all over
the town and
had a lovely
time I think.
London is just

Extracts from the Niwaru *Diary.*

wonderful it is wonderfully big, we hag out the bus and went to M͞r͞s Norths and went in and a dear old women came to the door and ~~to~~ showed us children at home I was awfuly Niwar sick and wanted to go back lady. next morning we went to see M͞r and M͞r͞s Pain they were very jolly and well all the children

Extracts from the **Niwaru** *Diary.*

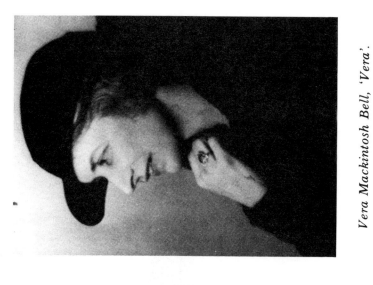

Vera Mackintosh Bell, 'Vera'.

Leslie Heron Beauchamp, 'Chummie'.

Katherine Mansfield and John Middleton Murry [1913].

Hôtel Château Belle View, Sierre.

Hôtel Victoria, Montana.

Ida Constance Baker, 'L.M.' [1976].

Katherine Mansfield [*1920*].

Chapter XIII

Garsington

The Café Royal in Regent Street, today so sophisticated, was quite different in 1916. It was a café-restaurant with a French atmosphere, mirrored walls, marble-topped tables, red plush seats, brilliant gilded decoration, and sawdust on the floor. It was open all day from 10.00 a.m. when breakfast commenced. Coffee was served in glasses and chips were sixpence a plate. A selection of daily newspapers was provided. Customers moved about from table to table, chatting with friends. It was a meeting place for artists, writers and would-be Bohemians. Among the regulars were Augustus John, in a broad-brimmed black hat, cloak and colourful neckerchief, models like Euphemia Lamb, Lilian Shelley, and Betty May. Miss May, a cocaine sniffer, having danced the night away at the Crabtree in Greek Street, would take a bath in someone's apartment and settle happily to breakfast with the papers. It was a spiritual home for many. There were other groups of course, British Museum types, well-heeled gangsters and society butterflies like Nancy Cunard, and Iris Tree. Frank Harris, Enid Bagnold, Bosie, the threesome, Cecil Gray, Van Dieren and Philip Heseltine were often there, so were D.H. Lawrence & Co. In fact, everyone who was anyone went there to watch the merry-go-round and perhaps drink cloudy absinthe or *crème de menthe frappé* through a straw, no doubt imagining they could see Toulouse Lautrec poised in sketching.

On the evening of Wednesday August 30th, Katherine, Kot and Gertler arrived there, having to share a table with an Indian law student, H.S. Suhrawardy, whom they did not know, but who recognised Gertler from Garsington. The

Indian was joined by a *long thin white herring of a woman with a terrific high bunch of crimson hair* and another coloured man, so wrote Gertler the next day to Ottoline. They began discussing Dostoevsky, the *New Age* and Lawrence's new book of poems *Amores*, which the woman had produced. Discussion must have changed to ridicule because Katherine, valiant but terrified, leaned forward and said, "Will you let me have that book a moment?" Then she walked out with it, followed by Kot and Gertler, leaving the amazed trio with rapidly ruffling feathers.

Kot immediately wrote about it to Lawrence, who answered on September 4th expressing a horror of the whole London scene.

Alas, after a visit from Frieda on September 16th, Kot broke off relations with the Murrys for two years. Apparently she told him something about Murry, Kot was always critical of him and very much Katherine's champion. It involved lies and jealousy; perhaps Murry felt Kot was a rival and an instigator of insurrections. Anyway Frieda told him in a letter on September 20th: *Don't be so miserable . . . Nobody could or would believe such small things of you. I think we had no true proportion last night. We both felt so bitter . . . You see, Jack has a terribly jealous nature. He was jealous of Katherine, pretended like the sneak that he is to be your friend, and his hate worked underneath all the time. There is a very great cowardice in Jack, I still feel very bitter about them both . . . . I feel Lawrence is their only moral support, he wrote to Jack: 'You Jack, are a little phenomenon of meanness' . . . there is so much that is good in them, must one not fight their dishonesty?. . . Her duplicity is . . . . a small part in Katherine, but if I love her I will hate her lies all the more . . .*

On October 4th: *. . . I hope you and Katherine will be friends again, you see she really loves Murry and then also she plays other people against him . . . She must become simple . . . But I do love her, if she tells lies, she also knows more about truth than other people and don't let us see too much the ugly things . . .*

And on October 15th: *. . . As Katherine does not write to me, I believe you must have told Jack what I said . . . They are as mean as they can be to everybody, then they turn round and* *say: 'Aren't people vile?' . . . Wherever they have been, they have turned people against me, tried to regard me as a quantité négligeable . . . they have done me infinitely more harm than I did to them . . . .*

Lawrence, testy in the background, wrote to Katherine on September 27th: *You said I insulted you in my letter — well I didn't . . . I can only say . . . there is a death to die for us all . . . .* and to Jack on October 11th: *. . . . what I hate in you is an old you that corresponds to an old me, which must pass away, the beastly thing — one day — we shall come together again . . . .*

To Kot on November 7th: *I have done with the Murrys, both, for ever . . . . so I have with Lady Ottoline and all the rest. Now I am glad and free . . . .* Lawrence was having a clean-out and on November 20th: *Today I have sent off the MS. of my new novel "Women in Love" . . . .I think it is a great book . . . .* The Lawrences and the Murrys did not meet again for two years.

On Thursday September 7th Katherine was at Garsington sharing a room with Carrington. Murry had started work at M.I.7 on the Monday. Carrington, born 1893 at Hereford, was the fourth child of a family of five, daughter of a railway builder for the East India Company. She was brought up in Bedford. Deeply attached to her father, she was critical of her mother, and found she did not like being female. She was in fact bisexual. At seventeen, after showing artistic ability, she was sent to the Slade School of Art, where she won prizes and a scholarship. Her Slade friends included Stanley Spencer, Paul and John Nash, Dorothy Brett and Gertler, who fell in love with her and proposed marriage in 1912. Her underlying bisexuality, really almost incomprehensible to both, caused much mutual anguish. Finally, incredibly, but not inexplicably, and in an instant, she fell in love with Lytton Strachey, after playfully preparing to cut his beard off as he lay in bed at Asheham, where they were guests of Leonard and Virginia Woolf in the autumn of 1915. This deep pathological bonding to a sort of father-type, lasted until Lytton's death in 1932 when, unable to face life without him, Carrington shot herself and died a few hours later from kidney bleeding.

Leonard Woolf, describing her, said: *she had a head of the thickest yellow hair I have ever seen, and as it was cut short round the bottom of the neck, it stood like a solid, perfectly grown and clipped yew hedge. She had the roundest, softest, pinkest damask cheeks and large china blue eyes through which one was disconcerted to glimpse an innocence which one could not possibly believe to exist this side of the Garden of Eden . . . .*

Ottoline, in her memoirs, described Carrington thus: *Fat lumpy face, a mop of fair sunburnt hair, elusive wandering blue eyes which rarely looked at one except when she wished to captivate and then she would look up like a child, with an odd uncertain rather furtive smile.* She was very attractive and a fine painter.

Writing to Gertler, Carrington described this visit to Garsington: *I went out into the garden. Katherine (Mansfield) and I wore trousers. It was wonderful being alone in the garden. Hearing the music inside and lighted windows, and feeling like two young boys — very eager . . . How I hate being a girl. I must tell you for I have felt it so much lately more than usual. And that night forgot for almost half an hour in the garden. And felt other pleasures, strange, and so exciting, a feeling of all the world being below me to choose from. Not tied — with female encumbrances and hanging flesh.*

To Lytton Strachey Carrington wrote, as from Shandygaff Hall (Garsington): *. . . Never have I seen the garden look so wonderful. A moon shining on the pond, covered with warm slime, bubbling and fermenting underneath and great black shadows cast from the trees over it all. And inside, music and these strange villagers with their babies, and young men in hard white collars and thick serge suits . . . Maria in her yellow trowsers (sic) lying covered in a black cloak in the passage,* distractedly *in* love with Ottoline. *We acted a play. Katherine sang some songs and danced ragtimes. We talked late into the night together after it was all over in bed . . . what fun we will have in Gower Street. She (Katherine) will play all the games I love best. Pretending to be other people and dressing up and parties!* Katherine had given her the snatched *Amores.*

Carrington was arranging to take over Maynard Keyne's house in 3, Gower Street for nine months, while he and J.T. Sheppard moved to Clive Bell's — Bell, as a conscientious

objector, was staying at Garsington. The rent was £27-10-0 per
year, Katherine and Murry were to occupy the ground floor,
Brett the second, and Carrington the attics at a rent of £9 a
year. Miss Chapman, 'Chappers', the housekeeper was to
occupy the basement. Katherine was now in Bloomsbury! They
all moved in on September 29th. The house was nicknamed
'The Ark'.

Murry, working very hard in M.I.7 to overcome his lack of
experience in translating German, found himself worked into
the ground. His only relief was escape to Garsington where he
came under the influence of Ottoline. By September 22nd he
was telling her in a letter that he suspected he was in love with
her.

Creating further erotic atmospheres Ottoline, with a
lantern, illuminated an improvised ballet danced on the lawn
by Gertler, David Garnett, Carrington, Brett and Murry.
Shortly after, unsuspecting Katherine returned to London,
leaving Murry behind; presumably he was having a few days'
holiday. After talking a long while with Ottoline about
Lawrence, Murry, according to Ottoline's memoirs, suddenly
asked her if 'he might come into her heart'. Later, when
walking in the garden, Ottoline called up to his lighted
window inviting him to join her in the garden, where they did
some more talking. He returned home the next day, then
silence ensued. Later he turned down an offer of a cottage at
Garsington. In the meantime, Katherine's letters to Ottoline
were chilly. Finally, Brett told Ottoline that Katherine was
angry with her. When in London, Ottoline visited 3, Gower
Street, and Katherine accused her of trying to entice Murry
from her. It seems on his return from Garsington, Murry had
collapsed on to the sofa saying that Ottoline was in love with
him. Whatever guilt he was feeling he continued to correspond
with her. Clive Bell wrote to Vanessa in December 1916:
*Ottoline is trying to get up an affair with Murry. She writes to
him and he leaves her letters about.* Murry was having a
difficult time. He told Ottoline he did not like living at The
Ark. His partial withdrawal from Katherine which had started
in Cornwall was still with him and was to get worse as he
became more self-absorbed and isolated, even to the point of
feeling nihilistic, an extension of his old youthful feelings of

unreality. Katherine was feeling little better. She was not working, there are only two brief notes in her notebook for the period November 1916 to May 1917, complaining of interruption from window-cleaners and inability to write.

Brett wrote daily to Ottoline recounting happenings and mentioning all callers, strangely, Lytton Strachey and Bertrand Russell. Brett admitted she kept her hearing aid 'trained to the cracks in the floor'. On November 2nd Brett, in answer to Ottoline, who had enclosed a letter from Katherine explaining that she had not written for so long because she was wretched, decided that Katherine must be *in love . . . . she is torn in two I believe — pity for the shy gentle clinging man she lives with and the passionate desire for freedom — new life, new faces . . . I long . . . . to tell her that I understand, but I can't yet . . . .* Brett probably believed that Katherine was in love with Bertrand Russell.

Much has been written about the friendship between Russell and Katherine, with suggestions that she was in love with him, that this could be deduced from the letters she wrote. None of these, to my mind, seem like the letters Katherine would write if she were in love. I think she would be flattered by Russell's interest in her work. They must have been discussing *The Aloe* because in a letter to him dated December 1st she said: *I have written to my little maid in Cornwall to send me the MSS.* Indeed, she sent it to him some time later in December, with a letter saying: *God! I have been unhappy today — in despair and walking idly over a dreadful world, having no landing place and no cover —* hardly a love-letter; and again: *I should have to be far away from this house to write freely; it depresses me horribly today.*

Russell at this time, and unbeknown to Ottoline, was in the midst of a passionate affair with Lady Constance Malleson, expressing longing for Ottoline's companionship in a letter, but also telling her that Katherine interested him mentally, that she had a very good mind but not much heart. Katherine's heart was not engaged, it was being eroded by Murry who was unhappy, Russell noted, when he dined with him at The Ark. Much was to do with his job. Murry had to read piles of German newspapers and write a political report. This was a most arduous task as his German was still a little shaky.

Collecting Katherine's letters together for posterity in 1949, Russell added a note to say there was no 'affair' nor going to be. At that distance from events there was no need to lie about it, in any case, truth was important to Russell, like telling Ottoline it was a pity her hair was going grey after telling her of his affair with Lady Malleson! One feels too that his opinion of Katherine was the truth, as he saw it: *it was at this time that I got to know her well. I do not know whether my impression of her was just . . . . but when she spoke about people she was envious, dark, and full of alarming penetration in discovering what they least wished known and whatever was bad in their characteristics. She hated Ottoline because Murry did not. It had become clear to me that I must get over the feeling that I had for Ottoline, as she no longer returned it sufficiently to give me any happiness. I listened to all that Katherine Mansfield had to say against her; in the end I believed very little of it.* (Russell's autobiography.) The note with the letter ran: *My feelings for her were ambivalent. I admired her passionately, but was repelled by her dark hatreds.*

About the time Katherine moved into The Ark, L.M. came home from Rhodesia with her father. She, no doubt jubilant, was met by Katherine and eventually saw the new abode in 3, Gower Street which she did not like much, especially the atmosphere, for there was a deal of spying going on from Brett for obvious reasons and Carrington, especially if Lytton paid visits and failed to go up to her attic. Ottoline also reckoned that Carrington spied on Katherine, watching her comings and goings, even saying that Katherine went out in disguise at night looking for exciting adventures.

L.M. went to stay with her friend from childhood days, Dolly Sutton, who lived in Chiswick, and with her help became a tool-setter in an aeroplane factory there, after a course in metalwork. Her supervisor and friend was Mr Gwynne, and her fellow workers included Stella Drummond, later Lady Eustace Percy, as tall as L.M. (about 6 feet) and Lady Mary Hamilton. Katherine found lodgings for her in Hampstead with a most kindly landlady, Mrs Butterworth, who saw to it that L.M., after a long and arduous day, came back to a good fire and meal. There are no comments on L.M.'s return in Katherine's journal and perhaps a faint nostalgia for the independence of youthful days influenced her later decision to part temporarily from Murry. L.M. thought Katherine was restless and seemed to want to be on her own. She knew too that Katherine felt stifled in The Ark.

Christmas 1916 drew near, and Katherine and Murry were invited to Garsington, the last carefree Christmas she was to know. The guests were to be Russell, Strachey, Clive Bell and Aldous Huxley who was already in residence, Marie Nys, Brett and Carrington. Ottoline had reservations about asking Carrington, who felt Ottoline had turned against her — quite true. This was due to jealousy over Carrington's regard for Lytton. One had only to watch Ottoline and Strachey playing tennis and listen to their girlish squeaks, to know how compatible they were. Lytton would also try on her shoes and strut about her bedroom. However, Ottoline relented and by Saturday December 23rd all were assembled. Brett, extracting every drop of happiness from the situation, had gone there the previous Wednesday.

Murry had arrived without presents; let us hope that Katherine had not. Carrington took long walks with Lytton on Christmas Eve, attending evensong to hear the Bishop of Oxford preach. Katherine was busy writing a play to be enacted on Boxing Day. Seven small sheets in pencil from her notebook survive in Wellington today. Meanwhile, Murry frantically concocted two Xmas billets-doux on Garsington notepaper, couched in terms reckoned to stun the receiver temporarily, so that they were unaware of the lack of a present.

To Ottoline he wrote: *Tomorrow I shall be the only wedding guest without a wedding garment: I who so deeply admire and so truly love you shall have no gift for you . . . .* He thought their love would never die. The note for Brett, whose Christmas was probably made by it, read: *This is my Christmas present — only what I am writing now — nothing more. And this is only to say that you are a darling, and that I hope we shall always be in the same house for Christmas until — forever — if every Christmas Eve you will either kiss me or let yourself be kissed by me.* One cannot help feeling sorry for him.

On Christmas Day, while others tramped about the fields

enjoying themselves, poor Katherine laboured at her play called *The Laurels*, quite a feat really. Lytton, in a big fur coat and a red worsted beard made by Carrington, was to be a grandfather called Dr Keit, Murry as Ivan Tchek was the lodger, he was a very good actor, Katherine as Florence Kaziany was Keit's daughter, with Carrington her illegitimate child. For once Tchek the lodger was not the guilty party; Aldous Huxley as Balliol Dodd probably was — we will never know. On the evening of Christmas Day, Lytton read his essay on Dr Arnold which was to be dished up eventually in *Eminent Victorians*. One evening Russell and Katherine sat talking well past midnight in the red room beneath Ottoline's bedroom. They had obviously discussed Ottoline at length because they looked so guilty when she commented on it, jokingly saying she could hear what had been said.

The day after Boxing Day and its no doubt uproarious evening, the guests departed, and a delayed Xmas present arrived for Ottoline, with a force of a torpedo and almost as lethal. It was the manuscript of *Women in Love*. Hermione Roddice, a caricature of Ottoline, left her deeply wounded, describing her as 'macabre, something repulsive . . . demonic woman, possessed by hatred and envy' — 'tall and rather terrible, ghastly', her dresses 'shabby and soiled, even rather dirty'. This book *written by someone whom I had trusted and liked haunted my thoughts and horrified me*, she wrote in her memoirs. She showed it to Aldous who also was 'horrified'. However, he was to do the same to Ottoline in his book *Crome Yellow*. These 'flannelled fools' enjoying Garsington to the full, seemed to have a blind spot about this sort of thing. Ottoline was so colourful and unusual a person, she could not easily be disguised in another character, 'warts and all', without a rumpus. Lawrence was in disfavour for a very long time — in fact, he never got back to Garsington again; pitiable, for I doubt whether he meant any real harm. Ottoline returned the MS and threatened Lawrence's agent with libel. *Women in Love* was not published until May 1921.

On January 12th the Murrys dined with Virginia Woolf. Another guest was Sydney Waterlow, Katherine's second cousin and brilliant son of Chaddie, sister of Elizabeth von Arnim. He had at one time pursued Virginia Woolf who thought him boring. Virginia had wanted to meet Katherine who had 'dogged her steps for three years' she wrote to Lytton on July 25th, 1916. In February she told Vanessa: *I have had a slight rapprochement with Katherine Mansfield who seems to be an unpleasant but forcible and utterly unscrupulous character, in whom I think you might find a 'companion',* and again on April 26th: *I am going to see Katherine Mansfield, to get a story from her, perhaps.* Leonard Woolf was planning to set up a printing press at his home, Hogarth House, Richmond. This would be tremendously interesting to Katherine, who was polishing *Prelude* for them. By June 27th Virginia was telling Vanessa: *I had an odd talk with Katherine Mansfield last night. She seems to have gone every sort of hog since she was 17, which is interesting; I also think she has a much better idea of writing than most. She's an odd character — admired what she could see of you of course.* By July 26th, it was agreed that they would print *Prelude*, which process began on November 13th, 1917. *It's very good I think,* wrote Virginia.

On her return to London, Katherine had arranged to see Russell, writing to him thus: *Sunday — January 1917 . . . I, too am looking forward to Tuesday. I have heard from Ottoline, she comes to town tomorrow for one or two days. I expect she will want very much to see you. I shall be the soul of discretion . . . I hope to move at the end of next week, but my cough is so disastrous in this kkaki weather that I can hardly conceive of leaving Gower Street except feet foremost . . . .*

Katherine had been looking for accommodation at Murry's instigation, who felt with a regular salary they could afford somewhere more self-contained. She wrote him a letter about her progress saying she was 'awfully tired and exhausted — not physically but mentally' and went on: *I draw back and shiver. Do you remember . . . All those houses, All those flats . . . we have taken and withdrawn from . . .? Let us . . . think of some other solution . . . My one overwhelming feeling is that we both must be free to write this year . . . our full life together must mark time for that . . . you know I love you.* Katherine in turn was withdrawing from Murry, alas. She had found a studio in Church Street, Chelsea. Murry took two dingy rooms nearby at 47, Redcliffe Road, Fulham. Though a depressing address then, the asking price in August 1982 for one of these houses in Redcliffe Road was £140,000!

On January 22nd she apologized by letter to Russell for sending a telegram, obviously cancelling their appointment, saying: *my cough is so vile that I'll not inflict it on others. I must try and cure it before it lays me quite too finally low . . . I want to move at the end of this week . . . if only it were not so cold and one did not cough so.*

Carrington, writing to Lytton on Saturday February 10th, described finding Katherine *in a sad plight yesterday sitting fully dressed in outdoor clothes on a bed, with a gas fire roaring in a tiny room, remains of 12 days meals for she hadn't left the room for that number of days! Her face was pale grey with deep red rims round her eyes. She admitted all the females in the houses were now raving lunatics and she likewise insane.*

Katherine moved to her studio during the next week. It seems to me that she had been quite ill for over three weeks, and it is possible that her tuberculosis, which was not diagnosed until December 1917 and was certainly too advanced for so short a history then, may have worsened that January or even before. Unaware, Lawrence was writing to Kot on February 9th: *The Ott, the Murries (sic) they are gone into the ground. Only for poor Katherine and her lies I feel rather sorry. They are such self-responsible lies. But then pity is worse than useless.*

L.M. was able to visit Katherine in her studio with its large window set high up, with a gallery overlooking the big main room at floor level in a sort of well. The kitchen was situated off the balcony, a bedroom was curtained off from the main room. J.D. Fergusson had a studio in the same street. There was a communal leafy garden.

After a long hard day at work, L.M. visiting Katherine, sometimes had problems in getting back to Hampstead. One night she had to join the down-and-outs in the crypt of St. Martin-in-the-Fields, behind the confines of the friendly substantial rope there. Inevitably she gave up her rooms and joined Katherine, staying out conveniently when Murry visited for his evening meal.

Katherine had begun to work. Orage was having problems

with the *New Age* because his writers were on active service.
He asked old friends for contributions, and Katherine obliged.
Between April and June she had nine pieces published:

Pastiche
Two Tuppeny Ones May 3rd, 1917
Please
Late at night May 10th, 1917
The Black Cap May 17th, 1917
In Confidence (uncollected) May 24th, 1917
The Common Round May 31st, 1917 (Later re-shaped and
    published in *Art and Letters as Pictures.*)
A Pic-Nic (uncollected) June 7th, 1917
Mr Reginald Peacock's Day June 14th, 1917
In September her translation of *M. Séguin's Goat* by Daudet
    September 6th, 1917 (uncollected)
In October — *An Album Leaf* September 20th, 1917
The Dill Pickle October 4th, 1917

Finally she finished revising *Prelude* and sent it to Leonard
and Virginia Woolf in September. The new name *Prelude* had
been suggested by Murry. Considering her emotional
dependence on Murry, her decision to live alone seems almost
pathological but it was a measure of the chill wind blowing in
their relationship, which was also reflected in her turning to
work for relief. It is likely too that her association with Russell
and their exchange of ideas had stimulated her writing vein.
    Mindful of Katherine's attitude to L.M., having her to stay
also suggests that living alone then was a problem. The
aftermath of illness and the emotional insecurity engendered
by the break-down in her relation with Murry had renewed her
old night-terrors. She was having panic attacks, walking the
streets until three in the morning to alleviate the anxiety.
When L.M. was away for three weeks in June, to look after her
sick sister just home from Africa, Katherine admitted she had
suffered greatly. On May 19th, during a temporary absence of
Murry, she ran for mental shelter to his rooms in Redcliffe
Road. She had had a panic attack as daylight faded.
    That spring of 1917 was unhappy for many in that bright
galaxy. Ottoline, a firefly skimming about from knight to

knight, had discovered that two could play the same game. Philip, about whom she had proclaimed, "I love Philip always, always without ending," had been unfaithful. Ottoline was devastated. Lytton, visiting Garsington on 21st February, 1917, told Virginia Woolf, *"Lady Omega Muddle is now I think almost at the last gasp — infinitely old, depressed, and bad-tempered — she is soon to sink into a nursing home . . ."* This she did. Phillip, as nice people often do in these circumstances, collapsed into his own guilt-ridden breakdown.

The Cannans marriage was also breaking up, basically due to the inexorable march of Gilbert's future florid, psychotic illness. Lawrence wrote a poignant letter to Mary after the final dissolution of her marriage, remembering the Cholesbury days and their evenings together mid the aroma of sage and onions cooking.

Lawrence was feeling very sore over *Women in Love.* He abreacted to Kot, regretting having exposed himself to all the rabble.

Murry's condition was worsening too — he felt that spring he was near to madness. He immersed himself in the whirlpool of work, burning the midnight oil. Life and love with Katherine was becoming meaningless, which state he had to keep from her.

He met up with J.W.N. Sullivan who had told Dan Rider he admired Murry's book on Dostoevsky and wished to meet him. As a result, Sullivan was taken on in M.I.7 to translate German and the isolated Murry unburdened himself to his new friend over stodgy afternoon teas in a Villiers street café. Sullivan was ambivalent towards Murry, but admitted that he could feel very close to him at times especially as they discussed Dostoevsky, when Murry, gazing at the ceiling would utter some strange remark like 'the inhuman is the highest form of the human.' It is obvious that Murry was repeating his Gordon sessions, while Katherine, of necessity, was again on the wing.

Ottoline asked Katherine to Garsington for Easter. It is interesting to note that she turned the invitation down, pleading pressure of work. However when Ottoline came up to London in May, she dined with them, and went with Katherine to a Balalaika Concert at the Grafton Galleries. They parted with Katherine's oft-repeated remark, "My corns are hurting, I must go to my old corncutter tomorrow. Good night darling."

Early in July Ottoline contracted measles from her daughter Julian, after which she had to convalesce in the Isle of Wight. On July 31st Katherine, who was complaining of 'rheumatism', saw her doctor who 'thumped and banged' her. Obviously he had been examining her chest. She told Virginia that she had been 'so ill . . . rheumatics plus ghastly depression plus fury'. In a letter about August 10th, 1917 she commiserated with Ottoline on her having had the measles, envying her convalescence by the sea and describing her longing for 'that wild untamed water that beats about my own forlorn island'. On a more cheerful note she described a sight of Augustus John at a show at Margaret Morris's theatre, 'with two very worn and *chipped* ladies', looking like a character out of *Crime and Punishment*.

Some time before August 11th Katherine went down to Garsington. Murry had asked Ottoline if she could find a place on the farm for his brother Richard. Presumably they both travelled down together, followed by Katherine. It was a happy visit, with dry sunny weather, the garden blooming with white phlox, zinnias, sunflowers and snapdragons. Ottoline thought Katherine seemed to be 'in a very happy mood . . . she was much simpler and seemed to trust me more'. Illness often simplifies a personality, and Katherine was far from well. They cut the ripe lavender and carried the sweet-smelling bundles into the house. Sweet geranium, verbena and rose petals were collected by the basketful for pot-pourri.

Writing to Ottoline on August 11th, thanking her, she remembered *the blue spears of lavender . . . you in your room, and your bed with the big white pillow and you coming down in the garden swinging the gay lantern . . . . Ever since I came back . . . I have been . . . working. It is the only life I care about . . .* and on August 15th: *. . . . who is going to write about that flower garden . . . There would be people walking in the garden . . . an exquisite haunting scent . . . conversation set to flowers . . . .* and she wrote the poem 'Night-Scented Stock' in memory of that garden in all its summer finery.

Night-Scented Stock

White, white in the milky night
The moon danced over the tree.
"Wouldn't it be lovely to swim in the lake!"
Someone whispered to me.

"Oh, do-do-do!" cooed someone else,
And clasped her hands to her chin.
"I should so love to see the white bodies —
All the white bodies jump in!"

The big dark house hid secretly
Behind the magnolia and the sparkling pear-tree,
But there was a sound of music — music rippled and ran
Like a lady laughing behind her fan,
Laughing and mocking and running away . . .
"Come into the garden — it's as light as day!"

Lawrence had begun to write to Katherine again and she told
Ottoline she was so fond of him that she couldn't and never
would shut her heart against him.

On Saturday August 18th, Katherine went to Asheham with
her typescript of *Prelude* to stay with Virginia, who met the
train at Lewes. The other guests were Lytton, Edward and
David Garnett. Asheham was a beautiful house standing alone
on the side of the Downs, about four miles from Lewes. It was
surrounded by trees and from the lovely floor-length Gothic
arched windows one could see for miles. It was lit by lamp and
candle, water was pumped into an inside tank daily, there was
an earth closet; but how beautiful the house looked! According
to Leonard, who liked Katherine but thought she disliked him,
they spent an 'uneasy' weekend in spite of her making him
really laugh with descriptions of her exploits on tour with
Garnet and the like, told it seems with a dead pan expression.
By nature he thought 'she was gay, cynical, amoral, ribald,
witty'. Katherine for her part thought Leonard 'so extremely
worthy, but I find him terribly flattening', so she told Ottoline.

The air was full of fine thistledown, blown about by a high, warm south-east wind. Men and women in the fields were working late, cutting the ripened corn by hand. While Lytton walked over to Charleston on the Tuesday to see Vanessa, whom Sydney Waterlow, who had rented Asheham earlier in the war, thought 'icy, cynical, artistic', Virginia and Katherine walked the 'Mongoose's walk', Mongoose being an endearment for Leonard. The track ran up behind the house to the top of the Down, with its heather and distant view of Lewes. One wonders how the conversation went. On Wednesday, another hot and windy day, Katherine left after lunch, travelling by fly from the Ram, an inn in Firle.

Writing to thank Virginia, Katherine thought Asheham was *very wonderful . . . It was good to have time to talk to you; we have got the same job, Virginia, and it is really very curious and thrilling that we should both, quite apart from each other, be after so very nearly the same thing.* Incidentally, Virginia, with her one and only novel *The Voyage Out*, had recently written two short stories, *The Mark on the Wall* and *Kew Gardens,* rather resembling Katherine's original idea to Ottoline about conversation being set to flowers in the garden at Garsington.

In September Murry had a week's holiday and Katherine seems to have enjoyed the golden days with him. Gertler, more or less a permanency at Garsington, wrote to Carrington about his life there with the ministrations of Brett, washing his hair and scrubbing his back in the bath. Murry had been a guest, *"A String in the Wind"* — *shifty, backboneless, fearful, ill, but rather nice and pathetic. Of course Asquith alights and his family . . . Elizabeth is awful . . . If you only knew how sick I am of the talk, talk, talk* — as for the *"Bloomsburians",* the *very sound of that word makes me sick . . . .* Elizabeth was Asquith's daughter; more of her later.

At Garsington, talk started in force at breakfast, and continued throughout the day in the garden, by the pool, on the terrace on warm evenings, around a log fire in the red room if chilly. At bedtime each guest, waving a candle in a silver candlestick, would slowly climb the oak staircase still talking, ultimately wandering off to their rooms, or following

Ott into her bedroom for more 'haircombing' by her fire; it sounds nice. Katherine would do her share of talking. Ottoline thought Aldous enjoyed Katherine's conversation but believed she thought him 'young and gullible; she was irritated and bored by his naïve stories and was very spiteful behind his back'. She didn't care for his Victorian laugh either.

On October 5th Virginia returned to Richmond, after three months at Asheham. She unearthed an old 1915 diary and began writing in it. It was to be 'written after tea, written indiscreetly'. The entry for October 9th ran: . . . *we took a proof of the first page of K.M.'s story The Prelude. It looks very nice.* It was to take a further nine months to print. On October 10th Virginia invited Katherine to dinner. An account appeared in her diary on Thursday October 11th. This oft-quoted entry about Katherine's perfume, compounded of malice and jealousy, will not be repeated here save to say that apropos of Leonard's interpretation, civet cats being thin on the ground, their essence is likely to go to the making of very expensive perfume indeed. Katherine's perfume was French, called Genêt Fleuri, gorse-blossom. I asked L.M. what it smelt like and with a smile she said she couldn't remember.

On October 11th Katherine wrote a long letter to Brett, with only a brief reference to the previous evening:

. . . . *I threw my darling to the wolves (Prelude) and they ate it and served me up so much praise in such a golden bowl that I couldn't help feeling gratified. I did not think they would like it at all and I am still astounded that they do . . . .*

In early November Murry, worked into the ground and neglecting to eat during the day, suddenly became sleepless. It seemed he did nothing about it, lying for hours in a state of beatitude. His weight dropped from 9½ stone to under 8 stone. One morning he found he could barely stand. The doctor, sent for by Katherine, put him on sick leave and considered he might be on the verge of tuberculosis. Resting from slavery, he wrote a poetic 'drama' in four weeks called *Cinnamon and Angelica*, in which each character was given

o

the name of a spice, an amusing and original idea, and perhaps in line with an exhausted brain given the peace of rest.

Katherine wrote to Ottoline asking if Murry might recuperate at Garsington, and as usual, Ottoline kindly obliged. Having seen him off on Saturday November 3rd, Katherine's letter of the 4th expressed relief at his being away from Redcliffe Road with its despised green 1/- bed from Cornwall.

Writing to Virginia and mentioning that Murry was at Garsington, she complained of her rheumatism ramping and raging — *I am so down in the depths that I cannot imagine anything ever fishing me up again.*

One day, in the green drawing-room at Garsington, Murry found Sir Sidney Colvin's *Life of Keats*, a life quite new to him. Reading *The Fall of Hyperion* and coming upon the lines: *Then saw I a wan face Not pin'd by human sorrows but bright-blanch'd By an immortal sickness which kills not* . . . he suddenly felt a special reference to his own condition: then the lines . . . *the sullen rear Was with its stored thunder labouring up* chilled him with foreboding. He had a premonition of disaster.

I doubt whether this reaction would have occurred in a state of health, but now the soil was prepared for the sudden panic, the sudden depressive thought, a frequent aftermath of physical illness, spreading in a sort of forest fire of agitation and melancholy. He wrote of this experience in his autobiography, with hindsight; but so deep was his feeling then, he later wrote a book on Keats, identifying with him, enshrining him, ingesting him as it were, even championing him in print, after a later biographer cast aspersions on Keats which Murry could not accept of his hero.

Ottoline in her memoirs remembered this period. In the red room after dinner . . . *Murry was talking in his vague meandering way about the beauty and neccessity of poverty and unhappiness in life . . . . the only life that was valuable was that of inner experience, which needed this outward irritant of disquiet and unhappiness as the pearl needs the grain of grit in the shell . . . I see Aldous now getting up in indignation . . . saying, "This is awful. It is disgusting" and going off in anger to his room . . . .* Aldous Huxley never did seem to like Murry and caricatured him brutally in his book *Point Counter Point*, also Katherine in *Those Barren Leaves*. One wonders why he had this fund of enmity within him. Probably the certain contempt that the Murrys felt for him showed at times.

After a fortnight Katherine joined Murry for the weekend. As she alighted from the high dog-cart she complained of feeling very cold. She stayed in bed all the next day in the attic room, Murry reading his play to her. Both agreed that they should no longer live apart, Katherine deciding to give up her studio and live in rooms next door to Murry. Alas, it was too late! Back in Chelsea a few days later, she wrote Murry that she had pleurisy and her doctor had put her to bed for a week.

On December 11th she had a visit from Aldous. L.M., quiet as a mouse behind the curtain on the balcony, was run to ground by Katherine shouting to her, much to Huxley's surprise. Ottoline kindly visited too, as did Fergusson, who was busy drawing an illustration for *Prelude*. She complained to Murry on December 13th that she was sleepless and excited. She was being visited by Chaddie and Aunt Belle, who filled the larder with food. L.M., disconsolate, was doing all she could, trying to make Katherine drink hot milk instead of Oxo, for instance. Murry, now 2lb. heavier, paid a second visit and found Katherine not really improving. She was feverish and had lost weight. Indeed he had never seen her so ill. He was very alarmed.

She told Anne Rice in Looe on December 22nd that her left lung was strapped up in plaster because of dry pleurisy, 'an old complaint', and that she was up but feeling like a 'gash balloon', the doctor having given her a certificate for convalescence in the South of France. . . . *But talk about the knock-out blow — I've had it!* He had told Katherine that her pleuritic left lung was 'better' but there was a 'spot' in her right lung — rather a serious one which required wintering abroad. He forbade her to travel to Garsington.

Dont mention Lungs, she told Murry, commissioning him to reserve her a room in the Hôtel Beau Rivage, Bandol. *They'd imagine I had come there to gallop away.* Practical and courageous, she had to admit that life had changed and she wished they could have married before she left. Murry was very downcast.

Katherine spent a quiet Christmas, sleepy and languid. Ottoline had sent her a beautiful pink silk eiderdown; typically, Murry's present of a jacket had not arrived. Aunt Belle sent an apple-green padded silk dressing gown, alas too commodious, and L.M.'s present was an expensive petticoat, the colour of 'raspberries and currants'. Sullivan, on duty at M.I.7, spent part of the day with Katherine, making up the fire and entertaining her over a bottle of wine; but her weakness seemed compounded by black irritability.

Murry returned to London in the New Year. Though deeply anxious over Katherine, he was now well physically. Misguidedly they both went to Harvey Nichols' to change the green dressing gown. Katherine was excited about going to Bandol and seemed happy. Looking back, Murry felt she might have recovered but for this formidable journey to France. Such activity would make her worse at that time; but the die was cast. Only our present day drugs and complete rest might have saved her. It was very serious that both lungs were affected. A lone traveller, she left London on January 7th, 1918 and arrived in Bandol three long days later; Murry could not have gained permission to travel from M.I.7, even if he had wanted to go.

Chapter XIV

Ill in Bandol

Katherine left Southampton in a blizzard at 9.00 p.m. on January 7th. The ship, anchored off Le Havre on a very choppy sea, did not discharge its passengers until thirteen hours later. Resting in a hotel there until 5.00 p.m. she started for Paris in an unheated carriage, with snow drifting through a broken window. The train arrived at 2.00 a.m., five hours late. Fortunately she had reserved a hotel in Paris so she was able to tumble into bed and sleep soundly. It was still snowing, and in deep happiness in spite of everything, she sent off a letter to Murry — . . . . *the spring of my joy is that we belong to each other . . . you are mine, and I am yours for ever,* walking through 'piercing cold' to post it. The streets were wet with slush.

For the overnight journey from Paris to Marseilles there were no friendly pillows; her left lung ached and burned, her feet hurt. It snowed as far as Valence, and then, after sunrise, the lush countryside gave way to the surrounds of Marseilles. Struggling with rugs and luggage she had to stand in a queue to get it registered and have her passport viséd.

Finally settled in the Bandol train with eight Serbian officers, there developed noisy scenes as French soldiers commandeered carriages, throwing out civilian occupants and their luggage. The Serbian officers defended Katherine and their carriage magnificently, and the train finally set off at 7.00 p.m., a six hour delay after such a bad night! She did not see the beautiful blue of the Mediterranean nor the red rocks of Bandol, as she arrived in the darkness at 9.00 p.m.

She fell into bed with hot soup, brandy and a hot water bottle
and into unconsciousness. There is nothing like the sleep which
overtakes one after such an experience.

The next day she found Bandol *as lovely as ever, glittering
with light*, but worn out she admitted to Murry she was lonely
and weak. It was bitterly cold in Bandol, and wearing a
woollen coat and Murry's geranium padded coat, her Xmas
present, with Ottoline's pink eiderdown around her knees, she
was still cold as she sat by the inefficient French fire. She felt ill
but was trying to work.

In the cold grey afternoon she set off to find the Villa
Pauline, sending a poignant account to Murry. As she walked
along the road, she suddenly realized she was suffering —
'terribly, terribly' — as she neared the beloved place. She
stood watching the pink house with its blue shutters, almond
tree and round stone table and thought how beautiful it all
looked. Madame Allègre greeted her but did not recognise her
at first. They sat talking at the table and as Katherine saw her
photograph on the wall, put there by Murry in those far-off
happy days, she 'nearly broke down'. On leaving she leaned on
the wall and watched . . . *the violet sea that beat up, high and
loud, against those strong dark clots of sea-weed . . . it began
to rain. Big soft reluctant drops fell on my hands and face.
The light was flashing through the dusk from the
lighthouse . . . .*

After her long walk, she had a very bad night. The exercise
had sent her temperature up, she sweated and coughed,
longing for morning only to find by her watch it was just 1.15
a.m.

Receiving this letter made Murry distracted. He bitterly
regretted the distance between them. All he could do to keep
their ragged banner flying was to write about the future and
their dream home, 'The Heron' so named after Leslie, a sort of
farmhouse they hoped to have some day.

The next letter was less tragic. She had begun to work a little
in spite of an aching back and devastating cough. She was
resting as much as possible and sleeping better. The pain in
her chest was altering, always a cheering sign. She told Murry
not to send L.M. and went on to complain of the very
well-meaning lady, Madame Geoffroi, who had journeyed to

see her, all the way from Avignon at Murry's behest. She had
met the Murrys in Bandol in 1916. Unfortunately she talked at
great length until Katherine was extremely fatigued, and
could scarcely bear the ache in her left lung.

Receiving Murry's sad letters on January 20th she admitted
she had been very ill. She said she had had a letter from her
mother in New Zealand sending her blessings and including a
recipe for bread, mentioning that after the war she
was going to do the cooking while Mr Beauchamp did all the
washing. They had moved to a new house in Wadestown called
The Grange, a beautiful house made of kauri wood, and both
loved the place, with its huge garden and extensive library
included in the transaction. Katherine's Grandma Beauchamp, had died on November 24th, 1917, the dear old lady
who had hung on Mr Beauchamp's every word, so devoted was
she to her son who had done so well for all of them. That day
Katherine had eleven letters, including a letter from her
doctor. It was nice of him to bother.

The staff were being decent too, the proprietress providing
hot wine for Katherine's cough, the little maid Juliette, *like a
double stock — tufty, strong, very sweet, very gay* bringing her
rosebuds and helping her to wash her hair. She found herself
having to apologize to Murry for writing so tragically, which
was trying. The weather had improved and the sky was like *an
immense Canterbury bell, darkly, transparently blue*. She was
feeling a little better but inevitably she had marked lassitude,
leaning on her pen, barely able to read, brushing her fringe as
a gesture for dinner, too tired to dress up. She noticed to her
consternation that she had gone grey over both temples
during the first few days in Bandol. She also complained of an
excited feeling, especially after working late at night. She alas
caught a hint of depression in Murry's letters — *I live for you
— you have all my love,* she told him.

Terrible to think of the pessimism and the gloom of the
recipient of such beautiful prose. This was a far-cry from those
dreary days at the Ark. Everything was changed by her illness,
all was tinged with this mental radiance, she was feeling so
much nearer her 'Pauline' — writing self.

The war grinding on obsessed her though, and she never felt
free from anxiety, imagining air raids in London, especially if

she did not get letters. In fact she became morbidly upset when the delivery of letters dried up. Like on January 30th, writing her second letter of the day: *I am faint with homesickness. Although it is so goldy warm, the tips of my fingers and my feet and lips and inside my mouth — all are dead cold . . . The road is all glare and my shoes make a noise on it as though it were iron. I feel sick, sick, as though I were bleeding to death. I . . . take out the Daily Mail . . . 'Air Raid in London . . . .'* She feared for Murry's safety. There was no letter the next day. She implored him to wire. She had decided to return in March instead of April. On Friday she got three hastily written epistles from Murry, which haste she remarked on drily in her rather cold reply, mentioning that she had pain over her left shoulder-blade. It is not difficult to guess why she was so diffident; the news from Murry must have sobered and altered her mood. Murry often let his fatigue and disillusion show through his letters, but she told him she had been working at last for the past two days.

On Sunday February 3rd she wrote telling him that the work excited her so much she felt almost insane at night after concentrating on it all day, suffering her old night terrors . . . *God! How tired I am! How I'd love to curl up against you and sleep. — — —*

On February 4th she posted the first part of her story *Je ne parle pas francais* in fear and trembling for its reception. It baffled her, its strangeness, its style seemingly dredged up from nowhere. She was much cheered on Tuesday to receive two happier letters about the Heron. *I am a changed child . . . how these letters have refreshed me!* She found Bandol stimulating mentally and her mind was alive with ideas for her writing. She told Murry she was in a state of work. To her joy a wire came from Murry saying her story was magnificent.

Alas, another telegram arrived too: *Am coming leave this afternoon Baker.* Katherine was horrified. It is a guide to the strength of Katherine's ambivalent feeling towards L.M. that, isolated and ill as she was, she preferred to manage alone and needed no support. She posted the second part of her story with the message: . . . *it's a tribute to Love, you understand and the best I can do just now . . . But what I felt so curiously*

as I wrote it was — ah! I am in a way grown up *as a writer* . . . .
She was.

Murry thought it a great short story. He also felt that it was unlike any of her former work, as though it had come from her unconscious mind, but sorrowfully Murry was aware of its underlying despair. The second part of *Je ne parle pas français* he found agonizingly painful, the abandonment of Mouse (Katherine) by her lover Dick Harmon (Murry). He could scarcely suppress *his* underlying despair in his letter. *I can go on only by forgetting for a little while, not* the letter to send to an ill girl.

Katherine, exasperated, had received 'two hysterical mad screams' by post from L.M: *Oh, my darling, make the doctor let me come* . . . *Oh, my darling* eat, in spite of her telling L.M. *not* to come.

Happily, another story had been written in the thick of it all, *Sun and Moon*, the charming tale which Katherine dreamed *even also its name* when she saw a supper table with its plate of melted ice cream and general chaos through the eyes of a boy of five.

L.M. arrived on the night of Tuesday February 12th, unwelcome, with her poor gift of squashed rum babas from Paris, to receive the unvarnished truth and details of the programme to be followed, contact at meals only and an afternoon walk together. This was stoically accepted. However, Katherine had admitted to herself the advantage of travelling back accompanied, and in the light of what happened, L.M. was a godsend.

Murry had been against L.M. going to Bandol and jealously felt that L.M. was trying to outdo him in love.

Her writing fell off with these events, she was sleepless and couldn't get comfortable in bed. Also she was consumed with hatred for L.M., telling Murry . . . *she is never content except when she can eat me* . . . *she'd* like *me to be paralysed* . . . *or blind — preferably blind* . . . *I* loathe *her so much for this* . . . *she's nicely finished my (really on the whole) odious friendship* . . . *I* can't *like her* . . . *she has persecuted me* . . . . *If there wasn't Jack* . . . *what she can't stand is you and I —* us.

It seems L.M. retaliated to some extent. Perhaps that was

just as well, because L.M.'s masochistic love was just the spark that fired and expended Katherine's sadistic response, and was the unending and unfailing supply of fuel which kept the friendship going to the end.

I must say that L.M. made some irritating remarks though. For example . . . *Katie mine, who is Wordsworth? Must I like him? It's no good looking cross because I love you, my angel, from the little tip of that cross eyebrow to the* all *of you. When am I going to brush your hair again?* . . . enough to make the toes curl in one's shoes!

Katherine was depressed and homesick, and some of Murry's pessimism continued to pervade his letters which sent her into a fever of anxiety.

About Tuesday February 19th, Katherine had a haemoptysis of bright arterial blood, which, though not heavy, was extremely alarming. Hearing of it in a brave letter from Katherine, just about finished Murry. He stumbled about in the streets at night, deserted during air raids, hoping a bomb would drop near him.

Katherine had a temperature and had lost weight. Valiantly she tried in her letters to support Murry. At the back of her sadness, she said, was absolute faith and hope and love. She felt, too, a sudden increase in her love for the world of nature, flowers, streams and clouds, and Murry, trying to respond, described his dream of them sailing to a desert island with their books, — poor Murry and poor, poor Katherine!

By February 22nd she was improving a little, her temperature had gone down and the haemoptysis stopped. Talking about the new German offensive to L.M., how the idea of it was always at the back of her mind, L.M., no doubt trying to introduce a lighter note, was reported to have said, *"Roger has got four teeth. Does that interest you? It is interesting, my Katie. And the gardener says the little black kitten is the* child *of the grey* lady *cat.* Writing to Murry about it she said she felt like Lawrence as though she were being destroyed.

However, she pinned her hopes on getting home for April 1st and made a great effort to write a new story. It was to be called *Bliss* a beautiful title. It was finished on February 28th and it had been a great pleasure to do.

On March 6th Katherine was joined by Madame Geoffroi and her husband who, though well-meaning, exasperated weary Katherine, who felt understandably antisocial, and scarcely able to bear the prospect of their three-day visit. Their chatter made her head ache. After they had gone, Katherine ordered a coffee, locked the door and smoked until midnight. The next day L.M., trying to make a hit, stayed out in dire cold and wind with a pack lunch, I suppose to give Katherine a little peace. L.M.'s sacrificial gesture came to naught, for Katherine was furious about it.

By March 12th L.M. was recalled by Mr Gwynne. This altered everything. Katherine prepared to leave with her. They required official permission and Murry duly sent the fake telegram summoning her home due to the illness of 'mother'. The consulate in Marseilles dismissed it saying that she required instead permission from the Military Permit Office in Paris. Katherine decided to ask her doctor in Bandol for a certificate advising travel to England on health grounds and with a companion. L.M.'s passage was assured because of war work. On what she called Black Sunday, March 17th Katherine sent L.M. to bring the doctor in order to get a certificate.

Meanwhile in England, that same night, Murry dined with Virginia Woolf. The other guests were Barbara and Nick Bagenall. In her diary Virginia wrote: *Poor Murry snarled & scowled with the misery of his lot. He works all day & writes when he comes home. Worst of all K.M. has been very ill . . . But I thought him very much more of a person & a brain than I thought him before. I think this was partly due to the contrast with Nick. The difference between a good mind & a mediocre one is very sharp — not that Murry is as easy or as agreeable. But he works his brains, always had worked them & thus cuts his way through a different atmosphere. I had a good deal of talk about books with him . . . . He will never write another novel he says. Poetry is a short cut & "Life seems to me now very precarious".*

Preparing to receive the doctor, Katherine dressed in a new dress and wearing her black swansdown neck-tie proceeded to be sweet and obliged when he came to see her, dictating and spelling the note as she leaned over him, feeling contempt for his flirtatiousness. She took it to Marseilles on Monday March 18th. She was feverish and felt very ill, but she gained permission to go as far as Paris. To cheer herself up she bought a bottle of Genêt Fleuri.

They left Bandol on March 21st, waiting for the 7.05 p.m. train to Paris at Marseilles. Katherine's back ached, and she had abdominal pain. L.M., with unerring inefficiency, had lost all her luggage on a two hour journey, by leaving it on Bandol platform. It was returned unharmed one year later by Cooks. After the long night journey to Paris they arrived to find the city under bombardment. They were held there three weeks. Postal and telegraphic communications between London and Paris were almost non-existent. Katherine required further permission to travel.

It took them until late afternoon to find suitable accommodation. It was Room 30 in the Select Hôtel, Place de la Sorbonne, next door to Sylvia Beach's book shop. Katherine, agonized, was without letters from Murry for eight long days. She wandered twice a day to Cooks for mail, to no avail; nights were disturbed with gun-fire. *I walk-walk-walk and go into cafés . . . get coffee . . . go back to the hotel and stare at my room — in a sort of stupor of fatigue and anxiety.* Even an eventual letter from Murry did not seem to cheer her. *. . . . I feel it is unbearable and that we have been treated too badly.* This letter was tear-stained. Murry answered: *My darling, don't be anxious about me . . . I am perfectly well: no chimney-pots have fallen on my head: no motor buses have run over me. That I worry and worry about you just now — well, that can't be helped and nothing will change that. I promise I'll make a valiant effort to keep heart; do you try to do the same. But oh, my darling —* a nice letter.

The bombardment was severe, firing was at eighteen-minute intervals. To shelter they started work in an underground canteen at the Gare du Nord. Katherine, coming off her first and last shift of 5½ hours, was speechless with fatigue. L.M. wisely continued there, for she was given free meals. Finally, on April 3rd permission to travel arrived from Bedford Square. The only delay now was procuring a berth on the next Channel ferry. However, Katherine was past feeling joy — she had had word from Murry that day which she called a note: . .

*if you knew with what fever I tore this open and found the two
middle pages empty!* All one can say is that Katherine, at all
times, wrote most fully, even when very ill, and leave it at that.

To pass the time Katherine played Demon Patience, even at
three in the morning with an anxious French mouse squeaking
in her waste-paper basket. There was talk of a boat leaving on
Wednesday April 10th she told Murry and enclosed her new
passport photograph, wearing round her neck Chummie's
greenstone. On it she looked thin with big frightened eyes.

On the boat, in their cabin, Katherine and L.M. playing
patience, were suddenly as one. Writing to L.M. afterwards
Katherine said: *Does it gleam to you, too — like a little jewel
beyond price — those hours on the boat when you sat on the
floor in a draught and I sat on the lounge and we put the red
on the black and wanted a seven? I was so happy __ were you?
Try and forget that sad and sick Katie whose back ached in her
brain or whose brain ached in her back. It's such a lovely
afternoon and very warm. I would like to turn to you and say
'Oh Jones, we are quite all right, you know'.* And that is the
way it was — a deep friendship in spite of everything.

Katherine arrived in London on April 11th. Murry, waiting
for her in a restaurant, was inwardly aghast at the sight of her:
she was hardly recognizable. She had lost a stone in weight,
being now 7½ stone. However she was blissfully *happy — but
really ill,* and seeing Dr Ainger, her New Zealand GP, was told
that she had definitely got consumption. On May 2nd the
decree nisi in her husband's divorce suit against her became
absolute and on May 3rd, in the presence of J.D. Fergusson
and Dorothy Brett, Katherine married John Middleton Murry
at South Kensington registry office.

In his autobiography, Murry said with bitterness: *Hence-
forward my life would be one long lie — of Love. To have no
faith, and pretend one; to have no hope and pretend it. —
Now between Katherine and me, a subtle and impassable
barrier had descended.* She went joyfully enough to Redcliffe
Road and was welcomed with a bear hug from Fergusson.
Murry's biographer, F.A. Lea, said that according to Murry's
colleagues at work he had looked as though he were being 'led
to execution'.

After the wedding they returned to Redcliffe Road. Seeing

Katherine 'a gaunt and bright-eyed shadow' Murry felt agonized, and as it always was to do, her cough seemed to jar on his spine. 'My one preoccupation was to get her away' — out of his sight, perhaps? Katherine, cynical and unhappy, wanted to stay; she rather liked the rootless, dingy but not dull street.

On May 9th Katherine had lunch with Virginia. In a letter to Ottoline she considered Katherine *very ill, but very inscrutable and fascinating. After a good deal of worrying by me, she confessed that she was immensely happy married to Murry, though for some reason she makes out that marriage is of no more importance than engaging a charwoman. Part of her fascination lies in the obligation she is under to say absurd things . . . .* She certainly was not going to show her wounds to Virginia, who wrote in her diary *. . . . we came to an oddly complete understanding . . . I get down to what is true rock in her, through the numerous vapours & pores which sicken or bewilder most of our friends . . . .*

Finally Katherine had to agree to go to Looe in Cornwall, while Murry looked for a house in Hampstead. Anne Rice, now living in Cornwall, had engaged a nice room in the Headland Hotel, overlooking the sea. On Friday May 17th Katherine left by train, anguished by Murry kissing her hand instead of her mouth, in case of infection. The beauty of the countryside in spring only made her feel more tragic. Anne and her husband Raymond Drey met the train at Liskeard and they continued by road. Anne, in her memoirs of Katherine, remembered meeting her. *Her appearance was wraith-like, touching and alarming, and the cough troublesome.* Though the room was charming, with a magnificent view of the sea from three big windows, Katherine was heartbroken. *It's ten o'clock, I am going to bed . . . now with the blinds down there floats in the old, old sound, which really makes me very sad. It makes me feel what a blind, dreadful, losing and finding affair life has been just lately, with how few golden moments, how little, little rest . . . It is agony to be away from you, but what must be must be. Forgive me if I have been — what was it? I find it so hard to be ill. But ah, if you knew how I loved you . . . .* The first of many letters to Murry from his 'loving wife' and surely one of the saddest letters ever written.

In a daze, coughing, feverish and in pain, she wept uncontrollably for the first three days as she surveyed the shipwreck of all her hopes for her marriage, which was to have 'shone apart from all else' in her life. Anne, finding her so distraught on the Sunday night, called the doctor. He came at 11.00 p.m. and found Katherine had left-sided pleurisy. She realized she had had pleurisy for three days before leaving London and should never have done so. She should have stayed put, right from November 1917! even if Murry did think his rooms were unsuitable. Bed has always been the best place for febrile tuberculosis, however dingy the street. After three days she was allowed up for a short period and on receiving a gay letter from Murry about smiling at a flowerwoman as he bought red roses for his aunt, she reacted by sending a 'snake' of a letter back. Curiously blind to the pain in Katherine's letters, Murry had written: *When I had read your letters I went off to my looking glass. Truly, honestly I didn't recognise myself — with a spotted bow-tie that looked — like a little dog who was smiling too. I could not be happier than I am. — — — — — when your train went out — — — — I knew the good thing was going to happen — — and I suddenly passed into a state of grace. Everything I did was a good thing. I made my Aunt better; I made the flower-woman laugh; — — Write to me as often as you can — — Most days, I shall probably send you only a post-card and a long letter on Sunday. But you will have a p.c. every day. I would write every day if it were not that I feel certain of the Heron again and I want, really want, to write articles for it — —.* Depressed and admitting that her 'vagrant self' was uppermost, her feelings coloured her reply.

> *. . . an idea*
> *Are you really happy when I am not there? Can you conceive of yourself buying crimson roses and smiling at the flowerwoman if I were within 50 miles of you? . . . even if you are lonely, you are not being 'driven distracted' — Do you remember when you put your handkerchief to your lips and turned away from me? Isn't it true that if I were 'flourishing' you would flourish ever so much more easily . . . . without the strain and wear of my actual presence. We could write each other letters and send each other work and you would quite*

forget that I was 29 . . . You are always pale, exhausted, in a
kind of anguish of set fatigue when I am by. Now I feel in your
letters this is lifting . . . .

He was never able to cope with this tragic happening right to
the end. His brother Richard, years later, told Professor
Alpers, "My brother simply didn't have what's needed there.
He'd hang around with a bloody awful face, and only make
her worse. He couldn't buck her up at all." There are many
like poor Murry, eased out of sick rooms by nursing staff. They
have faces like funerals, would make excellent undertakers,
and cause irate spouses to say darkly of their partners, "The
wind's in the west!"

Murry wept over the letter. Alas, some of it was true. In his
reply he admitted he was happy when she went away and felt
anguished when he saw her ailing. He was willing to wait years
apart to ensure her ultimate recovery.

It is odd that an intelligent man like Murry should think
that going miles away to a different bed, albeit with attention,
should be better than attention at home in the fold. One
wonders if he would have felt the same about a sick daughter,
if he could have survived the agonizing break with a very sick
child on her own like that, even if she were grown up; and
wasn't his plea that he would wait years, apart, really just a
a sort of relegation of Katherine to a shelf? Some men may not
have been able to face the separation, if they loved enough. It
is doubtful whether Katherine would have let him go, if the
positions had been reversed. She was the protector in that
partnership, she was the proprietor. Murry was the butterfly
caught in her net.

Katherine wrote on May 27th that his letter had 'really
nearly killed' her. *Hasn't all my suffering and misery been just
because of . . . my terrible — exhausting — utterly* INTENSE
love? She reminded him what an appalling blow it had been to
uproot after the agonizing separation of Bandol, that her
proposal of six weeks in Looe had been altered to four months
without consultation, that her letter was written from despair.
She voiced too, her disappointment over her marriage, that he
had never once held her in his arms and called her his wife,
regrettable! His following abreactive, insensitive letter we will

put down to his very real blind spot. He was rarely knowingly unkind. He described the effect her illness had on him, " . . . *my happiness withered in my heart — I shall never forget how it withered when I looked at you as you came into the restaurant. Perhaps I should have fought the devil of despair, but I am only Boge — —.* Not nice for a sick bride to read, especially in view of the utter bliss with which she would enter that restaurant! For Murry, Katherine's devouring love meant no separation and that he should stand by and simply watch her die. Yes, just that, like many other good husbands or wives have often had to do, particularly if they have been foolish enough not to insist on proper treatment.

For relief she turned to work and began to write *A Married Man's Story*, strong, mature and even sinister; alas, never finished. It was so absorbing, her depression eased and she began to have interest in the house Murry was trying to procure, which they called 'The Elephant' because it was made of greyish London brick. She had also written the 'delicate' story *Carnation* based on lessons at Queen's College.

Anne remembered painting the portrait of Katherine after a two hour sketch, the only known portrait, which now hangs in the National Art Gallery, Wellington. *She had a painter's eye for colour and design and the scheme of vivid reds was her choice. Strong colours gave her joy; she had no use for pastel shades. She posed with the serenity of a Buddha and only occasionally was the silence broken with the striking of a match to light a cigarette . . . she smoked far too much. How lovely her hair, coiled on top like a deep brown butterfly.* Anne was also to paint 'Ribni', Katherine's Japanese doll surrounded by marigolds.

In wonderful weather, the two girls went picnicking on a deserted beach all day. Alas, the heat and exercise exhausted Katherine and she had to rest on her balcony for the next few days, too tired even to walk to the post-box. She was still having bouts of black depression but managed and enjoyed a visit to Polperro. Her maid, a dear old lady called Mrs Honey, was foolishly suggesting she have a baby, she told Murry; she also described a hat-buying session, where she tried to explain to a Cornish pasty of a salesgirl, that she wanted a hat that appeared to be painted on the head — a cloche hat in other

P

words. She was also sending suggestions for colour schemes
for the Elephant and Murry, guilty over any black spots in her
letters, was assured that her blackness came from her health.

*I feel 'ill' and I feel a — longing for you: for our home, our
life, and for a little baby . . . my whole soul waits for the time
when you and I shall be withdrawn from everybody — when
we shall go into our own undiscovered darling country . . . you
are everything . . . and you are mine and I am yours,* a letter
born of an intensity of love not often experienced, and difficult
for Murry to live up to, difficult indeed for any man. Her
strength was her fantasy life, and Murry was the idealised lover
there. She continued to be overtaken by bouts of despair. In an
unposted letter to Murry on Sunday June 9th she described her
desperate nights, dreading the wane of day, pacing the floor,
looking in the mirror at 'that girl with the burning eyes'
thinking: *Will my candle last until it's light? . . . this terrifying
thought that one must* die, *and may be* going *to die . . . if I
could just stroll into your room 'all would be well'. But really I
have suffered such agonies from loneliness and illness
combined that I'll never be quite whole again.*

On the same night Murry dined with the Woolfs. Virginia
noted, *Murry was as pale as death, with gleaming eyes, & a
crouching way at the table that seemed to proclaim extreme
hunger or despair. "At Christmas," said Murry, "I was near
suicide; but I worried out a formula which serves to keep me
going. It's the conception of indifferentism. I have hope no
longer. I live in two layers of consciousness" . . . But to us he
seemed less nice, perhaps more anxious for effect.*

Anne came to continue with the portrait, Katherine wearing
her brick red frock 'with flowers everywhere'. Anne had
difficulty in finishing the portrait. She could not get the mouth
right, until she studied one of L.M.'s photographs.

Writing on a postcard of The Jolly Sailor Inn, West Looe, to
L.M. some little time before June 20th, Katherine tried to
liven up her wardrobe for Murry's coming.

*If you see J. before he comes down would you see that he brings
my velvet waistcoat (which "goes" with my velvet shirt, dear)
I'd also give my eyes for that crêpe-de-Chine "jumper" made of
Chaddie's evening coat and the black satin pinny dress to wear*

with it. These will only make a tiny parcel. If he hasn't room could you post them to me? Katie.

Though Murry was due to arrive for his week's holiday on June 21st Katherine, with 'rheumatism', made a sad journal entry on that day. *One looks hideous . . . one's feet swollen — and all one's clothes are tight . . . went for a walk and was caught in the wind and rain. Terribly cold and wretched.* The holiday together passed without comment. To L.M. on June 27th: . . .*My back is pretty fairish — not more than that . . . and my wings — well they are* there. *The left one is groggy — and the right one I don't know about. But I have got used to them now and take them in my* stride *as they are no good for my flight . . . I don't care a button for this place Jones . . . . I'd just as soon be in the Mile Road . . .*One feels that the holiday was probably not a success.

Returning to Redcliffe Road together at the beginning of July, Katherine made no adverse comment in her notebook. She even mentioned *my present state of health is a great gain. It makes things so rich . . . I seem to see, this time in London — nothing but what is marvellous . . .* She was back with Murry!

In Wellington, there had been rejoicing at Katherine's plans to marry. They had received kindly letters from both Mr and Mrs Beauchamp. Katherine's mother had sent money from her secret store as a wedding present, which, alas, had had to see Katherine through the Paris bombardment. However, in May, Mr Kay had cabled the bad news of Katherine's illness, which came as a great shock. To a family friend, Clara Palmer, on May 6th Mrs Beauchamp wrote:

Kathleen had to go to the South of France at the end of the winter, . . . and when she last wrote from Bandol-sur-mer she was getting better from pleurisy and rheumatism but unfortunately since her return to London we had a cable last week to say she was very seriously ill with advanced lung trouble, and required Sanatorium or home treatment at once. This was a great grief and shock to us as you may imagine. I had to repeat the cable to poor Harold who is on a short visit to Sydney . . . but of course I wired them authority for any extra

*special expenditure for the dear child, and I know everything
will be done for her that is possible, for she has been taken into
Belle's and Dora's fold by Chad long ago and is quite a pet with
them all. Chaddie has been marvellously good to her ever since
she arrived in England and Kass has so enjoyed the attention of
this loving and generous sister, but it seems that nothing much
can be done for her now but make the remainder of her life as
happy and comfy as possible. Of course if it was possible I
should go home to her by the next steamer, for I know she
would love to see me again, for she has at last learnt to love her
Mother and Father, and has written us adoring and adorable
letters lately, and so sweetly and quaintly put, poor poor
darling she has missed so much in life, but it was quite her own
choosing, fortunately she was the last to see Leslie off to
France, and she has never forgotten this privelege for she
simply worshipped her only brother and he had such loving
compassion for her always through all her misdeeds. Even
when at school he used to write and ask forgiveness for her in
the most learned and clever way.*

Mrs Beauchamp, who had been in Sydney, returned to
Wellington on March 21st, 1918, closely followed by Jeanne.
Alas, she was seriously ill. In the *Dominion* for Friday August
9th, 1918 there was an announcement: *The flags over the
banks and other financial institutions in Wellington shipping
offices, etc., were at half-mast yesterday as a mark of respect to
Mrs. Harold Beauchamp (wife of the chairman of the Bank of
New Zealand, and senior partner in the firm of Messrs. W.M.
Bannatyne and Co.) who died yesterday morning at her
residence 'The Grange' Wadestown. The interment will be
private.* She was cremated at Karori and her ashes were
preserved in a niche in the crematorium. Another item of news
had been reported in the *Dominion* a week previously,
connected with the sunlit days of the past. Nursing sister
Marion Ruddick of Ottawa had been awarded the Royal Red
Cross First Class for distinguished service.

Writing to Ottoline about the death of her mother,
Katherine said it was *a terrible sorrow. I feel — do you know
what I mean — the silence of it so. She was more alive than*

anyone I have ever known, and to Brett: *Yes, it is an* immense *blow. She was the most precious, lovely little being . . . and writing me such long, long letters . . . beginning "Dear child, it is the most exquisite day"* — she lived *every moment of her life more fully and completely than anyone I've ever known* — and *her gaiety wasn't any less real for being* high courage *. . . to meet anything with.*

Ever since I have heard of her death my memories of her come flying back into my heart — *and there are moments when it's unbearable to receive them . . . .* To Virginia: *. . . . My mother has died. I can't think of anything else. Ah, Virginia, she was such an exquisite little being, far too fragile and lovely to be dead for ever more.* To an old friend of the family she wrote on December 30th, 1918:

In spite of her frailty and delicate hold on Life one really felt that she was an undying soul. She was such a part of life, especially these last few years. She seemed to live in everything and to be renewed with every Spring. And it was so extraordinary how close she kept to her children. Her last letters were quite uncanny. We seemed to be thinking the same thoughts at just the same time . . . I wish we had not all lived so scattered — *and it is dreadful to think of poor Father without his wife and his "Boy". I shall be going abroad . . . for a more or less indefinite time. It will be such a relief to be strong again. I cannot bear an inactive life* — *and though of course I can do all my writing just as well with broken wings as with good 'uns', there are so many things beside that one longs to take part in. Kass.*

The Murrys had moved to the 'Elephant', 2 Portland Villas, Hampstead, on July 29th, 1918. It was a tall, gracious house looking across willow trees to the Vale of Health, with London in the distance. Her bedroom with the same view and her sitting-room, first floor back, were painted white, an ex-government table painted yellow served as a desk, with a foot-muff of fur and satin underneath. Nearby stood the large cupboard called 'The Black Monk'. There was a little *sommier,* under the frill of which played a black and white cat called Charles and later her two kittens Wingly and

Athenaeum. The covers of the *sommier* and chairs were *Lemon yellow with dashes of palm trees on them and parrots simply clinging to the branches. The parrots have I think a quite extraordinary resemblance to M(urry)*, she told Ottoline. On the mantelpiece stood a clock incorporating the figure of a little shepherdess, with strawberry skirt and green jacket, which proclaimed each hour with a delicate ping. By the fireside was a brass coal-scuttle.

Katherine thought the view from the front windows *simply superb — the pale sky and the half bare trees. It's so beautiful it might be the country. Russian country as I see it.* She would sometimes venture out on to the heath, wearing her black cape with three little collars on it like a coachman. It was lined with charmeuse of every conceivable peacock colour and fastened with a big clasp.

There were two maids, Gertie and Violet, and L.M. who had reluctantly but inevitably left her friends at the lathe to become housekeeper, muddling along in a job for which she was highly unsuited, but she did her best. Katherine's illness was a constant anxiety, with seemingly little support from Murry who would come home from work in the evening and *bemoan how terrible it all was, how dreadfully he was suffering and how he could hardly bear it.* So L.M. wrote in her memoirs.

Meanwhile, *Prelude* was on the wing; the first copies in their dark blue stiff cover were sent off on July 10th, 1918. Virginia, in her diary on July 12th said . . . *I myself find a kind of beauty about the story, a little vapourish I admit, & freely watered with some of her cheap realities but it has the living power, the detached existence of a work of art . . . .*, praise indeed!

Gertler to Kot, from Garsington on July 15th, thought *Prelude rubbishy but others say that, somehow after reading it through it sticks in one's mind and then one suddenly realises that it* is *rather exquisite . . . .* The jobbing printer who was advising and who later helped to set up the type said, "My, but those kids are real."

It seems that Murry had attempted to bridge the rift with Kot by asking him to Redcliffe Road, but in a letter to Gertler, Kot said: *it was simply impossible for him to meet the Murrys until he could completely forget the wrong attitude they had towards him — —*

Bliss appeared in the August number of *English Review. I threw down Bliss with the exclamation "She's done for!"* wrote Virginia, who was wildly jealous. . . . *her mind is a very thin soil laid upon very barren rock . . . superficial smartness . . . the effect was . . . to give me an impression of her callousness & hardness . . . Or is it absurd to read all this criticism of her personality into a story.* In August, Ottoline sent Katherine a mass of flowers and thanking her on 22nd, Katherine said that Murry *who is at the moment like the bathing dress, perpetually hanging out to dry after a* sad sad *wetting — gave a great gasp of delight.* The first entry in the journal on September 20th describing life at the Elephant, suggests that Katherine was basically sad, disillusioned, and subject to terrifying fits of temper. Tearing the page of a book she was reading she noticed afterwards, on looking in the mirror, that she was 'green' — *I am more like L(awrence) than anybody* — she was.

Trying to compose herself, sitting at her desk, she felt as though Chummie was sitting opposite. Later she went up to Murry's room, but came away despite his outstretched hand. She had no abiding place — 'where are my people? With whom have I been happiest?' she asked herself. 'With nobody in particular' — how sad it all was.

Anne came to tea at the Elephant. *On the broad window sill was a row of red geraniums. An interior modest and extremely tidy . . . she herself always appeared neat — no loose ends. She was propped up on a sofa and in a fit of coughing, she could still say 'It's a queer world darling, but in spite of everything, it's a rare joy to be alive'. Her conversation had the quality of her stories. On a later visit . . . I found Katherine a prisoner in bed, an ethereal person stretched under a black shawl, the embroidered birds and flowers gay in their vivid colours, and the thin hands clutching the fringe. 'I am never for one single hour without pain — and with probably the usual daily temperature'.*

Fortunately Anne introduced her to a new doctor, Dr Victor Sorapure, whom Katherine really liked and never ever criticised. Born in Jamaica in 1874, he was Consultant Physician to Hampstead General Hospital and had spent some considerable time working in New York. He did the

inestimable service to Katherine of finally diagnosing the cause
of the vicious 'rheumatism', instituted treatment by injections
and banished some of the dark cloud, lessening the pain. In
deep gratitude Katherine was to dedicate her story *The
Daughters of the Late Colonel* to him — *To Doctor Sorapure.
Were my gratitude to equal my admiration, my admiration
would still outstep my gratitude.* Alas, the dedication rescued
from the wastepaper basket with the manuscript by L.M.,
became separated and was never printed.

In October Katherine was seeing a specialist in tuberculosis
who told Murry that the only chance for her was strict
sanatorium discipline immediately; if not, she had four years
to live at the outside. She was also seen by her great-cousin
Doctor Sydney Beauchamp, brother of Elizabeth, on October
14th, her thirtieth birthday. She was in bed and febrile. His
verdict was the same. Why, one asks, was nothing done?
Murry, who should have insisted on taking the right decision,
followed Katherine's curious irrationality, curious in that
normally she was sensible, practical, and courageous. What
was one year of discipline to the torture of living later,
stranded on an Italian hillside in dire weather, and separated
from Murry? So the idea was dropped and the dying
continued. The answer lies in the following letter, written to
Murry some time in October 1918, when she was having
second thoughts about sanatorium treatment. . . . *.my fight
has been so hard that I just laid down my weapons and ran
away, and consented to do what has always seemed to me the
final intolerable thing i.e. to go into a sanatorium. Today, I
am determined . . . to live the sanatorium life here . . . .* She
planned to lie in a shelter in the garden all day, and have L.M.
as whole time nurse. . . . *for the first time today I am
determined to get well as mother would be determined . . .
Anything else, any institutional existence would kill me — or
being alone, cut off, ill with others ill . . . .*

She was in bed on October 20th, writing to Brett and
complaining of breathlessness. In another letter she said that
she had seen Lawrence! *For me, at least, the dove brooded over
him too. I loved him. He was just his old, merry, rich self,
laughing, describing things, giving you pictures, full of
enthusiasms and joy in a future where we become all*

*'vagabonds' — we simply did not talk about people. We kept
to things like nuts and cowslips and fires in woods and his black
self was not. Oh, there is something so loveable about him and
his eagerness, his passionate eagerness for life __ that is what
one loves so. Now he has gone back to the country.*

L.M. remembered the occasion well. It was a luncheon
party on November 14th. Lawrence, in a beard and looking
'like Christ', was pacing up and down the dining-room.
Katherine reminding L.M., who had a cold, that she was three
minutes late with the first course, added, "There is no need to
cry about it," as L.M. slunk from her room, eyes streaming.

Lawrence, on his return to Derbyshire, sent Katherine a
little bowl made of golden fluorspar. Writing from Mountain
Cottage, Middleton, Derby, on November 15th, 1918
Lawrence asked Katherine to *thank Ida Baker for the trouble
she took for me. One feels here like a man looking out of a
fortress.* Katherine never saw him again.

There was also, happily, a renewal of friendship with Kot,
who along with the Campbells received a mysterious telegram:
Come tonight, Katherine. Fearing the worst, they all arrived,
finding her thin and ill but bright with hospitality. For
Katherine a happy outcome of this was the collaboration with
Kot on Russian translation.

Virginia, visiting Katherine on November 6th, found her up
and dressed *but husky & feeble, crawling about the room like
an old woman . . . I think she has a kind of childlikeness
somewhere which has been much disfigured but still exists . . . .
Murry & the monster (L.M.) watch & wait on her till she hates
them both . . . .* Virginia was to visit weekly.

On November 11th, guns firing proclaimed PEACE.
Writing about it to Ottoline Katherine sadly wondered how
long it was since they had walked together in the garden at
Garsington. It was a whole long year ago.

Virginia had finished *Night and Day* on November 30th and
it was to be reviewed by Katherine. Visiting the Murrys that
day she thought there was something a little inharmonious in
both of them and an underlying lack of confidence. Virginia
left with Murry's poem, called 'A Critic in Judgement',
written in 1913 and which was finally published by Hogarth
Press on May 12th, 1919. She thought it 'intricate & involved &

as thick as a briar hedge'.

Visiting again on December 12th she noted Murry's silence, shyness she thought it, but he later confessed he had acquired a printing press on which his poems were to be printed by his brother Richard, who was learning 'art' printing at the polytechnic.

Six days later Katherine was telling Brett: *I am hardly alive. I have not been out for months and cannot walk up and down the stairs with any success — I feel — as though I have died — as far as personal life goes. I don't even want to live again. All that is over. I am a writer who cares for nothing but writing* . . . . The press was now installed in the basement and *Je ne parle pas français* was printed, November 1919.

Christmas 1918 came and Katherine told Brett it had been: . . . *superb — stockings — a tree, decorations, crackers, pudding, drink — most potent and plentiful — parcels pouring in and out. Murry seemed to wear a paper hat (a large red and yellow butterfly) from Christmas Eve until after Boxing Day — We gradually, under the influence of wine and chinese mottoes gave a party — Charades — Kot, Gertler, Campbell etc. Oh, I did* love *it so — loved everybody* . . . *The red chairs became a pirate ship. Koteliansky wore a muff on his head and Campbell a doormat tied under the chin.*

L.M. remembered Katherine *wearing a rather frilly soft dress of plum-coloured silk embroidered all over with tiny bunches of flowers.* Beatrice thought Katherine looked terribly thin and frail and described her cutting little bags of sweets from the Xmas tree and solemnly handing them round — 'a sort of Last Supper' which Kot disapproved of, thinking it was one of Katherine's 'stunts'. This was no stunt, it was symbolic. This *was* Katherine's 'Last Supper', her last Xmas in England with her old friends of happier days.

Lawrence wrote from his sister's in Ripley on December 27th, thanking Katherine for her present: *we read your letter in the wind* . . . *It made me feel weary, that we couldn't be all there, with rucksacks* . . . *setting off for somewhere good, over the snow* . . . *I do wish you were better* . . . .

From January 1st Katherine made no entry in her journal until May. Virginia's 'small bright presents' and letters went unanswered, a proposed visit for February 17th was cancelled by L.M. This prompted a diary entry on February 18th by Virginia: *It is extremely doubtful whether I have the right to class her among my friends . . . I have letters in which she speaks of finding the thought of me a joy . . . . the last dated December & it is now February. The question . . . decidedly pains me . . . . we have been intimate, intense perhaps rather than open . . . .* Virginia was peeved, fascinated and suffering from jealousy. Her heart was engaged, Katherine's was not. Professor Quentin Bell told Professor Alpers that he thought there was perhaps some element of 'a little love affair' in Virginia's feeling for Katherine.

Inviting Virginia to tea on February 24th, Katherine explained her silence. She had been receiving injections, probably vaccine prescribed by Doctor Sorapure, which made her febrile for forty-eight hours. Katherine would be too shattered physically and mentally to bother about Virginia.

Murry had been invited to be editor of the *Athenaeum* at a salary of £800 a year and at tea that day Katherine asked Virginia to contribute. Ottoline was in town too, and dined with Virginia, who found Ottoline had *the slim swaying figure of a Lombardy poplar . . . . & a feeble mincing step on the street like that of a cockatoo with bad claws.* Ottoline also visited Katherine for lunch and commented on L.M: *why does the mountain (L.M.) hold the plates in such a strange way?* Poor L.M. was trying to hide her vegetable-stained hands well under the plates and grimly remembered the occasion at the age of eighty-eight, even imitating Lady Ottoline for the author and pointing out too that Morrell was pronounced 'Moral'.

On March 19th Virginia met Murry at her club to discuss the *Athenaeum*. She thought him improved in health, *more freshly coloured . . . . his eyes shone . . . his silences were occupied with pleasant thoughts.* They talked zestfully for 1¾ hours, mainly about his poetry. As soon as Virginia mentioned her new novel *his eyes came down from the ceiling at once,* and after asking the title, quickly excused himself. Virginia thought him *much of a small boy still . . . in spite of his tragic airs.*

Virginia visited Katherine on Saturday March 22nd. *The inscrutable woman remains inscrutable,* as she started up a great discussion. Katherine was to review four novels weekly for the *Athenaeum*, and Virginia privately hoped she would not do *Night and Day*. Virginia thought *something dark and catastrophic has taken place since we met. So much she hinted but said she wished now to forget it — something that had absorbed her, apparently . . . .*

Murry recruited J.W.N. Sullivan and Aldous Huxley as his assistants on the *Athenaeum*. Huxley was not deemed able enough to be sub-editor by Murry and Katherine, who regarded him as a beginner. This possibly rankled and generated some of the enmity between him and the Murrys. He attacked them in print for years. About Katherine he wrote, January 27th, 1963, to Allan J. Crane: *yes I knew Katherine Mansfield fairly well and liked her stories. She was an unhappy woman, capable of acting any number of parts but uncertain of who, essentially, she was — a series of points and arcs on the circumference of a circle that was uncertain of the location of its centre.*

He was much harsher to Murry:

1st March 1962 To Myrick Land.
Murry's was an acute and subtle mind and there was something curiously fascinating about his conversation. Moreover he would radiate a kind of religious enthusiasm — about Dostoevsky . . . about 'Metabiology', about Lawrence. At first people tended to catch fire from his enthusiasm, this flame of earnestness. But after a while they began to discover that the flame was only a stage effect, that the enthusiasm and the earnestness were not spontaneous — for Murry and Katherine Mansfield too had a strange way of churning themselves violently and indefatigably in the hope of transforming a native inability to feel very strongly or continuously into a butter pat of genuine emotion, true passion, unquestioning faith . . . .
Hypocrisy says La Rochefoucauld is a tribute that vice plays to virtue. Murry's brand of hypocrisy was rather different — it was the tribute that emotional impotence pays to faith and passion. Lawrence was at first taken in by the hypocrisy — and the genuine charm; then, when he saw through it, he was appalled and indignant, all the more indignant for having been taken in.

They all met at the Elephant in the evenings, Sullivan's pipe making Katherine cough. Among the contributors were T.S. Eliot, Bertrand Russell, E.M. Forster, George Santayana, Virginia and D.H. Lawrence.

Writing to Kot on March 11th, Lawrence mentioned he had been asked for a contribution and that he felt mistrustful of Murry. On March 14th he admitted *he* had been very ill. He seemed very antagonistic towards Frieda and was even wildly considering leaving her, feeling she bullied him. Alas, Murry accepted only one of Lawrence's pieces. *I heard from Murry,* he told Kot, *very editorial — he sort of 'declines with thanks' the things I did for him. He will publish one essay next week . . . that is the first and last word of mine that will ever appear in The Athenaeum. Goodbye Jacky, I knew thee beforehand — but don't say anything at 2, Portland Villas.*

Lawrence's essay 'Whistling of Birds' appeared on April 11th, signed Grantorto; his other material was returned with a copy of *The Athenaeum* which unfortunately included his letter to Murry; *nasty bit of oversight,* Lawrence considered, also adding his opinion of *The Athenaeum* for Kot: calling it wet and be-snivelled.

Virginia, taking tea with Katherine and Murry, noted that Murry *sat there mud coloured and mute livening only when we talked his shop.* Virginia expressed dislike for Grantorto on 'Whistling of Birds' and though she longed to hear what they thought of *her* article, neither obliged, *her hard composure is much on the surface.* Virginia suspected that Murry had told Clive Bell he did not like her article 'The Eccentrics' which duly appeared on April 25th. She found it much easier to talk to Katherine than Murry, and noted that Katherine was much troubled by her cough which she likened to a 'big wild dog'.

The peace of the Elephant was shattered over Easter by the fair, with its swings and roundabouts and attendant noise nearby. Virginia and Leonard, visiting Katherine on Easter Monday, found her 'haggard and powdered' and hating the uproar of the fairground. Murry and Richard were also there and all partook of 'a stiff tea'.

Leonard in *Beginning Again* remembered visiting the Elephant. *To see them together, particularly in their own house in Hampstead, made one acutely uncomfortable, for Katherine seemed to be always irritable with Murry and enraged with Murry's brother who lived with them, and, according to Katherine, ate too much. Every now and then she would say sotto voce something bitter and biting about the one or the other.*

Virginia was considering renting the tower house at Higher Tregerthen, on the recommendation of Katherine, who at a distance of nearly three years remembered only its nice features.

There were further observations on Murry in Virginia's diary for May 9th, after visiting Katherine: *he has not yet shed all the husks of clever youth. One feels him very informed essentially, & capable of running on in an excited uneasy state about life such as I can recall in my own past. One tacitly assumed it to be a mark of genius.*

On May 19th Katherine took up her notebook again with its last entry on New Year's day. It was 6.00 p.m. and she sat alone in her room, thinking of her mother, how she would come in through the garden at home calling, 'Children! Children!' *My little mother, my star, my courage, my own. I seem to dwell in her now.* She just wanted time to write about it all she wrote, then she didn't mind dying. By the Tuesday night she was febrile, and had pleurisy with blood-stained sputum.

Eventually reaching calmer waters she was able to tell Ottoline that she and Murry seemed to work like niggers at *The Athenaeum*. To Dorothy Brett she admitted that she had to keep solitary, couldn't go out much and shunned parties and gossip. *Were I perfectly sincere I'd have to confess that I was always acting a part in my old palmy days. And now I have thrown the palm away . . . .*

Dorothy Brett had acquired a house in Pond Street, Hampstead, conveniently near the Murrys. She seems to have adopted both of them, in fact she was a born 'hanger on'. She had more or less left Garsington and Ottoline, and now according to L.M: 'her wish was to be an intimate member of the Murry household' and was never off the doorstep. She was, of course, in love with Murry.

On June 12th a severe review of Murry's poem 'The Critic in Judgement' had appeared in *The Times Literary Supplement*, while Virginia's *Kew Gardens* had been well received. At tea with the Murrys on June 14th, Virginia found them both extremely depressed, though Murry was pretending not to care about his review. She thought Katherine 'so ill and haggard' as she told Virginia that she planned to go to San Remo in September and that Murry was to live in the country. Thinking of the bleakness of their future, Virginia departed, *leaving them to their spare lonely meal, nothing seeming to grow or flourish round them; leafless trees.*

On June 28th Katherine wearily told Ottoline that she was having trouble with her cook who was eventually sacked for drinking, and that she was still ill. *Oh these nights — sitting up in bed, waiting for the black trees to turn into green trees. And yet, when the dawn comes, it is always so beautiful and terrible . . . that it's almost worth waiting for . . . .* Now that Katherine was going abroad, Virginia felt her visits were numbered, seeing her only three more times that summer. She felt she was liking Katherine more and more and that they had reached some kind of durable foundation but she found Murry 'pale and sad, as usual'.

Katherine now had the new kitten called Wingly. He was a great comfort. Anne Rice had recently had a baby son and writing to congratulate her, Katherine mentioned that her father was arriving on August 14th, and that she would be glad to be out of England, she hated the place . . . . *the only thing I have got out of it all these months is pennies. I have earned quite a few . . .* at what cost! Jeanne accompanied her father and was to stay on in England, to Chaddie's delight.

Mr Beauchamp bought a house for Chaddie and Jeanne near Lyndhurst in the New Forest. It was called Woodhay, had a lovely garden and orchard and had cost £2000.

Katherine saw her father on August 17th for the first time since 1912. It would be a poignant meeting. Katherine, describing the day for Ottoline, found him *just as I had imagined, but even fuller of life, enthusiasm, with his power of making all he says vivid, alive and full of humour.* It seems Murry surpassed himself that day: *never spoke once to him, paid him not a moment's attention. It could not have been more fatal,* Katherine told Ottoline. This behaviour from a man who had at times lived on Katherine's allowance and did not support her even now to any great extent, seems incredible. No wonder Mr Beauchamp was to call him later 'a perfect rotter' and to make sure that the handsome cash allowance of £300 per year ceased at Katherine's death, in contrast to that of his other daughters' allowances, which were in the form of income from capital held in their names and which could be left to their husbands. However, to be fair to Murry, he suffered from difficulty in communicating. Virginia Woolf noted that: *He scarcely speaks; makes one feel that most speaking is useless; but as he has a brain of his own I don't mind this. Besides it is more shyness than purpose.*

Poor Katherine, married just over one year, was disillusioned with Murry but still loved him 'for all the strangeness' between them. He was thoughtless, neglecting to show her new books he had acquired, was sometimes late for meals, uncommunicative, banging the bedroom door when he had no clean towel, and 'why is lunch late?' — terrible for a sick wife. *He ought not to have married. There never was a creature less fitted by nature for life with a woman . . . life without work . . . I would commit suicide . . .* she wrote bitterly in her notebook.

Sylvia Lynd wrote an account of a visit to Katherine in August 1919 for the *Weekly Westminster Gazette*, January 20th, 1923.

She was shown into the salon on the first floor. Katherine was dressed in a purple dressing gown trimmed with emerald green buttons and a carmine velvet sash. She wore mules of pale brocade with high heels. She was very pale and prettier than Mrs Lynd remembered. Her rings were loose on her thin fingers as she made the tea. With her neat black head and pale face silhouetted against a purple wall, she was like a china figure.

So Katherine prepared to go to Italy. She put on her gauzy toque and had her passport photograph taken, surely the saddest, most tragic little face ever, but she was going to seek the sun, and leave behind the England she detested. On September 9th she wrote a letter to Murry and left it with Mr Kay.

If I were you I'd sell off all the furniture and go off on a long sea voyage . . . Any money I have is yours of course. I expect there will be enough to bury me. I don't want to be cremated and I don't want a tombstone or anything like that. If it's possible to choose a quiet place, please do. You know how I hate noise . . . All my Mss I simply leave to you . . . But don't let anybody mourn me. It can't be helped. I think you ought to marry again and have children. If you do give your little girl the pearl ring. She must have been feeling very low and bitter to write thus, but there is a little flicker of humour there also.

She, L.M. and Murry set off on September 11th, 1919 to stay at San Remo in a hotel under English management. Then trouble began. Guests complained to the manager, guessing the cause of Katherine's devastating cough. He asked her to leave but kindly offered to rent her his villa, the Casetta Deerholm at nearby Ospedaletti. They accepted gratefully and Murry left on October 2nd. Alas, Katherine received a bill for the fumigation of her hotel room!

Chapter XV

Ospedaletti and Menton

The Casetta Deerholm was built on a rough aromatic hillside of fig and olive trees, thyme and rosemary, above Ospedaletti, with a great spread of sea in front and that spoiler of a good sea view, the coast road, well tucked in below and out of sight. It was small with two rooms and a kitchen downstairs and two bedrooms upstairs. Alas, there was no water as yet; cooking was done by charcoal stove and heating by open wood fire. The small garden with its slip of a lawn, had been cut out of the hillside, a sort of terracing, with a cotton bush gracing the gate. There was a veranda at the side of the house. On a lower level there were a few hotels, Katherine occasionally negotiating the way there; but alas, the weary climb home was almost more than she could manage, for she was breathless on exertion, even on dressing and brushing her hair, because disease had put so much lung out of action.

Without this dark shadow and the repercussions from her faulty relationship with L.M. it should have been a lovely spot to work in; but winter was approaching, the high exposed position of the Casetta lent itself to piercing winds, driving rain, cruel draughts, and consequent anxiety over heating bills. The warmth from expensive green wood fires poured up the chimney, instead of heating the stout metal of a closed stove.

At first L.M. had to carry water from a spring, and cooking by charcoal was difficult for her. She used sand from the hillside to clean the blackened copper pans. Inevitably some meals were late, especially when trying to make do with damp olive roots and paper for cooking. However, water was installed by October 10th. The weather was still warm and insects abounded, methodically biting Katherine who had to sleep under a mosquito net. By day she spent hours in the garden watching the sea and 'that lift of white seen faraway' on the horizon, which moved her terribly.

By October 13th it was cold, foggy and wet. The next day was her thirty-first birthday. Murry sent her a spoon, Chaddie and Jeanne an enamelled matchbox. L.M. gave her a bottle of Genêt Fleuri. Strangely there was only a letter from Mr Beauchamp, who perhaps felt sore. He was coming to stay with his cousin Connie Beauchamp and her friend Jinnie Fullerton at the Villa Flora in Menton. Katherine, stimulated by the change, had been sending cheerful letters home, but by October 16th, under the influence of *'sudden intense heavy cold'* she admitted she was *'just a little bit tired . . . . hold me close till I am warm',* she implored Murry.

She was receiving books each week for review for *The Athenaeum*; she was grateful for the income and the mental stimulus of the task. However, by October 22nd she had to confess she had been ill in bed with a temperature, which was inevitable; she had set off a sick woman. A cold hillside and sea view were not likely to improve this state; she would have been more comfortable in the Elephant.

Then relations broke down with L.M. They were not speaking except for housekeeping directions. They had been quarrelling. *I go mad,* she wrote to Murry, *just like L(awrence) used to. Here I have thrown things at her . . . called her a murderer, cursed her. Her three standing remarks: 'Give me time!' 'I'll learn by degrees, Katie' and 'You must first teach me, that's all' . . .* That was some of the trouble, L.M. was feckless at times, inadequate, and very inexperienced in homecraft, but mostly, L.M. set Katherine's teeth on edge. She was depressed and lonely enjoining Murry to love her as much as she loved him. Letters from Murry seemed to be delayed seven days and tended to come in batches of two. She implored him to write.

The local doctor, a German called Bobone, was called in and seemed to disregard the depression, he didn't listen. He informed Katherine that the apex of her right lung was affected, the left infiltrated to the third rib and gave her a prescription.

By November 3rd there was snow on the mountains, and thunderstorms churned up rough seas, the noise of which was almost unendurable. Mr Beauchamp at Menton was suffering from a chill and was in bed. He planned to motor over to see Katherine on Wednesday November 12th. Katherine was unable to keep her depression out of her letters home, complaining further about not getting Murry's letters *let us try to make this our last separation,* and recalling happier days . . . . *Ah, how terrible life can be! I sometimes see an immense wall of black rock, shining in a place just after death perhaps — and* smiling — *the* adamant of desire — a terrible letter to receive. Desperate, Murry answered her, reiterating that he wrote every day.

Murry's colleagues noticed his tragic looks and his work reflected his despair. He showed Tomlinson a poem he'd written.

> . . . Scratch through the silver of illusions glass
> Their name at least that a faint light be thrown
> Upon the further chamber's basalt floor . . .

"*Your* floor," Tomlinson had chuckled, "*would* be bloody basalt." So he told Katherine in a letter on November 11th, trying to make her laugh.

In the week of November 10th Katherine had to review Virginia's novel *Night and Day.* She didn't like it and thought it *a lie in the soul . . . the war never has been . . . I feel in the profoundest sense that nothing can ever be the same again — that, as artists we are traitors if we feel otherwise . . . inwardly I despise them all for a set of* cowards . . . she told Murry. On November 11th Katherine was visited by Dr Ansaldi from San Remo, who was over-optimistic but reiterated the need for rest.

Mr Beauchamp at Menton was bemoaning the cold weather from his sick bed. He wrote to Katherine that he couldn't keep warm even with a hot water bottle. On Wednesday November 12th his party duly arrived at the Casetta at 10.30 a.m. filling the place with furs and coats and ten pairs of spectacles, which they all tried on. L.M. anxiously made the lunch, chops awash with onions, followed by fruit and cream. In the afternoon they all motored to San Remo, Mr Beauchamp as cheer-leader, talking in Maori down the speaking-tube to the chauffeur. Amid the gales of laughter, Katherine, in another world, was happy also. While the women went shopping, she sat with her father in the sun-warmed car. He thought they were like a couple of hot-house plants ripening. It was touching that they had these moments together. His life, like Katherine's, was now so changed, his beloved wife gone, also his treasure Chummie, his girls dispersed all over the world and now his rather special child, albeit his little black sheep, fading away. All the bounce seemed to have gone out of him. He had been depressed and a bit footloose. Saying goodbye to Katherine with his symbolic nosegay of five daisies and an orchid tied with grass, he held her in his arms, called her his precious child saying that she was just like her mother.

Describing the happy day for Murry, Katherine added that they had all seemed horrified by the cold weather and all disapproved of the chilly Casetta. Murry, who had dined with Mr Beauchamp in London two weeks ago, replied saying he wished he had been more friendly towards him then. Alas Murry had felt hostile that evening.

However, in spite of the isolation and discomfort, Katherine had declined the suggestion that she move to Menton. She valued her privacy too much. After a further chill, Mr Beauchamp finally left Toulon for Naples on November 22nd. He was to marry, the day after arrival in Auckland on January 5th, 1920, at the registry office, his wife's close friend, Mrs Laura Bright, a rich widow.

The noise of the sea began to irritate Katherine, keeping her awake at night, and the intense cold frightened her. *I breathe it and deep down it's as though a knife softly pressed in my bosom and said, 'Don't be too sure'. That's the fearful part of having been near death. One knows how easy it is to die . . .* she told Murry.

These feelings worsened her irritation with L.M. which erupted into black hatred. Katherine called the feeling her 'deadly enemy'. This propensity was part of the fabric of her personality. Russell recognised this in her, 'her dark hatreds'.

L.M. bore the brunt of this 'black fit' because she was there and really triggered it off. However well-meaning L.M. was, she was a great irritator.

Katherine described her feelings in her letter to Murry on November 20th: *Christ! to* hate *like I do. It's upon me today . . . . It's simply a blind force of hatred. Hate is the* other *passion. It has all the opposite effects of love . . . it makes you long to DESTROY . . . Her great fat arms, her tiny blind breasts, her baby mouth, the underlip always* wet *and a crumb or two or a chocolate stain at the corners — her eyes fixed on me — fixed — waiting for what I shall do so that (she) may copy it. Think what you would feel if you had consumption and lived with a deadly enemy!* No wonder L.M. tended to stare at Katherine. She would show the concentration of a knife-thrower's assistant in order to dodge the missiles thrown at her. She would also be watching to see which way the wind was blowing. It must have been a great strain. No wonder she journeyed into San Remo to eat cakes.

Murry was now sharing the Elephant with Sydney Waterlow, and working hard rescuing *The Athenaeum*. Katherine was well aware of the effort going into it. Truly his life was very hard. However, for the December 5th issue of the paper his review of the fourth anthology of *Georgian Poetry* edited by Eddie Marsh, and *Wheels* by the Sitwells, was outstanding and disturbing. In it Murry roundly ridiculed the old style of poetry and thus made way for the new. In his criticism he had exempted Lawrence, De la Mare, Wilfred Owen and W.H. Davis. He had, alas, hurt his kind friend Eddie Marsh.

By December 1st Dr Ansaldi was called in again. Katherine had a temperature of 102°. She was so sick and lonely she had even decided to go to Menton, contacting Jinnie about it. Writing to Murry on December 3rd she enclosed some verses . . . *last night under the inspiration of a fever attack I wrote these verses. Keep them for me, will you?* She was obsessed with the fear of death. Unfortunately, before leaving England she had read some poem of Murry's in his private book, where he had contemplated the idea of her death. In his journal he wrote: *She had come upon it unaware, and it had pierced her heart.*

Her main poem, called 'The New Husband' went thus:

Someone came to me and said
Forget, forget that you've been wed.
Who's your man to leave you be
Ill and cold in a far country?
Who's the husband — who's the stone
Could leave a child like you alone?

You're like a leaf caught in the wind,
You're like a lamb that's left behind,
When all the flock has pattered away;
You're like a pitiful little stray
Kitten that I'd put in my vest;
You're like a bird that's fallen from the nest.

We've none of us too long to live,
Then take me for your man and give
Me all the keys to all your fears
And let me kiss away these tears;
Creep close to me. I mean no harm
My darling. Let me make you warm.

I had received that very day
A letter from the other to say
That in six months — he hoped — no longer
I would be so much better and stronger
That he could close his books and come
With radiant looks to bear me home.

Ha! Ha! Six months, six weeks, six hours
Among these glittering palms and flowers
With Melancholy at my side
For my old nurse and for my guide
Despair — and for my footman Pain
— I'll never see my home again.

Said my new husband: Little dear,
It's time we were away from here.
In the road below there waits my carriage
Ready to drive us to our marriage.
Within my house the feast is spread
And the maids are baking the bridal bread.

I thought with grief upon that other
But then why should he aught discover
Save that I pined away and died?
So I became the stranger's bride
And every moment however fast
It flies — we live as 'twere our last!

Abandoned by Murry, death was her new husband. It was a *cri de coeur*, written in a fever, simply a reflection of her depression, no more than that. I doubt whether it was intended as a 'snake' or written in anger, more likely desperation, misguided though, especially as this particular poem set in motion a crisis from which part of Katherine never recovered.

Murry, his self-deceiving armour-plate pierced at last, guilt-ridden, for he had started an affair with Brett that winter, probably unwillingly, but which was to continue fitfully for years and contain an abortion, was unconsciously seeking a show-down, which he got. He made swift arrangements to travel to Ospedaletti, sending the following harsh letter to Katherine which shot her in the wing:

8 December, 1919.
This morning in bed I got your Thursday letter and the verses called 'The New Husband' . . . . I don't think that at any time I've had a bigger blow . . . Even now they hardly seem like a letter and verses — more like a snake *with a terrible sting. But it's kind of you to tell me you have those feelings, far better . . . than keeping them from me. You have too great a burden to bear . . . What is certain is that this can't go on . . . my faith at present is that my coming out . . . will put you right. But I dont see why it should. I feel that everything depends on me; that I have to do something quite definite, very quickly. But I don't know what it is . . . I'm ready to chuck the paper . . . but I must see my way to money . . . it's fundamental to any decision I take . . . you know my position as a bankrupt . . . I'm absolutely incapable of work, now . . . I must tell you the truth. I'm not made of steel . . . it's becoming a great effort to do what I have to do sanely . . . . No, no, no, — all this is too hard. I don't mean it . . . .*

The trouble was, he did. Across the letter, Katherine wrote:

This letter killed the mouse . . . banished the Dream Child for ever. Before I had received it I had learned to live for Love and by Love . . . a kind of third creature. Us was what I lived by. After I had read it . . . my own self returned and all my horror of death vanished. From this date I simply don't care about death! . . . . I simply feel alone again, Voilà

In her notebook: *These letters . . . cut like a knife through something that had grown up between us. They changed the situation for me, . . . forever . . . Gone is my childish love — gone is my desire to live in England. I don't particularly want to live with him . . . I am become — Mother. I don't care a rap for people. I shall always love Jack and be his wife but I couldn't get back to that anguish — joy — sweet madness of love . . . I am (December 15th 1919) a dead woman, and I don't care . . . Honesty — is the only thing one seems to prize beyond life, love, death, everything . . . O those that come after me, will you believe it? At the end truth is the only thing worth having . . . I'd say we had a love-child and it's dead . . . J says: Forget that letter! How can I? It killed the child . . . .*

And to Murry on December 9th:

. . . However ill I am, you are more ill. However weak I am, you are weaker . . . You make me out so cruel that . . . . I feel you can't love me in the least — a vampire. I am not . . . granted that I have sent you this 'snake' . . . are you justified in punishing me so horribly?

In spite of protestations from Katherine telling him not to come, Murry arrived in Ospedaletti on December 16th with a king-size headache, probably repeated attacks of migraine precipitated by anxiety. According to L.M: *he brought no happiness. The days of those two weeks were shadowed . . . . he spent his nights in the little spare room. Katherine said I must wait till all was quiet and then creep with my rugs into her room to sleep as usual on the sofa.* Good old L.M!

After Murry left, Katherine sagged with exhaustion and

misery. She was ill and sleepless. *Appalling night of misery deciding J. had no more need of our love*, she wrote on January 10th. Thrown back on her writing she began *The Man Without a Temperament*. Strangely, she discovered her feelings of friendship for L.M. returning, and at that L.M. blossomed. Katherine finished the story on January 11th, writing from 9.30 a.m. until 12.15 p.m. Then, too exhausted to sleep, she lay listening to 'the drowned souls' in the sea, thinking that she and Murry were no longer as they were. Cast back on herself with little or no future she was engulfed in depressive rumination, dwelling on the past, 'going over all the old life before . . . the baby of Garnet Trowell'. She had terrible fits of weeping 'haunted' by thoughts of Jack.

An English doctor, efficient and firm, called Foster, who had seen her on December 8th, agreed when he saw her again that she should move to Menton but that she must rest completely for two months. His verdict was that there was serious disease in the left lung of long-standing, the right was quiescent. He proposed to notify the authorities and requested her to sterilize her knife, fork and spoon. It seems obvious that he feared she was an open tuberculosis case, i.e. with positive sputum. However, this was not so.

On January 16th she began another story, subsequently called *The Wrong House* but never finished. They finally left the Casetta on January 21st for a nursing home, L'Hermitage, in Menton. She wrote to Ottoline the day before, unburdening her misery: *my heart has been affected . . . . by misery. I have simply wept for days. The appalling isolation, deathly stillness, great wind and sea, and this feeling that I had consumption and was tainted, dying here. If I moved, even to the doorstep — my heart beat so hard that I had to lean against the door, and then no sleep — nothing but going over . . . one's whole past life . . . I tried to explain this to M(urry) but — he did not understand at all . . . . I thought . . . that 'one' understood . . . I was wrong. For nearly six years I have felt loved. Now it is gone — tragic!*

Her room, which was to be 30 francs a day, was large and overlooked the gardens and mountains. The relief was enormous, she had escaped from 'that hell of isolation'. Jinnie and Connie, two very nice women, 'English ladies' (Katherine's description), were there to meet her. L.M. was to try to get a job. Her room at the Pension Anglaise was 15 francs per day. Katherine was very short of money and was asking Murry to sell her collected stories for only £20. He sensibly contacted Michael Sadleir of Constable's. In the meantime he had been made an OBE, yet note a letter to Katherine on December 5th: *I wish to God I were a man. Somehow I seem to have grown up, gone bald even, without ever becoming a man; and I find it terribly hard to master a situation.* Somebody, somewhere, knew his worth. He was editor of the *Daily Review* of the Foreign Press and now chief censor.

There was an obvious change in Katherine's letters to Murry, a hardness had crept in, accentuated by money problems. On January 26th Murry wrote to Katherine about walking in Sussex the previous weekend, ostensibly to look for a house in the country. He was unwise enough to make it very plain he had enjoyed himself: *drunken with the magnificence of the Downs,* asking airily, *How's money?* In the new hardened state Katherine rather unreasonably took exception to this and told him so. She asked him to contribute £10 per month towards her expenses, a thing she had never done before. It seems incredible that she had to ask Murry for support. No wonder Mr Beauchamp was aggrieved. Anyway she considered his letter 'an abnormally selfish one' which it wasn't really and she ended her letter: *I've nothing to say to you Bogey. I am too hurt* . . . .

His reply on February 7th, 1920 was abject, trying to excuse his inner deadness which in the circumstances must have been very real.

In her next letter she actually said she couldn't write to him every day, feeling that he did not read her letters, she preferred to work instead. What a change! She wired him to send £10; his reply: Though things are tight, *I will send you a cheque for £20 tomorrow, if you will repay me when you get the money for your book.* This brought a sharp reply on February 4th: *Perhaps I did not make it clear that I asked you for the £10 a month* . . . *I am afraid from this note you may advance it for me and then take the book money. But I am afraid that will not do. Will you please tell me* why *money is tight?* According to his biographer Frank Lea, Murry always thought of himself as poor . . . waste horrified him and he drew security from gardening and woodwork. Some people find it difficult to eradicate the haunting fear of poverty engendered in childhood, no matter how successful they become. In Murry it was ingrained.

On February 7th she wrote: *It's only since I've been away you have withdrawn yourself from me and ever since I broke down at the Casetta and appealed to you things have never been the same . . . Oh, darling . . . Do care . . . wait till I'm strong before you run away for a bit . . . .*

February 7th had been a bad day for Katherine. She had received a terrible pathological letter from Lawrence, calling her a reptile! He hoped she would die. He also called Murry a worm.

One wonders why Lawrence should indulge in such dastardly vituperation for no apparent reason. His rejection by Murry had generated a smouldering fire within him, like a volcano, which burned ceaselessly and erupted sporadically from internal pressures. It is also possible that Lawrence was dysrhythmic, a state where the electrical brain rhythms are irregular and made more so by external factors such as alcohol, excessive intake of fluids, flashing lights, and over-exertion, which in some can trigger off brain-storms, epileptic fits, delusions of jealousy, aggression, even occasional homicide. This is hypothetical, of course, in Lawrence's case but it is obvious that from time to time he seemed to suffer from a disturbed mental state, which his long-suffering friend Jessie had witnessed and called his 'dark side', a sort of frenzy 'exploding inside' using 'wild words'. She recalled an occasion at Robin Hood's Bay when Lawrence 'stalked . . . like a strange wild creature and kept up a stream of upbraiding' for no apparent reason.

I had a patient once who was perfectly well throughout the week, but frequently developed delusions of jealousy on a Saturday night after drinking a large quantity of beer. By Monday he was sheepish but well. His electroencephalogram showed dysrhythmia, and he was therefore liable to electrical build-up from the trigger mechanism of alcohol.

Witter Bynner in his book Journey with Genius reckoned

that Lawrence was liable to flare up after wine. He described a luncheon occasion with Frieda and Lawrence at the Monte Carlo Hotel in Mexico City, when, as they were sipping chianti, Lawrence suddenly stood up, accused Frieda of having her legs open to every man in the room, then threw his wine in her face. Actually Frieda was sitting at a corner table well covered by the table cloth. And there we will leave our 'promiscuous hater' for the moment.

Murry answered with the good news that Constable was publishing her book of short stories for £40. It was to be entitled *Bliss* and consisted of Katherine's best stories up to 1920, with two new ones *Revelations* and *Escape*, written in Hampstead. He told her he had bought her an overcoat, then requested her to wire him if she still loved him; very upsetting, that. Then a letter came from Murry asking her not to give him up entirely. This wounded Katherine, always very sensitive to any hint of withdrawal of love. She wept all day, feeling that he was perfectly prepared to be given up and that he wanted to be free. In her notebook she wrote a long account of her anguish, her aching throat, trying not to cry in front of the other patients, taking a faded little brougham to the post to send him a telegram and having to buy sal volatile at the chemist to keep her going. Fortunately she saw Jinnie in the street, who no doubt noticed her distress and kindly took her to the doctor, presumably for sputum tests and then arranged to gather her into the fold at the Villa Flora at the end of a week.

Murry replied to her wire and desperate letter, on February 10th. He was very upset saying he was at the end of his tether. He denied being cold, insisting that he wrote with his blood protesting his love for her. Murry, who had also received a blistering letter from Lawrence, wrote to Katherine saying he would hit him when next he met him — poetic justice. Katherine wrote to Lawrence saying . . . *I detest you for having dragged this disgusting reptile across all that has been,* and she described for Murry how when she read Lawrence's letter she *saw a reptile, felt a reptile . . . he is somehow filthy. I never had such a feeling about a human being . . . .*

Katherine, upset, sleepless, and feverish, pondered on her relations with Murry, her mainstay, now sadly tattered. It is obvious that there had been some sparring at the Casetta, frank truths exchanged, fine between two healthy partners, distasteful when one partner is dying. *Yes, I felt in Ospedaletti that you refused to understand and I have felt since I have been abroad this time that you have turned away from me — withdrawn yourself utterly from me . . . .* Sensibly she tried to surmount the irreversible tragedy, '. . . out of evil good shall come' and called pax, but she was maimed.

Katherine moved into the Villa Flora, the beautiful house which Jinnie ran as a nursing home. Katherine had to pay a similar fee for her room but there were many advantages, lovely log fires, a personal maid, congenial company and a baby Pekinese dog. Connie, most kindly and solicitous, arranged for her dressmaker to make Katherine a new dress and referred to her as her 'hedgesparrow'. In such a kindly and luxurious atmosphere, Katherine began to blossom a little and though still ill, was happier and less dependent on Murry. He considered her letters from the Villa Flora less spontaneous than her other beautiful, if fraught, loving letters of the past. It was true, the girl who wrote those other letters was buried at the Casetta. Things would never be the same again; the golden goose was killed.

Both Jinnie and Connie were Catholics and they hoped to convert Katherine, but this did not materialize in spite of the following experience. One day in April, L.M. received a letter from Katherine to say that while lying on a hillside, she had had a sudden conviction that there was a God and she intended to become a Catholic. *Once I believe in a God, the rest is so easy . . . I mean to make life wonderful if I can. Queer, Jones, I've always had a longing to* heal *people and* make them whole, *enrich them: that's what writing means to me — to enrich — to give — I want to do it in life too. I shall tell Jack this, some time . . . Perhaps I shall just leave him to find out. But you can't live near me and not know it . . . I tell you for another reason too — and that's because you are my 'sworn friend' — Jones, I am not at all well yet — terribly nervous and exacting and always in pain — But I will get over it — But I need you and I rely on you — I lean hard on you — yet I can't thank you or give you anything in return — except . my love. You have that always.*

Katie.

This letter was a treasured possession of L.M.'s and it reveals a significant facet of their stormy relationship. L.M. procured a nursing assistant's post in a nursing home in Menton and was able to visit Katherine in the evening.

Unfortunately, while at the Villa Flora Katherine learned that her father considered he was doing a great deal for her, which information may have been merely the result of a misread remark. This caused a rift which lasted nearly two years. Mr Beauchamp strenuously denied the charge, as shall be seen later.

Though it was still just February, the weather at Menton was wonderful after the cold of Ospedaletti and Katherine was taken on picnics into the mountains. She was now trying to persuade Murry to postpone getting a house in the country, and proposing to spend the next two winters abroad, another sign of change. Formerly she could not bear the idea of separation. She also wished to have L.M. with her. Murry was wanting to leave the Elephant; he couldn't stand the place. Obsessed with his day-dream of a house in some lovely spot, one can imagine his grinding disappointment.

Though Katherine was more settled, she had had an attack of arthritis, principally in her right hip-joint, the pain was severe. Fortunately her cough was much improved. Murry's fatigue was showing through his letters. This upset Katherine. *It's a great effort to love just now, isn't it? Ah, Bogey* — she wrote on March 7th.

On March 8th Murry wrote to Brett saying that her loving him had made him realize how sacred his marriage was. He had been on a country expedition with her, looking at a cottage he told Katherine, who answered a little tartly that she couldn't spend seven months in a cottage, that she preferred being in her home in Portland Villas: *you write to me as though I had been away 8 years . . .*

She was further upset by a letter from — (probably Brett) telling her of 'orgies' and the 'drink' and the parties. She implored Murry not to let Richard see the 'orgies' or wine parties and . . . *The 'girl you left behind you' really did die after all in that Casetta and is buried there for ever . . . .*

Murry had eventually bought a small cottage called Broomies on Chailey Common; alas they never lived in it, but

Katherine began to be pleased about their acquiring it.

On April 6th she told Murry they were all motoring to Nice. She described how they had early lunch in hats then the maids brought cushions and rugs for the car. Connie had brought Katherine six hats. She did not like Nice with its large glittering shops. I wonder if she thought a little about that other young artist, Marie Bashkirtseff, in her white dress in a green arbour by a marble fountain, in the garden of Villa Acqua Viva, all those years ago? Katherine loved the Riviera though; it reminded her of New Zealand.

On April 7th she went to lunch with Sydney and Violet Schiff, whom she had met through a publisher called Grant Richards. Sydney wrote under the name of Stephen Hudson and was an authority on Proust. He translated the eighth and final part of Proust called *Time Regained* which was published in England in 1931. Born 1868, his grandfather was Jewish, and a very successful banker. Sydney's father came to the London Stock Exchange, founding the firm of A.G. Schiff and Company. Sydney went farming in Canada, but, coming from an artistic, cultured background (his father had entertained musicians, artists and publishers most lavishly), he had always had a desire to write. Back in England at forty-one, his first marriage having failed, he had the great fortune to meet and fall in love at first sight with the beautiful Violet Beddington, one of nine daughters of intensely musical parents, living at 21, Hyde Park Square, London. One sister, Ada Leverson, was the friend of Oscar Wilde whom he called the Sphinx. All the girls sang, they were friends of Puccini, Caruso and Scotti. Sydney and Violet were married in 1911 and spent their time between London and their beautiful 'Villa Violet' at Roquebrune. His friends included Marcel Proust, Beerbohm, T.S. Eliot, the Sitwells and Aldous Huxley. He had encouraged Gertler and Gaudier-Brzeska, and had collected paintings of Picasso, Gertler, John Nash and Wyndham Lewis.

Early in April Sydney drove over to the Villa Flora to meet Katherine for the first time. He came in a Victoria feeling she would love the drive. He found the large villa in a palm-filled garden. He was shown into a spacious salon where he was joined by Katherine. They sat together on a sofa with a gilded ornate back. Dainty fresh and elegant with transparent skin

and rather a hectic colour she looked fragile but radiant when
she laughed. Her dark brown hair, mid length, curled beneath
her hat. She spoke clearly in a soft low voice which was a little
hoarse. They drove off to Roquebrune where she was
introduced to Violet. Katherine removed her hat. Her hair
was drawn back and held by a comb, as usual she was wearing
a fringe. Sydney thought she looked younger without a hat.
After champagne and during lunch they were joined by
Violet's friend Madame Bibka Prévost elegant in grey
crêpe-de-Chine and carrying mimosa. She was going to have a
baby. As Violet sang 'Wie bist Du, meine Konigen' tears welled
up in Katherine's eyes. She hurriedly took her leave much to
Bibka's astonishment.

One can only assume that with the music and the sight of
Bibka, Katherine was overwhelmed with grief at the death of
all her fine hopes.

On Saturday April 24th there was a dinner party for
eighteen at the Villa Flora for Katherine's last evening. She
was to wear her purple silk dress and real pearl ear-rings, an
Easter present, a far cry from the terrible Casetta days. She
arrived home a few days later.

R

Chapter XVI

Last Summer At The Elephant

To mark the occasion of their second wedding anniversary, Katherine visited the office of *The Athenaeum* to collect Murry. They wished to purchase a coffee pot. Katherine sent a lively account to the Schiffs on May 10th: *the untidiness of John's desk was the first crushing blow . . . Huxley wavering like a candle who expected to go out with the next open door . . . Sullivan and E.M. Forster very vague, very frightened. I heard myself speaking of lemon trees and then I said that in one valley I knew there was a torrent. Nobody cared . . . I ran downstairs back into the car with Murry . . . He was sure the shop would be shut because I'd talked . . . so he looked out of his window and I looked out of mine . . . .*

In the next letter to the Schiffs she mentioned she had been ill: *. . . in physical and mental pain that could not be spoken of . . . here's a woman . . . who . . . has made demands on a man who confesses he has very little vitality to spare . . . who finds . . . he doesn't . . . desire her kind of life — but wants to be a scholar and live quietly . . . how well I understand this jealous passionate love of himself . . . I have been living in a dream . . .* however *deeply one is shaken — Art remains . . . Men come up in the evening . . . they sprawl on the sommier . . . take chance shots with the cigarette ash and never reach the inside of the fender . . . .*

Murry had always been narcissistic, and self-absorbed. Katherine noticed he was drawn to any mirror in a room to contemplate his reflection. Martin Green, in his book *The von Richthofen Sisters*, considered Murry 'the winsome faunlike Narcissus of British intellectual life'.

Katherine sounded disillusioned. She had also become suspicious of Brett's relationship with Murry. At tea one day, Brett thought Katherine looked sad and frail. She then accused Brett of having an affair with Murry, upsetting the hot water over her legs as she did so. She was crying bitterly. Brett vehemently denied this, but failed to convince Katherine. On another afternoon, while Brett was playing bowls with Murry, Katherine 'arrived in a taxi. She was cold, remote, furious, and drove off looking straight before her like a stone image . . . .'

Between 14th and 21st May, T.S. Eliot and his wife Vivienne dined with the Murrys. Vivienne Eliot, born 1888, had married T.S. Eliot in 1915 after a short acquaintance. She came from a cultured background, her father was a distinguished painter. She was slim, small, with light brown hair and grey eyes, very vivacious, seductive, alas also a little irritating. Because of a basic mental instability which led eventually to a psychosis and breakdown of the marriage, she was frivolous and argumentative, 'a spoilt kitten type' according to Virginia Woolf. She had some sort of association with Russell who recognised her mental symptoms, considering she was 'a person who lives on a knife-edge' and on this basis took her under his wing, paying for her dancing lessons, taking her on holiday and buying her silk underwear. T.S. Eliot, a protégé of his, was by now painfully aware of his wife's problems and grateful for any attention or kindness shown to her. Murry had got Eliot to write for *The Athenaeum* and had already entertained them both. Vivienne found the Murrys 'scintillating' and their evenings 'incomparably brilliant'.

Alas, Katherine did not like Mrs Eliot, and writing to the Schiffs about the occasion, she described her suffering:

The Elliots (sic) have dined with us tonight. They are just gone — and the whole room is quivering. John has gone downstairs to see them off — Mrs. E's voice rises — "Oh don't commiserate Tom; he's quite happy." I know it's extravagant. I know, Violet. I ought to have seen more but I dislike her so immensely. She really repels me — she makes me shiver with apprehension . . . I don't dare to think of what she is "seeing". From the moment that John dropped a spoon and she cried, "I

say you are *noisy tonight* — *what's wrong"* to *the moment,*
when she came into my room and lay on the sofa offering idly:
"This room's changed since the last time I was here." To think
she has been here before. *I handed her the cigarettes saying to*
myself "well you won't find it changed again." Isn't that
extravagant. And Elliot, leaning towards her, admiring,
listening, making the most of her — *really minding whether*
she disliked the country or not —
I am so fond of Elliot . . . I felt a deep sympathy with him . . .
But this tea shop creature. Murry comes up after they are gone
— and he defends her. He tells me of a party he gave here and
how she came and was furious with him and how he drank to
get over the state of nerves she had thrown him into "I like her;
I would do the same again." Just the sort of note Murry *would*
strike in the circumstances and not the note to end an evening
on, in case of disturbing Katherine's night's sleep. Katherine
went on: *I feel as though I've been stabbed. Now it's dead still*
— except for the far off noise of the trains drumming round
the hollow world. Poor Katherine, and poor unstable,
insensitive, undiplomatic Vivienne, who was to be abandoned
ultimately.

Virginia paid two calls in May and early June. She had not
liked Katherine's review of *Night and Day*, she saw 'spite in it'
and had been highly irritated by her writing. *I'm not going to*
call this success — *or if I must, I'll call it the wrong kind of*
success. Written in the unhappiness of the Casetta, Katherine
hated *Night and Day*.

Katherine received Virginia coolly, it would be awkward
after that review. Virginia thought Katherine *of the cat kind;*
alien, composed, always solitary — *observant* — *someone*
apart, entirely self-centred; altogether concentrated upon her
'art': almost fierce to me about it. However, on Virginia
mentioning *Night and Day* Katherine piped: *An amazing*
achievement, why, we've not had such a thing since I don't
know when — and straight away invited Virginia to lunch to
discuss it. Virginia again felt at ease with her, *a common*
understanding between us — *a queer sense of being 'like' . . . I*
can talk straight out to her.

Katherine also entertained Gertler to tea. He too, was ill,

having suffered a haemoptysis in April, after a no doubt hectic visit to Paris. He was to go into a sanatorium at Banchory in November. Sadly he never really recovered and committed suicide in 1939.

In June *The Athenaeum* began to publish short stories. For June 11th Katherine contributed *Revelations*. Her desk was snowed under with work, piles of books to review and manuscripts to read. On Tuesdays she sat at her typewriter with a cup of beaten eggs in wine for lunch, not stirring until the task was completed.

Between April and October 1st, 1919 Katherine had collaborated with Koteliansky on translating the letters of Anton Chekhov, which appeared in *The Athenaeum* in thirteen instalments. From the beginning she loved and cherished Chekhov.

She had also reviewed 150 novels, which brilliant and at times slightly hectic pieces were published posthumously in book form, entitled *Novels and Novelists in 1930*. Katherine was so taken with a first novel, *Dark River* by Gertrude Millin published in 1920, that she wrote to the authoress about it. In *The Athenaeum* review she wrote:

Perhaps a novel is never the novel it might have been, but there are certain books which seem to contain the vision, more or less blurred or more or less clear, of their second selves of what the author saw before he grasped the difficult pen.

To Miss Millin: *I wish I had said more about your book. I have felt ever since the notice appeared that I really didn't do it justice — didn't express as I should like to have expressed how "original" it was — how different from the many novels, how anxious it made the reader feel to know more of the author's work . . . I kept feeling "If she can keep this up, if she does keep this up in her next book — if she goes on 'freeing' herself and exploring her own gift this woman is going to be a rare writer"!*

Miss Millin in her memoirs, *The Night is Long*, said that Katherine's letter *was the only thing that gave me any happiness about "The Dark River" — coming when it did, it meant much to me.* Gertrude Millin was a white South African and her novel was an account of life on the *sucked dry, used up, thrown aside scrap of the earth's surface, the River Diggings.* As a Colonial, this would strike a chord in Katherine and no doubt made her reflect on her Grandpa Beauchamp's life on the goldfield at Ararat and her father's birth there. She was to write again to Gertrude Millin from Paris in 1922.

Another visitor was her cousin Elizabeth, who after the death of Count von Arnim in 1910 had been living in Switzerland. There, in October 1910, she and a devoted maid had surveyed the countryside for possible sites on which to build a chalet, travelling each day from the Château Belle Vue Hotel in Sierre. They found a beautiful spot near Randogue-sur-Sierre just below Montana, with a glorious view over the Rhône Valley towards Mont Blanc. When finished it was called Chalet Soleil, there were sixteen bedrooms in the upper two stories, with the Nassenheide Library housed on the ground floor. A separate small chalet in the garden was Elizabeth's place of work. This garden became massed with flowers. Hoards of visitors came and went, including Bertrand Russell's formidable brother Francis, Earl Russell, who steamrollered Elizabeth into an unhappy marriage with him. It was dissolved in 1920.

She had been writing steadily since *Elizabeth and Her German Garden* and on June 29th, 1910 had seen the stage version of her book *Princess Priscilla's Fortnight* open at the Haymarket Theatre. Three of her four lovely daughters 'in a beaming row in white muslin' were present on the first night.

Now, with ten novels behind her, she came no doubt with great curiosity and admiration to look her cousin Katherine over. Much water had flowed under the bridge since her rather stiff reception of the young Beauchamp cousins in 1904.

Katherine was not enamoured and wrote rather harshly about Elizabeth to Violet Schiff in an undated letter: *a thousand devils are sending Elizabeth without her German Garden to tea here tomorrow . . . I expect she will stay at longest half an hour — she will be oh, such a little bundle of artificialities — but I can't put her off . . . .*

Elizabeth, now fifty-three and still very fascinating, who gave Dame Ethel Smythe 'the feeling of standing under a cool

and gentle waterfall on an extremely hot day', was to be a good
friend to both Murry and Katherine. Frank Swinnerton found
her *small, fair, lazy-voiced, she seemed at a first male glance
to be no more than a child. Then one observed that the child
was precocious. And then that she was terrifying . . . some men
trembled under the gaze of her rather prominent merciless
pale blue eyes, and collapsed altogether before the demurely
drawling boldness of her tongue . . . Her judgement of men
and women, however, being unsentimental, were often
destructive . . . I have never known any woman with the same
comic detachment of mind . . . .*

Her finest novel *Vera* published in 1921 and depicting her
life with Russell, fascinated Katherine. Elizabeth admitted to
Murry much later that she had admired Katherine abjectly.

In July Katherine had to resort to more injections of vaccine.
Dr Sorapure's treatment had merely mitigated the arthritis.
She attended a clinic in Harley Street, presumably Dr
Sorapure's private consulting rooms. She had the inevitable
reaction and was confined to bed, telling Violet about it: *The
'trouble' has been I've had an overdose of vaccine and it laid
me low. Ten million — or twenty million — hosts of
Steptococci attacked and fought one another . . . .*

On August 12th she noted:

 *. . . I cough and cough and at each breath a dragging
boiling bubbling sound is heard . . . I sip water, spit, sip, spit. I
feel I must break my heart . . . life is . . . getting a new breath
. . . And J. is silent, hangs his head, hides his face with his
fingers* as though *it were unendurable. 'This is what she is
doing to me! Every fresh sound makes* my *nerves wince.' I know
he can't help these feelings . . . If he could only for a minute,
serve me, help me, give* himself *up . . . I feel I never could get
well with him . . . .*

One can only assume that with the music and the sight of
the pendulum; the punch in the weak midriff as a sort of tonic
for Katherine. Murry told her he was considering taking rooms
in Brett's house for the winter: *the lack of sensitiveness as far as
I am concerned — the selfishness of this staggers me . . . who
could count on such a man! To plan all this at such a time . . .*

she noted in her distress.

She had also read Brett's letters to Murry. They horrified her. *Brett in her letters to Murry is unbalanced. This morning when she wrote how she wanted to rush into the cornfield — horrified me. And then he must smack her hard and she threatens to cry over him until he's all wet. Poor wretch! She's 37, hysterical, unbalanced, with a ghastly family tradition — and he has 'awakened' her. Her face is entirely changed: the mouth hangs open, the eyes are very wide: there is something silly and meaning in her smile which makes me cold. And then the bitten nails — the dirty neck — the film on her teeth! Whatever he may feel about it the truth is she flattered him and got him! She listened and didn't criticise and sat at his feet and worshipped and asked for the prophet's help and he told her the old old tragedy . . . .* This entry in Katherine's notebook was suppressed by Murry when preparing the Journal.

Of course, Brett had the mental chassis for this sort of thing. She made the same meal of Lawrence in New Mexico, much to Frieda's fury. Lawrence, writing to Brett on January 26th, 1925 from Oaxaca said: *Your friendship for Murry was spiritual — you dragged sex in and he hated you. He'd have hated you anyhow. The halfness of your friendship I also hate and between you and me there is no sensual correspondence . . . .* One got the unvarnished truth from Lawrence.

Writing to Rojer Fry on August 1st Virginia said: *I'm coming up tomorrow to say goodbye to Katherine Murry. Have you at all come round to her stories? . . . I'm too jealous to wish you to, yet I'm sure they have merit all the same . . . .* She was to review *Bliss.* After seeing Katherine for the last time, Virginia felt she was really going to miss her.

Towards the end of August, Katherine visited the theatre to see the play *Mary Rose.* She enjoyed the evening, so she told Violet. I wonder if this was the occasion when the American saw his little shipboard girl of the duck-embroidered frock, now grown up, but ill and weary?

In September Katherine prepared to leave for Menton. Connie and Jinnie had bought a large villa, Villa Louise, with a lovely garden in Garavan, the bay to the east of Menton, with presumably a small staff villa built into the hillside called Isola

Bella. They had kindly offered it to Katherine. She was to love it. She and L.M. left on September 11th, 1920 arriving two long days later, driving up to the villa in an open carriage from Menton station in glorious Riviera sunshine. On September 12/20 Gertler wrote to Carrington: *Brett? What does she do? She plays tennis with Murry and likes him very much.*

Chapter XVII

Isola Bella

Katherine's book *Bliss* had been published in September and eight reviews were sent to her at the Isola Bella. After only three days there, she learned to her consternation that Murry had had a communication from Sobieniowski, wanting £40 for a collection of her old letters which she very much preferred to have destroyed. This anxiety was eventually settled by L.M. who kindly paid the bill. The letters did not arrive until November 2nd, however.

Katherine loved Isola Bella. There was a large terrace with a stone balustrade overlooking the sea where Katherine spent much of her day. There were four bedrooms upstairs with balconies, the salon had two french windows, one with a view of the large beautiful garden, the other opening on to the terrace. A large date palm looked in at Katherine's bedroom window. There were mimosa, orange trees and a magnolia in bud. She thought the view was very lovely. Her bedroom wallpaper was decorated with baskets of pink flowers.

It was hot in Menton, the mosquitoes were active in the still evenings, and Katherine, aching and feverish, had also developed enteritis — inevitable after a long train journey with questionable food on the way. However she had acquired a French maid, Marie, who was to cook like a dream and by September 18th she was up again. *I have never been so thin . . I simply melted like a candle with that fever . . .* she wrote in her letter-card to Murry, a mutual arrangement to cut down the writing. This was abandoned, inevitably.

Murry was now sharing the Elephant with Milne of the British Museum, the maid Violet looking after them, with

Wingly racing about getting lost.

Katherine continued to do her book reviews for which she was paid £10 for four. She also wrote her stories, going to bed early, and, protected by a mosquito net, worked far into the night. *The Daughters of the Late Colonel* was finished at 3.00 a.m., December 13th. L.M. was ready for her, a tray of tea and egg sandwiches to hand.

Though she was probably glad to escape from England, Katherine admitted she missed Murry more than she expected and felt that their relationship was crumbling while they were apart — too true.

Receiving 'reams — from Brett', 'ruffled' Katherine's feathers: *she is keeping you at tennis because of the good it does you . . . You are not to be allowed to work too hard . . . and in future you and I and she and Gertler are all going to live in some untidy chateau with Richard 'for a tornado' upsetting my exquisite ways and eating all the jam. This made me . . . rage so furiously together.* Poor Katherine, this insensitive stuff was enough to send her temperature up.

By the 29th she was depressed over her feverishness and lassitude, wishing for Murry's company and feeling an *awful sense of insecurity . . . One puts out one's hand and there's nothing there (Are these three years a dream?)*

By October 11th however she had written a new story, *The Young Girl*. Once more she had dreamed it up. It duly appeared in *The Athenaeum*. She was feeling a little stronger. Alas, Murry forgot her thirty-second birthday, October 14th. It seems incredible in the circumstances. *I confess it was a bit of a jar yesterday to have no birthday . . . First time since we've been together . . . Tell Wing that he didn't remember either . . .* she wrote sadly. It seems Murry had also failed to send her payment for her reviewing.

Jinnie and Connie had now arrived at the Villa Louise which afforded Katherine a little relief in her physical and spiritual isolation, out of which she sent Murry one of her remarkable letters which must have impressed him deeply:

— — — *suffering, bodily suffering such as I've known for three years. It has changed for ever everything — even the appearance of the world is not the same — there is something added.* Everything has its shadow.*Is it right to resist such suffering? Do you know I feel it has been an immense privilege . . .It has taken me three years to understand this — to come to see this. We resist, we are terribly frightened. The little boat enters the dark, fearful gulf and our only cry is to escape — "Put me on land again". But it's useless. Nobody listens. The shadowy figure rows on. One ought to sit still and uncover one's eyes. I believe the greatest failing of all is* to be frightened. *Perfect Love casteth out Fear. When I look back on my life all my mistakes have been because I was afraid . . . Was that why I had to look on death? Would nothing else cure me? You know, one can't help wondering sometime . . . No, not a personal God or any such nonsense. Much more likely — the soul's desperate choice . . .*

Am I right in thinking that you too have been ridden by Fear (of quite a different kind). And now it's gone from you and you are whole. I feel that only now you have all *your strength — a kind of* release . . . .

Katherine's boat was pulling steadily away from Murry's shore.

It was turning cold but it was exhilarating: *a kind of whiteness in the sky over the sea. I loved such days when I was a child* . . . she wrote on October 22nd. Katherine had seen Dr Bouchage, a young local doctor of thirty-three, who also suffered from tuberculosis. He reminded her of Chekhov. The verdict was much the same: disease of long-standing, half an hour's exercise only, the rest of the time on the *chaise-longue*. Katherine was preoccupied with her soul, asking Murry if his soul troubled him. *I feel that only now (October 1920) do I really desire to be saved . . . I* long *for goodness — to live by what is permanent in the soul . . . I never felt the longing for you as I do this time — but for such other reasons . . . .*

She was expecting Murry for December 20th and had proposed, calmly, that they give the Elephant up at Xmas, while L.M. was in England for three weeks, then in the same breath said she couldn't think what made her even consider it; but change, inexorable, was occurring. Her letters were generally less hectic, there seemed now to be no desperate dependence on Murry's letters arriving.

There was still controversy with L.M. but much less heat.

L.M. seemed to be a lady of leisure: *now that she has nothing on earth to do, she does absolutely nothing but make* French knots *in her bedroom and ask questions like: 'Can you tell me a book that will explain what makes the sea that funny yellow colour so far out. What is the* authority?'

By November 2nd Katherine was immersed in another new story and consequently was feeling pressurized and melancholic. It was *The Stranger*, which was published in *The London Mercury*, January 1921. She admitted to Murry that work excited and fatigued her and she felt she ought not to do it. She also blamed the opium in her cough mixture; alas, that great comforter the cough mixture has some such side-effects.

Murry had been to see Elizabeth Countess Russell and had sent Katherine a long account. With her unerring eye she summed up for Murry a profile of her cousin: *She only wants a* male appearance . . . *Forgive my frankness: she has no use for a physical lover . . . . Her very life . . . her gift, her vitality, all that makes her depends upon her* not surrendering . . . . For her part Elizabeth thought Murry 'very sweet and feminine in feeling and masculine in brain'. T.S. Eliot had the same feeling about Murry. When they were talking together, Eliot admitted he felt as though he was talking to a woman.

Katherine continued to love Isola Bella deeply: *My heart beats for it like it beats for Karori*. She had been offered the place for a year from May 1921, at a rent of 6000 francs (then 57 francs to the pound). To Murry she declared: *You will find Isola Bella in poker work on my heart* . . . . She had found, as never before, that it was *the* place to work in. Straightway she wrote *Miss Brill* the story about that pathetic maiden lady and her tired little fur with its 'dim eyes'. Amidst the joy over the villa, there was the inevitable 'snail under the leaf'. In his letters, she felt Murry had gone away. She implored him to come back to her.

Then the storm over the photograph broke. Murry had been contacted by the *Sphere* regarding a photograph of Katherine for the advent of her new book *Bliss*. He sent them the charming early photograph where she is wearing her greenstone birthday ear-rings. Unfortunately he had forgotten that she detested it. Over-critical, she objected to the 'beastly

eyes — long poodle hair and a streaky fringe'. She accused
Murry of carelessness and lack of appreciation of her work.

> . . . *I have been ill for nearly four years — and I'm changed,
> changed — not the same. You gave twice to your work . . .
> what you gave to my story. I don't want dismissing as a
> masterpiece. Who is going to mention 'the first snow' I haven't
> anything like as long to live as you have.* I've scarcely any time,
> *I* feel. *Richard will draw posters 100 years. Praise him when
> I'm dead. Talk to me. I'm lonely. I haven't one single soul.*

Murry thought 'the first snow' alluded to *The Stranger*: *But
her words, so light, so soft, so chill seemed to hover in the air,
to rain into his breast, like snow.* I think the allusion is taken
from Chekhov's *Nervous Breakdown* letter about Grigorovitch
being 'the only one who noticed the description of the first
snow'.

In her anger against Murry, she requested him not to
publish any work she left in England, to destroy the
photograph (a pity, it is charming) and expressed a wish to be
free of journalism. She also said she intended to find an agent,
namely J.B. Pinker, who easily placed her future stories.

It was now November 28th and the weather had changed. It
was very cold and snow lay on the mountains. Katherine's ire
slowly dissipated. She wrote a new story, *Poison*, which Murry
did not quite believe in. It contained a woman-of-the-world
hardness, which was inevitable after such an emotional storm
— over little, granted, but not unexpected. One sympathizes
with Murry but not much. It was like a man to send the wrong
photograph and very like a woman to object as Katherine did!

Murry had had a new book published — *Aspects of
Literature* — which he sent to Katherine at the end of
November: *your book is ASTONISHING as a whole . . .* she
told him. *There's a note in it . . . clear and challenging and
absolutely new, my boy . . . .* Alas, there were other new
aspects of Murry appearing. After reviewing *The Autobiography of Margot Asquith*, he had become entangled with
their daughter Princess Elizabeth Bibesco who had taken up
writing short stories.

Born 1897 and married on April 30th, 1919 to Prince

Antoine Bibesco of the Roumanian Legation, she lived in 33, Warwick Square, London. Ottoline had entertained the Asquith party at Garsington when they blew in one Sunday in June 1916, annoying her *rushing over the house, and saying everything was 'so' beautiful,* too *adorable! as they kept standing about in the red room, I said to Elizabeth, 'Do you never sit down, Elizabeth? . . .' later she made a-dead set at Lowes Dickinson. She took him out into the garden . . . poking her face into his, convinced that she was charming and bewitching him with her brilliant conversation, he poor fellow getting more and more miserable . . . .*

Virginia, commenting on October 12th, 1918 in her diary, thought Margot Asquith *as tense as a stretched bow . . . and as for poor pasty Elizabeth she seemed to have come straight from behind Marshall & Snelgrove's millinary counter.*

Lilian Gish, on the other hand, who met the Princess at Pickfair in Hollywood, and saw her come down to dinner in a lovely night-gown over a slip with a silk scarf draped about, thought her pretty, 'witty and amusing'.

Ottoline, commenting in her memoirs on another occasion, said Elizabeth was *like a quick ticker-tape machine, ticking out aphorisms and anecdotes . . . There seemed no heart, or character inside and no understanding of tragedy or comedy. The mechanical clapping of her tongue went on in my brain like a tune on a barrel-organ. She seems merely a collector of celebrities. She has never been young and never will be. She isn't unkind and I feel has rather a nice tolerant nature, but she is too conceited and vain.*

On Saturday December 6th, 1919 Virginia met Elizabeth Bibesco again when lunching with the Cecils. *Elizabeth was nicer and less brilliant than I expected. She has the composed manners of a matron, and did not strain to say clever things. I thought her slightly nervous when we drew into the window to talk. Perhaps she does not like the woman's eye to rest upon her. She is pasty and podgy, with the eyes of a currant bun, suddenly protruding with animation. But her animation is the product of a highly trained mind; a mind trained by living perpetually among more highly trained minds. "Memory comes to take the place of character in the old" she said . . . . This was said, I remember, owing to my rash abuse of Lady*

Glenconner . . . her aunt of course. She turned round, a little uneasily, to disclaim all admiration for Lady G. I suppose she wishes to stand well with the intellectuals.

Augustus John in his memoirs, remembered dining at The Magestic in Paris with Elizabeth and three young diplomats. Apparently after coffee and brandy Elizabeth managed to silence even the corps diplomatique with her bright talk. He was relieved when the bottle was empty, scarcely able to escort her back to the Ritz. The men would be worn out! and even bored to tears.

The punchline comes from Julian Vinogradoff, Ottoline's daughter, and Juliette Huxley, who in an interview with Dr Jeffrey Meyers both described Princess Bibesco as 'an extremely unhappy nymphomaniac'. Her portrait by Augustus John hangs in the Laing Art Gallery, Newcastle-upon-Tyne.

Reacting from the photograph storm, Murry seemed a bit disorganised. After dining with Anne Rice he found himself kissing her goodbye, also another guest, Mrs Bonamy Dobrée. This harmless action seemed to him to warrant a letter of apology, but he tore it up. Two days later he actually spoke to a prostitute near Leicester Square, declined her proposition, but invited her to dine with him at Malzy's while she listened. The following night he visited Brett at 10.00 p.m., by arrangement, suffering revulsion afterwards. Five days later he was invited to dinner at Mary Huchinsons, when Princess Bibesco, another guest, gave him a lift home and he found himself kissing *her* on the cheek too. She sent him a story which he said he might publish, and she then called at his office. So the hurdy-gurdy started up. He actually sent the story to Katherine, who on December 4th returned it with a letter:

. . . I hasten to return this story which I haven't read and wouldn't read for £5 . . . And please, darling don't tell me about Elizabeth Bibesco . . . the love-story in the motor-car and so on . . . oh, Don't tell me!

By December 6th Katherine completed a new story *The Lady's Maid*. She was languishing with reviewing: *Isn't it grim to be reviewing — when one might be writing one's own stories which one will never have time to write . . . Forgive me . . . the ancien couteau burns faintly in my left lung tonight . . . .*

He had promised to send her a typewriter but had not, writing in long-hand fatigued her so. Discussing her problems of overwork with Dr Bouchage, he had persuaded her to give up reviewing. She was suffering from palpitation and was having to rest more.

Guilt-ridden over Bibesco, he must obviously have been ingested by then, Murry wrote to Katherine some more about the Princess, fearing his meeting her might have had an adverse effect on her illness.

Exasperated, Katherine sent a wire dated December 12th: *Stop sending me these false depressing letters be a man or don't write me Tig.*

By the 13th Katherine had completed *Daughters Of The Late Colonel*. Writing about it later to Ottoline on March 4th, 1922:

I shall never forget lying on that wretched little sofa in Menton writing that story. I couldn't stop. I wrote it all day and on my way back to bed sat down on the stairs and began scribbling the bit about the meringues.

Then, with the deadly aim of a rattlesnake, a letter arrived for Katherine which laid her very low. It was from Princess Bibesco, criticizing her for holding on to Murry, asking how as *a sick woman, away in France, and quite unable to make any kind of life or happiness for Murry, how dared she try to hold him.* Also contained was 'a suggestion of intimacies', according to L.M., who was a shocked observer. Dated December 19th Katherine put down her feelings in the tragic piece called 'Suffering': (Mss papers 119/10 ATL.)

. . . There is no limit to human suffering . . . I thought last year in Italy: Any shadow more would be death. But this year has been so much more terrible that I think with affection of the Casetta! . . . suffering can be overcome . . . Accept it fully. Make it part of life. *The present agony will pass — if it doesn't kill . . . Now I am like a man who has had his heart torn out . . . It is as though a ghastly accident had happened. If I can cease reliving all the shock and horror of it . . . I will get stronger . . . .*
The fearful pain of these letters will fade. I must turn to work.

S

I must put my agony into something, change it. 'Sorrow shall be changed into joy' . . . . I write that. I look up . . . the sky is pale, and I catch myself weeping. It is hard . . . it is hard to make a good death . . . . In another entry: *I've been poisoned by these "letters". How* can *he know someone so 'strange' to me? to us? Not only know her, but cherish her?* This piece was signed 'Katherine Mansfield'. A further note reads: *In the white lace, the spreading veil and the pearls, she looked like a gull. But a quick hungry gull with an absolute insatiable appetite for bread. 'Come, feed me! Feed me! said that quick glare.*

Katherine had obviously looked at the wedding photograph of Prince and Princess Bibesco. It was all there, the lace and pearls, and with her unerring eye, Katherine had discovered the secret.

As previously arranged Murry arrived at the Isola Bella on December 21st. It should have been such a happy day. He found Katherine very seriously ill. He blamed overwork. There was also a broken heart. Wiping the slate a little cleaner he wrote to Brett on December 22nd to decline the rooms in her house. *It seems as though I'm too fond of you in one way, ever to make anything of a physical relation with you . . . We must wait and see.* Murry resigned from *The Athenaeum* which duly merged with the *Nation*.

Katherine, fainting by the wayside, received her book *Bliss* and a letter from Virginia, who had reviewed it.

December 19th 1920

My dear Katherine
I wish you were here to enjoy your triumph — still more that we may talk about your book "Bliss" — For what's the use of telling you how glad and indeed proud I am? However I must to please myself send a line to say just that.
                    Yours ever
                    V. W.

To Vanessa, Virginia wrote on January 7th, 1921: *I'm not in the least jealous of Katherine (Mansfield), though every review praises her . . . .*

A blast from Lawrence in Taormina to Mary Cannan mentioned *Bliss: the Nation said K's book was the best short story book that could be or had been written. Spit on her for me when you see her . . . As for him I reserve my language. I hear from London the Athenaeum lost £5000 a year under our friend . . . Vermin, the pair of 'em.* And on 24th February: *are those miserable Murrys still about?*

Katherine answered Virginia's letter on December 27th: *Please don't talk of triumph, even in jest. It makes me hang my head . . . . it came on Xmas day . . . a two-fold gift. I think of you often — very often — I long to talk to you . . : you are the only woman with whom I long to talk work . . . But leagues divide us . . . one lives by the sky again — by the changes of cloud and light. Whenever I think of Asheham it is of clouds — big golden clouds, hazy, spinning slowly over the downs . . . .* Perhaps she was also thinking of the flying thistledown and the golden, healthy days at Asheham, seemingly so long ago. One feels that Virginia would have been a most welcome visitor during that unhappy time.

Following the appearance of *Bliss*, Katherine wrote to Orage after years of silence:

9th February 1921
Dear Orage,
  This letter has been on the tip of my pen for many months. I want to tell you how sensible I am of your wonderful unfailing kindness to me in the "old days". And to thank you for all you let me learn from you. I am still — more shame to me — very low down in the school. But you taught me to write, you taught me to think; you showed me what there was to be done and what not to do.
My dear Orage, I cannot tell you how often I call to mind your conversation or how often, in writing, I remember my master. Does that sound impertinent? Forgive me if it does.
But let me thank you Orage — Thank you for everything. If only one day I might write a book of stories good enough to 'offer' you . . . . If I don't succeed in keeping the coffin from the door you will know this was my ambition.
        Yours in admiration and gratitude
        Katherine Mansfield.

*I haven't said a bit of what I wanted to say. This letter sounds
as if it was written by a screw driver, and I wanted it to sound
an admiring, respectful, but warm piping beneath your
windows. I'd like to send my love too, if I wasn't so frightened.*

                                                                    K.M.

On December 27th Katherine was noting: *I went out into the
garden just now. It is starry and mild . . . I sat on the cane
chair and leaned against the wall. I thought of Jack contained
in the little house — within reach — there was a time when this
thought was a distraction . . . It took away from my power to
work . . . I, as it were, made him my short story. But that
belongs to the Past . . . I thought also of the Princess . . . .* And
later: *What would he have said and* felt *at B's letters? He
would have felt what I felt. Let no man suffer so again! For
mingled with all the suffering is the anguish of despair because*
one is ill. *How could anyone let such a thing happen to me at
such a time? . . . Do they treat me as posthumous already? Oh,
the agony of life! How does one endure it?*

Murry left on January 11th to arrange to give up the
Elephant, returning on January 19th when he heard Katherine
had had a relapse. He returned to London early in February
and attended a 'farewell dinner' given for him by Clive Bell on
February 11th at 46, Gordon Square. Virginia, who sat next to
Murry, wrote an account of it in her diary: *He posed, I
thought; looked anguished & martyred . . . I asked about
Katherine. Poor man! he poured himself out. We sat on after
the others had gone. "But I lacked imagination" he said "I
never saw, I ought to have understood. I've always held one
was free to do as one likes. But she was ill, & that makes all the
difference. And it was nothing — nothing at all."*

*This referred of course, without names to the Bibesco
Scandal, with which London, so they say, rings.*

*"And I adore Katherine — She's absolutely the most
fascinating person in the world — I'm wholly in love with her."*

*Apparently she is worse — dying? God knows. This affair
seems to have brought on a crisis. She is desperately depressed,
thinks her book bad, can't write; accuses herself; I imagine is
beside herself with jealousy. Murry asked me to write to her.
She feels herself out of things, left alone, forgotten. As he
spoke with great feeling, & seemed to be very miserable, &*

anxious to apologise (was it for this that he wished to see us all
— to prove that there was nothing in it?) I liked him, felt with
him, & I think there can be no doubt that his love for
Katherine anyhow is sincere. All the rest seems of no great
importance beside it. Sydney's version is of course over
emphatic . . . .

Murry finally settled his affairs by the middle of February
and rejoined Katherine. Over this period Katherine's letters
were short and flat, she was too ill to write in her usual vein. A
gland in her neck became painfully inflamed, which required
repeated tapping and draining. A large quantity of pus was
removed.

Murry in his journal January 4th, 1951, wrote of this time:
I felt a horrible sort of double guilt — for hurting Katherine
and for hurting Elizabeth, by writing her the cold and formal
letters on which Katherine insisted . . . Katherine would not
hear a word in defence of Elizabeth and I resented being
compelled to behave brutally towards her. Finally I explained
to Elizabeth that I was completely in love with Katherine, and
that she was seriously ill, and that whatever she wanted me to
do, I must do . . .
And as I remember, Elizabeth took it very well. Later — *All*
the same it was a little hard. While she was well, I had to be
the companion of her "innocent" self; and when she was ill I
had to be "the man without a temperament". Journal, May
23rd. 1954. It is amazing that even then there was no
criticism of the dastardly action of Princess Bibesco towards his
dying wife, nor her subsequent betrayal of himself even at that
distance, only mealy-mouthed regret for hurting the Princess.

Katherine was further shattered by the fact that Murry had
seen Princess Bibesco again (to say goodbye?). Also the story in
The Athenaeum for January 14th 'The Ordinary Man' by
Bibesco, prompted a wire from Katherine declining to send
any further contributions. From this episode emerged Murry's
lukewarm novel *The Voyage*, based on the affair. In March, in
spite of the 'goodbye', a letter came for Murry from the
Princess which Katherine read. She sent an account to L.M.

. . . . Elizabeth Bibesco has shown signs of life again. A letter
yesterday begging him to resist Katherine 'You have withstood
her so gallantly so far how can you give way now' And 'You

*swore nothing on earth should ever come between us' . . . I
hope he will go on with the affair. He* wants to. *'How can I
exist without your literary advice ?' she asks. That is a very
fascinating question. I shall write to the silly little creature . . .*

This she did!

24th March 1921

*Dear Princess Bibesco
    I am afraid you must stop writing these little love letters to
my husband while he and I live together. It is one of the things
which is not done in our world.
You are very young. Won't you ask your husband to explain to
you the impossibility of such a situation. Please do not make
me have to write to you again. I do not like scolding people
and I simply hate having to teach them manners.*

*Yours sincerely
Katherine Mansfield*

In the same month she wrote in her notebook: *I thought, a few
minutes ago, that I could have written a whole novel about a*
Liar. *A man who was devoted to his wife, but who lied. But I
couldn't. I couldn't write a whole novel about anything . . . I
feel as though I am* dirty *or* disgusted *or both. Everything I
think of seems false.* One wonders what Prince Antoine
Bibesco was doing all this time; he was reputed to be a
charming man. Princess Bibesco became an alcoholic and her
husband nursed her devotedly to the end, which was in 1945.

Katherine was now disillusioned with the Riviera which she
had so much loved. Writing to Ottoline on February 2nd, 1921
she said she had: turned *frightfully against it and the French
. . . . I wish the horrid old Riviera would fall into the sea . . . as
to England . . . . I never want to see it again . . . Did one know
all the wrong people? Is that why nobody remains to me —
except de la Mare?*

Walter de la Mare had visited Katherine at the Elephant.
She had loved talking to him and he, in admiration, wrote a
poem about her entitled 'To K.M.' published in *Selected
Poems* (Faber). By March, L.M. had gone to England to pack
up the effects of the Elephant.

I have been in bed for six weeks, Katherine wrote to Ottoline, mentioning also her other anxieties: *something happened, a kind of earthquake . . . . I lost faith and touch with everybody . . . I was almost out of my mind with misery last year . . . . M. is here for the moment . . . . His typewriter ticks away here . . . .*

Katherine was spitting blood again. *It makes one feel that while one sits at the window the house is on fire.*

On March 9th to L.M. in England: *I wish I were back in the Hampstead house . . . allowed to linger on the stairs . . . It should have been a perfect little house: it never came to flower. And the view of the willows — bare now — and the room that was mine — so lovely — the light was always like the light of a pale shell . . . .* She told L.M. to throw the shepherdess clock into the dustbin, the clock whose tiny, fairy-like chime had so much charmed her; seemingly it was broken, like Katherine's heart, all very sad. She noted also that Brett was writing to Murry about their 'child' Arthur (Richard Murry): *Jack will marry her one day . . . can't you see Jack with Lord Esher, his father-in-law? also Brett's £550 which is bound to be more! I long to have this happen . . . it would be — beautiful if one were alone . . . I am angry with 'people' with Brett & Co. with Vera for writing me a false, cold hearted snobbish letter "so glad you are nearing normal again." Typical!* Katherine's sister Vera, so far away in Canada, couldn't have been in possession of all the facts.

Poor Katherine was having further glandular infection. *My gland is a great deal more swollen,* she told L.M. *the blood goes on tapping and squeezing through like a continual small hammering, and all that side of my head is numb.* She had to have repeated aspirations to ease the pain of pressure within.

In a letter later she told L.M. about an incredible happening. She had paid the surgeon's bill for the operation. It was 100 francs. Murry had agreed to pay for the coach, 20 francs. When making out the week's bills, he asked Katherine for half the coach fare — 10 francs — plus half the tip of 2 francs! *. . . fancy not paying for your wife's carriage to and from the surgery! I really am staggered. I think it is the meanest thing I ever heard of . . . the lack of fine feeling. I suppose if one fainted he would make one pay 3d for a 6d glass*

of salvolatile and 1d on the glass . . . . Kot, whose over harsh
opinion of Murry was that he was 'a gheat scarndyel', would
have had him 'beaten-plainly!'

She went on . . . . *I am infinitely worse than when I left
England . . . I wish I could consult Sorapure* — she couldn't
because the bill was left unpaid. Poor Katherine, working hard
to pay for her dreadful illness, had run out of money. *I must
make every effort to get* — *better* soon — *Jack 'accepts' it . . .
he* NEVER *tries to help* . . . *I was not born an invalid . . . I
long for* — *Do you understand? I feel every day must be the
last day of such a life* . . . *Ida. Help me to escape!*

Sullivan was visiting them and hoping to get a house nearby.
He rather irritated Katherine by going into the dining-room,
helping himself to an orange, then tossing the peel into the
fireplace. However, Murry was glad of his company, they
talked of money incessantly and together they visited Sydney
Schiff.

Katherine had decided to go to Switzerland and was making
preparations to leave Menton. Writing to L.M. on March
18th, 1921 she asked her to look for a small chalet near
Geneva: *help me to get to Switzerland soon* — *will you? And
always we must behave as though J. were a visitor. Not a
person to consult, or to expect from or to count on. If he comes
along* — *he comes and that's all.*

Life at the Isola Bella was finished. Connie and Jinnie had
become rather shadowy figures, especially as Katherine had
decided not to become a Catholic. It seems also, that someone
else wanted to rent the villa. In the first week in May, Murry
returned to England to give lectures at Oxford. L.M. finished
her sad task of winding up the Elephant, arranging to board
Wingly and Athenaeum with a vet, and then locked up.

On May 4th L.M. escorted Katherine to Baugy in
Switzerland. Always stimulated by change of scene, Katherine
wrote one of her long letters to Murry, telling him she loved
him very much and longed to hear from him. He had stopped
off at Bandol and had gone to see the Villa Pauline and the
Allègres, sending postcard views to Katherine.

On May 7th she had received *The London Mercury*
containing *The Daughters Of The Late Colonel*, and she was
anxious to see the reviews. On May 14th she ascended from

Lake Geneva to the Hotel Château Bellevue, Sierre, an old castle, to meet Dr Stephani of Montana. There is no report of his opinion.

Murry wrote from Oxford on May 19th: *it's a world I left years and years ago . . . We're utterly strange to each other . . . How intimately I have* grown in *to you lately! With everyone else . . . I am a kind of bemused spectator. Life seems like the slow dropping of water into a deep well . . . A curious deep happiness is hidden somewhere inside me. Well, darling — we've had a strangely mixed time together — but if it had been a time of unmixed suffering it would still have been worth the price to get to the condition we're in now.*

This letter must have made Katherine happier.

The lectures were to form a book of classical criticism called *The Problem of Style*, which was to be reprinted more than any other of his works.

One of the students there was William Gerhardi who, in his *Memoirs of a Polyglot* remembered Murry lecturing *superbly and engrossingly — not a word of his fell on stony ground. At a literary club he also spoke on Tchekov . . . very quietly, seated in a low armchair stroking the carpet pensively while he searched for some phrase which, when found, really expressed the secret of Tchekov's enchantment. He also made some sly allusion to the work of his wife, Katherine Mansfield; and when I read a story of hers I was so pleased with it that I wrote her a letter.* This she answered on June 23rd: *I cannot tell you how happy I am to know that 'The Daughters of the Late Colonel' has given you pleasure. While I was writing that story I lived for it, but when it was finished I confess I hoped that my readers would understand what I was trying to express. But very few did. They thought it was 'cruel': they thought I was 'sneering' at Jug and Constantia; or they thought it was 'drab' and in the last paragraph I was 'poking fun at the poor old things'. It's almost terrifying to be misunderstood. There was a moment when I first had 'the idea' when I saw the two sisters as* amusing; *but the moment I looked deeper (let me be quite frank) I bowed down to the beauty that was hidden in their lives and to discover that was all my desire . . . All was meant, of course, to lead up to that last paragraph, when my two*

flowerless ones turned with that timid gesture, to the sun.
'Perhaps now . . .*' and after that it seemed to me, they died as*
surely as Father was dead.

He also sent her his manuscript of *Futility* which both she
and Murry liked, and suggested a publisher, Cobden-
Sanderson, who accepted it. Gerhardi was deeply grateful to
Katherine and appearing on television in 1982, sixty years on,
said so, to my delight.

Gertler, writing to Kot on June 25th, also had news of the
Oxford lectures: *'Toronto' (Frank Prewitt, a Canadian poet)*
. . . says — they were a great success, especially among the
young ladies, and that he had a great ovation on the last
one . . . .

Murry joined Katherine in the Château Bellevue Hotel on
June 10th. She and L.M. had been up to Montana, 5000 feet
above sea level, to see the Chalet des Sapins belonging to the
mother of the local doctor, a Scot called Hudson, who had
treated Katherine in Sierre. It seemed ideal and it was taken
for a year. So began the most productive period of Katherine's
writing life, July to December; also Murry's, who wrote *The*
Things We Are, The Voyage Part I, and *Countries of the*
Mind.

Virginia was very hard on *The Things We Are*, sending it on
to Ottoline. On August 1st, 1922 she wrote: *I beg to say that*
the damp spots are not my doing. They come from within. He
has a mania for confession. I suppose his instinct is to absolve
himself in these bleatings and so get permission for more
sins . . . .

Soon they contacted Countess Russell, Murry taking a letter
from Katherine apologizing for not answering Elizabeth's
letter. He walked to the Chalet Soleil with it on Saturday June
15th, arriving at 11.00 a.m; they talked until lunch, then
Elizabeth came up to see Katherine in the afternoon.

Chapter XVIII

Chalet des Sapins and Paris

The Chalet des Sapins, remote and set in pine trees, overlooked a wide deep valley with mountains towering behind. There was a bathroom on ground level, a living/dining-room on the first floor, with Katherine's bedroom on the second floor which led on to a large balcony with enclosed glass sides. Ernestine Rey, a local Swiss girl, did the housekeeping. L.M. stayed in the village, later getting a job in a clinic there. In August she gallantly returned to London to collect Wingly, who travelled back to Montana in a collar and lead, to Katherine's utter delight. Black and white, and one of Dr Johnson's 'a very fine cat indeed' types, he eventually weighed 12lb.

I visited Montana in deep snow in December 1978 but failed to find the chalet, which was a pity because it is now an annexe to the Pension Helvetia run by Ernestine's niece Mme Rosette Simon. Guests can reserve Katherine's room. I saw the ice-rink where Murry spent much time spinning, and the Victoria Palace Hotel bathed in low cloud, where Katherine attended a clinic on July 13th and 18th. The great wide valley below was white and remote. On descending to Sierre, I saw the Château Belle Vue Hotel, with its profusion of decorative purple cabbage-like plants in the courtyard in front. They were drooping in the rain. I walked around the garden which overlooked the railway station in the valley below, and sat on a seat which perhaps figured in a photograph of Murry and Katherine taken in the summer of 1922. I noted the elegant empty dining-room, with its glossy wooden floor. The whole place seemed deserted, the reason for which I discovered later.

It is no longer a hotel but the Town Hall.

Writing to Ottoline on July 21st, 1921 Katherine told her of Elizabeth and her basket of apricots and to Brett in August she described how Elizabeth loved flowers: *her love of flowers is really her great charm . . . Elizabeth looks coolly at the exquisite petunias and says in a small faraway voice 'They have a perfect scent.' But I can feel I can hear oceans of love breaking in her heart for petunias and nasturtiums and snapdragons . . . .* Some petunias smell of carnations, delicately so.

Murry spent much time down at the Chalet Soleil. It would be a paradise, with its great library. He would return to Montana at twilight with piles of books under his arm. Elizabeth visited Katherine, bringing huge bouquets of flowers, and wearing beautiful clothes; *frocks like a spiders web, a hat like a berry — and gloves that reminded me of thistles in seed,* she wrote to Brett, describing 'a ravishing wrinkle' which appeared on Elizabeth's nose when she smiled.

However, there was not always accord between them, and rapport seemed impaired at times. They had led such different lives, Elizabeth from sophisticated society, Katherine simpler but the more gifted. On Katherine happily telling her she was writing a story about an old man, Elizabeth mistakenly said she did not like old men, 'They *exude* so'. Katherine was filled with such horror that she accused Elizabeth in her notebook of having a 'vulgar little mind'. Later she put the remark down to shyness.

Reading the *Journal* in 1927 Elizabeth wrote to Murry admitting she had been afraid of Katherine even though she adored her and felt a sense of embarrassment and inferiority in her company.

However, when Elizabeth's novel *Vera* was published in September 1921, both Katherine and Murry gave her genuine praise, Murry called it 'a Wuthering Heights written by Jane Austen'. Katherine thought the end *extraordinarly good . . . I admired the end most, I think . . .* she wrote to Brett.

Both worked all morning and from tea to supper. Murry did articles for the *Nation* and *Times Literary Supplement*. Clement Shorter of the *Sphere* had commissioned Katherine to do six stories at 10 guineas each. Katherine was deeply critical of these stories with their incongruous illustrations. To Brett, August 29th, 1921: *my stories for the Sphere are all done — I have had copies with illustrations. Oh, Brett, all my dear people looking like — Harrods 29/6 crêpe-de-chine blouses and young tailors' gents, and my old men — stuffy old woolly sheep.* To Ottoline she wrote: *I don't believe they are much good. Too simple. It is always the next story which is going to contain everything, and that next story is always just out of reach.*

Murry went rambling in the afternoon, and read aloud to Katherine at night. Sometimes she was able to join him on his walks, sitting in the forest among wild strawberries and violets. In a letter to Ottoline: *I have never lived in a forest before, one steps out of the house and in a moment one is hidden among the trees. And there are little glades and groves full of flowers — with small ice-cold streams twinkling through . . . .* She spent much time on her balcony looking over the tops of the pine trees to the mountain peaks on the other side of the valley, the Weisshorn in the far distance and Les Violettes — skiing terrain — watching 'the deep sharp shadows in the ravines and stretching across the slopes'. They took breakfast on the balcony. They cut each other's hair. *We try to make it a rule not to talk in bed.*

By August 8th she was thinking up a special New Zealand story. *It's called "At The Bay" and it's full of sand and seaweed, bathing dresses hanging over verandas, and sandshoes on wooden sills . . . . And it smells (oh I do hope it smells) a little bit fishy . . .* she told Brett.

On Saturday August 6th, Murry was thirty-two, so young, both of them, for so much tragedy. However, his presents were a panama hat, some blotting-paper, a cake and a ruler. There was tea with candles and liqueur chocolates. There was a piano in the chalet and no doubt Katherine played it that day. Towards the end of August, Katherine had a high temperature and vomiting. She blamed this on the hard writing — *what it is to live in such a body!* By early September she was writing 'for nine solid hours'. Wingly had arrived with 'immense eyes . . . he is like a little anchor . . . .' She was feeling 'an extraordinary feeling of ease here', she told Violet Schiff. *I've never known anything like the feeling of peace and when one isn't working the* freshness *in the air, the smell of pines, the taste of snow in one's teeth . . . . I feel much better . . . even tho' I still can't walk and still cough . . . .* It would be a bracing spot.

On September 24th she had a long chat by letter with Sylvia Lynd about marriage: *I believe in marriage. It seems to me the only possible relation that really is satisfying. And how else is one to have peace of mind to enjoy life and to do one's work. To know* one another *seems to me a far greater adventure than to be on kissing acquaintance with dear knows how many . . . it's far more 'wonderful' as time goes on . . . even to watch Murry darning his socks over a lemon . . . .*

In September, as a result of the extra work requested by her agent Pinker, Katherine found she needed help from L.M., offering her £10-12 per month. She agreed, but had to go back to England for a short time to look after her sister, home from Rhodesia to have her baby. Mentioning a plan to escort an English girl to Montana on her return, L.M. received a typical, tyrannical letter from Katherine which illustrates a facet of their involved friendship.

29th September 1921,
. . . . I suppose it gives you a trumpery sense of power, to take on one job and pretend . . . you're perfectly free for any other that comes along . . . You're the greatest flirt I ever met, a real flirt . . . It seems so utterly indecent at your age to be still all aflutter at every possible glance — I'm not going to flirt back, Miss, and say how I want you as part of my life and can't really imagine being without you. The ties that bind us! Heavens, they are so strong that you'd bleed to death if you really cut away . . . Be my friend! Don't pay me out for what has been . . . I've no doubt I'll get a card today saying your idea is to go to Africa . . . I really mean it is detestable . . . .

Early in October, Katherine was in bed again with a temperature and under its effect she noticed that the world seemed 'almost unbearably beautiful'. She blamed too much riding along very rutted roads, in a carriage pulled by a horse which stopped every three minutes to turn round and 'ogle' her and Murry. On October 14th Katherine was thirty-three;

among her presents was a handkerchief from Jeanne.
Thanking her for it, Katherine wrote on October 14th, 1921:

My dear little sister,
  *Your handkerchief is such a very gay one it looks as though it
had dropped off the hankey tree. Thank you for it, darling. I
remember one birthday when you bit me! . . . when I got a
doll's pram and in a great rage let it go hurling by itself down
the grassy slope outside the conservatory. Father was awfully
angry and said no one was to speak to me. Also the white
azalea bush was out. And Aunt Belle had brought from Sydney
a new recipe for icing. It was tried on my cake and wasn't a
great success because it was much too brittle . . . . You made
me long to have a talk with you in some place like the lily lawn.
Ah, Jeanne, anyone who says to me "Do you remember?"
simply has my heart . . . going back to the dining room at 75,
to the proud and rather angry-looking seltzogene on the
sideboard, with the little bucket under the spout. Do you
remember that hiss it gave and sometimes a kind of groan?
And the smell inside the sideboard of Worcester Sauce and
corks from old claret bottles? If we are ever together down the
Pelorus Sounds come off with me for a whole day — will you?
and let's just remember. How Chummie loved it too! Can't you
hear his soft boyish laugh and the way he said, "Oh-
abso-lute-ly!"*

Jeanne still remembers that letter and a wealth of feeling
sounds in her, 'Oh that poor darling!'
  On the evening of her birthday Katherine finished *The
Garden Party. The Mercury* had accepted *At The Bay: the
longer I live the more I realize that in work only lies one's
strength and one's salvation,* she told Brett. Murry believed
that many of her stories were written straight off without 'false
starts' or alternative draughts. The original manuscript was
written at great speed towards the end and consequently the
writing was almost illegible. Katherine maintained that once a
story was thought out, nothing remained but the *labour.* She
noted on January 17th, 1922: *It's always a kind of race to get in
as much as one can before it* disappears.
  The first two weeks of November were rather barren, she felt

she lacked concentration and was wasting time. *Stories wait for me,* grow tired, *wilt, fade, because I will not come.* She had written only one story, *The Doll's House,* since her birthday. So on November 21st she began *The Weak Heart,* a New Zealand story which was never finished. This was most unusual. She was weary and haunted by the idea of death which feeling she commented on in her notebook.

November 24th: *Tonight, when the evening star shone through the side-window and the pale mountains were so lovely, I sat there thinking of death. Of all there was to do — of life — which is so lovely — and of the fact that my body is a prison. But this state of mind is* evil. *It is only by acknowledging that I, being what I am, had to suffer* this *in order to do the work I am here to perform . . . .*

On November 26th she began *Daphne,* alas also unfinished. Some snow had fallen in October 'like white bees'. All began knitting, Murry mixing the wools to get what he called 'a superb astrachan effect', Katherine felt that knitting turned her into an imbecile. They all wore 'red Indian boots, fur lined', she wrote to Brett on November 5th. *At present the Big Snow hasn't fallen. All is frozen hard, and each tree has a little mat of white before it . . . .* It was extremely cold, but the central heating burned day and night. One remembers the cold she suffered in Ospedaletti with inadequate heating. She and Murry were reading Jane Austen's *Emma* with great pleasure and Katherine had also begun Proust. During her depressed period at the beginning of November, her thoughts had turned to her father and her long silence since the day in Ospedaletti. She wrote him a long letter.

November 1st 1921
Father darling,
I must get over this fear of writing to you because I have not written for so long. I am ashamed to ask for your forgiveness and yet how can I approach you without it? Every single day I think and wonder how can I explain my silence. I cannot tell you how often I dream of you. Sometimes night after night I dream that I am back in New Zealand and sometimes you are very angry with me and at other times this horrible behaviour of mine has not happened and all is well between us. It is

simply agony not to write to you. My heart is full of you. But the past rises before me, when I have promised not to do this very thing that I have done and it's like a wall that I can't see over.

The whole reason for my silence has been that, in the first weeks I was ill and waited until I was better. And then events conspired to throw me into a horrible depression that I could not shake off. Connie and Jinnie made me understand how very much you considered you were doing for me. They made me realise that for you to give me £300 a year* was an extreme concession and that as a matter of fact, my husband was the one who ought to provide for me. Of course I appreciate your great generosity in allowing me so much money and I know it is only because I am ill in the way that I am that you are doing so. But it is highly unlikely that I shall live very long and consumption is a terrible expensive illness. I thought that you did not mind looking after me to this extent. And to feel that you did — was like a blow to me. I couldn't get over it. I feel as though I didn't belong to you, really. If Chaddie or Jeanne had developed consumption husbands or no husbands they would surely have appealed to you. One does turn to one's father however bad one is. Have I forfeited the right to do so? Perhaps . . . There is no reason, Father dear, that you should go on loving me through thick and thin. I see that. And I have been an extraordinarily unsatisfactory and disappointing child. But in spite of everything, one gets shot in the wing and one believes that 'home' will receive one and cherish one. When we were together in France (sic) I was happy with you as I had always longed to be but when I knew that you grudged me the money** it was simply torture. I did not know what to say about it. I waited until I saw if I could earn more myself at that time. But it was not possible. Then I had waited so long that it seemed impossible to write. Then I was so seriously ill that I was not in a state to write to anybody. And by the time that crisis was over it seemed to me my sin of silence was too great to beg forgiveness, and so it has gone on. But I cannot

---

*In the margin Mr Beauchamp wrote: *Quite untrue. H.B.*
**In the margin at this point: *Quite untrue. Never made such a statement to anyone. H.B.*

*bear it any longer. I must come to you and at least
acknowledge my fault. I must at least tell you, even though the
time has passed when you wish to listen, that never for a
moment in my folly and my fear, have I ceased to love and to
honour you. I have punished myself so cruelly that I couldn't
suffer more. Father don't turn away from me, darling. If you
cannot take me back into your heart believe me when I say I
am*

Your devoted deeply sorrowing child
Kass

Across the top H.B. wrote: R(eceived) *7th January 1922.*
A(nswered) *Idem* and two days later: *I can emphatically state
that in* thought, word, *& deed I have never begrudged any of
my children the amounts I have paid them by way of
allowances. On the contrary, I have always considered it a*
pleasure *and a* privilege *to do everything possible for their
comfort, happiness and worldly advancement.*

H.B. 9th January 1922

In a letter to Sydney Schiff on December 3rd there was the first
mention of Dr Manoukhine and his treatment: *when does one*
really begin *a journey — or a friendship — or a love affair?* To
Brett on December 5th she admitted she was tired and
'horribly unsettled' over the idea of the new treatment. Dr
Manoukhine, a Russian now living in Paris, was treating
tuberculosis by irradiating the spleen. Koteliansky had written
to Katherine about him, to Murry's deep regret, but it was in
answer to two letters from Katherine requesting the doctor's
address. She had sent him a photograph and was trying to
make amends. Kot, no doubt depressed, had been critical of
her for losing pages of his translations.

Writing to him on December 5th she told him she had
written to Dr Manoukhine: *Do you know I have not walked
since November 1920? Not more than to a carriage and back.
Both my lungs are affected; there is a cavity in one and the
other is affected through. My heart is weak too. Can all this be
cured. Ah, Koteliansky — wish for me!*

By Xmas all was well between them; he sent her chocolates
and cigarettes, and she reminisced in her thank you letter

about the Xmas party at the Lawrences' in those far-off days at
Cholesbury. On December 24th she sent him a postcard of
Montana to say she had heard from Manoukhine. She so
wanted to be well, and at the moment she was ill in bed.

Thanking Ottoline for her swan-decorated handkerchiefs,
Katherine described her Xmas: *We had a proper Christmas —
even a Tree thanks to the Mountain, who revels in such things .
. .The house whispered with tissue paper for days, a pudding
appeared out of the bosom of the air . . . the crackers,
however, would not pull, which cast a little gloom over M. who
relishes crackers, and the mottoes which were German were
very depressing . . .* I am glad it is all over . . . .

Wingly was in the news too: *since he came here he has
turned into a real Persian with an enormous ruff and feathers
on his legs,* she told Raymond Drey on December 27th, asking
him if he knew of a good dentist in Paris. She said she was
going there very soon: *my teeth are falling like autumn leaves.
They have very large wooden buns here for tea with nails in
them and powdered glass on top . . . I defy anyone to grind
them to powder without an accident.*

By January, six feet of snow had fallen and it was very cold:
all is still, white, cold, deathly, eternal. Like James Elroy
Flecker, who found the dark, snow-laden Swiss pines
depressing, Katherine hated the snow after a while.

During January she had been reading *Cosmic Anatomy*, a
review copy sent by Orage to Murry. It concerned the
Structure of the Ego, and was by a Dr Wallace, a contributor
to the *New Age.* For some reason Katherine was very interested
in it and contacted Orage about it. Murry was totally opposed.
"Why does Jack hate it so?" Katherine wondered as she tore
herself away from it to get some work done. Wallace suggested
that the mind could control, transcend and even survive the
body after death.

On January 11th she wrote the story *A Cup of Tea* in four or
five hours. On the same day she heard that the *Dial* had
accepted *The Doll's House,* such success, if only she had been
well! It was also accepted by the *Nation.*

She was trying to work on *The Dove's Nest.* She had been in
bed six weeks! *I can't shake off the congestion and all the
machinery is out of order. Food is a horror . . . If I can get well*

enough to go to Paris, it's all I ask . . . she told Brett on
January 20th. By January 25th, 'deadly tired', she finished
Taking the Veil. It had taken only three hours to write, after
much thought and was born of a vivid childhood memory of
the convent near home. It was published by the *Sketch*. She
longed for 'inner calm' in which to do her writing like
Elizabeth, unruffled, and all alone in the big chalet. The
Chalet des Sapins Katherine found noisy, with banging doors,
chattering and the sound of footsteps on the stairs — very
off-putting that, with the dreaded duster approaching. *I find
it devilish, devilish, devilish!*

In a letter to Mrs Marie Belloc Lowndes, who proposed to
spend ten days with Katherine, she expressed a wish to write of
'family love' in the inevitable turning to thoughts of the warm
security of an idealized home situation.

Switzerland February 1922
Katherine Mansfield to Marie Belloc Lowndes
   *I have such a romantic vision in my mind of your house in
Barton Street. Thank heaven for dreams. I have been there on
a warm spring afternoon, and there has been a room with open
windows where you have sat talking, wearing the same
embroidered jacket . . . Outside one was concious of trees — of
their green gold light . . . But it's all far away from my cursed
Swiss balcony where I am lying lapping up the yellows of eggs
and taking my temperature in the eye of Solemn Immensities
— mobled Kings.*
*Illness is a great deal more mysterious than doctors imagine. I
simply can't afford to die with a very half-and-half little book
and one bad one and a few stories to my name. In spite of
everything, in spite of all one knows and has felt — one has this
longing to* praise life, *to sing one's minute song of praise.*
*Will one ever be able to say how marvellously beautiful it all is?
I long above everything, to write about family love — the love
between growing children — and the love of a mother for her
son, and the father's feeling. But warm, vivid, intimate — not
"made up", not self-conscious . . . Goodbye, I hope you are
happy — I hope you are well?*

And in similar vein she wrote to Gertrude Millin:

Let me tell you my experience. I am a 'colonial': I was born in New Zealand. I came to Europe to "complete my education" and when my parents thought that tremendous task was over I went back to New Zealand. I hated it. It seemed to me a small petty world, and I longed for "my" kind of people and "larger" interests and so on. And after a struggle I did get out of the nest finally and came to London, at eighteen, never to return, said my disgusted heart. Since then I've lived in England, France, Italy, Bavaria. I've known literary society in plenty. But for the last four — five years I have lived either in the South of France or in a remote little chalet in Switzerland, always remote, always cut-off, seeing hardly anybody, for months, seeing really nobody except my husband and our servant and the cat and "the people who come to the back door". It's only in these years I've really been able to work and always my thoughts and feelings go back to New Zealand — rediscovering it, finding beauty in it, re-living it. It's about my Aunt Fan who lives up the road I really want to write, and the man who sold goldfinches, and about a wet night on the wharf, and Tasana Street in Spring.

She had so many ideas, and was too ill to get them all down.

Though still in bed, she was planning her trip to Paris and asking Anne Rice to recommend a hotel with a lift that went up as well as down. *Last time I stayed at one that Cooks recommended with one of those glass topped beds and strong tea coming out of the hot water tap. They plucked me to my last pin feather . . . .* It was her plan only to consult Manoukhine, then return in the spring for treatment. Though aching all over and almost too weak to stand, she went through her papers destroying and tidying. It was her way before a journey: *I prepare as though for death. Should I never return all is in order. This is what life has taught me.* She did not return to the chalet, alas.

On January 26th she received two letters from 'V. and J.' presumably Vera and James. In her notebook, she wrote bitterly: *I felt these two letters had nothing whatever to do with me. I would not care if I never saw V. again. There is something in her assumed cheerfulness which I can't bear. I'd never get on with her. And J. — is it fancy? — just a touch of carelessness. I feel they are so absolutely insincere. What on earth would I do at Woodhay?* Vera and her husband were on a visit to Chaddie and Jeanne. She had not seen Katherine for years, and perhaps, writing from such a distance both in time and space, had no real idea of the extent of Katherine's suffering. It seems there had been lifelong sibling rivalry between them, probably one-sided, inevitable when one of the siblings was Katherine! — an insoluble problem.

Katherine was ready to leave for Paris by January 30th. There had been another heavy fall of snow. She and Murry drove in a sleigh to the station. He was very fit with his stay in Switzerland, he skiied and skated and was no doubt attractively sunburned. Katherine thought he looked 'excessively handsome' these days. *I never saw a more splendid figure.* She left in a happy state of mind, expecting to be back soon, but wondered wistfully if she might be seeing the countryside for the last time. It was a great comfort to know that the *Westminster* had accepted *The Garden Party.* L.M. was looking after her as well as she could, but there was the inevitable quarrel. They were staying at the Victoria Palace Hotel, 6, Rue Blaise Desgoffe, Rue de Rennes.

On the evening of January 31st Katherine went to see Manoukhine. Sadly, she realized her heart was not in it, she was in conflict over having disturbed their life together at Montana. Dr Manoukhine was suggesting she start treatment straightaway. Writing to Murry on Tuesday 1st February she wished they could have seen the doctor together and asked Murry to come for 2 days to help her decide.

With her usual thoroughness she asked Manoukhine for further details of the treatment. It was very expensive, 300 francs a session of X-rays to the spleen, fifteen sessions in all. Katherine had her hard-earned £103 from her stories, that was all. She saw Dr Manoukhine with his French partner Dr Donat, who held out hope for recovery. Katherine's heart was still somewhat heavy. *A dark secret unbelief holds me back* . . she told Murry, but she was in the middle of a new story and longed for his reply with advice.

With the unerring accuracy of a bird in flight came the swift reply, declining to come: *Heard from M. saying he prefers to remain in Montana. All his letters now are the same. There breathes in them the relief from strain. He does not believe a word about M(anoukhine) and talks of coming to 'fetch' me in May.* Katherine, under the terrible effect of the first application of X-rays, was feeling ill, ill as was to be expected with such terrible treatment.

The first available evidence of damage by radiation was in 1895. By 1908 there were thirty deaths recorded from intractable ulceration and tumours. Surveys have shown that radiologists more often develop leukaemia. An acute, whole-body reaction occurs within twenty-four hours of being irradiated. This is 'radiation-sickness' presenting with nausea and vomiting. If the dose is big, the reaction appears earlier. Two to four days later, diarrhoea and ulceration of the throat and intestine occur; in two to four weeks, haemorrhages into the bowel, skin, joints and kidney, which can lead to death. This, then, is something of what Katherine had to endure on top of her inexorable destructive disease and lack of support from the blinkered Murry.

He had not even asked how things were going but talked about trying to finish his novel and write articles. After a rather straight reply from Katherine, Murry began to vacillate and sent a telegram to which Katherine replied with even more candour on February 9th: *Please do not come here to me . . . I want you to have your freedom as an artist. You asked for it at Menton . . . after you left for Montana you asked for it again . . . your own personal feeling was not at this most critical of all moments in her life I could not leave Wig. Golly-no! It was my work — May would be too late — my novel — and so on . . . I now know that I must grow a shell away from you . . . I want now intensely to be alone until May . . . I am going to see a little flat tomorrow . . . Don't send the DAILY NEWS about E.B.* Murry had foolishly mentioned a review of Elizabeth Bibesco's first collection of short stories; 'I have only myself to blame'. Murry replied on February 9th, saying he deserved the letter, but explained that he was terrified of being uprooted. He denied wanting his freedom as an artist, indeed he felt he could not work without her presence. Murry left for Paris arriving early on February 10th.

In his journal, August 10th, 1948, recalling this time, he was abject. *God! how terrible are one's failures in* love. *They haunt*

the secretest places of one's soul for years and years — for ever.
*Even though they are, in a sense, tiny and almost trivial, they
are enormous and absolute. And what good would it do to
"open them to God"? God himself cannot pardon them.*

L.M. had been tramping the streets looking for and finding
a flat: 'very nice where five girls with bobbed hair lived with
their uncle'. Katherine went to see it, noted 'uncle' had
departed leaving two cigars, and told L.M. on leaving, "But
it's a bawdy house!" L.M. replied, "I quite see what you mean!"
Katherine described all this in detail for Elizabeth. L.M. left
for Montana.

Murry and Katherine settled in. They had two rooms and a
bathroom at the end of a passage, pleasantly marooned,
working, playing chess, and drinking their own tea.
Murry was nursing her as best he could. Writing to L.M. on
February 14th she said: *It is remarkable — more — how such a
dreamy nature can care for another as he looks after me. He
even brushed my hair last night . . . .* Katherine had started on
her last major story *The Fly*, that great story with its
unillumined landscape of depression and despair, about a fly
drowning in ink and a bereft bank manager, completed on
February 20th. She had hated writing it. It was considered one
of the fifteen finest short stories ever written, by a masterly
critic of the short story, E.T. O'Brien and was 'her clear-eyed
admission that life goes on' (Professor Ian Gordon).

Back in Montana L.M. was trying to settle Katherine's
affairs. Much correspondence ensued, some of it expressing
exasperation. One letter, about February 20th, suggesting
L.M. try to sell Murry's skis at the Palace Hotel, contained
nine directives, one of which was testy. *Please call me K.M. —
not K. I never feel like K.* On February 20th: *why don't you
learn to ski! Jack wonders too. What a chance!* Katherine's
clothes arrived sporadically and once, to her fury, she received
a pair of stockings and a belt by expensive letter-post.

There were further reactions from the treatment, some
disorientation and confusion when she hardly recognised
Murry on waking from sleep. By February 13th she had a
'feeling of violent confusion', her back ached, her throat was
sore and she was without hope. She was missing the
ministrations of Ida, having to look after her clothes and wash

up cups.

On February 23rd *The Garden Party*, her book of short stories, duly appeared, which reached its third edition by April 2nd. H.M. Tomlinson in the *Nation* thought it 'a happier book than "Bliss" '. *The Times Literary Supplement* considered it stronger and that . . . pity had entered in.

Mary Agnes Hamilton in *Time and Tide* thought the book was polished and cruel. The *English Review* praised it and considered Katherine a 'feminine Maupassant'.

Writing to William Gerhardi on March 3rd she asked him if he had read the review in *Time and Tide*. *It was written by a very fierce lady indeed. Beating in the face was nothing to it. It frightened me when I read it. I shall never dare to come to England. I am sure she would have my blood like a fish in Cock Robin. But why is she so dreadfully violent? One would think I was a wife beater, at least, or that I wrote all my stories with a carving knife. It is a great mystery.*

Writing to a friend in March, Elizabeth eulogized over *The Garden Party.* She thought it marvellous and 'bleeding with reality'.

Two ecstatic letters came from Chaddie and Jeanne, both are written in large flowing handwriting, quite different to Katherine's, which though often illegible was more characterful.

Woodhay, Lyndhurst, Hants, February 26th 1922
My darling K.,
I expect my letter will be one of hundreds that will be pouring on you just now, what an exciting moment it must be receiving so many congratulations. You must almost feel you are doing a Princess Mary and being married. I do want mine to be a very feminine and heart felt congratulation dear, you know how deeply I feel your successes and have always felt and known it would come. In todays "Observer" there is a very complimentary article on you, they simply couldn't say more. J. and I were most excited about it, and it has made us very keen to possess your new book. I am sure Jack must be very proud and very happy, please give him my love and say how happy I am for you both. J. and I think you were very wise dear to send that wire, of course we quite understand, and will

come over to you whenever you are ready for us. May sounds a lovely month to be in Paris and with you there it will make it a very happy time to look forward to. I am so glad you advise your hotel for us to come to, as it will be far nicer all being under the same roof, it will make all the difference.

My dear 'V' has returned to Canada, she and Mack sailed last Saturday, she full of regrets at not having seen you. Poor child her time here was one long rush she hardly seemed to have time to talk except when she was getting up or going to bed! Why are Canadians and Americans so keen to cram every moment of their lives so full with work and pleasure, it quite paralyses me and leaves me almost panting in the background! Jeanne and I took V in hand and made her get some really attractive clothes, she hadn't collected any for years, she is rather inclined to run to seed unless we insist of her thinking of herself and spending money on herself, far too good natured for this world! She won't be across this summer with the boys as Father will be going over to see them towards September after he has viewed us all. She hopes to come next year and bring Andrew and Johnnie it would be good to have them and I will just love you to see them dear, I know they will interest you very much. I do wish I had a Johnnie for you to play with. I know you would make such a lovely Aunt to him — We came back from London last Saturday after seeing V off! We had had a very happy ten days at the club. We found all our crocus out in the front drive to greet us, a golden strip, so beautiful, now the mauve and white are appearing, such a joy to see flowers again. How one misses them in the country in the winter. I am just like you I adore flowers nothing seems to give one greater pleasure.

Well dear, the child and Kuri have gone to bed after having eaten two oranges (only J. not Kuri). I must go to as I have to have an early start and go into Southampton to a dentist tomorrow. I so dislike S'hampton it is such a dull place just full of people one would see on the Picton boat. Do let us hear from you again soon dear, we so love your letters. So take every care of yourself and how much we are thinking of you and feel sure this new treatment is going to make you a new being. All my love and again telling you how happy I am for all your great success . . . .

                                                        Marie

From Jeanne, Woodhay, February 26th, 1922:

My dearest K —
the Sunday Observer gave us news of your 3rd book and
what an excellent criticism too, we are so anxious to get the
book — Jack must be feeling very happy and proud of you —
and what a relief to your mind now that it is launched — I
expect you will receive so many congratulations that only your
head will be seen over a wave of letters!
Your new china tea pot fills me with envy, we inherit the love
of them from dear little mother, when ever she saw one she
liked she mentally used to pour out tea, to test the spout — a
fine art it is the pouring out of tea, it must be done slowly and
the tea pot held at the right angle —? what a difference it
makes to the taste? — You said in your letter to me that you
read between the lines something was perhaps going to happen
this year? — Nothing that I know of dear, but still 'one never
knows', and one goes on hoping. It is very joyful news to hear
how well you are going to be in May, we will certainly come
and see you then. I shall start a money box for the visit — the
pillar box kind that Aunt Li used to keep at 'Tarana' for her
3d-s-.
Belle Trinder was in here today very shiny and tanned and she
always jingles golf balls in her pockets. Harry is filling out his
'Pink coat' and stiff white collar and Patsy very plain is playing
ping-pong — what a typical 'county' household — Much love
'K' dear to you and I do feel so happy for you —
Your loving Jeanne.

Katherine was quite right in her divinations. Jeanne married
Captain Charles Mitford Renshaw, formerly Captain Persian
Rifles, at St. Margaret's, Westminster on October 17th, 1922.

Vera's husband died at fifty-seven after a highly successful
career. Thereafter she moved in diplomatic circles; there were
thirteen embassies in the block of flats where she lived in
Ottawa. She was involved in nursing administration and was
given *carte blanche* by the Prime Minister, Mr Massey. She
died at the age of eighty-eight from a stroke which took away
her power of speech.

On October 10th, 1923, Chaddie married Cecil Marmaduke
Pickthall of the Foreign Office, giving up Woodhay to live in

Chelsea at 9, Trevor Square. She loved staying with Jeanne and it was on one of those visits that she developed an acute abdomen, for which she was admitted to the local hospital, dying there within a week.

I am and shall be for the next ten days rather badly ill, Katherine told Brett on March 15th. *M. has just come in with two bunches of anemones, two small tea plates and a cake of rose thé soap . . . . I* cannot *work for the moment and Shorter has ordered 13 stories, all at one go, to be ready in July . . . Oh, your cinerarias. I wish I could see them . . . We used to have blue ones in pots in a rather white and gold drawing room . . . . Oh, how beautiful Life is . . . .*

A shopping list for cosmetics for Katherine whilst in Paris, 1922, still survives. I found it among her letters to L.M. in the British Library:

50 Sachets de toilette simple parfum Oeillet	11.25
Crepe de nuit	15.0
Boite de trois pains de savon	
Rosée de Beauté Flacon leger	20

Katherine had received a letter from her father in answer to her explanatory one and she answered it on March 18th:

My darling Father,

I can't express to you my feelings when I read your letter. How can you possibly find it in your heart to write like that to your undeserving little black sheep of a child only God knows. It wrings my heart to think of my ungrateful behaviour and I cannot understand how I have been the victim of my fearfulness and dread of misunderstanding. You have been — you are — the soul of generosity to us all. Then how, loving you as I do, feeling your sensitiveness and sympathy as I do, can I have made you suffer? It is a mystery, I sometimes wish that we could have been nearer to each other since I have been grown up and not the intolerant girl who returned to New Zealand with you years ago. But fate has willed otherwise . . . .

God bless you darling.

I am, ever your loving and grateful child,

Kass

She also told him that New Zealand was in her very bones and that she thanked God she was born in New Zealand.

Meanwhile, the irradiation reaction continued, with painful burning sensations in her hands, feet and bones, and a splitting headache. She told Elizabeth on March 24th that she had not been out of her hotel once in eight weeks, except to go to the clinic.

Finally by March 22nd L.M. in Montana had turned the chalet into a guest house, with the help of a young Swiss girl, Susie de Perrot, daughter of the Suchard chocolate firm, her sister and two Irish girls called Aylesbury. Katherine for once was full of praise. Commenting on the arrival of her clothes, Katherine told L.M: *all my things look rather as though they had been washed through the customs — they are very much exhausted. But even a change is such a relief that I fully expect a low hiss of admiration when I go to lunch today in different shoes* . . . . She was also trying to get rid of some of her old clothes, clothes from happier days, 'little jackets and so on'. A large parcel was duly collected by the Aylesbury girls, who gave Katherine news of L.M., expressing their admiration for her. Ida had also sent Katherine her writing-case, which reminded her *of the Ida I love, not because of what it cost. But the 'impulse' — the gesture — what you call the 'perfect thing'. It carries me back to Isola Bella. Oh, memory! And back I go to the Casetta and the olive tree before and the cotton tree along the twisted fence and the red roses and big starry-eyed daisies. Menton seems to hold years of life . . . however painful a thing has been when I look back it is no longer painful . . . . Now when I hear the sea at the Casetta it's unbearably beautiful* . . . . She also mentioned that she was having to visit a dentist to have fillings replaced, and striking a gay note she intended to have her hair done with henna, so that it would glow like a chestnut. She was to visit Manoukhine in his flat and there meet a writer called Bunin, who was supposed to have met Chekhov. Alas, this Russian was rather hazy about Chekhov, much to Katherine's disappointment, especially in view of the effort required to get there at all.

Some time during the stay in Paris, Katherine saw Francis Carco for the last time. It seems that he ran into Murry at the Café d'Harcourt, the old hunting ground. He noted that Murry looked older, with a lined, thin face, no longer fresh and bright-eyed. Strolling and talking rather lamely, they agreed to meet again. Later, passing the Café de l'Univers in Place du Theâtre-Français, Carco saw Murry and Katherine sitting near the door. Murry had not told Katherine of their previous encounter, so that the meeting was rather uncomfortable. Carco was horrified by Katherine's appearance. He thought her dark eyes still flashed with their old warmth but she looked ill and he could scarcely bear to see her poor little thin hands which she tried to hide under the table. Declining Murry's invitation to take a drink, Carco hurried off. It was all too sad for them.

About March 29th Katherine met James Joyce, whose book *Ulysses* had been reviewed by Murry in the *Nation*. Katherine had taken two weeks 'to wade through' the book and was 'dead against it'. She was shocked by it, but admitted there were 'amazingly fine things in it'. Sydney Schiff, staying in Paris with Violet, had arranged the meeting with Joyce, and Katherine, sending them an account, said she had felt out of her depth, almost stupefied. Yet Violet was able to tell Wyndham Lewis that Joyce considered that 'Mrs. Murry seemed to understand his book better than her husband'.

Katherine wrote to Brett about Joyce: *Joyce had not one grain of a desire that one should read it for the sake of coarseness, though I confess I find many "a ripple of laughter in it"*, then went on to talk of Wyndham Lewis, who for some reason of his own was to be odious to poor Katherine. *I'm interested in what you say for Wyndham L. I've heard so very very much about him from Anne Rice and Violet Schiff. Yes, I admire his line tremendously . . . but it's queer I feel that as an artist in spite of his passions and his views . . . he lacks a real centre . . . what one aims at is to work with one's mind and one's soul together . . . . Wyndham Lewis would be inclined to call the soul tiddley-om-pom . . . .* Katherine had a very keen eye.

By April 8th she was able to go out and buy a new hat at Bon Marché, describing the expedition for L.M: *hundreds of women . . . like some terrible insect swarm . . . the hats were loathsome. Jack as usual on such occasions would not speak to me and became furious. If I said 'Do you like that?' he replied 'No horribly vulgar!' If I timidly stretched out a hand he hissed*

'Good God!' in my ear . . . drove to another hat shop. 'Get this damned thing over!' was Jack's excuse . . . my one stipulation was I didn't mind what kind of hat I bought but it must have no feathers. And I finally decided on a little fir cone with two whole birds on it.

The irradiation effect was nearly over. At the end of April she went for a drive in the Bois, delighting in the flowering cherry trees. There were still two weeks of treatment to go, however. Ever hopeful she told L.M., on April 30th: *I intend next spring to go to London, take the Bechstein Hall and give readings of my stories — I've always wanted to do this . . . it would be a great advertisement. Dickens used to do it. He knew his people just as I know old 'Ma Parkers' voice and the Ladies Maid.*

On May 3rd she wrote to Brett that she was beginning her long serial of 24,000 words with *A scrumptious wedding, rose pink tulle frocks for the bridesmaids, favours on the horses' heads, that marvellous moment at the church when everyone is waiting, the servants in a pew to themselves.* The Cook's hat! *But all, all divinely beautiful if I can do it . . . gay, but with that feeling that 'beauty vanishes, beauty passes, though, rare it be . . . .'* This proved to be, alas, the unfinished story *The Dove's Nest*, on which she worked at Randogne to no avail, leaving only the original part written in the Chalet des Sapins.

On May 11th Katherine and Murry went with the Schiffs to tea in the Bois; Katherine loved watching the women dancing in the open, under the flowering chestnut trees. It was wonderful to be back in the world again. On the same day Katherine wrote to L.M. about the results of the treatment — would that the improvement had continued!

Dear Ida,
    as far as I can tell this treatment has been . . . completely successful. I hardly ever cough. I have gained 8 lbs. I have no rheumatism whatever . . . my voice has changed back . . . the only thing that remains is that my heart is tired and weak . . . I get breathless and cannot walk yet except at snail's pace with many halts. We are going to the Angleterre (Hotel at Randogne 750 feet below Montana near Chalet Soleil).

Towards the end of May, L.M. with a heavy heart, closed the chalet and travelled home via Paris, with Wingly on a lead. She found Katherine in an untidy room. Murry, like many writers, tended to spread papers on the floor as well as the table. Katherine would be thrilled to see Wingly, who with eyes large with interest, carefully examined the room. L.M. did not stay long, but showed Katherine her little account book. Katherine was as upset as L.M. and admitted, at the sight of it she 'could have howled like a dog'. *I had better end this letter quickly for the old feeling is coming back — an ache, a longing — a feeling, that I can't be satisfied unless I know you are near . . . not because I need you — but because in my horrid odious, intolerable way I love you and am yours ever . . .* and that really sums up this long friendship. L.M. reached England and found a permanent home for little Wingly, much travelled and harrassed like his poor mistress. He was to live with L.M.'s aunt in Lewes.

Brett had joined Katherine and Murry in Paris and wrote to Kot — all about the meeting. Katherine had greeted her at the foot of the stairs holding out her hands. She was fragile and 'wonderfully beautiful'. Brett could not help loving her.

Chapter XIX

Switzerland and London

Missing L.M.'s kindly support, Katherine and Murry set off for Randogne on June 4th, 1922. Murry was hopeless as a courier. He gave away a 500 franc note belonging to Katherine, as a 50 franc tip, left her precious travelling clock on the train, lost the registered luggage tickets and his fountain pen. There were no couchettes — both sat up all night — no washing facilities, no food on the train, no porters and the train was overcrowded due to the Montreux Fête de Narcisse. At Sierre, Katherine, exhausted, was able to rest at the Hotel Château Belle Vue, then lunch and sleep until the Randogne train. When the voiture arrived, Murry was out, Katherine was asleep, nothing was packed and the bill was unsettled. The final part of the journey was by cart, on a rutted road, in heavy cold rain. The rooms in the Hotel Angleterre weren't too attractive but after rest, Katherine could absorb the peace and freshness of the countryside from her balcony: *that journey nearly killed me literally,* she wrote to L.M. *He had no idea I suffered at all, and would not understand why I looked 'so awful' and why everybody seemed to think I was terribly ill. Jack can never understand . . . I feel I cannot live without you . . . I cannot move about at all . . . my heart thuds in my ear . . . and bangs twice as fast all day. It is hateful to again have to give up baths, to again have to dress sitting down and sipping water and so on . . . .* At Katherine's request, made in desperation, L.M. joined them at the Angleterre towards the end of June, occupying a room some distance away from their quarters in the more or less empty hotel.

Katherine was exhausted and unable to work. She contacted

her cousin Elizabeth: *here I am with dry pleurisy, coughing away . . . . my only trouble is John. He ought to divorce me, marry a really healthy young creature, have children and ask me to be godmother. He needs a wife beyond everything . . . what a perfect glimpse we had of the Chalet Soleil as we bumped here in the cold mountain rain . . . all your lovely house is hidden in white blossom. Only heavenly blue shutters showed through. The little 'working' chalet is in an absolute nest of green . . . .* Elizabeth visited them on June 13th finding Murry asleep in a garden chair outside, and Katherine, rounder-faced, sitting in the glass veranda, coughing incessantly.

Four days later Murry went to tea with Elizabeth, showing her his new book *Countries of the Mind*. It would be a happy day for him. Elizabeth, working on *The Enchanted April*, had finished it that day; a light, charming book, but Katherine was very critical of it when she read it in December. Elizabeth visited Katherine again on the 19th, and found her pinched and cold in the unheated gloomy hotel. She begged her to come to the Châlet.

Writing to Koteliansky Katherine admitted to a feeling of indifference to everything, a new feeling and very significant. The weather had turned cold, the valley was full of cloud, there was a sound of water flowing. Katherine could not work, and typing tired her. Sadly, she realized she could not finish *The Dove's Nest*. *I seem to have lost all power of writing*, she noted. *Sometimes I think my brain is going. But no! I know the real reason. It's because I'm still suffering from a kind of nervous prostration caused by my life in Paris.* It was a great relief to have L.M. *I'll never never say another word of impatience. I don't deserve such a wife. All is in order already . . . .*

In a letter to her father on June 26th, she described the cold misty weather and envied him his voyage to England in the *Aquitania*. He was due in London in August. *I have a very soft spot in my heart for the "Niwaru"* . . . do you remember how mother used to enjoy the triangular pieces of toast for tea? Awfully good . . . on a cold afternoon in the vicinity of the Horn . . . . Mother in her little sealskin jacket with the collar turned up.*

On June 29th Katherine and L.M. moved down to the Hotel Château Belle Vue. Murry stayed behind at Randogne visiting Elizabeth daily and Katherine at weekends. Then they played at billiards. Alas their relationship was breaking down. Katherine had become deeply restless and unable to work. Each had a depressing effect on the other. I think there was another simple, additional explanation. Brett was arriving at Sierre on July 5th, to stay with Katherine for a month. Neither Murry nor Katherine would want to face a ménage à trois.

Brett painted in the hotel garden. In the mornings, Katherine had arranged to be incommunicado. She would sit on a chair facing an aloe tree, or walk about very slowly. Brett remembered her wearing a cerulean blue jersey she had sent her, and a little dark brick-red hat. Occasionally in the afternoon they all went for a drive in a carriage. L.M., reminiscing, thought that Brett kept Katherine talking too late at night. Katherine showed Brett, after much searching, the hotel room which had appeared in one of her recent stories, *Father and the Girls*.

It was at that time she wrote *The Canary*, the 'hero' of which was a little bird who seemed to have a whole repertoire of songs, such a sad story, and her last, marking the end of her creative life. She had also written the tragic and beautiful poem 'The Wounded Bird', the last verse of which is unbearably sad:

At night, in the wide bed
With the leaves and flowers
Gently weaving in the darkness,
She is like a wounded bird at rest on a pool.
Timidly, timidly she lifts her head from her wing.
In the sky there are two stars
Floating, shining . . .
O Waters — do not cover me!
I would look long and long at those beautiful stars!
O my wings — lift me — lift me!
I am not so dreadfully hurt . . . .

On July 30th kindly Elizabeth, deeply aware of the tragedy of this dying girl, struggling to write and to type in order to earn money to keep going, gallantly offered to lend her £100 until further funds duly arrived. Katherine accepted the loan gratefully, paying it back some little time before she died. Elizabeth had been visited a few days previously by Murry who was in the depths of despair.

Brett left for England on August 3rd. Writing to Kot, Katherine said she felt like 'campbelling' about her: *she is a terrible proof of the influence one's childhood has upon one . . . I do not think she will ever be an adult being. She is weak; she is a vine; she longs to cling. She cannot nourish herself from the earth; she must feed on the sap of another. How can these natures ever be happy? . . . she is seeking someone who will make her forget that early neglect, that bullying and contempt. But the person who would satisfy her would have to dedicate himself to curing all the results of her unhappiness — her distrust, for instance, her suspicions, her fears . . . hidden in the slave there are the makings of the free man. And these makings are very nice in Brett, very sensitive and generous. I love her for them. They make me want to help her as much as I can . . . .*

She had also been thinking of Lawrence after reading *Aaron's Rod* and asked Kot if he had read it. *He is the only writer living whom I really profoundly care for. It seems to me whatever he writes, no matter how much one may 'disagree', is important . . . he is a living man . . . .* And again on July 17th: *I want to talk for hours about — "Aaron's Rod" . . . It is a living book; it is warm, it breathes. And it is written by a living man, with conviction . . . I feel nearer Lawrence than anyone else. All these last months I have thought as he does about many things . . . now I have made myself a glass of tea. Everytime I drop a piece of lemon into a glass of tea I say 'Koteliansky' . . . they are thinning the vines for the last time before harvest . . . And in the orchards apples are reddening; it is going to be a wonderful year for pears . . . .*

On August 7th Katherine wrote a letter to Murry to be sent to him via the bank after her death.

Dearest Bogey
I have been on the point of writing this letter for days. My heart has been behaving in such a curious fashion that I can't

*imagine it means nothing. So, as I should hate to leave you
unprepared, I'll just try and jot down what comes into my
mind. All my manuscripts I leave entirely to you to do what
you like with. Go through them one day, dear love, and
destroy all you do not use. Please destroy all letters you do not
wish to keep and all papers. You know my love of tidiness.
Have a clean sweep Bogie, and leave all fair — will you?*

*Books are yours of course . . . . monies, of course, are all
yours. In fact, my dearest dear, I leave everything to you — to
the secret you whose lips I kissed this morning. In spite of
everything — how happy we have been! I feel no other lovers
have walked the earth more joyfully — in spite of all.*

Farewell — my precious love,

I am for ever and ever

Your

Wig

On August 14th she made a formal will which was witnessed by
two of the hotel staff. She left her gold watch and chain to
L.M., her Spanish shawl to Anne Estelle Rice, her fur coat to
her mother-in-law, her large pearl ring to Richard, and her
Shakespeare to Elizabeth. She left all books to Murry,
requesting he give one each to Walter de la Mare, H.M.
Tomlinson, Dr Sorapure, A.R. Orage, Sydney and Violet
Schiff, J.D. Fergusson and D.H. Lawrence; her writing-case to
Chaddie, her piece of greenstone to Jeanne, the brass pig to
her father, her bible to Vera; her Italian toilet boxes and
carved walking-stick to Koteliansky. *All manuscripts notebooks papers letters I leave to John M. Murry likewise I should
like him to publish as little as possible and to tear up and burn
as much as possible. He will understand that I desire to leave as
few traces of my camping ground as possible.* Writing to
Richard about the ring on August 14th, she said: *My idea in
leaving it to you was that you should give it — if you care to —
to your woman whoever she may be . . . . But Jack gave me the
ring and I feel it would be nice to keep it in the family.*

That very day, Lawrence was in Wellington, *en route* from
Australia to New Mexico. He wrote 'Ricordi' on a postcard and
sent it to Katherine, c/o Ottoline.

The same day, Katherine wrote to Brett about staying with

her in Pond Street, Hampstead. She told her she had been 'horribly ill' and wanted to see Sorapure. She implored Brett not to tell anyone she was coming, not even Kot. She was too ill to face the world. She and Murry had reached the parting of the ways.

Katherine, Murry and L.M. left Randogne on August 16th for London. Murry was to stay in Boris Anrep's house next door to Brett. He was desolate; Katherine in 'spiritual crisis'. On August 18th Katherine saw Dr Sorapure, who did not think her heart was diseased. Probably the problem all along had been a tachycardia, a quick action of the heart due to pyrexia and toxic causes. In addition she may from girlhood have experienced extra-systoles, an irregularity in heart rhythm — alarming but not serious — where the heart has to miss a beat to compensate for an extra-systole, a small extra beat to the regular rhythm. She had always feared she would die of heart disease.

On August 21st Mr Beauchamp took lunch with Katherine, Chaddie and Jeanne. Writing the next day to thank him, Katherine remarked how young he looked. *Just a note to say how happy I was to see you yesterday . . . The girls looked so well and charming too. Wee Jeanne though, looks almost too young to have a real live husband. She ought to be married in a daisy chain with the wedding service read from a seed catalogue, as it used to be when we were children. It's a sad pity that New Zealand is so far, dearest Papa. How nice it would be if we could all foregather more often. By this same post I am sending you a copy of my book.* It was *The Garden Party.*

She wrote to Elizabeth that her father would live for hundreds of years, growing redder and firmer and fatter forever. *As to his "fund of humorous stories" it doesn't bear thinking about . . . I said to my sisters while we powdered our noses together. "Dont you find his stories a little tiring" and they cried (they always say the same) "oh but the old dear does so enjoy telling them and he really is most amusing!" The only reply was to cross oneself . . . .* She also mentioned 'John's little grand tour' had died at Sierre. He had planned to visit Italy. Murry had said, "Why shouldn't I come to London with you? *(Pause)* Dash it all. I will come. *(Pause)* I'll toss for it. Heads

London. Tails Italy. (*Pause*) It's tails. That settles it. I go to London tomorrow . . . ."

Katherine seemed to have decided to stay in London for three months, and take further treatments of irradiation from a doctor there. After seeing Sorapure she was feeling just a little better. On August 23rd Koteliansky visited Katherine. After he had gone she wrote him a letter: *You know I am deeply sorry for Murry; he is like a man under a curse . . . that is why I am determined to remain his friend and to make him free of his own will . . . I must not speak against him to you . . . It is better to be silent about him — in these last months away from all his associates here I think he has got much more like he used to be . . . Now that I am no longer in a false position with Murry, now that I am, in the true sense of the word 'free' I look at him differently. His situation is very serious. But who am I to say anyone is beyond hope — to withdraw my hand if there is even the smallest chance of helping them . . . .*

L.M. was also in Pond Street, sleeping on a small folding bed outside Katherine's door. This was done in secret because L.M. believed that 'Katherine did not want Murry to know of her night terrors', fearing to be 'alone' lest 'she go out of her mind with misery'. It seems, on the face of it, that Katherine had accepted Brett to a large extent after the Bibesco affair. There is nothing more calculated to diminish animosity towards a rival than the emergence of a new rival. Also, the Pond Street flat was a valuable asset. However, one evening during a visit from Kot, there were residual signs of resentment. Kot described the occasion for Miss Mantz. Hearing the sound of Brett talking to Murry in a room above, and his deep voice answering her, Katherine's eyes filled with tears as she enjoined Kot to listen. She asked him to promise that when she was dead, Murry would never marry Brett. Kot solemnly promised. One supposes that she preferred not to know her successor. Perhaps, too, she considered Brett too old to marry Murry, especially for starting a family. There was also the difficulty in communication due to her deafness.

On August 27th Katherine lunched at Anne Rice's house. Anne left a loving memoir:

. . . *One more meeting and I had a premonition it was going to*

*be the last. There was an unreality about her and I felt sadly
the end was not far off; there was a serenity, a surrender, the
supreme acceptance 'It's time to go'. Our luncheon was
planned by the cook and her husband Wagner, in the capacity
of butler . . . in a cerise eye-shield and a brightly coloured
waistcoat and — rolled up shirt sleeves . . . Wagner . . . drew
the curtains leaving us in . . . darkness . . . The entrée was
dramatic. A belated Christmas pudding, drenched in brandy,
was lit up alarmingly. Katherine could still laugh. I very much
wanted her to see the nursery decorations . . . slowly she made
the climb clinging to the banisters. I have always felt a
lingering remorse at the effort it must have cost her . . . .*

A luncheon engagement was made with Orage for August
30th at 6, Pond Street. They drank white wine. Brett, peering
out of her upstairs window, took a dislike to the back of his
head! The way was being laid. On September 1st Murry and
Katherine went for the weekend to Vivian Locke-Ellis's house
at Selsfield, a beautiful modernized seventeenth century
mansion near East Grinstead. She returned to London and
Murry stayed on, visiting Katherine at the weekend. The gulf
was ever widening between them now.

Orage was looking for renewal, especially as the *New Age*
was dying. Early on he had been a theosophist and was
fascinated by the teachings of P.D. Ouspensky a Russian
philosopher and journalist, whom he had met in London
before the war. After returning to Russia, Ouspensky, working
for the British Government representative Mr F.J. Pinder, sent
a letter to the *New Age* describing the deteriorating conditions
in Ekaterinodar in the Kuban Peninsula of Southern Russia,
which was governed by the White Russian, General Denikin.
An anti-Bolshevik, Ouspensky pleaded for British support and
eventually Denikin's forces were evacuated to Turkey in 1920.
With the help of Orage and a Times correspondent there Carl
Bechofer-Roberts, Ouspensky after much hardship reached
London.

During the uprising Ouspensky had met another refugee,
George Ivanovich Gurdjieff, a Caucasian Greek born in 1872,
who was in charge of a 'Hindu Ballet' in Moscow. This was in
1915. In 1910, Gurdjieff had founded the Institute for the
Harmonious Development of Man in Moscow, based on the

idea that man was imbalanced in his intellectual, emotional and physical centres by civilization. To attain harmonious development, man required special mental and physical exercise which would modify his machine-like existence and help a new and satisfying unified being emerge. In doing so, new powers could operate, and the whole personality extended. Gurdjieff had travelled widely through Turkey, Tibet, India, Mongolia, Jerusalem and India, absorbing details of rituals and religious dancing. He was also an authority on carpets, having watched whole communities engaged on their making, to the accompaniment of singing and dancing. In addition he had learned how to mend beautiful old carpets. Indeed, at one time he had been a carpet salesman. Otherwise his background was veiled. Discerning Katherine, when she eventually met Gurdjieff, thought he looked like a carpet dealer from Tottenham Court Road. Short and bald with a sweeping moustache and penetrating black eyes he spoke broken Russian with a Caucasian accent, and had very little English. His native languages were Armenian and Greek. He wrote in Armenian. During the revolution, Gurdjieff had had to remove his institute to Essentaki, Tiflis, and Constantinople respectively, where Ouspensky worked with him, giving lectures. By July 1922, having been unable to continue working in Russia because of the political situation, Gurdjieff became established in La Prieuré des Basses-Loges at Fontainebleau.

In London Ouspensky formed a group financed by Lady Rothermere, which met in a theosophical lecture room at 28, Warwick Gardens, Earl's Court. The group included a psychiatrist Dr James Carruthers Young formerly a surgeon, who had worked with Jung in Zurich. T.S. Eliot, David Garnett and J.D. Beresford were also interested. The Prieuré was bought by Gurdjieff with money from Lady Rothermere. After meeting Orage on August 30th, Katherine joined the Ouspensky Circle. She saw him on three further occasions.

Murry, who had despised *Cosmic Anatomy*, was totally opposed to the Ouspensky Circle. He could scarcely bear to discuss the matter with Katherine and finding the ever widening rift between them intolerable he finally left to live with Vivian Locke-Ellis at Selsfield.

September was crowded with appointments, lunch and teas with her father and sisters. She also saw Marion Ruddick. Katherine commenced X-ray treatments with Dr Webster; there were to have been eight, but she discontinued after only three sessions, due to adverse reaction and a feeling that she preferred to be treated by Dr Manoukhine. Kot came along to Pond Street, as did Richard, who did a drawing of Katherine. She had dinner with Sullivan and Vivian Locke-Ellis. On September 7th Katherine lunched with Sydney and Violet Schiff. Alas, Wyndham Lewis was also present. It was a traumatic occasion for Katherine. For some reason, Lewis had been contemptuous of Katherine's views. Perhaps it dated back to 1913 when Katherine had compèred the cabaret at the 'Cave of the Golden Calf' in Regent Street. He had done the décor for Strindberg's widow Freda, whose night-club it was. Sure-footed in those days, perhaps she had shot him down on some occasion; let us hope so.

At lunch it is possible that she had discussed Gurdjieff and he, in his heartlessness, making no allowances for a poor creature ravaged by mortal illness, must have poured scorn on her ideas. Murry told Violet in a letter on December 21st, 1948: that Wyndham Lewis had upset Katherine for days afterwards. Katherine, protesting, wrote Violet a note about it which was duly sent on to Wyndham Lewis, who in his reply cruelly ridiculed Katherine's involvement with Gurdjieff's doctrines and jealously called her stories 'vulgar dull and unpleasant'.

As Professor Alpers put it 'this encounter marked the end of Kass Beauchamp's relations with creative artists of her time . . . .'

On September 20th Katherine received her 'Ricordi' message from Lawrence. She was glad to get it.

On September 27th she broke the news to Murry that she was going to Paris for eight to ten weeks for treatment. She asked him up for the weekend, but also mentioned she would be seeing Orage. It seems Murry did not come. He therefore did not see her again until the day of her death.

On Monday October 2nd Katherine left England for ever.

L.M. accompanied her and they settled in their old 1918 Hotel Select, Place de la Sorbonne. They had had a *divine crossing, very still silvery sea with gulls moving on the waves like the lights in a pearl* . . . she told Brett. She saw Manoukhine on October 4th and had a further treatment. Rashly he promised her complete and absolute health by Christmas! On October 6th she received a letter from Jeanne about her forthcoming marriage to Captain Renshaw. Her father had written too, from Port Said, quoting a poem by Enid Bagnold: 'I am a sailor sailing on summer seas'. *All the same a marvellous wash of the blue crept up the page as I read his letter* . . . she told Murry.

To Brett on October 9th, she admitted her cough was so much worse: *I am a cough — a living, walking or lying down cough* . . . . In her notebook she confessed she was thinking of Murry — *We are no longer together. Am I in the right way, though? No, not yet. What remains of all those years together? It is difficult to say. If they were so important, how could they have come to nothing. Who gave up and why?*

To Murry she wrote, on October 11th: *A new way of being is not an easy thing to live* . . . *I have to make such big changes. I feel the only thing to do is to get the dying over* . . . *And then all hands to the business of being reborn again* . . . . *Looking back, my boat is almost swamped sometimes by seas of sentiment. 'Ah, what I have missed! how sweet it was, how dear,* . . . *how precious.' And I think of the garden at the Isola Bella and the furry bees and the house wall so warm. But then I remember what we really felt there — the blanks, the silences, the anguish of continual misunderstanding. Were we positive* . . .*? No, we were not. We were a nothingness shot with gleams of what might be* . . . *Well, I have to face everything as far as I can and see — what remains* . . . .

On October 13th, thanking him for his birthday poem, she told him she was going to Fontainebleau. Murry was downcast. He felt their ships were sailing away from each other.

On Saturday October 14th she was thirty-four. She received telegrams from Murry, de la Mare, Locke-Ellis, and a letter from Brett. Ida bought her an armful of mimosa. Dr James Young came up from Fontainebleau to examine her chest, and

gave her the 'go-ahead' for the Prieuré. With him was Mr F.J.
Pinder, who was translator for Gurdjieff. Manoukhine had
written to Gurdjieff saying she was not fit to stay at the
institute. Orage, having given up the *New Age* with the last
issue on September 28th, told his crestfallen secretary Alice
Marks, "I am going to find God." He arrived at the Select
Hotel to greet Katherine on her birthday; she would be glad to
see him.

She had been very low in the morning, suffering terribly
from radiation sickness: *one feels like wet stone . . . Then . . .
one burns . . .* she told Brett. *I am far more desperate about
my illness and about life than I ever show you . . . I have no
belief whatever in any kind of medical treatment . . . I'm
exactly where I was before I started. I "act" all the rest because
I am ashamed to do otherwise, looking as I do . . . .* In her
notebook for October 14th she wrote an account of how she
felt, to be sent to Murry, but changed her mind. He found the
piece among her papers, which must have affected him deeply.

*. . . . Yesterday I thought I was dying . . . my spirit is nearly
dead. My spring of life is so starved that it's just not dry . . . I
am an absolutely hopeless invalid . . .*
*Ah, I feel a little calmer already to be writing . . . I am so
terrified of what I am going to do . . . Think of five years'
imprisonment. Someone has got to help me to get out . . . And
who is going to help me? Remember Switzerland: 'I am
helpless.' Of course, he is. One prisoner cannot help another
. . . I have heard of Gurdjieff who seems to know infinitely
more about it. Why hesitate? Fear . . . fear of losing Bogie? . . .
Face things. What have you of him now? . . . He talks to you —
sometimes — and then goes off . . . He dreams of a life with
you some day when the miracle has happened . . . . Yet there is
a deep, sweet, tender flooding of feeling in my heart which is
love for him and longing for him. But what is the good of it as
things stand? Life together, with me ill, is simply torture with
happy moments. Therefore . . . Act for yourself . . . But now
that I have wrestled with it . . . I feel happy — deep down.*

The next day she sat in the Luxembourg Gardens *cold,
wretchedly unhappy . . . . everything horrid, from Anfang bis*

zum ende, a most tragic entry and almost the last in her notebook. On October 17th, Katherine and L.M., without luggage, went down to Fontainebleau, ostensibly to see over the place for two days. They saw Gurdjieff, who invited Katherine to stay for a trial period of two weeks. She was given a large, beautiful room with a view of the garden, known as the Ritz.

Chapter XX

Fontainebleau

The Prieuré, on the edge of the forest of Fontainebleau, had belonged to Mme Laborie, widow of Maître Laborie, defending counsel in the Dreyfus case. Originally an old Carmelite monastery, rebuilt by King Louis XIV as a gift for Mme de Maintenon, it had been left fully furnished and largely unoccupied, since 1914. The thirteen acres of grounds surrounded by a high brick wall, were neglected and overgrown. There was a small row of houses surrounded by trees called Paradou, where lived Gurdjieff's mother, married sister and brother, a Dr and Mrs Stjoernval, and a Mr and Mme de Salzmann. The whole community ate in the large dining-room, where King Louis XIV had been entertained; it was furnished with the original furniture, there being a large table for twenty-five, and two side-tables for twenty. Over the mantelpiece hung a photograph of Gurdjieff's father in beard, moustache, and astrakhan hat. Gurdjieff dined at the middle of the big table. The food was excellent; Gurdjieff was apparently a connoisseur. Exotic alcoholic drinks were also served, such as slivowitz, kumiss and kifter.

The day began at 6.30 a.m. with a peal from the bell-tower, when breakfast was served; lunch was from 12.30 until 2.00, tea at 4.00, with a large dinner at 6.30, after which exercises and dancing began, continuing until 11.00 p.m. Everyone in turn became kitchen staff from 5.00 a.m. to 11.00 p.m. There was no hired staff. All work was done by the pupils. It was a patriarchal life at the Prieuré, and the enigmatic Gurdjieff, with his magnetic personality, radiated tremendous force which had a mass hypnotic effect. This is a very powerful force and can influence even the sceptical. Combined with this was colossal energy, creativity and intensity of purpose, always attractive to the less well-equipped. People simply jumped to his bidding. One really has to admire this Asiatic 'card'. Here he was, probably largely uneducated, being bought a wonderful old mansion to live in, where other people paid him to live, while they worked for him like galley-glaves for nothing, sometimes until 3.00 a.m., building, digging, constructing and cultivating.

Under this auspices, the guests built a Turkish bath, and a huge study house from a disused hangar, on the framework of which were fixed rough laths. The spaces between were filled with a mixture of mud and chopped straw. This was dried by the heat of stoves, then painted. The roof was of tarred felt, beneath which were fixed cucumber frames as windows encircling the room. Caucasian designs were painted on the glass in red, blue, green and yellow. The floor was of pounded earth and was to be covered, as were the walls, with sixty-three glorious Eastern carpets and sixty-three fur rugs. Gurdjieff was good on carpets. There were seats in two tiers all around the room, covered with mattresses and skins. There was a raised stage for dancing, made of earth and covered with linoleum, at the far end of the room. It all looked like a dervish tekke. Above the door was a small gallery holding Eastern stringed instruments and drums, and nearby was an alcove especially for Mr Gurdjieff, hung with dark red curtains and a rich wall-carpet. It contained a divan covered with cushions on which he lolled in state. It was not quite finished by the time Katherine arrived.

Dr Young worked as hard as anybody. Orage, put to strenuous digging for six weeks, admitted he was almost weeping with fatigue. Just when nearing the end of his tether, he was taken off the task and invited to coffee in a café by Gurdjieff. Dr Young admitted he was aware of a certain amount of hypnotism involved, even in his case: *otherwise I should not have been able to lay aside my critical sense so easily. Gurdjieff was a very powerful personality — a type of man I had never met before. To some he could do no wrong . . . . .* He considered Gurdjieff's path was the path to power for himself, involving mental and physical bullying as taught in Mongolian monasteries. A student at the Prieuré remembered Gurdjieff *heaping obscenity wrath and denunciation on a crumpled and distraught Orage*, whose mind seemed dominated by Gurdjieff so that he remained a slave to him for seven years, during part of which time he lectured for Gurdjieff in America and actually once had George Bowden in his audience. In after years, on hearing music that had been played at Fontainebleau, Orage was moved to tears.

The dancing was interesting, dervish dances of a sort of masculine action were performed by the men. The women's dances were from Northern India and China. A priestess dance portrayed a religious ceremony, another followed the movement of a machine. The gymnastic exercises from Tibet and Kafiristan were 'electrifying' according to a pupil, Charles Stanley Nott — *they were new yet familiar. I longed to do them.* There was a 'Stop' exercise, where students had to cease moving and hold the pose.

Finally, to sum up, a letter of significance quoted below reached Dr Young from a fellow pupil: *I no longer have the faintest doubt about Gurdjieff and his institute. Signs of hoofs and horns are all over the place, and my deep and instant distrust which increased with every day I spent there . . . the note of fear rather than love . . . . Did you meet a Russian named P. who was there recently? . . . I hear he had to retire to his room nightly to conceal his explosions of laughter . . . he noticed 'fear' in the general attitude of pupils . . . I simply cannot believe that a genuine teacher would indulge in so much bunkum . . . . Doubts one might feel, yet hardly that type of doubt which Gurdjieff's fantasy, cheapness, spectacular use of show, of megalomaniac hints of this and that to come, etc., etc., inevitably do produce in one.* I very much like the reaction of the Russian named P. For Dr Young, leaving after a year: *much that was valuable was met on the way — not a complete waste of a year.*

So L.M., her heart very heavy, even though Katherine was 'radiant, her eyes shining' from an evening spent by a log fire in the salon, prepared to leave the next morning, returning to the Hotel Select. She never saw her darling Katie alive again. She eventually commenced working on an estate farm at Lisieux in the middle of November. She duly dispatched

Katherine's clothes, and was sent 1000 francs to buy further
warm garments, making, alas, a number of mistakes.

October 24th, 1922. Katherine wrote: *I'd like another
sleeping jacket — a very warm one — and a Tuteur for
teaching the 'cello.*

October 28th: *can I have a pair of galoshes and a pair of
garters.*

October 30th: *I dislike very much the coral coat and can
never wear it. It looks so vulgar . . . I dislike also . . . the
jumper you bought for the tricot coat and skirt and if I am
sincere the coat and skirt itself. I look like a skinned rabbit in
it. Please stop buying and stop asking me questions about
clothes.*

November 2nd: *Forgive my harshness. Of course I have
thought better of it and I am ashamed . . . I do want one other
thing. A perfectly plain chemise frock . . . to do exercises in the
evening . . . . cashmere . . . gaberdine . . . dead
simple . . . preferably dark blue . . . it musn't
show my legs through.*

November 4th: *The black coat is . . . much
too small . . . I* have *the black velvet jacket —
why a black plush? I wish I could send it back to
you — I so hate hard things — that stand out like plush . . . .*

November 13th: *The blue dress is about 2 miles too long. It
trails. I shall have to take it up about ½ yard for dancing . . I
need . . . some ribbons for head bands . . . can you rescue my
little old blue velvet coat with black satin collar edging and my
purple velvet one. Oh yes, I really need 3 aprons, coloured
ones as easy to wash as possible . . . and three coloured
handkerchiefs for my head and . . . a copy of each of my two
books . . . .* By November 23rd Katherine had had enough!
*Please buy me no dress . . . and no shoes. This is final! I can't
risk the wrong things again . . . .*

For Katherine it was a new life, an exotic diversion. She was
living with Russians, immersed in things Eastern. Her room
she thought a 'glorified Garsington', the *food like a Gogol feast
. . . Mr. Gurdjieff is not in the least like what I expected. He's
what one wants to find him really.*

She rose at 7.30 a.m., washed in ice-cold water and lit her
fire. Her breakfast was coffee, bread, butter, quince jam, eggs

and gorgonzola cheese. For lunch at 11.00 a.m. there was light delicious fare such as veal in cream sauce, with wonderfully cooked vegetables; after dinner at 7.00 there was the dancing in the salon by the enormous log fire. Dr Young kindly made up her fire at night, while she patched the knee of his trousers.

She made friends with a Russian girl, Olga Ivanovna, who brought her wood. Olga, who had had an English governess when a child, could speak English well. She accompanied Katherine on her walks, and noticed they had to stop often. Olga, who was to marry Frank Lloyd Wright, the famous American architect, remembered her first sight of Katherine with her intense dark eyes, very white face and dark hair cut short with a fringe. She thought that face wonderful.

Jeanne's wedding made me feel sad, Bogey . . . Thank you for telling me about it, she wrote to Murry on October 20th and on October 24th: *Don't feel we are silently and swiftly moving away from each other! Do you really? And what do you mean by us meeting 'on the other side'? Where — Boge? You are much more mysterious than I!* Trust the lugubrious Murry to strike such a note in his letter.

I want to try and escape from my terrible illness . . . . It is a great happiness to be here . . . . She had been walking in the garden in autumn sunshine, observing the foundations for the Turkish Baths, and visiting the animals on the farm. She was instructed to 'watch' in the kitchen, with its twenty pots on the stove and Gurdjieff tasting the shredded cabbage. She thought the dancing wonderful and longed to be able to do it. On October 28th she even asked Murry's forgiveness for not writing often. Things were quite different now, she was indeed 'silently moving away' — *our happiness does not depend on letters . . . . we LIVE here — every moment of the day seems full of life . . .* anxiety *I never feel . . . .*

Gurdjieff instructed a young Lithuanian girl, Adela Kafian, to look after Katherine. Adela could not speak English, so they conversed in simple French. She became devoted to Katherine.

After five weeks Katherine felt a longing to write but realized she would not for a long time. She had been befriended by Mr Salzmann, a painter and friend of Olga Knipper, the widow of Chekhov. This intrigued Katherine. It was now intensely cold and the place was heated only rarely.

Her room had been changed to a small simple one in the workers' quarters, and sitting on the bed with Olga Ivanovna, Katherine felt like a poor young girl as Olga dried her yellow dancing stockings by the fire. Olga knew Katherine slept badly and after everyone had settled, she would steal into Katherine's room and find her sitting up by the fire. Then Olga would stay until Katherine dozed off. She also noticed that there were times when Katherine was depressed and dissatisfied with herself. *I am wicked*, she told Olga, *I shall never be able to change. Why should I dislike some people to such an extent that it is simply nauseating to me? Mrs N., for instance. Even meeting her in the corridor is enough to spoil my whole day.* Katherine was still battling with some free-floating hate; L.M. was safely out of it. Olga realised, too, that at times Katherine was emotionally dependent on her, and remembered a particular day when longing for fresh air and outdoor work on the study house, she left Katherine, in spite of knowing she needed her company and seemed on the verge of tears at her going. On returning, Olga found Katherine a little brittle and asked for forgiveness, only to receive a confession from her that she had criticised Olga to a Mrs P. for leaving her without wood because she wanted to hurt her, "Did I not tell you I was wicked?" To compensate, Katherine asked Olga to accept a scarf of her choice. It was of black silk with an orange pattern around the edges. All was well again.

By November 19th she was scraping carrots in the kitchen, she told Murry and thought what a contrast there was between this and her bed in a corner at the Chalet des Sapins where she would lie and wait for Murry to visit her. She loved the bustle, with everyone busy and went on: *I badly need a good* washing. *Remarkable how clothes fall into their proper place here. We dress in the evening, but during the day . . . the men look like brigands. Nobody cares . . . Oh, Bogey, how I love this place!* She lived in her fur coat. It was now the end of November and becoming progressively colder. She wondered how Lawrence was and what he would think of the institute.

Ouspensky saw Katherine, about the middle of November. She thought him a 'very fine man', He thought she seemed near to death. Bechhofer-Roberts, visiting the Prieuré, thought Katherine seemed happy: *A frail doomed silhouette watching the dancing . . .*

She saw Orage almost every day. Both Katherine and Orage had changed from those early competitive days of 1910. There had been some inner division in him. Under the influence of Ouspensky's doctrines, he had told Rowland Kenney, a member of the group that he thought it possible that 'the literary man, the artist, the philosopher' in him might be 'all artificial' and that his real vocation could be that of 'cobbling old boots'. To Murry, who met him on that last day at the Prieuré 'he seemed changed, much gentler. It is interesting too how Orage could become Gurdjieff's abject follower for seven years, producing very little in the way of writing, and that he who had said endearingly about writing 'always keep a trot for the drive', should leave so colourless an account of Katherine's last days. His presence in the institute would be a comfort to her. During their long talks Katherine would ask, "What has come over us!" admitting she tore up the stories she started, almost immediately. She said she wanted to write differently and was highly critical of her previous work.

On November 11th, Katherine's eternal snail under the leaf manifested itself in the loss of three weeks' laundry, which had been stolen; her crêpe-de-Chine nightgown, pyjamas, pantalons, tops, woolly petticoat, eighteen handkerchiefs etc. Ida was commissioned to replace them and to make a crêpe nightgown. . . . *just a hole cut in the middle the sides sewn up and a ribbon from the sides to tie at the waist at the back* . . . . Like her Grandpa Beauchamp, Katherine was very practical. She also wanted Ottoline's eiderdown. She told L.M. that she went to bed about 1.00-2.00 a.m. and that her hands were ruined by scraping vegetables. L.M. in her new job on an estate-farm at Lisieux near Deauville, was working with the cows. Katherine disapproved, feeling it was too isolated: *you need people . . . to take you out of yourself . . . why are you so tragic? . . . The part of you that lived through me has to die — then* you *will be born* . . . . Commencing early December, L.M. loved the farm. *I could have been very happy working there* . . . . *had it not been for the immense hidden weight of sorrow.*

The Turkish Bath was now finished; ladies bathed in the afternoon, men at 7.30 p.m. once a week, and Gurdjieff, who joined the men, stipulated that each man had to tell three funny stories. Katherine enjoyed talking to the Hartmanns in their room before dinner; he, small, bald, with a pointed beard and wearing a whitewash-spattered blouse, had been a page in the Tzar's court, and was a musician; his beautiful wife had been an opera singer.

Murry, who perhaps had suggested a visit at Xmas, was put off. She felt she wasn't well enough physically.

The enterprising Mr Gurdjieff had had a couch built on a railed-off gallery above three cows in the cow-house, where Katherine could lie inhaling the sweet smells of such a place, which, strangely, in the East, was thought to be beneficial to tuberculous patients. There were two divans covered with Persian carpets and Mr Salzmann had decorated the whitewashed walls and ceiling with flowers, birds and a tree in yellow, red and blue paint. There were animals on the branches, too, with faces like the pupils — Orage was portrayed as an elephant. Katherine lay all day in the gallery and later she was to sleep there too. This was the first time that resting had been mentioned in her letters. She loved listening to the beasts and 'the singing wiry silvery sound of milk falling into an empty pail . . .' In the same letter she asked for a photograph of Murry. When it was Adela's turn to work in the cow-house, she decorated the staircase with leaves and would wait until Katherine came, walking very slowly up the stairs and carrying a notebook. After milking Adela would take Katherine a glass of the sweet warm milk.

By December 17th she was moved back to the beautiful room. On the previous Saturday Gurdjieff had come to the stable and asked her how she was so she told Murry. She also added that she no longer had a fringe.

It was December 23rd and Gurdjieff was planning an English Xmas providing a sheep, a pig, turkeys, a goose, wine, spirits, and a Christmas tree. The feast was to be on Christmas Eve. In her memoir of Katherine, written in Russian, Adela remembered Katherine joining them by the Xmas tree, wearing a purple taffeta dress embroidered with little flowers, simple in cut with shoulder straps. Her hair was short and combed over her forehead. She recited and enacted some piece after which the whole company surrounded her.

Unknown to Katherine, Adela had dug up a small Xmas tree in the grounds and had put three candles on it, for Katherine's room. Seeing her preparing to leave, Adela sped ahead to light the candles. Smiling and surprised, Katherine sank into her chair, while Adela wrapped her up in her long, warm, blue and white striped scarf. Then sitting at her feet, her arms embracing Katherine's knees, they watched the spluttering candles on the little tree. As one went out Katherine said, "That's me."

Murry had sent Katherine the Rothenstein drawing of himself, a charming likeness, which she thought 'extraordinarily good'; writing her last but one letter to him on Boxing Day, she reiterated: *I want to be Real . . . this place has taught me so far how unreal I am. It has taken from me one thing after another until . . . all I know really — is that I am not annihilated and that I . . . believe . . .*

On December 22nd Katherine wrote to L.M. to wish her a 'Happy Xmas', telling her of 'the real old-fashioned English Xmas' planned for sixty people.

I'm doing all I can for the little children so that they will be roped in for once. I've just sent them over coloured paper and asked them to help to make flowers. It's pathetic the interest they are taking.

Our pudding was made in a baby's bath, stirred by everybody and Mr. Gurdjïeff put in a coin. Who gets the coin gets our darling new born calf for a present. The calf — 1 day old — was led into the salon to the beating of tambourines and a special melody composed for it . . .

. . . You must not worry about me . . . It's exactly as though you took a piece of my flesh and gnawed it. It helps neither you nor me . . . . I must end this letter. If you'd like me for a friend as from this Xmas I'd like to be your friend. But not too awfully serious, ma chère. *The whole difficulty in life is to find the* way *between extremes . . . .* Katherine was still fighting that rear-guard action!

In a blotter was another letter to L.M. written after Xmas, probably on New Year's Eve, but not posted. It was in a sealed envelope, grey, lined with purple-blue:

. . . you have been in my mind today . . . as you see I am

sending you 100 francs. Play with it . . . I have lost my money complex. We are in the throes of theatre building which ought to be ready on January 13th. Gurdjieff has bought 63 carpets for it and the same number of fur rugs. The carpets . . . displayed . . . in the salon last night are living things — worlds of beauty. And what a joy to begin to learn which is a garden, which a café, which a prayer mat . . . My thoughts are full of carpets and Persia and Samarkand and the little rugs of Beluchistan. I am looking for signs of spring already. Under the espalier pear trees there were wonderful Xmas roses, which I saw for the first time this year. They reminded me of Switzerland . . . I have moods when I simply pine for the S. of France . . . When this time is over I shall make for the South or the East and never go North again.

My blue dress is in large holes. Those cashmere cardigans look as if rats have gnawed them. As to my fur coat — it's like a wet London cat . . . I caught one of the goats nibbling it.

Write and tell me how you are will you? Dear Ida?

With love from K.M.

To Elizabeth, undated:

. . . here is the £100 you lent me. I am sending it as you see at the last moment while the old year is . . . turning up his toes . . . .

. . . I cannot tell you what a joy it is to me to be in contact with living people who are strange and quick and not ashamed to be themselves. It's a kind of supreme airing to be among them . . . . I haven't written a word since October . . . I am tired of my little stories like birds bred in cages . . . . Goodbye dearest Cousin. I shall never know any one like you. I shall remember every little thing about you for ever

Lovingly yours
Katherine

On December 31st she wrote to Chaddie and Jeanne but the letter was unfinished and unposted. She also wrote to her father, describing the institute and her gallery in the cow-house. *I must look a great Pa — woman perched up aloft.* She told him she was staying for six months. *The New Year is*

*already here. I must leave the fire and go to bed. God bless you
darling father. May we meet again at not too distant a date.
Ever your devoted child Kass.*

Her last letter to Murry was in pencil, dated December 31st,
1922 and was a hurried note asking him to come to stay at the
Prieuré as Gurdjieff's guest from January 8th or 9th until the
14th or 15th, telling him what clothes to bring and details of
the journey. She signed it, 'Your ever loving Wig'. Olga
remembered Katherine's excited mood on New Year's Eve as
she told her that she was back again with all her old feelings,
habits and desires. She wanted to invite her husband to stay,
start writing again and wear her hair in a fringe once more.

Murry arrived at the Gurdjieff Institute in the early
afternoon of January 9th and was shown to her room. She was
very pale but radiant. He thought she had changed profoundly
in the three months since he had seen her, that she seemed
unearthly. He had never seen anyone more lovely than she
appeared to him that day. She thought she would be leaving
the institute soon and wanted to live in simplicity in England
with him and he cultivate the land

She showed him the little gallery in the cow-house, then the
study house where they had tea with Olga. Murry met the
Hartmanns, the Salzmanns, Orage, Adela and Dr Young, who
was to become his great friend. Indeed, Murry was impressed
with the simplicity and dedication of the whole group. When
he offered to help with the painting, Katherine noted with
amusement that his co-painter was her hated Mrs N. It had
begun to rain and Olga wanted to get an umbrella. Katherine
answered, "Oh, no, I love the rain tonight, I want the feeling
of it on my face."

After dinner, the dancers assembled in the salon. Katherine,
sitting by the fire, seemed to Olga to be strange and far-away,
her eyes unseeing and looking above the crowds. After the
music she gently bid Olgavanna goodnight.

It was ten o'clock. Katherine told Murry she was tired. They
slowly climbed the stairs together. About half-way up she
began to cough, and Murry, taking her arm, helped her into
her bedroom. Suddenly, blood gushed from her mouth. She
gasped, "I believe . . . I'm going to die." Murry put her on the
bed and rushed out for the doctor, meeting Adela on the way,

who found Katherine sitting on the edge of the bed, her hands over her mouth, with blood oozing through her fingers. Adela gave her a towel: *gasping for breath she called for her husband.* Two English doctors and a Russian arrived. They thrust Murry out of the room, 'though her eyes were imploring me'. He sat in anguish outside the door. Adela went to her room and wept on the bed. Olgavanna, still painting in the study house, suddenly heard Orage calling, "Please come quickly: Katherine is bad, very bad." She ran all the way to her room and found Katherine on her bed surrounded by doctors applying hot water bags. She was dead, her hand was still warm. It was just ten thirty.

This fatal haemoptysis would probably have occurred whether she spent her last three months at Fontainebleau or not. She might have lived only a little longer. She went into the institute out of desperation, because all physical treatment had failed. The Gurdjieff Institute fulfilled a need for another way and its exotic atmosphere would be diverting.

Among those who received a telegram the next day were the Schiffs.

Fontainebleau 10th 15.25
Schiff 18, Cambridge Square W.1 London.
Darling Katherine died suddenly tuesday night funeral Fontainebleau protestant church friday four o'clock.

Jack

L.M., heartbroken after she received hers, caught the afternoon train. She found Katherine lying in a raw white-wood coffin in a small chapel. Lovingly she draped the coffin with the embroidered black silk Spanish shawl, to hide its starkness. The silk shawl now lies in the Bibliothèque Municipale Menton, in a glass case along with a manuscript letter and a carved ivory box. Back in Katherine's room, she took the gold watch and chain from the mantelpiece, which had been willed to her. Then she packed up Katherine's possessions. Going out into the garden, she looked for the Christmas roses Katherine had written about, and visited the balcony in the cow-house.

In England, Kot went over to see Brett. He was crying and

unable to get permission to go to France. Richard, Sullivan and Brett travelled over together, as did Chaddie and Jeanne. Brett placed a basket of lily-of-the-valley bearing a large pink bow at Katherine's head. She was horrified by the coffin. In the study house, Murry took Brett up to Gurdjieff who, in an astrakhan hat, was sitting on the floor. He looked at Brett who stared back. He then stood up and shook hands.

On Friday January 12th in the cold Protestant Church, an old white-haired clergyman read the service over Katherine in French, then the hearse, drawn by two black horses wearing funeral plumes, moved slowly off, followed by ramshackle cabs driven by drivers in shaggy brown fur coats and a line of private cars. They took the long way round to the cemetery at Avon, out of respect, and past many dirty little children, old men and women. L.M., unable to bear the slow pace of the journey which went on for miles, got out of the cab to walk. At the cemetery, Murry could scarcely stand, he was almost carried to the graveside. There, in the fading light of that winter afternoon, Katherine was lowered into a deep grave. L.M. dropped a bunch of marigolds 'a flower she loved' onto the coffin and Gurdjieff some nuts and raisins, which he believed contained the germs of renewal.

On their return, the mourners gathered in the study house, where L.M. remembered there were 'an immense number of dishes carried around to everyone'. Later in the salon, feeling completely numb, she saw that Murry 'was talking far too much and laughing hysterically'. Someone came over and suggested she take him upstairs to rest, which she did. *Katherine would have wanted me to look after him as much as I could.*

Before leaving the next day, Adela remembered Murry coming to say goodbye. He gave her Katherine's engagement ring, a cluster of rubies, set in gold also the purple taffeta dress Katherine wore so happily on her last Xmas. As she carried it along the corridor, a little robin flew through the window over her head, and out again. On the anniversary of Katherine's death Murry returned to Avon and at the side of her grave, Adela returned the beloved ring to Murry, feeling that it was right to do so.

Virginia Woolf made a three-page diary entry on January 16, 1923 on hearing of Katherine's death:

*One feels — what? A shock of relief? — a rival the less? . . .
When I began to write, it seemed to me there was no point in
writing. Katherine won't read it. Katherine's my rival no
longer . . . I was jealous of her writing — the only writing I
have ever been jealous of. This made it harder to write to her;
and I saw in it, perhaps from jealousy all the qualities I dislike
in her . . . Hers were beautiful eyes — rather dog-like, brown,
very wide apart, with a steady slow rather faithful and sad
expression. Her nose was sharp, a little vulgar. Her lips thin
and hard . . .
Did she care for me? Sometimes she would say so — would kiss
me — would look at me as if (is this sentiment?) her eyes would
like always to be faithful. She would promise never to forget.
That was what we said at the end of our last talk . . . . For our
friendship was a real thing, we said, looking at each other
quite straight. It would always go on whatever happened.
What happened, I suppose, was fault findings and perhaps
gossip . . . the small lies and treacheries, the perpetual playing
and teasing, or whatever it was, cut away much of the
substance of friendship. One was too uncertain . . . Yet I have
the feeling that I shall think of her at intervals all through life.
Probably we had something in common which I shall never
find in anyone else.*

Murry returned to Wayside Cottage, Ditchling; L.M. stayed
with Brett in Pond Street. Soon hostilities began. L.M. was
typing Katherine's manuscripts, and being secretive about it,
covering the papers with a cloth when Brett came into the
room. Brett objected to L.M. wearing Katherine's hat;
significantly L.M. was re-christened 'Bill'. Abreacting in a
letter to Murry, whom she had hoped to marry, which idea he
firmly squashed as early as February 1st, Brett made the
mistake of calling L.M. 'a great porpoise of a woman'.

He answered on April 4th, 1923 sharply reproaching her.
Murry was gathering what ammunition he could in order to
extricate himself from a now impossible situation.

However, the heartbroken Brett eventually found a new
hero, albeit a more peppery one, in D.H. Lawrence who, with
rather dragging feet, accepted her in his Rananim expedition
to New Mexico in 1924. Murry, for obvious reasons, declined
to join the crew. Brett died in El Prado, New Mexico, in

August 1977 and in an interview with her biographer John Manchester and hearing much better with her modern efficient hearing-aid, smilingly recalled how handsome and charming Murry had been. Life in New Mexico had suited her admirably; hordes of sight-seers came annually to visit the D.H. Lawrence Memorial Chapel and stopped by to cull from Brett her memories of 'The Four Musketeers', D.H.L., F., J.M.M. and K.M.

D.H. Lawrence wrote to Murry from New Mexico on February 2nd, 1923, on hearing of Katherine's death:

Del Monte Ranch, Questa

Dear Jack, —

I got your note just now, via Kot, about Katherine. Yes, it is something gone out of our lives. We thought of her, I can tell you, at Wellington . . . Yes, I always knew a bond in my heart. Feel a fear where the bond is broken now. Feel as if old moorings were breaking all. What is going to happen to us all? Perhaps it is good for Katherine not to have to see the next phase.

. . . It has been a savage enough pilgrimage these last four years . . . I wish it needn't all have been as it has been: I do wish it.

D.H.L

Much later, while listening to Witter Bynner read a letter he had received from Murry, Lawrence cried testily that Katherine Mansfield was worth a thousand Murrys but he neglected and abandoned her then returned to make a meal of her. He thought Murry would do the same to him.

Murry invited L.M. to Wayside Cottage, paying her £6 a month to sort out Katherine's papers. She then became a housekeeper for a time to Elizabeth Countess Russell, who was living in the New Forest near Woodgreen. From 1942 L.M. lived in a delightful secluded thatched cottage, set in peaceful watery meadows at the end of a leafy lane. I found her still there in 1976, living alone with a small, truculently possessive black dog called Megan. The hedgerows on the way were full of violets and primroses. It was a glorious day in early May. L.M., a tall but stooping figure with a fine fair complexion and soft grey hair, sat in a chair by a small table. She was almost blind. The room, with its low-beamed ceiling, was tastefully furnished and strewn with the softest, most expensive woollen shawls. She was kind and hospitable — an 'English lady'. She said she had no difficulty in recalling her time with Katherine — "It's not long ago. It's just the other day." She died on July 4th 1979.

In the New Year honours for 1923, Mr Beauchamp received a knighthood for services to New Zealand finance. On the news of Katherine's death he donated 47, Fitzherbert Terrace, worth then £6000, to the nation to be a National Picture Gallery. He gave the Turnbull Library £200 to purchase her first editions. He also had built a bus and tram shelter at the end of Fitzherbert Terrace which, alas, had to be rebuilt further down the terrace due to the ravages of the new motorway construction. In 1929, nine years before his own death, this proud, courageous old man had the pain of learning from a New Zealand admirer of Katherine, who had visited the grave at Avon, that it was not in perpetual ground but in the fosse commune which was usually re-used. Sir Harold arranged with his son-in-law Captain Renshaw to travel to Avon to investigate. It appears that Murry either had forgotten to pay the bill for Katherine's funeral, or in his insistence on a simple funeral had not realised that this might be a tragic outcome of such simplicity. Captain Renshaw put everything right. Now Katherine lies very near to the plot where Mr Gurdjieff and his family are buried, which is somehow as it should be.

Chapter XXI

After Fontainebleau

Murry felt numb and unreal for weeks.

By February, in desperation, he decided, though fearful, to spend some time completely alone in a cottage in Ashdown Forest, to sort himself out. There, after hours at a table by the fire, he had a mystical experience. The room seemed filled with a presence, which produced in him a deep conviction that all was well with Katherine. This experience, though often written about in a derogatory fashion, was very real to Murry, and this was proved years later when he was given an anaesthetic for the first time for a septum operation, 1928-29. He discovered that the mystical experience and the anaesthetic experience were the same.

In a state of euphoria born of the spiritual rebirth after such a happening, a sort of relief after the storm with its attendant mental hyper-activity, he planned and commenced his new magazine *Adelphi* with Kot as business manager, publishing Katherine's work. In the first issue in June 1923 which contained a large portrait of her in the front, a copy of the one she detested incidentally, Katherine continued to contribute for the next two years. Spurred on by Countess Russell, who told him to publish all he could, Murry brought out *The Dove's Nest and Other Stories* in June 1923, containing the fine stories Katherine was too ill to finish. I think Murry was right to publish all he could of Katherine's work. Done under the lash of physical disease, it had for that very reason to be given a chance to live and not be left 'unsung' in some drawer. *The Poems* and the collection of earlier stories *Something Childish*, followed. The *Journal* was published in 1927, then the *Letters* in two volumes in 1928.

The *Journal* he knit up for himself from the mass of unsorted holograph material left by Katherine which filled four large cardboard cartons, consisting of notebooks, diary entries, jottings on margins or at the end of stories, a hundred sheets of notes, unposted letters, sketches of unwritten stories. These fragments were mostly undated, Katherine and Murry rarely dated their correspondence, yet Murry dated them more or less accurately once they were sorted and deciphered with the help of L.M. The material was arranged and wedded up throughout the *Journal*, the whole becoming a masterpiece, a sort of mosaic under Murry's expert editing. Though not at times totally accurate biographically, veracity, like a note of music, runs through its pages for anyone with a trained ear to pick it up.

He suppressed some material of course. In the Juliet notebook she wrote, while in Paris 1914:

One night when Jack was with Goodyear and I had gone to bed and he said that what he really wanted was a woman who could keep him — yes that's what he really wanted, and then again, so much later, with Campbell, he said I was the one who submitted. Yes I gave way to him and still do — but then I did it because I did not feel the urgency of my own desires. Now I do (added late 1915) and though I submit from habit now it is always under a sort of protest which I call adieu submission. *It always may be the last time.*

In 1954 Murry published a definitive edition of the *Journal*, adding eighty-one extra pages. Murry idealised Katherine in the *Journal* and so began what has been called the Mansfield Myth, which was no such thing but simply a reputation established posthumously. This lovable, tragic young artist had simply caught the imagination of many, and continues to do so in spite of her faults and falsities. The small lies, though not commendable, were largely a by-product of her vivid fantasy life. She was an entertainer, an enricher of life and had to dramatize, to gild the moment with some mental fire, exaggerating and falsifying. In her letters she was, at heart, the earnest little Karori schoolgirl, sitting down in her frilled starch pinafore to write her best composition ever. If some of her letters seem to play to the gallery, to be coloured to suit the tone of the receiver, why not? She was giving of herself; like any actress worth her salt, she had to be in the limelight, smiling up at the gallery, head back, arms outstretched, wondering, "Anybody here who still loves me?" in the best Mrs Patrick Campbell manner.

The *Journal* was translated into French in 1932 by Marthe Duproix, the definitive edition in 1956, which sold 5000 copies. It was further translated in:

Italy	1933, 1949, 1957
Poland	1935
Spain	1940, 1959
Japan	1943, 1954
Sweden	1970

To date, her stories, *Journal* and *Letters* have been translated into twenty-two languages.

In France, with the advent of the 1956 edition of the *Journal*, the Isola Bella was made into a memorial by the New Zealand Government and the Municipality of Menton. There is a bronze plaque on each side of the door, one of which records her birth in Wellington and death at Fontainebleau. The other is engraved with her words to Murry that Isola Bella will be found in poker-work on her heart, and a list of stories written there:

> *The Daughters of the Late Colonel*
> *The Young Girl*
> *The Stranger*
> *The Lady's Maid*
> *Poison*

Le Livret du Mémorial Katherine Mansfield, consisting of 112 pages was issued and Jeanne had to make a speech in French in front of the Isola Bella at its opening as a memorial. The Villa is an annexe to the Pension Louise nearby and one can stay there. The 'cave' below, once the gardener's shed, is now the 'Mansfield Room'. Once a year, some lucky young writer is sent from New Zealand to work and stay at the Isola Bella.

Plaques were put up at the Chalet des Sapins, the Villa Pauline and the Hôtel Beau Rivage. The plaque on the Hôtel Beau Rivage reads:

Il est trois heures. Je viens d'achever Felicite. Dieu sait que j'ai été heureuse eu l'écrivant.

Jeudi 28 Février 1918

This was the beginning of a letter to Murry to say she had finished *Bliss*. At a ceremony at Fontainebleau organized by Les Amis de la Forêt de Fontainebleau M. Vignand, chairman of the Societé des Gens de Lettres formally opened the new Katherine Mansfield Footpath, the Katherine Mansfield Rock and the Katherine Mansfield Crossroads on June 11th, 1939, in the forest of Fontainebleau. The Elephant attained its plaque circuitously. The charming family living there now were surprised to learn from a friend that Katherine had lived there once and straight away they contacted the L.C.C. who duly obliged. The Casetta Deerholm was destroyed by enemy action in World War II. Now a new villa stands on that steep aromatic hillside with the sea spread before it.

According to Miss Ruth Mantz, who went through Katherine's papers with Murry while engaged on the biography, Katherine began a story called *Maata* in Paris in 1914. In 1940, Mr Pat Lawlor of Wellington, whilst in conversation with a Maori friend who knew Maata, discovered that she had the MS of an unpublished novel, along with a large collection of letters from Katherine to her. He arranged to meet Maata in his office.

He found Maata dark skinned and attractive, looking quite different from the ordinary Maori woman. He noticed that her eyes were rather hard. She spoke well, in a low voice. She was neatly dressed. Maata said she corresponded with Katherine until she died. She said that she had the MS of the unfinished novel entitled *Maata*, about 60,000 words which she, Maata, was to complete. However, Maata had not brought the manuscript and seemed disinclined to let him see it. She returned in two weeks to discuss possible publiction but still did not produce the MS. In November 1943 Lawlor wrote to Murry about this manuscript. Murry replying said that

Katherine had wanted to write a novel called MAATA and had completed the first chapter. He believed however that she had had no contact with Maata since 1911.

In a later book, *Old Wellington Days* 1959, Lawlor wrote that portions of the *Maata* MS had been sold in London. He went on to give a touching account of Chesney Wold, now 350, Karori Road, which he visited to find it empty and desolate, 'the sport of vandals . . . . awaiting the axe of the demolition order'. It had been empty for fifteen years. On going inside and climbing the rickety stairs he saw *the sagging wallpaper was revealing layers and layers of earlier paper back to the lurid Victorian designs . . . .* He noted the shattered coloured glasses on the veranda windows, there was no sign of the aloe tree, but *nature had left that little boxwood hedge referred to so lovingly in 'Prelude' . . . .* Happily, a lady, reading of the sad demise of Chesney Wold, decided to save it and bought it for £1700, so halting the demolition order.

He found that 75, Tinakori Road was now 133 and had been converted into Lednam Residential Flats. Inside were 'traces of a fine old home seared'. The garden above the old concrete gateway had been bulldozed and a large macrocarpa tree, a holly tree and an oak were sadly in need of trimming. 47, Fitzherbert Terrace became number 23 and was taken over by the New Zealand Forest Service. A nearby 'off shoot street' was named Katherine Avenue. At the city end, near the old zig-zag path down to Thorndon Quay, was built the Katherine Mansfield Memorial. Lawlor found the house at Day's Bay 'on its little stretch of beach', largely unchanged and well cared for. It had been purchased from Sir Harold by the brother-in-law of a Miss Moginie. It was *the third dwelling in a group of three houses facing the harbour on turning the road into Day's Bay.*

In 1950 Murry prepared a complete edition of Katherine's letters. It was one third as long again and contained only letters to him. All deleted passages were restored.

Two years later, while engaged on a review of the F.R. Leavis book on D.H. Lawrence, which piece was 'considered the best essay on Lawrence ever written' according to F.A. Lea, Murry read all of D.H. Lawrence's works. In his journal October 1955 he wrote: *I go on reading Lawrence. In spite of myself it gets me down. I am torn between a heart-rending sense of the pity of it, and a kind of exaltation at the splendour of it . . . What have I to do with Lawrence? What has Lawrence to do with me? And yet it is true, I should not be what I am, or where I am, without him. Just as Katherine is, he is part of me. My life would have been utterly different without those two . . . I think he is glad that a fragment of him lives on in me.*

As earlier instructed by Katherine, Murry gave her large pearl 'daisy' ring to his 'little girl', born to Violet his second wife, on April 19th, 1925 and christened Katherine Middleton Murry, known as Weg. *I always felt, quite simply, that Violet's daughter was Katherine's daughter . . . .* and later:

. . . . I love to think . . . that Katherine has watched all my life . . . . and is watching my life; my communion with her through love is so simple and direct and intense at such a moment that all my life is subsumed under it. It is gathered up in such a moment and purified and vindicated. I am known even as I know. And there rises within me like a clear silent spring the knowledge of the truth of her parting message.

"In spite of everything — how happy we have been! I feel no other lovers have walked the earth more joyfully — in spite of all.

Farewell — my precious love . . . ."

The following poem was written by a young girl from New Zealand, Iris Guiever Wilkinson, pseudonym Robin Hyde. Born in 1906 in Capetown, she came to live in Wellington when a few months old. She attended Wellington Girls' College, fulfilling her longing for London and England as she set off on January 18th, 1938 via Hong Kong, Moscow, Warsaw and Berlin, arriving six months later in September 1938. On route she caught sprue, an exhausting tropical disease, and was too sick to accept a valued job in journalism on the *Daily Mirror*. She died on August 23rd, 1939 in her 34th year and was buried in Kensington New Cemetery, Gunnersbury.

Katherine Mansfield
by Robin Hyde
(Iris Guiever Wilkinson)

Our little Darkness, in the shadow sleeping
Among the strangers you could better trust,
Right was your faring, Wings: their wise hands gave you
Freedom and song, where we had proffered dust.
Dust is a thing of road and sheepfolds, rising
Where men and sheep are driven on to gate;
A wavering smoke, too faint and blown for signals,
Mica-bright staring crystals, love and hate,
A blindness in the eyes, a pain for feet.

Dust is the unthrown wrestler at our gate.

So wrapped in what they gave you, rest you, sweet:
Be tranquil, seagull conjured into swan:
We have in mind who used you ill or well.
The dark dust-taken hair slopes fallen back
From mermaid forehead: once for all lie slack
The winning fingers. Rest you, in those arms
Held out at Fontainebleau, rank flower and weed,
Idlers and gossips, shapes of strife and heat
Who find your marble cool to lean upon.

Deep underneath the seas is swung a bell
Of travelling note: oh, very far away,
Clear as you dreamed, gleam tiny bush and bay.

And after marble, dust fulfils a need.

Acknowledgements

I wish to thank Mrs Jeanne Renshaw, sister of Katherine Mansfield, for her unfailing kindness; also, Mr Peter Day for advice and letters about LM.

Every effort has been made to communicate with all copyright holders.

I am grateful to the following for kindly granting me permission to quote from copyright sources:

copyright 1978, the Estate of Katherine Mansfield, The Society of Authors as the literary representative of the Estate of Katherine Mansfield for extracts from *Letters of Katherine Mansfield*;

The Society of Authors as the literary representative of the Estate of John Middleton Murry for extracts from his published works and those of Katherine Mansfield and for extracts from letters of John Middleton Murry;

Alpers, Antony, *The Life of Katherine Mansfield*, Jonathan Cape, London 1980;

Asquith, Lady Cynthia, *Diaries: 1915-1918*, edited by E.M. Horsley; *copyright* 1968 by Michael and Simon Asquith, Hutchinson Publishing Group Ltd., and Alfred A. Knopf, Inc.;

Bagnold, Enid, *Autobiography*, William Heineman Ltd.;

Baker, Ida Constance, *Katherine Mansfield: The Memories of LM*, by kind permission of Peter Day and Michael Joseph Ltd.;

Brett, Hon. Dorothy, *Lawrence and Brett, A Friendship*, Secker and Warburg Ltd., John Manchester, Executor of Estate of Hon. Dorothy Brett;

Brett, Hon. Dorothy, *Reminiscences of Katherine Mansfield*, Brett and Manchester, John Manchester, *ADAM* (*1972-3*);

Lawler, Patrick, *Old Wellington Days, 1959* Whitcoulls Publishers, Christchurch, New Zealand;

More Wellington Days, 1962 Whitcoulls Publishers, Christchurch, New Zealand;

Leighton, Roland, fragment of poem 'Villanelle'; David Roland Leighton;

Mackenzie, Sir Compton, *My Life and Times*, Octave IV, The Literary Estate of Compton Mackenzie, Chatto and Windus. The Hogarth Press;

Mrs Igor Vinogradoff for Morrell, Lady Ottoline, *'Ottoline'*, *The Early Memoirs of Lady Ottoline Morrell*, edited by Robert Gathorne-Hardy, *copyright* 1963, Faber & Faber Ltd., and Alfred A. Knopf Inc.;

'Ottoline at Garsington', *Memoirs of Lady Ottoline Morrell*, 1915-1918; edited by Robert Gathorne-Hardy, *copyright* 1974, Faber & Faber Ltd.;

Nehls, Edward, ed. *D.H. Lawrence 'a Composite Biography'* 3 Vols. 1957, 1958, 1959, The University of Wisconsin Press, Madison;

Orton, William A., *The Last Romantic,* Macmillan Publishing Company, Holt, Rinehart and Winston, New York;

Parker , Millie, *Broken Strings*, February 23rd 1923, The *New Zealand Herald*, Auckland;

Rice, Anne (Mrs O. Raymond Drey), *Memories of Katherine Mansfield,* David Drey, *ADAM 300* (1965);

Russell, Bertrand, *Autobiography of Bertrand Russell*, George Allen & Unwin (Publishers Ltd.);

Swinnerton, Frank, *Backround with Chorus,* 1956, *The Georgian Literary Scene* 1969, Hutchinson & Co. Publishers Ltd.;

Woolf, Leonard, *Beginning Again*, The Literary Estate of Leonard Woolf and the Hogarth Press;

Downhill All the Way, The Literary Estate of Leonard Woolf and the Hogarth Press;

Woolf, Virginia, *The Diaries of Virginia Woolf*, ed. Ann Olivier Bell; Vols. I and II, 1977 and 1978;

The Question of Things Happening — *Letters of Virginia Woolf*, ed. Nigel Nicolson and Joanne Trautmann, Vols. I and

II, 1975 and 1976, The Literary Estate of Virginia Woolf and the Hogarth Press;

Miron Grindea, editor of *ADAM* for extracts from Katherine Mansfield's *Letters to Sydney and Violet Schiff*, *ADAM* (1965) *Fifteen Letters to Virginia Woolf, ADAM* (1972-73);

To the editors and proprietors of the newspapers of New Zealand I am especially indebted:

Auckland Weekly News

The *Dominion*, Wellington

Weekly Gazette

New Zealand Graphic and *Ladies' Journal*

The *Weekly Graphic* and *New Zealand Mail*

The *New Zealand Herald*, Auckland

Select Bibliography

I Katherine Mansfield
  Collected Stories, London, 1973
  Journal of Katherine Mansfield, 'Definitive Edition' ed. J.M.
  Murry, Constable, London, 1954.
  The Letters of Katherine Mansfield, ed. J.M. Murray, 2
  vols., Constable, London, 1928.
  Letters of Katherine Mansfield to John Middleton Murry,
  1913-1922, ed. J.M. Murry, Constable, London 1951.
  The Scrap Book of Katherine Mansfield, ed. J.M. Murry,
  Constable, London, 1937.
  The Aloe, ed. J.M. Murry, Constable, London, 1930.
  Novels and Novelists, ed. J.M. Murry, Constable, London,
  1930.
  Poems, ed. J.M. Murry, Constable, London, November
  1923, Knopf, New York, February 1924.

II John Middleton Murry
  God, Being an Introduction to the Science of Metabiology,
  1929.
  Son of Woman, the Story of D.H. Lawrence, Jonathan
  Cape, London, 1931.
  Between Two Worlds, an Autobiography, Jonathan Cape,
  London, 1935.
  Katherine Mansfield and Other Literary Portraits, 1949.
  *The Letters of John Middleton Murry to Katherine
  Mansfield*, ed. by C.A. Hankin, Constable, London, 1983.

III Alpers, Antony, *The Life of Katherine Mansfield*,
  Jonathan Cape, London, 1980.
  Baker, Ida Constance, *Katherine Mansfield: The Memories
  of LM*, Michael Joseph Ltd., London, 1971.
  Beauchamp, Sir Harold, *Reminiscences and Recollections*,

New Plymouth, New Zealand, 1937 (With a chapter on Katherine Mansfield contributed by Guy H. Schofield).

Berkman, Sylvia, *Katherine Mansfield. A Critical Study*, New Haven, 1951.

Charms, Leslie de, *Elizabeth of the German Garden*, London, 1958.

Carco, Francis, *Les Innocents*, Paris, 1916.

    Montmartre à vingt ans, Paris, 1938

    Bohème d'artiste, Paris, 1940

Carrington, Dora, *Letters and Extracts from her Diaries*, ed. David Garnett, 1970.

Carswell, John, *Lives and letters*, Faber and Faber, London, 1978.

E.T. (Chambers, Jessie), *D.H. Lawrence: A Personal Record*, Jonathan Cape, London.

Darroch, Sandra Jobson, *Ottoline*, Chatto and Windus Ltd., London 1976.

Ede, H.S., *Savage Messiah* (a life of Gaudier-Brzeska), 1931.

Gerhardi, William, *Memoirs of a Polyglot*, London.

Gertler, Mark, *Selected Letters*, ed. Noel Carrington, 1968.

Glenavy, Beatrice Lady, *Today We Will Only Gossip*, Constable, London, 1964.

Green, Martin, *The von Richthofen Sisters*, London, 1971.

Holroyd, Michael, *Lytton Strachey, 'a Biography'* Harmondsworth, 1971.

Lawrence, D.H., *The Collected Letters of D.H. Lawrence*, ed. Harry T. Moore, New York, 1962.

'Prologue to Women in Love' in *Phoenix II*, ed. W. Roberts and Harry T. Moore, 1965.

The Quest for Rananim, D.H. Lawrence's letters to S.S. Koteliansky ed. George Zytaruk, 1970.

Lawrence, Frieda, *The Memoirs and Correspondence*, E.W. Tedlock J. New York, 1964.

Lea, F.A., *John Middleton Murry*, 1959.

Mairet, Philip, *A.R. Orage, 'a Memoir'*, 1936

Mantz, Ruth Elvish, and J.M. Murry, *The Life of Katherine Mansfield*, 1933.

Merlin, Roland, *La Drame Secret de Katherine Mansfield*, Paris, 1950.

Meyers, Jeffrey, *Katherine Mansfield, a Biography*, 1978.

Morrell, Lady Ottoline, *Ottoline, The Early Memoirs, Ottoline at Garsington* 1915-1918. Both Ed. Robert Gathorne Hardy, 1968-1974.

Nehls, Edward, ed. *D:H: Lawrence, 'a Composite Biography'*, 3 vols. The University of Wisconsin Press, Madison, Wisconsin 1957, 1958, 1959.

Nott, C.S, *Teachings of Gurdjieff. The Journal of a Pupil,* 1969.

Orton, William, *The Last Romantic,* 1957.

Swinnerton, Frank, *The Georgian Literary Scene,* 1969 *Background with Chorus,* 1956.

Woolf, Leonard, *Beginning Again: An Autobiography of the Years 1911-1918,* Hogarth Press, London, 1964.

Downhill All the Way, An Autobiography of the Years 1919-1939, Hogarth Press, London, 1961.

Woolf, Virginia, *The Diaries of Virginia Woolf,* ed. Ann Olivier Bell, vols. I and II, 1977 and 1978.

The Question of Things Happening: Letters of Virginia Woolf 1912-1922, ed. Nigel Nicholson and Jeanne Trautmann, vols. I and II, 1975 and 1976.

IV Articles

Grindea, Miron (editor) *ADAM International Review,* No. 300 (1963-1965) 1-14, 76-118 (Special Issue on Mansfield and Beatrice Hastings, forty-six letters by KM).

ADAM International Review, 370-375 (1972-73), 1-128 Special issue on Mansfield containing letters to her by V. Woolf, Richard Murry and Bertrand Russell.

Hastings, Beatrice, *Straight Thinker,* Bulletin June 1932.

Hudson, Stephen (Sydney Schiff), 'First Meeting With Katherine Mansfield', *Cornhill Magazine,* 1017: 202-212, Autumn 1958.

Kafian, Adela, 'The Last Days of Katherine Mansfield' in *Adelphi,* October-December, 1946, pp. 36-39.

Leeming, Owen, 'Katherine Mansfield's Sisters' (transcription of interviews recorded in London) in *New Zealand Listener,* 1 March, 29 March, 5 April, 11 April, 1963.

Olgivanna (Mrs Frank Lloyd Wright, née Lazovich), 'The Last Days of Katherine Mansfield', in *Bookman,* New York, 73: 6-13 March, 1931.

Orage, A.R., 'Talks with Katherine Mansfield', in *Century*

Magazine, No. 87: 36-40,November 1924.
Young, James Carruthers, 'An Experiment at Fontainebleau, a Personal Reminiscence', in *New Adelphi, n.s., 1:*
26-40, September 1927.